LOVE
AND
RUIN

LOVE
AND
RUIN

TALES OF OBSESSION,
DANGER, AND HEARTBREAK
FROM *THE ATAVIST MAGAZINE*

EDITED BY EVAN RATLIFF
INTRODUCTION BY SUSAN ORLEAN

W. W. NORTON & COMPANY
INDEPENDENT PUBLISHERS SINCE 1923
NEW YORK | LONDON

For information about permission to reproduce selections from this book,
write to Permissions, W. W. Norton & Company, Inc.,
500 Fifth Avenue, New York, NY 10110

For information about special discounts for bulk purchases, please contact
W. W. Norton Special Sales at specialsales@wwnorton.com or 800-233-4830

Manufacturing by RR Donnelley
Book design by Chris Welch
Production manager: Lauren Abbate

ISBN 978-0-393-35271-9 (pbk.)

W. W. Norton & Company, Inc.
500 Fifth Avenue, New York, N.Y. 10110
www.wwnorton.com

W. W. Norton & Company Ltd.
Castle House, 75/76 Wells Street, London W1T 3QT

1 2 3 4 5 6 7 8 9 0

TO MATT POWER

CONTENTS

EDITOR'S FOREWORD

In the world of biology, an atavism is a reversion to a lost trait in a modern lineage. It's a kind of evolutionary teleportation, like a whale born with vestigial leg bones, or an extra nipple in humans, that happens when genes recombine. Five years ago, when we created *The Atavist Magazine*, we aimed to do something similar with the storytelling tradition of great magazines and nonfiction books—to recombine and revive them where they were least expected to thrive: online.

At the time, telling serious stories digitally was considered quixotic at best and utterly futile at worst. As the flood of digital life seeped into our lives and pockets, so too came calls for the stories we consumed to be increasingly simplified and bite-sized, to accommodate a perceived decline in our attention spans. "Longform" written storytelling—of characters and deeply reported facts and intricate plots—was, it was said, going the way of the black rhino. Our magazine is built on questioning that wisdom, asking whether a small group of editors, writers, designers, and fact-checkers might bring to life true, gripping narratives that were compelling enough to capture readers in the digital age.

In its conception, *The Atavist Magazine* is simple. Each month we offer one longform, nonfiction, narrative story, a tale containing intimately etched characters, surprising twists, and universal human struggles. We present each one digitally, on the Web, with a unique design—enabled by software we create ourselves, called the *Atavist* platform—meant to be consumed on your computer, your tablet, or your phone.

To do that, however, requires that we place equal measures of trust in our authors and our audience. For our authors, it means giving them the freedom to explore deeper narratives than those in a typical magazine. Because we avoid the "house style" that often creates a paint-by-numbers effect in magazine features, it means placing each author's own voice at the center of the story. The result is an eclectic mix of styles, as akin in some ways to a series of short books as to the traditional magazine feature, but united by the fundamental approach at their heart.

We've needed to trust, as much, in our readers. Not only that you were out there—an idea that was not popular on the Internet in 2011—but that you, inundated by the ephemera of Twitter and Facebook, still yearned for true tales of love, betrayal, and human failing. That if we could hook you with great writing, we could keep you for much longer than any publisher on the Internet would dare expect.

Five years on, this collection is a testament not just to the work that a small group of writers and editors has put into the world, but to the smart, engaging audience that still exists for stories like these.

There is some irony, of course, that we are now committing these stories to paper. *The Atavist Magazine* has been entirely digital from the beginning. Indeed, we are known as much for establishing a new style of longform design on the Web—often featuring video, interactive graphics, and sound—as for the pieces animated by that design. But we don't see the two as a contradiction. In fact, stories meant as a breakwater against the creep of online ephemerality are naturally at home in print, the medium that originally inspired us to create them.

Given the confines of these two covers, though, it was no simple prospect to choose the pieces here from among the fifty-plus issues of *The Atavist Magazine*. Here you will find narratives that stand outside time, including those from reporters who spent months or years tracking down subjects, earning their trust, and piecing together their accounts.

For the title story, "Love and Ruin"—winner of the 2015 National Magazine Award for Feature Writing—James Verini embeds the story of one couple's romance, and one woman's dedication to Afghanistan, into four decades of the country's history. In "The Sinking of the *Bounty*," Matthew Shaer reconstructs a ship's final voyage and the Coast Guard investigation into her demise, an account of heroism and hubris in the eye of a hurricane. Essayist Leslie Jamison, in "52 Blue," examines the unusual community of people obsessed with a whale that sings at a frequency—52 hertz—never before heard by scientists and inaudible to other members of its species. She comes away with an absorbing meditation on what it means to be alone, and how we seek meaning from the natural world.

There are within these pages, as well, writers who have burrowed deep into archives in search of the great lost figures from an earlier era. In "American Hippopotamus," Jon Mooallem uncovers the story of two superspies and sworn enemies from the early twentieth century who unexpectedly became allies in an insane plot to feed a hungry America. Adam Higginbotham, in "A Thousand Pounds of Dynamite," delivers a darkly hilarious account of a bomb left inside a Lake Tahoe casino in 1980—and the bizarre extortion plot that disintegrated with its detonation.

Finally, there are writers in these pages who have mined their own lives for wrenching but illuminating memoirs of romance, loss, and recovery. You'll find David Dobbs tracking down his mother's lost love from sixty years ago, and Brooke Jarvis recounting her time in America's last leper colony. Both Cris Beam and Vanessa Veselka examine the fragility of memory and the haunting fog of the past, each in their own way, by unwinding their twisted family histories.

What binds these stories together is the keen eye with which their writers capture people and events, and their knack for hooking us into a story and never letting go. We hope you'll find it to be storytelling in its best, most atavistic, sense.

Evan Ratliff
Editor-in-chief, *The Atavist Magazine*

INTRODUCTION

by Susan Orlean

Let us first dispense with the issue of the name. For some reason, no one has settled on a name for stories that amble inward and outward but are built of real facts from real life—in other words, the kinds of stories *The Atavist* has been laying out, like jewels on a velvet pillow, for the last five years. The label "creative nonfiction" has had a good run, but it has always made me uncomfortable: too many people interpret the word *creative* to mean that the genre entails fabrication and invention. "New journalism" is kind of snappy, except this kind of writing is not really very new. Daniel Defoe was writing "new journalism" in the not-very-new year of 1704, when he published *The Storm*, and there have been practitioners working at it in every century since. "Narrative nonfiction" is a nice solid name but a bit of a mouthful. At the moment, "longform" seems to be the most popular description, but I worry: Doesn't it make the stories sound like they're just too damn long?

When I'm asked what kind of writing I do, or what kind of writing I like, I tend to stumble and feint, avoiding a name altogether. "I like *interesting* stories," I explain. "Stories that aren't necessarily big news stories. Stories that are rich and deep even if on the surface they seem slight. And I love stories that have been overlooked, that turn out to be windows onto worlds or chapters of history that we never noticed were there. And then I like to find out more about them, about their context and resonance, and why I—or anyone—might find them interesting, and how we might be able to draw greater conclusions from them about the nature of life and human civilization and the meaning of—" This is usually when the person who asked me bolts for the door and I'm left midsentence, trying to explain myself. Longform answer, I guess.

I would like to propose another name: "magpie journalism." Magpies, the little hunch-shouldered *Pica pica*, with their semiformal black-and-white bodies and long, slender tails, have a penchant for collecting shiny things. It's fascinating that they have this odd habit. What is even more fascinating is that they ever manage to find anything to satisfy the urge. After all, magpies live in the woods, surrounded by muted greens and grays and browns. Is there anything sparkly there? If there is, it's so hidden that it would take a special eye to notice it in that blur of earth tones, buried by layers of ordinary forest litter. It takes a particular keenness to tease out a bit of flash and retrieve it for display. Are shiny things somehow essential to magpies' survival? Probably not, since a piece of tin foil or a coin or a can doesn't serve any purpose we know to be indispensable: they can't be eaten or provide shelter or solve any of the usual bird problems of staying alive. But still, something drives the magpie to keep searching and to keep laying out its treasures for the rest of the world to see.

So here you have the treasures of *The Atavist*'s magpies, who have dug around in the quotidian and found the remarkable. Their mightiest tool is the capacity to notice. All these stories arose serendipitously, after some chance encounter or scrap of information fell into the writer's hands, and he or she noticed it enough to realize there was something interesting in there. These are not stories that a publicist proposed via an email blast with bullet points; nor are they twee human-interest stories that an editor devised to brighten the gloom of the news hole. They are stories that were glimpsed and then grabbed and shaken until they unfurled, stories that many other writers might not have noticed at all. And what big stories they become! A strange pebble leads to a deep, unexpected history of Afghanistan; a whale becomes the template for human loneliness; a deathbed mention of a man's name unfolds into a story of war and discovery. The fact that many creative nonfiction/narrative journalism/new journalism/longform stories start small is a wonderful trick, because the good ones then get big without the reader freaking out about committing to an epic. The best ones, in fact, take in the whole world.

There is a moment in the process of writing pieces like these when many of us have a crisis of faith. Why should anyone care about this story? Is it just too minor, too obscure, too trifling? It doesn't wrestle with urgent issues; it doesn't deliver breaking news or argue a crucial matter. No one will die if they don't know about, say, a misbegotten plan a century ago to raise hippos for meat.

And yet. The gauge here isn't utility. Reading is so much more than that: the magic in reading is the imperative to learn, to be transformed, to inhabit even briefly another psyche, another situation, and to see life as you would not have seen it otherwise. The magic is to be able to time-travel, not as a spectator to canned, airless history, but as a participant in the details of another moment in culture, to really feel it and taste it and sense it on an animal level. The canoe full of gunpowder blasting away a future generation of leaders in the Battle of Sitka, the tumbledown cemetery beside a Hawaiian leper colony—the images like these awaiting you in the stories here, thanks to *The Atavist*, are the kind that hurl you out of your reading chair and into another realm. That, in and of itself, is important and sufficient. To be reminded that there is a universe outside your own tiny experience is marvelous. It enlarges you. You are better, and smarter, and more humane, and more empathetic, for it. You will dazzle at dinner parties with your trove of amazing facts, collected herewith. These magpies have found you bits of silver, and you can take them with you, a forever gift of something that shines.

LOVE
AND
RUIN

JAMES VERINI

PROLOGUE

It has no official number in the archaeological record, nor an agreed-upon name. Some curators at the National Museum of Afghanistan in Kabul, where it resides, have called it the Limestone Head. Others call it the Carved Pebble. Still others call it simply the Head, and while there is no question that the artifact they're talking about depicts a head, the answer to the question of just whose head it depicts—which person or deity its unyielding eyes and screwed mouth reflect—is lost, like so much else in Afghanistan is lost, to some insolently mute vault of time.

The Head is carved into a limestone pebble two and a half inches high by one and a quarter inches wide. It dates from around 10,000 B.C.E., placing it in the Upper Paleolithic and making it one of the oldest pieces of sculpture ever found on the Asian continent. We know that it turned up in a gorge near the village of Aq Kupruk, in the northern foothills of the Hindu Kush. Beyond that we know nothing. The best that the most thorough scholarly paper written about the Head—published by the American Philosophical Society in 1972, seven years after it was discovered—can say for its subject is that it is "apparently humanoid." Was it devotional, decorative, whimsical? "Was the head made for a onetime limited use or was it intended for long-term retention and repeated use? . . . Since it will not stand, was it intended to be carried about?" The Head won't say.

But its dumbness beckons. The Head's sculptor was far cleverer than an artist living twelve thousand years ago had any call to be. The eyes are not crude circles (all you'd really need in the Upper Paleolithic, you'd think) but are composed of a series of subtle line strokes, as though they are contemplating us wearily. The nose, the American Philosophical Society paper observes, "begins with a wide angular cleft rather like that of the nose cavity in a skull and seems almost to be intentionally 'unrealistic,'" while the "deeply engraved line of the mouth itself apparently arcs upward in what seems to be a smile." The paper concludes that the Head does not come from an "individual or cultural 'infantilism.'" Yet the overall effect, millennia later, is a kind of infancy. It's somehow fetal looking, the Head. Some observers see on its face a smile, others a frown, and still others that inscrutable expression, neither frown nor smile, that a wise child makes when he peers into you.

The archaeologist who unearthed the Head, who might have had the most questions about it, had the fewest. Louis Dupree was certain it depicted a woman—and furthermore, that it had been carved by one. "What else?" he said to a *New York Times* reporter, rather tauntingly, in 1968, when he brought the relic to the American Museum of Natural History. "Women ruled the hearth and the world then. The men were away hunting." *Of course* it was a woman.

That was how Louis Dupree talked—to *Times* writers, to fellow archaeologists, presidents, statesmen, interrogators, spies. He even talked that way to his wife, Nancy, who, when asked whether it was true her husband swore like sailor (and a sailor he had been before becoming an archaeologist), would sometimes sigh longingly and reply, "Worse."

In the field he worked casually. In 1962 he carried out the first major excavation at Aq Kupruk, an immensely important site, essentially by himself. For the follow-up dig, three years later, when he discovered the Head, he splurged and brought along as diggers and assistants a pair of graduate students, a pair of precocious high schoolers, and his cook.

"We were very, very careful with it," Charles Kolb, one of the graduate students, recalled of the Head. Except for Dupree, that is.

Although it was very possibly the most important find of his career, he never properly catalogued it (thus its lack of a single name or record number). Then, in Kabul, he took it home with him, where Nancy, a writer of guidebooks and an amateur scholar, came to adore it as much as he did. Dupree's daughter took a shine to it, too, and called it Daddy's Head. The name stuck.

The Afghan official who granted Dupree permission to take Daddy's Head to New York told him, "If you lose it, you'll owe us half a million dollars." The careful procedure Dupree employed to transport it overseas involved putting it in his jacket pocket, folding the jacket, and stuffing the jacket into the overhead shelf on the plane. Nancy spent the flight looking up nervously at the bundle.

Upon its return from the United States, Daddy's Head was installed at the National Museum in Kabul. Between their excavations, research trips, lecture tours, and teaching stints abroad, Louis and Nancy would visit it there. They'd stare at it for what seemed like hours, talking about the history it must have witnessed. One photograph of the couple shows them sitting at a table, gazing at the artifact as Louis holds it in his fingers (gingerly but on equal terms). They appear mesmerized, as though Daddy's Head is almost physically drawing them back in time. The photo was taken in 1971, as they were falling more deeply in love with one another and, together, with Afghanistan. They peered into the country's wondrous, terrible, unknowable past. Daddy's Head, they liked to think, was opening its vault of secrets.

In 1978 a Communist cabal seized power in Afghanistan. Louis was imprisoned and deported. The next year the Soviet Union invaded. Its troops pulverized the country, reducing much of its history—the unearthed chapters and those still buried—to rubble. Louis helped the Afghan resistance while Nancy worked with refugees. The struggle against the Soviets gave way to civil war, and their beloved National Museum was in the crossfire.

Nancy and others tried to save the artifacts in the collection. But she didn't find Daddy's Head. The Taliban ended the civil war but followed that by closing schools, ransacking libraries, and destroying much of what was left of the collection. She wondered if all the work she and Louis had done to preserve Afghan culture had been in vain. She assumed she would never see Daddy's Head again.

ONE

I first encountered Nancy Dupree in a ghostly sort of a way. On a Tuesday night in 2003, while soldiers my age were in Afghanistan fighting the Taliban, I was sitting in a theater in Los Angeles watching a production of Tony Kushner's *Homebody/Kabul*. The play's first scene is given over entirely to a monologue spoken by a Mrs. Dalloway–type character. Why she is addressing us, and from where, she leaves unspoken, as she does her identity—she does not name herself and is known in the program only as the Homebody— but we're aware from the Homebody's first words that the central fact about this woman is that she is deeply taken by, even lost to, Afghanistan. In the convolutions of her speech and mind, the Homebody is wise and helpless, composed and scattered, ancient and infantile. "Our story begins at the very dawn of history, circa 3,000 B.C.," she begins as the lights come up but interrupts herself at once to explain, "I am reading from an outdated guidebook about the city of Kabul."

The Homebody's monologue is brilliant but tortuous, almost infuriatingly so. She departs the narrative of Afghan history for jags about party etiquette and antidepressants, uses words no audience member could be expected to know and then apologizes for them. She is, in other words, very human. So much so, it's clear—or anyway was to me that night—that she must be based on a real woman.

Curious, I eventually contacted Kushner and learned her backstory. In the 1990s he had been browsing the stacks at the New York

University library, looking for material about Afghanistan, when he stumbled across a volume titled *An Historical Guide to Kabul*. He opened the book and didn't close it until he'd read to the end; the Homebody and the play had emerged. The guidebook's author's name was Nancy Hatch Dupree.

I started asking around about her.

"If the Afghans ever go back to deities, she'll be one," the former American ambassador to Afghanistan Ryan Crocker told me of Dupree. "They all know what she's gone through with them and on their behalf."

Ashraf Ghani, the Afghan intellectual and presidential candidate, described her as "a grandmother figure and mother figure in Afghanistan. Somebody who's given us our cultural heritage. Someone who's played a living witness to our history."

Kushner, who since writing the play has become friends with Dupree and serves on the advisory council of her foundation, called her a woman of "dazzling erudition." (Nancy has never seen *Homebody/Kabul*. "I hear it's good," she tells people.)

The Grandmother of Afghanistan—that is not original to Ghani. It is what Afghans call Dupree, aware that she is technically American. In fact, if she could be said to have any single vocation, this may be it: she is a self-appointed but also widely acknowledged guardian of Afghan culture, the country's bluffest and most beloved expatriate busybody. Among other things, she is the author of dozens of books and scholarly articles on Afghanistan's history, architecture, politics, music, literature, and art; a founder of the Society for the Preservation of Afghanistan's Cultural Heritage; the creator of a library extension service that distributes books to schools and government bodies around the country; the creator of the most extensive digital archive of Afghan historical materials; an occasional adviser to ministers and generals; and an advocate for Afghan women's and children's rights.

Natives and foreigners alike have been trading stories and legends of her ever since she first arrived in Afghanistan over a half-century ago. There was the episode in the 1960s, for instance, when Nancy saved Bagh-e-Bala, the onetime summer palace of the emirs, from destruction, partly out of scholarly devotion to the building and partly so she could host her wedding there. In the 1980s a young Saudi man approached her, looking for help bringing in equipment to dig tunnels where mujahideen fighters could hide between attacks on Soviet troops. Dupree was not an official, he was aware, but he had heard that she knew everyone of importance in Afghanistan, and that she had the rind to get what she wanted from any one of them. Nancy was too busy to help him, but she recalls the man, who went by the name Osama bin Laden, being "very shy and polite."

More recently, while ordering lumber for a construction project, Nancy ran up against a moratorium on logging that Hamid Karzai had instated. After she called him and made her frustrations known, Karzai ordered the moratorium lifted temporarily. "He was just a little nobody when I first met him," she told me of the president of the Islamic Republic of Afghanistan.

Karzai had other reasons to be helpful. The lumber was for a library Dupree was building at Kabul University, for which he'd already helped raise $2.5 million. She has been planning the library, the project that could most properly be called her life's work, and collecting its contents for thirty years. Those contents represent one of the most comprehensive, if not the most comprehensive, archives of post-1979 Afghan historical documents and scholarship anywhere. The library is the more impressive because it is a repository of knowledge about a time during which knowledge was concertedly destroyed in Afghanistan—a memory bank for a generation of Afghans whose clearest personal memories are of exile. She sees it as her greatest gift to her adopted home, as well as her last attempt to save Afghanistan's past, as it were, from itself.

Like other Americans, in the years after 9/11 I read and thought a lot about Afghanistan, that country—in the Homebody's words—

"so at the heart of the world the world has forgotten it." In the fall of 2012 I heard that Dupree's library was, after so many years in the making, finally scheduled to open. I also heard that her health was failing. I called her and told her I wanted to come to Afghanistan. She wasn't overly excited at the prospect, but neither did she exactly object. I booked a ticket for Kabul.

TWO

On a hot September morning, I stepped from one of Kabul's loud, dusty streets to the Kabul University gate. Dark episodes in recent Afghan history originated on the university campus. It was here that Communists and Islamists first did battle in the ideological skirmishes that led up to the Soviet invasion, here that the warlords who would destroy the country—and who still run much of it—first rubbed shoulders. Ashraf Ghani told me that when he came to the university, "people were literally killing each other there. There were warring student gangs." One of his first acts as chancellor was to remove forty-three tons of scrap metal from the school, he said, most of it pieces of blown-up tanks. The tanks have been replaced by a lot of healthy-looking trees, and fewer, less-healthy-looking buildings. Today the campus has a liberal vibe that contrasts with the rest of the country. Female students wear cursory headscarves or none at all; they and their male classmates look at and sometimes even talk to each other.

Twenty feet from the gate I got lost. Dupree had anticipated this, apparently: soon a silver sedan pulled alongside me. The silhouette of what might have been a child appeared in a back window. I'd never met Dupree, only spoken with her on the phone. Her avian voice hadn't prepared me for the diminutive woman I found. A collapsing robin's nest of gray hair didn't quite get her to five feet, and she couldn't have weighed more in pounds than her age in years, eighty-six at the time. Her eyes were sunken, her face a topography of wrinkles. (I was reminded of the Homebody's description of an Afghan whose "skin is broken by webs of lines inscribed by hardships, siroccos, and strife.") But her cheeks were girlish and full, her mouth small and coy.

Hidden inside a light blue *salwar kameez* and a long scarf, Dupree seemed already to be in midconversation when I settled next to her in the back seat. That morning had produced a dustup over fabrics that she wanted for the library, she was saying, and "people just do not realize you don't accomplish things overnight here. They come from somewhere else and expect everything to fall into place. But it takes so much bloody time." Looking out the window, she added, "That's why everything here is kind of . . . half-assed."

We drove to her temporary office, which she'd been working out of for years, in a converted garage. With a cough, she eased into a chair behind the old dining room table that serves as her desk. Her staff, at small desks around the room, greeted her as Nancy Jan. (*Jan* is a Dari diminutive that means, roughly, "dear.")

A cook brought out plates of rice pilau from the kitchen (a closet with a hot plate) as the library's designers arrived to discuss the fabric situation. Dupree had been informed there was not enough of the red pattern she'd ordered long before for all the upholstery and curtains in the library and now was, she announced, "really browned off. We could have done this six months ago!"

"Two years ago," said Dupree's executive director, Waheed Wafa, a tall, warm-voiced man whose face exuded beleaguerment. Like many educated Kabulis, Wafa grew up with the Duprees' books. Also like many educated Kabulis, he had been beaten by the Taliban. When the U.S.-led coalition invaded, in 2001, he became a fixer for *The New York Times*, then a reporter. Dupree hired him in 2011.

Wafa produced a fan of swatches, potential replacements, and held up a reddish one. "That's dullsville," Dupree said, waving a hand dismissively. She jumped to the issue of acoustics. Without enough good fabric to absorb sound, the library would be too loud.

"What about urns?" Wafa suggested. Knowing Dupree's mood could be improved by a story of Afghan ingenuity, he told one: During the Taliban years, he said, his friends in the Kabul underground used to hold meetings in a room they thought was secure. But one day they realized Talibs were listening outside. So they lined the walls of the room with large urns, to muffle their voices.

"Oh yes, yes!" Dupree said, getting into the story, and smiling for the first time since I'd met her. After some gentle cajoling from Wafa and the others, she agreed on potential vendors. "Okay, that's done. Decision made. Bang!" she said, slapping her hand on the table. Her staff looked up from their desks hopefully. A date was set to go to the market, and the group left.

Later, Wafa told me the new library was still months from completion. Since Dupree was relying on the Afghan government to pay for much of it, she was also relying on the government to pay the workers who were supposed to be finishing it. It hadn't been, and they weren't. I asked him when it might open. "God knows," he said, dragging on a Marlboro. He'd recently upped from a half-pack to a whole pack per day, he confided.

A few days later, Dupree and a thickset, bearded man in his mid-thirties named Mashall, who manages her box-library program, drove to Charikar, a town about forty miles north of Kabul, to check in on a provincial council and a few schools. As we were departing, I asked if it was safe in Charikar. "We don't ask questions like that," she said. "If you think about that, you'll go nowhere. And that's why the Americans don't go anywhere."

Like many Afghans, Mashall has come to know Afghanistan only in adulthood. Before that he lived in Pakistan, where he'd moved as a child after his village was bombed in the Soviet war. He grew up in Peshawar, where he met Dupree in 1999. "When people see Nancy on the TV," he said, "they say, 'She's still working, she's still here.'

We say to our women, 'Look at Nancy Dupree, she's eighty and still working.'"

Dupree waved a hand. "When people see me, they say, 'Good God, that woman is still alive?'"

She looked from the window onto a cinder-block sprawl that had been a meadow, the site of a cavalry battle in the First Anglo-Afghan War, in the early 1840s. Dupree recounted how she and a friend used to ride horses there and reenact the fighting. "I swear there must be people in that village who tell stories about these two crazy women who rode around charging at each other."

We passed Bagh-e-Bala, the domed hilltop palace that the emir Abdur Rahman built to escape the heat of the Kabul Valley at the end of the nineteenth century. "That's where Louis and I were married," she said.

THREE

Nancy Hatch was born in Cooperstown, New York, in 1926 and raised in Travancore, a small feudal kingdom on the southern tip of India, during the last gasps of the Raj. Her mother, a onetime stage actress, studied traditional Indian theater and wrote a guidebook to Travancore. Her father, who'd fought in the First World War with the British, worked on education projects for UNESCO around Asia. "He taught me a tremendous amount," Dupree said. "One thing was, if you hold on to something too long, it fails."

Living in India in the 1930s and '40s, she told me, "was like growing up on a movie set. The maharaja was very fond of my father. I was the same age as the maharaja's brother. Every time there was a new birth of leopards or tigers at the zoo, they'd bring the cubs to the palace, and I'd go to the palace with my little white gloves and big hat." She left to study at Barnard College and after graduating performed as a harpist. She gave that up to enroll in the Chinese and

Japanese studies department at Columbia University, then followed her father into UNESCO, working as an adviser to the governments of India and Ceylon (now Sri Lanka).

At Columbia, she met an aspiring diplomat named Alan Wolfe, a suave and capable product of Manhattan wealth. They married in Ceylon. The match was not ideal, according to some friends. Wolfe was "definitely not Nancy's type," said one of them, Mary Mac-Makin. "Though the fact that he was in the Foreign Service was such a draw for her. I think that's why she married him." According to MacMakin, Nancy was "a party girl" but "a brain, too."

Wolfe joined the Foreign Service after the war. In 1962 he was assigned to the Kabul embassy. "He wasn't happy. I was very happy." Though on paper Wolfe was a cultural attaché, in truth Afghan culture was of only secondary interest to him. That was because, off the books, he was the CIA's new chief of station in Kabul.

A rising star in the agency, Wolfe was, if not the best-liked operative in the clandestine services, surely among its most ambitious. An underling once described him to a journalist as "the kind of guy who only speaks to Cabots, Lodges, and God." A former agent who worked under him described to me his first meeting with Wolfe. "Wolfe was dressed in a very good suit, Brooks Brothers I'm sure," he said. He walked around the room, making a point to look at his pocket watch every few minutes. "I'm expecting a call from Kissinger," Wolfe kept saying.

Soon after they moved to Kabul, Alan and Nancy met Louis Dupree. Born in 1925 to descendants of French Huguenots on the family tobacco farm at Dupree's Crossroads, North Carolina, as a boy, Dupree thought he would become a Presbyterian preacher. He also believed in integration, and the two were immiscible in the Jim Crow South. As a youth leader in the church, said Nancy—with the air of hagiography that characterizes much of her recollection of Louis—he invited a black boy to a service, and "when the church elders told him he couldn't do that, he said, 'Fuck you.'"

"This was way before Martin Luther King," she added.

With the outbreak of World War II, Dupree dropped out of school to attend the Coast Guard Academy, then joined the Merchant Marine. At sea he read everything he could. In 1944 he joined the army, trained as a paratrooper, and was dispatched to the Pacific, where his most challenging mission, according to stories he would later tell, found him dropping behind enemy lines in the Philippines to recruit Bontoc Igorot natives to fight the Japanese. Dupree was awarded a Purple Heart and a Bronze Star.

After the war, he won a scholarship contest for veterans and, with no high school diploma, was admitted to Harvard, where in eight years he completed bachelor's, master's, and doctoral degrees in anthropology. The Harvard archaeologist Carleton Coon took Dupree under his wing. One of the last great American academic generalists, Coon was, like Dupree, interested primarily in prehistoric Asian archaeology, but he convinced his pupil that to really understand the world, he must be versed not only in archaeology but also in history, geography, biology, linguistics, ethnomusicology, political science, and whatever else he had time for. Dupree agreed. His dissertation, on Paleolithic tools, took up two volumes.

Early on, he displayed a knack for portentous finds. At an excavation in Iran, he and Coon discovered skeletal remains that helped debunk the theory, dominant in archaeology at the time, that humanity's origins lay in the Far East. In the summer of 1949 he and a friend were sent by the Museum of Natural History to carry out the first American dig in Afghanistan. Within a few months, Dupree and a colleague had found the medieval city of Peshawarun, long thought vanished, in Afghanistan's southwestern desert. They stumbled upon it while searching for a drink of water, they explained. Later Dupree found the oldest human remains ever discovered in Afghanistan, dated to 30,000 B.C.E., and the oldest tools, dated to 100,000 B.C.E.

Dupree and his colleagues were regularly written up in newspapers, but they were anachronisms; the swashbuckling era of archaeology was ending. Dupree's contemporaries were scientific specialists who employed new technologies and meticulous record keeping—all of which bored Dupree no end. "He wasn't really up on the Paleolithic literature or the most recent anthropological theories," said Rick Davis, an archaeologist who worked for Dupree. Charles Kolb said the handling of the Aq Kupruk artifacts was shambolic: when it came time to divide the excavation's yield—including Daddy's Head—among the Afghan and American partners, they simply laid out the thousands of pieces they'd found and commenced haggling.

What Dupree lacked in punctiliousness, however, he compensated for with toil, good cheer, and a leonine confidence. "He was a real commander [and] was very direct," said Davis. "He facilitated and encouraged so many people who came to Afghanistan, even people with the most slender credentials. He'd introduce these wayfaring scholars to these local people."

Ashraf Ghani was one of many young Afghan scholars whom Dupree helped and encouraged. "He was an incredibly gracious man," Ghani said. "It was the openness of his mind. He exemplified a tolerance for critique, for ideas."

He was "a very profane character," the American ambassador to Afghanistan in the mid-1970s, Ted Eliot, said. The first time Eliot's wife dined at Dupree's home in Kabul, a high-ranking Afghan official was also present. Eliot's wife privately expressed her worry to Dupree that the Afghan regime was spoiling for a war with Pakistan. Dupree, well into his cups, brought the official over to Mrs. Eliot. "So what about it?" Dupree asked him. "Are you going to start a fucking war with Pakistan?"

"That was typical," Eliot said.

Such impieties aside, by the 1960s Dupree was, by general consent, the leading Western expert on Afghanistan's history. Some said the leading expert. His "knowledge of the country was extraordinary," Kolb said. "He understood it from the prehistoric era through the current political situation."

FOUR

Abdur Rahman, the builder of Bagh-e-Bala, liked to call his country Yaghistan: Land of Insolence. And indeed, while there was much about Afghanistan to attract the polymath bon vivant Dupree, its chief appeal to his rebellious nature may have been precisely that. "The insolence of the Afghan, however, is not the frustrated insolence of urbanized, dehumanized man in western society," Dupree would write in the introduction to his most important book, *Afghanistan*. "But insolence without arrogance, the insolence of harsh freedoms set against a backdrop of rough mountains and deserts, the insolence of equality felt and practiced (with an occasional touch of superiority), the insolence of bravery past and bravery anticipated."

Afghans like to claim that Cain and Abel founded Kabul and that Cain is buried there. If so, he was only the first of many murderous dynasty builders to arrive. He was followed by the Aryans, the Kushans, the Persians, Alexander the Great and the Greeks, the White Huns, the Arabs, Tamurlane and the Mongols, the Ghaznavids, and yet more Persians. Afghanistan emerged as a loose coalition of territories under a monarchy only in the mid-1700s, and its boundaries were not formally delineated until the 1880s, when they were decided on by British and Russian cartographers. Seeing the country as a mutually beneficial stretch of insulation between the Raj and the tsar, they gave little thought to the myriad cultures and faiths that unwittingly found themselves inside the new borders: Pashtuns, Turkmen, Tajiks, Uzbeks, Hazaras, and Baluchis, who variously practiced Sunni, Sufi, and Shiite Islam, Buddhism, and even some Zoroastrianism, along with expert grudge-holding and famously bloody battles over succession. The colonially minded American historian Theophilus Rodenbough, writing in 1885, observed that "the love of war is felt much more among Afghans than by other eastern peoples."

Britain and Russia spent much of the nineteenth century vying for control of Central and South Asia in the sadistic enterprise known as the Great Game. Rodenbough proudly related that during the First Anglo-Afghan War, "Kabul and other towns were leveled with the ground; [Afghan] troops were blown from guns, and the people were collected together and destroyed like worms." However, the Afghans had one elusive advantage over their would-be occupiers: they were not, had never been, a feudal people. Afghan political life was arranged around complex authority-sharing conclaves known as *jirgas* and *shuras*. When trouble arose, elders, chiefs, and religious leaders would act together to protect their territories. In this way, they had rebuffed one attempted conquest after another. Uninterested in cohering in peacetime, in war Afghans were something to watch; the British may have blown their enemy from cannons, but eventually they left in humiliation.

In the 1930s Afghanistan—for as long as anyone could remember, a byword for exotic isolation—began opening up to the world. On the eve of World War II, King Mohammad Zahir Shah aligned Afghanistan with the Axis powers and then, seeing which way the wind was blowing, switched to the Allies, thus avoiding being drawn into actual conflict by either. The Dari term for this is *bi-tarafi*, or "without sides." Some observers called it self-preservation, others a way of playing world powers off each other, still others plain deceit. Dupree liked to call his adopted home the Switzerland of Asia, where "spies swapped lies and information and played cat-and-mouse with counter-agents and counter-counter-agents."

By the time Dupree settled in Kabul, in the 1950s, its upper classes were dressing in Savile Row suits and sending their sons to Oxford. In 1958 the prime minister, Mohammad Daud Khan, became the first Afghan leader to visit Washington, and the next year Dwight Eisenhower returned the favor, the first American president to venture to the Afghan capital. Embassies opened. Diplomats, academics, archaeologists, and explorers arrived. Kabul University expanded.

The Peace Corps set up shop. Kabul became a spur on the Hippie Trail, the path of enlightenment and drug tourism that snaked from Europe to India.

Dupree was in the middle of it all. When not out on a dig, he taught courses and lectured about Afghanistan, compiled reports, advised governments and corporations, filmed documentaries, and wrote or edited scholarly articles and books (some 218 of the former and 22 of the latter by the end of his career). In between he socialized endlessly. More than any other foreigner, he knew Afghans, all kinds of Afghans; he was as charmed by goatherds as he was by the royal family. They all had something to teach him, he felt. He assumed that Afghans found him charming, too, and indeed many did. What he failed to see—what other Americans who knew and loved the country less did see—was that while Afghans liked him, that didn't mean they trusted him. "Their long history with foreigners taught them that you never knew who would be in charge next," Ted Eliot, the former ambassador, said.

FIVE

Louis Dupree and Alan Wolfe were the only Americans in Kabul who could match one another cocktail for cocktail and tale for tale, and by the mid-1960s they had become good friends. "He was very smooth," Mary MacMakin said of Wolfe. "A good talker, a good dancer, a good drinker—drinking especially." And Dupree, who had a connection at customs and brought in liquor by the crate, seemed "impervious to alcohol."

To much of the rest of the world, as to the country's more cosmopolitan citizens, the opening of Afghanistan was an encouragement, proof that the Cold War could be avoided in certain corners of the globe. Dupree's social calendar seemed proof of this: on a given night, he might be found dining in the company of the American ambassador or the Russian one. But to Wolfe—a gentleman spy in the classical mold who spoke seven languages and thought a great deal about meaning in history—Afghanistan wasn't just another front in the Cold War; it was a deceptively important one, and one to which Washington wasn't paying sufficient attention, he believed.

And to a degree, he was right. Russia's preoccupation with Afghanistan had persisted through the fall of the Romanovs and the October Revolution. "The road to Paris and London might lead through Kabul," Leon Trotsky remarked, to the agreement of his boss, V. I. Lenin, who said, "The East will help us to conquer the West. Let us turn our faces toward Asia." For a time the Afghan royal family was receptive to the Kremlin's overtures, particularly after Lenin wrote the king a pandering letter in which he expressed his conviction that Afghanistan had been chosen by history for a "great and historic task," namely to "unite all the enslaved Muslim peoples." Afghanistan was the first country to recognize Soviet Russia, in 1917, and two years later the USSR was the first nation to recognize an independent Afghanistan.

But the Afghans perceived, rightly, that the atheist Moscow regime was out to topple Islam along with all other religions. They also suspected that the Bolsheviks' intentions for Afghanistan weren't all that different from what the old regime's had been: where the tsars had seen Afghanistan as the passageway to a larger empire, the Bolsheviks saw it as the means to further revolution. Neither much appealed. This suspicion was confirmed when Lenin backed a plan to recruit an army of disaffected Muslims and use Afghanistan as a staging ground to attack British India. Relations soured further in the 1930s, when Stalin ordered the Muslim leadership in Soviet Central Asia decimated and instituted forced collectivization, sending hordes of refugees into Afghanistan.

The Afghan government wanted help in modernizing, however, and during the Cold War help came from one of two places. Finding American requests to sign mutual security pacts and contain "Communist aggression" too demanding, Kabul turned to Moscow. Beginning in the 1950s, Soviet arms, advisers, and economic aid came rushing in. Afghans traveled to the USSR for academic and military training. Washington countered with projects and weapons of its own, but it never caught up.

Wolfe was acutely aware of all this. How much he privately told Dupree about his work was known only to the two friends. Publicly, they were at the center of Kabul's international social scene. This being the 1960s, that scene was characterized not only by heavy boozing but by adultery. Afghan officials bedded foreign diplomats' wives; foreign diplomats bedded Afghan officials' wives; wives bedded wives. Nancy and Annie Dupree, Louis's wife, rebuffed any number of offers. In the midst of it, the two women, who were very different—Nancy was childless and famously flirtatious, Annie more traditional and shy, with three children—bonded. It was with Annie that Nancy reenacted the battles on horseback in the meadow.

Soon after arriving in Afghanistan, Nancy accompanied the American ambassador to see the giant Buddhas at Bamiyan. Appointed to act as an unofficial historian for the trip, she attempted to read up on the statues but was appalled to find that no guidebooks to Bamiyan existed. At a cocktail party upon their return, she cornered the Afghan minister for tourism, Abdul Tarzi. She recalled the encounter this way: "Now, instead of being a diplomat's wife, I said, 'Mr. Tarzi, it's a scandal. That is one of the wonders of the world, and you don't have a proper guide, you don't have anything.' And in typical Afghan style, this Mr. Tarzi drew himself up, and he said, 'You're quite right. Why don't you do something about it?' A French archaeologist who was part of the discussion said, 'Madam, do you like ladies' coffee parties?' I said, 'Not really.' He said, 'Do you play bridge, Madam?' I said, 'That's a waste of time.' 'Then,' he says, 'I suggest you take up this challenge of Mr. Tarzi's.'"

She did. Tarzi liked the manuscript for *The Valley of Bamiyan* so much, he had the tourism ministry publish it. She went on to write guides to Balkh, Herat, and the National Museum. The books were increasingly handsome; Afghanistan was becoming a tourist destination, and as Nancy put it to me, "They needed to be printed in some kind of form that these rich bitches would take notice of." *An Historical Guide to Kabul*, the book that thirty years later would possess Tony Kushner, was published in 1965. Annie proofread it. In the acknowledgments, Nancy wrote, "I owe her for more than these labors, for her understanding of and sympathy for the city has been a constant guide since my arrival."

What happened next is still obscured by mystery and rumor. No two people tell the story the same way. Finally, the one fact that can be verified is the only essential one: at some point, the couples switched partners.

SIX

Some friends of the Duprees and Wolfes believe Annie and Alan fell in love first, leaving Louis and Nancy to do the same. Others maintain that it was the reverse. Charles Kolb had long suspected that Louis and Nancy were having an affair. She visited the camp at Aq Kupruk for no apparent practical reason. Kolb recalls flying into Kabul in 1966 to resume work at Aq Kupruk. Louis picked him up at the airport and, with his customary bluntness, announced, "I've divorced Annie and married Nancy."

"That's all he said about it," Kolb told me. "I said, 'Okay.'"

When I asked Nancy about it, she did what she usually did when she didn't want to discuss something—she recalled the most famous and most anodyne episode from the affair and then abruptly ended the conversation. When she finished writing *The Valley of Bamiyan*, she told me, she sent the manuscript to Dupree for fact-checking.

For some time she heard nothing back. Finally, he summoned her. When she arrived at his home, he was sitting behind a large desk in a room full of plants that had been moved inside for winter storage. He handed her the manuscript without looking at her. At the top of the first page he'd written, "Adequate, but nothing original."

"After a curt riposte, I turned on my heel and stomped off," she recalled. "I got to the door, and he said, 'Come back here.' So I went back. And I never left."

They were married in the winter of 1966, in a blizzard. Minister Tarzi stood in for her father during the negotiation of the bride-price, which Louis set at ten thousand sheep. "Even in a situation like that," she told me, "he was a joker."

Alan and Annie Wolfe left Kabul, and Louis and Nancy Dupree became its expat nucleus. They lived in a compound in the modern Shar-e-Nau district. Nancy worked in the main house, Louis in a building in the courtyard. So many visitors stopped by that they had to instruct their guards not to admit anyone who hadn't made an appointment. In the evenings, they hosted a recurring cocktail party known as the Five O'clock Follies.

Otherwise the Duprees could be found traveling Afghanistan's rough mountains and deserts in Louis's red Land Rover. "He was always looking for new caves," Nancy said. "And I was always happy to go along because I might see something. And if there was something I needed for the guidebooks, he was always happy to go along, because he might find another cave. Every time one of us would finish an article, he'd open a bottle of champagne. It was real companionship." Together they fell in thrall to a country where, in the Homebody's words, "one might seek in submission the unanswered need."

"I was happy then," Nancy told me. "Going around and learning everything new with Louis Jan. So enthusiastic, like a teenager."

In 1973 Louis published his magnum opus, *Afghanistan*, the culmination of a quarter-century of work and travel. It's still the definitive survey text on the country. For all his lack of sentimentality and his admiration of Afghan insolence, Dupree was an optimist, and the book's keynote is one of hope for the country's future. *Bi-tarafi* had allowed the Afghans not only to stay neutral in the Cold War, Dupree argued, but also to coax mortal enemies into cooperating. In their efforts to use Afghanistan as a proxy battlefield, the United States and the Soviet Union had ended up helping it. "The Soviets assisted the Afghans in building roads from the north, the U.S. from the south," he wrote. "The Soviets helped construct the landing strips and buildings for the new International Airport at Kabul; the Americans installed the electrical and communications equipment.

"But since the West and the Soviet Union are both interested in winning, the question of 'Who's winning, the Americans or the Russians?' should be considered," he went on. "In all honesty, one must answer 'Neither—the Afghans are winning.'"

Nancy likes to deny what everyone knows, which is that she was essential to the research and composition of *Afghanistan*. She claims she merely transcribed it. "You've seen his book?" she asked me one day. "I typed that dumb thing three times over—on a manual typewriter! Three times, and I was happy to do it."

The false modesty of this claim was demonstrated when her *An Historical Guide to Afghanistan* was published. Where *Afghanistan* is a monument to fact, her book is an exercise in style and wit, and it's still an indispensable guide for diehard Afghanophiles, who—like Kushner—don't read it so much for the information as for her voice. ("We were totally committed to her guidebooks as we traveled around the country," Ted Eliot, the former ambassador, told me.) In the acknowledgments she wrote, "From my husband, Louis Dupree, I draw a constant charge of excitement and enthusiasm for this land and its people. Together we find new depths and new values. I shall be well pleased if this book succeeds in conveying our continuing affection for Afghanistan."

SEVEN

After the two-hour-long drive north, Nancy, Mashall, and I arrived in Charikar in the late morning. From Western news coverage, one can get the idea that, twelve years after the American invasion, the Taliban are still confined to Afghanistan's peripheries. This isn't the case. The Taliban control much of the countryside, it's true, but the group also wields influence and fear in just about every city and major town, including Kabul. Nancy's first stop was at the office of the provincial council in Charikar, which had been attacked recently. The office sits behind blast-shielding berms and a pair of guards whose faces suggest they don't expect to be much help when the next bomb explodes.

For years Dupree has been sending books, thousands of them, to provincial councils—on history, administration, farming science, public health, and anything else she can have printed—in the hopes that local officials will use them to better govern. "Mr. Karzai and the government, they don't like it, because it takes away from their own power," she says. "But until the people get a voice, Afghanistan's not going anywhere." After three and a half decades of war, however, the country is still mostly run by small groups of old men, many of them illiterate.

She and Mashall were led into a narrow, dark room lined with overstuffed green felt chairs and coffee tables. A policeman with a limp put out bowls of pistachios and poured tea as provincial officials, all of them old and hirsute—*reesh safeda*, or whitebeards, they're called—shuffled in. Without greeting Nancy, they sank into chairs. She had forgotten most of her Dari, so she asked them questions through an interpreter.

"Is Kabul listening to you?"

Murmurs.

"Are you getting the money for the projects you want to do?"

Fewer murmurs.

"Do you listen to the women and get them money?"

Silence.

The whitebeards knew who she was, and perhaps they even appreciated her help, but they couldn't have been less interested in her presence. Dupree elicited somewhat more adamant murmuring when she asked about the recent murder of a local woman. An official spoke to the interpreter, who turned to Dupree and said, "They are totally against the things which are bad." Dupree frowned. The official was now talking into his phone. The meeting was over.

As the officials shuffled out, a younger man introduced himself as the secretary. In precise English, he explained that the council valued her books. They had tried to set up a public library, as she'd requested, but people borrowed the books and neglected to return them. So he'd moved them into a locked office. Now officials neglected to return them.

As he and Dupree talked, he unburdened himself. "The problem in Afghanistan is everything is based on theory," he told her. The council had no money. He hadn't been paid a salary in a year and half. A local merchant had donated the big green chairs. Dupree listened intently, made suggestions. She said she wanted him to connect the council to her organization online, so she could distribute the newsletter he wrote and send him materials. He looked at the floor. "We don't have Internet."

"This is so typical," she said to Mashall as they left. "He's got the spirit. He wants to do something, not for himself, but for other people. But he can't break out."

EIGHT

In 1973 in *Afghanistan*, Louis had expressed great hope for the country's future—too much, as it turned out. He didn't mention that radical Communism and radical Islamism were on the rise, nor that the halting attempts at modernization and religious and social reforms undertaken by Mohammad Daud Khan—who'd been removed from the prime ministership by his cousin, King Zahir Shah, nearly a decade earlier—hadn't made it out of the cities. The gaps between the increasingly secular urban elite and the poor, illiterate, and devout peasantry were more glaring than ever. In 1972, when the country was overcome by famine and hundreds of thousands died, an official remarked, "If the peasants eat grass, it's hardly grave. They're beasts. They're used to it." The next year, after Dupree had completed his book, Daud staged a palace coup and took back control of the government.

Louis knew the autocratic but generous-spirited Daud as well as any foreigner did. "You must understand one thing in the beginning: Afghanistan is a backward country," he'd once told Dupree during an interview. "We accept this. We know that we must do something about it or die as a nation." Daud wanted America to support Afghanistan, he said, but not at the price of its independence. "We first turned to the Unites States for aid, because we believe in the American ideology. The idea of freedom for all is the idea that we have for Afghanistan . . . but any aid which any country gives to us must be with no strings attached."

Daud delivered the same message, with less tact, to Soviet premier Leonid Brezhnev. By the late 1970s, Moscow was largely keeping Daud's government afloat, but still he liked to "light Soviet cigarettes with American matches," as one KGB officer put it. "We will never allow you to dictate to us how to run our country," Daud reportedly told Brezhnev, dispensing with the subtleties of *bi-tarafi*, after the Kremlin had instructed him to expel workers from NATO countries.

In 1978 Afghan Marxists murdered Daud and his family. Mayhem of the sort not seen since the Anglo-Afghan wars ensued. Officials, academics, businessmen, landowners, journalists, religious leaders, and anyone else deemed a threat to the socialist revolution were rounded up, tortured, and executed.

Louis, of course, knew the Marxist cabal well, including the new president, Nur Mohammad Taraki, a sadistic KGB provocateur of long standing. Taraki, a firm believer in terror, liked to say, "Lenin taught us to be merciless towards the enemies of the revolution." Despite this, Dupree was at first sanguine about his intentions—or startlingly naïve, depending on whom one asked.

Dupree's delusional attitude derived in part from experience, one suspects, and in part from pride, but more than either from his love of the Afghans. He similarly assumed he wouldn't be targeted, regardless of the persistent rumors about him, because so many Afghans loved him. "Louis's conviction was that every Afghan knew he was a friend of Afghanistan and they wouldn't hurt him," Ted Eliot said.

One day in November 1978, Louis and Nancy went to the National Museum to pay a visit to Daddy's Head. That afternoon, after Louis had returned to the hotel suite where they were staying at the time, secret policemen knocked on the door. An Afghan translator Dupree worked with had been arrested and, after being tortured, had identified Dupree as a spy. Others followed suit—maybe to save their skins, maybe because they knew something.

In Kabul, it had long been suspected that Dupree's relationship with Alan Wolfe extended beyond friendship and the eventual exchange of spouses. During the Cold War, it was common for American scholars to gather information for the CIA, and Dupree was a perfect candidate for recruitment: three Harvard degrees, military experience, unparalleled knowledge of the country. He'd been surrounded by spies of one type or another for much of his life. (Carleton Coon, his mentor at Harvard, had been an agent in the Office of Strategic Services, the CIA's precursor.) And Dupree never really left military service. Before moving to Kabul, he'd worked as a researcher in troop behavior for the air force, writing field manuals and course curricula, and later taught at West Point. He didn't officially retire from the army until 1967.

It would have surprised no one, in other words, if Dupree had worked with the CIA. He always denied the rumors—adamantly, sometimes angrily. According to some people who knew him well, however, that may have been a front.

As Kabul station chief, Wolfe had been tasked with providing the CIA with intelligence on the Russian-made hardware being used by the Afghan military. Most of it was in the north of the country, as is Aq Kupruk. The archaeologist Charles Kolb said that on their way to and from the excavation site, Dupree and he took detailed notes on the Russian equipment they saw. Dupree photographed it with a high-speed camera. Kolb believes he was doing this for Wolfe and that Wolfe or the CIA may have funded Dupree's work in some capacity. "We were always looking for military installations," Kolb told me. "He was working with Alan and providing information to Alan directly." He also believes Dupree's popular parties were a means for the pair to gather intelligence. His "soirees were very eye-opening, because you got people together who were theoretically political enemies, but in that environment they would talk. It was very good for Louis to learn what was going on and for Alan Wolfe to get what he needed."

NINE

"Dupree, the biggest CIA agent!" the interrogator called out when the police brought the archaeologist to a seized government building. On a desk, while Dupree was questioned, sat a Kalashnikov, its barrel pointed at him. He was moved to another building, where a man took calls, calmly tabulating political assassinations, as two guards smiled at Dupree and drew their fingers across their necks.

The next day he was interrogated for nine hours. He was instructed to make a list of all the Afghan intellectuals he knew. Suspecting it would be used as a kill list, he refused, telling his captors, "I know practically everyone." He was told instead to make a list of all the Kabulis he knew. He consented, and the first name he wrote down was that of Nur Mohammad Taraki, the new president and possibly the man who'd ordered him arrested. No more lists were requested. Asked what he would say if someone accused him of working for the CIA, Dupree replied, "If you want to accuse me of working for the CIA, don't go through this God damn nonsense," according to an account of his incarceration that he later dictated to Nancy. "Just go ahead and accuse me."

The translator who fingered him was brought in. The man was shaking, and according to Dupree, "his face was not his face. It had about a month or more of growth of beard. It was totally misshapen, his eyes were not his own, his lips were swollen and almost dropping down to his lower jaw. He could hardly talk."

An interrogator questioned the translator in front of Dupree.

"Is Dupree CIA?" he demanded.

"Yes, everybody knows Dupree is CIA," the translator whimpered.

Uninvited, Dupree jumped in. "Did I ever tell you I was CIA?" he asked.

The translator said no.

"Did I ever try to recruit you for CIA?"

No again.

After five days, Dupree was brought to the Ministry of Interior. Women demanding to know where their husbands and sons had been taken were being thrown around by their burkas. An official recognized Dupree and, forgetting himself for a moment, shook his hand. Then he stiffened and handed Dupree a statement to sign. "You are hereby informed that you are ordered out of the country never to return," it read. "If you ever do return to Afghanistan, you will be responsible for the consequences." Dupree signed it, but not before appending a statement of his own in the margin: "I would like

to add that I have great love and affection for the people of Afghanistan and I hope that eventually a true experiment in socialism will
succeed in Afghanistan for the benefit of all the people."

He found Nancy, who'd somehow kept it together during his
incarceration. They drove in the red Land Rover to the border. There
they were officially expelled from Afghanistan.

To this day, she maintains that none of the rumors about Louis
had any basis in fact—that he'd never been connected with the CIA
in any way. The translator and others named him, she said, because
he was a gossiped-about American and because they didn't want to
die. "Some of these characters, I've run into them," she said. "It takes
them a long time, but eventually they'll get me into a room all by
ourselves, and they'll let it all spill out. They feel so guilty because
they turned him in. But it was life or death for them. They were killing people all over the place."

TEN

Louis and Nancy drove over the Khyber Pass to Peshawar, where
other expatriate and Afghan friends who'd made it out were gathering. They moved into Dean's, a Victorian hotel, a hangout for people
with information about what was happening in Afghanistan. Their
rooms came to be known as the Dupree Suite. They tried to approx-
imate their old life, confident that soon enough everything would
calm down and they'd return.

But the Afghanistan they'd known was disappearing. In February 1979 the American ambassador was kidnapped by Islamic
extremists and later killed in a shootout. Washington began sup-
plying anti-Communist rebels. In September Taraki's prime minister had him strangled in his bed and took power. The next month
Afghans went into open revolt against the Moscow-backed regime
and its heavy-handed religious and social reforms. Officials, Soviet

advisers, and their families were tortured and murdered, their bodies paraded on pikes in the streets. On Christmas Day the Soviets invaded.

From its start, the invasion's brutality was matched by its clumsiness. The Kremlin promised a months-long operation; a ten-year occupation followed. In that time over 600,000 Russian troops would be sent to Afghanistan. Fourteen thousand of them would be killed, according to official estimates (unofficial estimates go as high as 75,000), and 400,000 injured or taken ill. Roughly a million and a half Afghans—most of them civilians—would die, and numberless villages and towns would be leveled.

All of it was in vain. It was not long before Russians were referring to the war in Af-*gavni*-stan: Afshitstan. The Afghans simply would not submit. Calling on the old traditions of the *jirgas* and the *shuras*, they created an endlessly brave and hugely effective network of resistance, joined by deserters from the Afghan army and fighters from around the Muslim world. At first they fought with nineteenth-century muskets and World War II–era Lee Enfield rifles and made bullets by hand from spent shell casings. One Afghan attempted a suicide attack by setting himself on fire and rushing at a Russian tank. Eventually, a disorderly coalition of world powers and adversaries that included the United States, China, Pakistan, Israel, Britain, Egypt, and Saudi Arabia provided the mujahideen, as they called themselves—warriors of God—with serious weaponry. Decades worth of grudges against the USSR were avenged on television screens around the world, as grainy footage of shoulder-launched rockets turning Russian helicopters into fireballs emerged from the Hindu Kush.

American support for the resistance was run out of CIA headquarters. Among its choreographers there was Alan Wolfe, who had moved to Washington with Annie. By now he was the chief of the Near East Division, known as its grand old man. Shortly after the 1978 coup, Wolfe flew to Islamabad to confer with agents. He told them a story. "I came home the other day, and my wife and I were having our evening martini, and *The Washington Post* was on the coffee table," Wolfe said. "The photo on the front page was of the new Afghan flag being raised in Kabul. I picked it up and showed it to my wife. 'They're fucking with our country, dear!' I can't have that. I am going to change that fucking government, toss those commie bastards out on their asses."

"I sat there looking at Wolfe as he spoke," the agent who worked under him told me. "It was clear to me that this was one of those moments that you hear about but rarely are lucky enough to witness."

On the ground, the Afghan resistance was run by Pakistani intelligence from Peshawar, where armies of refugees, many eager to fight, were massing. Nancy worked in the overflowing refugee camps, while back at Dean's, rebel leaders conferred with Louis, whose understanding of guerrilla warfare and connections with influential leaders across Afghanistan were invaluable. He no longer harbored any illusions about the Communists. Word spread. One day someone walked into the hotel with a copy of the *Los Angeles Times*. In it was an op-ed, by a Russian political commentator, entitled "CIA Perfidy Necessitated Rescue by Soviet Union." It read: "In May, 1979, the American intelligence men in Pakistan who were engaged in training Afghan rebels were led by the well-known CIA operative Louis Dupree."

ELEVEN

There is no evidence Dupree led a rebel army, much as he probably would have liked to, but he did much else to assist the mujahideen. He had known most of its field commanders since they were young men. He sneaked into Afghanistan to advise and fight with them. "Actually," claims Nancy, "it was Louis who taught them how to make a Molotov cocktail."

When he wasn't with the rebels or in Peshawar, Dupree traveled to American universities and think tanks to lecture about the war and urge people to get involved; cofounded groups to support the fighters and refugees; and wrote reports and op-eds. He always stressed that this was not a proxy fight between capitalism and Communism, that Afghanistan was not a "client" of the West—a position offered with increasing bluster as the mujahideen became celebrities in Georgetown sitting rooms. Afghanistan was its own country fighting for its own future, Dupree reminded his audiences.

In 1981 he was in a near fatal car accident. In the hospital for a year, he underwent two brain surgeries. Still partially paralyzed after being discharged, he went to Washington to urge lawmakers to send the rebels more weapons. Testifying before the Senate, he said, "This is, in my opinion, the most important political and moral issue that faces us at this time and is probably the most important since the Second World War."

In Dupree's personal papers, one finds dozens of letters he sent— to politicians, employers, deans—on behalf of Afghan exiles. More poignant, however, are the letters written to him by the exiles themselves. "Since the year that the Russian took over Afghanistan, many people have been died and many were slaughtered by Russians army," wrote a student turned fighter named Hafizullah who'd fled to Iran. "I was charged for the crime that [I] worked for and with Americans in Kabul. Now I am in Tehran have no passport and I am eager to come over to USA for my further studies or if not possible to take refugee there at that part of the world."

Life got worse for the Duprees, too. Still suspected of being a spy, Louis was expelled from Pakistan in 1979. "I have been followed, harassed and hounded by various elements in the Pakistani government," he wrote in a letter of complaint to (who else?) Pakistani president Mohammad Zia-ul-Haq. "Somewhere in the bowels of the Pakistani bureaucracy exists a hard-core belief that I am a CIA agent." Eventually, he was readmitted.

Although Louis took up a professorship at Duke University, he and Nancy never entertained the thought of moving permanently to North Carolina. When I asked her why, she said, "These people were in trouble. Refugees were coming in." She choked up. "How could you turn your back on them at that time?"

By 1985, the year Mikhail Gorbachev became general secretary of the Soviet Communist Party, two things were obvious. The first was that the USSR had lost the war in Afghanistan. Though the conflict wouldn't officially end for another four years, withdrawal talks were already under way. The second was that Afghanistan was, in a more profound sense, lost. Five and a half million people—one-third of the population—would flee the country by the end of the decade, and another two million would be displaced internally. Louis called it a "migratory genocide." Whole swaths of the country were laid waste; mosques, libraries, schools, museums, and archaeological sites were razed. It was as though some horrible wind had swept in from the north and erased epochs.

As the crisis worsened, so did Louis. Still disabled from the car accident, he was diagnosed with lung cancer. He remained the final authority on Afghan history, however, so when a consortium of charity organizations dealing with the preservation of Afghan culture needed to assemble a bibliography of scholarship on the country, he was the obvious choice. No sooner had he submitted the bibliography, however, than he convinced the consortium it wasn't what they wanted. What they wanted, he said, was the stuff produced during the war: the underground newspapers, the home footage of fighting, the testimonies of Russian defectors, and so on—the documents that would tell a generation living in exile what their country was like while they were gone. "In the camps around Peshawar, they had an unprecedented phenomenon—Afghans from all over the country, populations that had never interacted with each other, gathering in one place," Nancy said. "The possibilities to cre-

ate a legacy of learning for when they repatriated were enormous."
She and Louis began collecting. It was the start of her library.

Louis was always sure the refugees would repatriate and reclaim
their country from the Soviets. "He had every faith," said Nancy.
"He said, 'The Afghans will throw them out.'" In January 1989,
as he lay dying in Durham, North Carolina, the last Soviet tanks
rolled out of Afghanistan. The mujahideen had captured everything
except Kabul.

"Well, darling, you were right," she told him.

Louis looked up at her. "The problems are just beginning."

People traveled from around the world to attend the memorial service at Duke. Dupree's eulogy, read by the director of its Islamic and
Arabian development studies department, Ralph Braibanti, was
entitled "Tribute to a Mujahid." Louis and Nancy, he told the mourn-
ers, had "appeared in a moment in history when the culture they
so admired was in crisis. It was this transmigration of their spiritual being that enabled each of them to preserve some part of the
national character which now became part of their persona."

In the service program was printed a photograph of Louis taken a
few years before, during a mission with the mujahideen. He's wearing large, professorial eyeglasses, an Afghan vest, and a traditional
pakol cap, gray hair flowing from its brim. He looks haggard but
highly pissed off. Aged but eager. A boyish mischievousness dances
across his face, halfway between a smile and a frown. *I know a lot,* his
unyielding eyes and pursed mouth seem to say, *but I'm not going to tell
you a fucking thing.*

After Louis died, Nancy wound up his affairs, taught his classes
through the end of the term, and broke down. But she didn't just
miss Louis; she missed Afghanistan. They had been her two greatest loves. So when she was invited to return to Peshawar to head an
Afghan cultural organization, she thought it might be an opportunity to carry on his work, and she accepted before she could refuse.

Civil war persisted for seven years after the Soviet departure. Kabul, which had made it out of the occupation mostly unscathed, was torn apart. The rebel leaders Louis had helped were now warlords. They battled block by block for control of the city while the last Soviet-backed president, Mohammad Najibullah, tried in vain to hold on to power. Rockets slammed into the National Museum, and soldiers and militiamen looted the collection. In 1993 Nancy traveled to Kabul to assess the damage for the United Nations. "Artifacts [were] strewn among the rubble, and filing cabinets of museum records and catalogs indiscriminately dumped," she later recounted in an article. "Hasps had been unscrewed and locks ripped off steel storage boxes, and drawers and crates had been methodically emptied onto the floor." It was rumored that thieves were using her guidebook to the museum to value stolen pieces. Seventy percent of the collection, she estimated, was gone. Among the missing pieces, it appeared, was Daddy's Head.

In 1996 the Taliban swept the warlords from Kabul and at first were more respectful than anyone had dared hope. The Taliban leader, Mohammad Omar, appointed a cultural minister and decreed the smuggling of relics illegal. He allowed the UN to repair part of the museum. But in 2001 he changed course, ordering the Bamiyan Buddhas—the subject of Nancy's first guidebook—destroyed. When footage of Talibs blowing up the statues was broadcast around the world, it became clear that hard-liners loyal to the polite Saudi she'd met years before, Osama bin Laden, had taken control. Next, Omar ordered what remained of the museum's collection destroyed. Heavies from the Ministry for the Propagation of Virtue and the Prevention of Vice arrived, hammers in hand.

Later that year, however, the United States invaded. In 2004 the museum reopened. The curators returned to work. They took the salvaged artifacts from their hiding places and began the slow process of recataloging them. Nancy, who had been splitting her time between Peshawar and North Carolina, began the process of moving back to Kabul the same year. One day she received an email from a curator who had "found a remarkable little bundle wrapped in brown paper," Dupree said, recounting the message. "She tore off the paper only to come to another layer of paper, newspaper. She continued peeling the bundle, and under the newspaper she found toilet paper and then tissue paper."

Inside the tissue paper was a small, very old rock. There were markings carved into it. The features were faint.

Daddy's Head, Dupree said to herself.

TWELVE

After Louis died, one of the things Nancy did to keep her mind off him was continue the collection they'd started during the war. She scoured bazaars and antiques stores and bookstalls in Pakistan and Afghanistan. She visited old mujahideen and exiles and aid workers to see what they had. She hired unemployed men to help her. She stored the old books, reports, pamphlets, newspapers and magazines, tracts, treatises, photos, film reels, and slides she gathered in Peshawar. "If it had Afghanistan in the title, it wasn't safe around me," she said.

Of course, it didn't work. In every new find, there was something to remind her of Louis. *Louis would have liked this,* she would say to herself, handling a book, or, reading an account of a particular battle, *Louis would have disagreed with that.* Finally, she admitted to herself that the collection was her way not of moving on from Louis but of remembering him. More than that, of memorializing him and his love of Afghanistan.

While her new library awaited completion in late 2012, her collection sat in Kabul University's main library, a sad affair in the middle of campus. Most of the materials were stored in locked, fragrant cedar cabinets. In the back of the building was the small, stuffy archiving room. On the days I visited, young male archivists (and one woman) could be found studying and scanning, copying and uploading, unbinding and rebinding. One day I looked over the shoulder of an archivist as he paged through a Taliban propaganda newspaper from 1996 whose headline read "Congratulations to the People of Afghanistan About the Capture of Kabul by the Taliban."

Operations were overseen by Rahim, a dour, wiry man whom Dupree hired in Peshawar. He and a group of helpers smuggled the collection into Afghanistan. They stuffed about thirty thousand items into sacks and loaded them onto the backs of horses and men for the trek over the Khyber Pass. It took six months. Rahim said it was worth it. "We learn many things from Nancy," he told me. "Many information about Afghanistan we get from Nancy." Now they have about ninety thousand items.

In 2005, when he was university chancellor, Ashraf Ghani donated a plot of land on the campus to Dupree to house the collection. When I asked him why, he told me the collection "represents the proposition that to overcome the past we need to understand it. The past is haunting Afghanistan. We have too much history—history that has not become historical. History that lives. Our perceptions of history are clouding our future. We've done horrible things to each other, and those things need to be put to rest, and this collection is part of that."

Browsing the cabinets one day, I found myself thinking of a line from the Homebody's monologue:

My research is moth-like. Impassioned, fluttery, doomed. A subject strikes my fancy: Kabul, you will see why, that's the tale I'm telling—but then, I can't help myself, it's almost perverse, in libraries, in secondhand bookshops, I invariably seek out not the source but all that which was dropped by the wayside on the way to the source. . . . Old magazines, hysterical political treatises written by an advocate of some long-since defeated or abandoned or transmuted cause; and I find these

irrelevant and irresistible, ghostly, dreamy, the knowing what
was known before the more that has since become known
overwhelms.

It had been obvious enough to me, watching it at work, that her
organization was inefficient. Her staff was well intentioned but poorly
trained and overly worshipful of her. Nancy herself was Homebody-
like, unable to focus on any single task or line of thought for very long.
Just how inefficient I learned on my last days in Kabul. Wafa, her executive director, admitted to me that the organization was broke. Nancy
had blown through a $3 million grant from the State Department a
year ahead of schedule. The Norwegian government had stepped in
with a bridge loan, but now that was nearly gone, too.

An auditor hired by the grant administrator to assess Dupree's
organization told me she "is completely exhausted and wants to let
go, and she's trying to hand it over, but her board can't be bothered."
The whole thing was being held together, barely, on the strength
of her legend, he believed. "The American government has spent
$3 million supporting the cult of an old lady." An employee of hers
told me the organization "will collapse when Nancy is gone," a con-
tention with which the auditor agreed. Indeed, many of the people
around her seemed to believe this.

Penury nagged at her. Grasping deans at the university were making noises about commandeering her new library. She worried that
Karzai, having paid for some of it, might use it for his own purposes.
After trips such as the one to Charikar, she suspected that Afghans
were indifferent to her projects. She seemed to become sicker and
more impatient by the day. Her coughing fits grew deeper and longer,
her outbursts more plangent and scattershot; it was as though everyone reminded her of how little time she had left, and thus everyone
was a waste of time. It wasn't long before she was blowing up at me
when I walked into her office each morning. She would lapse into the
first person plural, as though she were yelling at herself, too. "You

don't seem to be interested in the things we are doing!" she said one day. "What are we doing here? Why?! What's our purpose?"

THIRTEEN

For weeks I had been bothering Dupree to take me to the National Museum. I wanted to see Daddy's Head with her. Finally, she relented, and I could see as soon as we arrived why she hadn't wanted to come. The museum still pains her. Everything in it reminds her of Afghanistan's past, of her past, of Louis.

At the entranceway stands a second-century marble relief of the Kushan king Kinishka that is particularly close to her heart. She likes to call Kinishka, a scholar and arts patron, her hero. The statue's head is gone, smashed by a Talib. "This poor little fella," she said as we walked by him. Inside we passed a damaged Buddha. "I, ah—" she said, then turned away, on the brink of tears.

Upstairs, after looking at a display of gold coins ("I kept telling Louis to find me some gold," she joked), we emerged from the gallery to find burly military contractors with assault rifles taking up positions on the staircase. They looked as though they expected the statues to come to life. Nancy didn't flinch. Nor did she betray interest when their charge—an official, clearly American, in a baggy suit, mustache, bad haircut—bounded up the stairs. He introduced himself as a deputy ambassador of something.

"Another ambassador?" she said.

"There are so many of us," he replied gamely.

Afterward I asked Nancy what she thought of him. "He's an ambassador," she said. By this I took her to mean: *My patience for my countrymen, and their preposterous exertions in this doomed place that I love so much, is at an end.* And it was a position for which I could hardly blame her. On the contrary, the ignorance and futility—there is no other term for it: *the abject failure*—of the American adventure in Afghanistan is obvious as soon as one sets foot in the country. Our attempts to rebuild institutions and infrastructure have come to little; hugely expensive projects sit skeletal and looted, the countryside poor and benighted; Karzai's ministers live like pashas in Kabul. This is to say nothing of a reinvigorated Taliban or of the daily bombings, maimings, and beheadings. All of it at the expense of the American taxpayer, America's reputation, and worst of all, everyday Afghans, the people whom Dupree has been trying to help for most of her adult life.

"We have really destroyed this very sensitive characteristic of the Afghan character, which is self-sufficiency," she told me one day. "They used to be proud of the fact that they did things for themselves. But now they've had so much money thrown at them, they've had so many advisers telling them what to do, that from the village on up, these young people don't want to think for themselves. *Let the foreigners do it.*"

Dupree feels this failure deeply, and as she is an American adopted by Afghans, it takes a double toll on her, embarrassing and infuriating her in equal measure. She knows that she is part of this failure, that as the quintessential expat do-gooder in Kabul, she somehow embodies it. She worries that one or the other of her homelands might blithely do away with her legacy. Her library finally opened in March of last year, several months after my visit. But even as the building's completion approached, she spoke of it as a tenuous thing. "It would only take one mullah with a match or one American daisy cutter," she told me, "and it would be finished."

Dupree had reluctantly agreed to speak with me one last time. Shortly after I got to her office, however, so did a young Afghan-American woman, two hours late for an appointment. Dupree had been yelling about her—"Where the hell is this person? God damn it, damn it, damn it!"—but when the woman finally arrived, apologizing profusely, Dupree issued a contrition-banishing wave of the hand and invited her to sit down.

It was her first time in Kabul, the woman explained, and she'd gotten lost. She was a graduate student, about to begin research near Kandahar. She had nothing pressing to ask of Dupree, nothing to offer her, but Dupree put aside what she was doing—and me—to speak with her about nothing much. Soon they were trading stories and laughing. She took the woman out to tour the campus. When I returned to the office three hours later, they were having lunch. Dupree was talking about Louis. It was the happiest I'd seen her. I left quietly.

On my way off campus, I stopped at the new library, recalling something the auditor had said about it. "She wanted to make sense of what her legacy would be," he'd said, "so she's become obsessed with the building." He was probably right—and the obsession had paid off. It was a beautiful building. Its granite walls and stolid wooden beams and flagstone portico were somehow already perfectly weathered. Inside, there was no furniture, no curtains, no books. It felt new and old at the same time. It knew a lot but would say nothing. Students were already walking by it as though it had been there forever, and soon enough none would remember its provenance. Though it is Nancy's monument to Louis, to their love of Afghanistan, she has refused to put their name on it. It is called, simply, the Afghanistan Center at Kabul University.

I walked into the interior courtyard. A solitary worker was cleaning a new windowpane. Nearby his young son was sitting with a neat pile of tattered textbooks. The school year had started, and he wanted the books to last through the long winter ahead. He was carefully wrapping each cover in brown paper.

52
BLUE

LESLIE JAMISON

ONE

December 7, 1992: Whidbey Island, Puget Sound. The world wars were over. The other wars were over: Korea, Vietnam, the Persian Gulf. The Cold War was finally over, too. The Whidbey Island Naval Air Station remained. So did the Pacific, its waters vast and fathomless beyond an airfield named for an airman whose body was never found: William Ault, who died in the Battle of the Coral Sea. This is how it goes: The ocean swallows human bodies whole and makes them immortal. William Ault became a runway that sends other men into the sky.

But at that naval air station, on that day in December, the infinite Pacific appeared as something finite: audio data gathered by a network of hydrophones spread along the ocean floor. These hydrophones had turned the formless *it* of the ocean and its noises into something measurable: pages of printed graphs rolling out of a spectrograph machine. These hydrophones had been used to monitor Soviet subs until the Cold War ended; after their declassification, the navy started listening for other noises—other kinds of *it*—instead.

On December 7 the *it* was a strange sound. The acoustic technicians thought they knew what it was, but then they realized they didn't. Petty Officer Second Class Velma Ronquille stretched it out on a different spectrogram so she could see it better. She couldn't quite believe it. It was coming in at 52 hertz.

She beckoned one of the technicians. He needed to come back, she said. He needed to take another look.

The technician came back. He took another look. His name was Joe George.

Second Petty Officer Ronquille told him, "I think this is a whale."

Joe thought, *Holy cow*. It hardly seemed possible. For a blue whale, which is what this one seemed to be, a frequency of 52 hertz was basically off the charts. Blue whales usually came in somewhere between 15 and 20—on the periphery of what the human ear can hear, an almost imperceptible rumble. But here it was, right in front of them, the audio signature of a creature moving through Pacific waters with a singularly high-pitched song.

Whales make calls for a number of reasons—to navigate, to find food, to communicate with each other—and for certain whales, like humpbacks and blues, songs also seem to play a role in sexual selection. Blue males sing louder than females, and the volume of their singing—at more than 180 decibels—makes them the loudest animals in the world. They click and grunt and trill and hum and moan. They sound like foghorns. Their calls can travel thousands of miles through the ocean.

The whale that Joe George and Velma Ronquille heard was an anomaly: his sound patterns were recognizable as those of a blue whale, but his frequency was unheard of. It was absolutely unprecedented. So they paid attention. They kept tracking him for years, every migration season, as he made his way south from Alaska to Mexico. His path wasn't unusual, only his song—and the fact that they never detected any other whales around him. He always seemed to be alone.

So this whale was calling out high, and he was calling out to no one—or at least, no one seemed to be answering. The acoustic technicians would come to call him 52 Blue. A scientific report, published twelve years later, would describe his case like this:

No other calls with similar characteristics have been identified in the acoustic data from any hydrophone system in the
North Pacific basin. Only one series of these 52-Hz calls has
been recorded at a time, with no call overlap, suggesting that
a single whale produced the calls. . . . These tracks consistently
appeared to be unrelated to the presence or movement of other
whale species (blue, fin and humpback) monitored year-round
with the same hydrophones.

Much remained unknown, the report confessed, and difficult to
explain:

We do not know the species of this whale, whether it was a
hybrid or an anomalous whale that we have been tracking. It is
perhaps difficult to accept that . . . there could have been only
one of this kind in this large oceanic expanse.

TWO

The drive from Seattle to Whidbey Island took me through the
plainspoken pageantry of Washington State industry: massive piles
of raw logs and cut lumber, rivers clogged with tree trunks like fish
trapped in pens. I passed stacks of candy-colored shipping con-
tainers near Skagit Port and a collection of dirty white silos near
Deception Pass Bridge, its steel span looming majestically over
Puget Sound—hard-sparkling water glinting with shards of sun-
light nearly two hundred feet below. Craggy cliffs rose on either side
over the water, studded with crooked straggler pines clinging to the
steep rock. In front of me on the two-lane highway, a biker wore a
jacket full of skulls.

On the far side of the bridge, the island felt pastoral and otherworldly, almost defensive. LITTER AND IT WILL HURT, one sign read. Another said, SPACE HEATERS NEED SPACE. The lawns were full of goats and rabbit hutches.

Whidbey Island often calls itself the longest island in America, but this isn't strictly true. "Whidbey is long," the *Seattle Times* observed in 2000, "but let's not stretch it." It's long enough to hold a kite festival, a mussel festival, an annual bike race (the Tour de Whidbey), four inland lakes, and an annual murder-mystery game that turns the entire town of Langley, population 1,035, into a crime scene. In 1984 the island was a refuge for a white supremacist named Robert Jay Mathews—leader of a militant group called the Order—whose home burned down around him when a pile of his own ammo caught fire during a shootout with the FBI. His body was found next to the charred remains of a bathtub. Every year, it's rumored, his followers gather on the day he was killed, at the site where his home once stood, to commemorate his death.

The Naval Air Station, on the northern end of the island, specializes in electronic attack, which means manipulating the electromagnetic spectrum: sending out radio and radar frequencies to locate and neutralize enemy operations, or using these same techniques to defend against similar tactics. The station also monitors the intricate array of hydrophones known as the Sound Surveillance System (SOSUS), part of an undersea surveillance network that ranges across the Atlantic and Pacific Oceans, from Nova Scotia to Hawaii, seafloor-mounted hydrophones connected by underwater cables to facilities that process the audio data onshore. SOSUS was initially built for one reason: to track Soviet subs. Its earliest hydrophone arrays were installed on the seafloor between Greenland, Iceland, and Britain—a naval-warfare choke point known as the GIUK Gap, the waters that Soviet subs would have to cross if they were heading west.

SOSUS tracked its first diesel sub in 1962, its first Victor- and Charlie-class subs six years later. The system was expanded through the 1960s and helped locate the only two U.S. nuclear submarines ever lost at sea.

But once the Cold War ended, operations were downsized, and much of the equipment was declassified. The hydrophone arrays still did military duty, but the navy started looking for other uses for them, too.

Joe George, the technician who first identified 52 Blue in 1992, still lives in a modest hillside home perched on the northern end of Whidbey, about six miles from the Naval Air Station. When I visited, he answered the door smiling—a burly man with silver hair, no-nonsense but friendly.

He'd offered to show me around the naval base. Though he hadn't worked there for twenty years, he was still able to get us past security with his navy ID. He told me he uses it whenever he comes back to the base to drop off his recycling: the profits go toward a Morale, Welfare and Recreation Fund that pays for bleachers and baseball diamonds for the base. We passed by the looming hangars where the planes are kept, "prowlers" and "growlers," all designed for electronic warfare.

Whidbey Island is currently home to seventeen active-duty electronic attack squadrons, including the oldest electronic warfare squadron in the navy, the VAQ-130 Zappers (mascot: Robbie the Dragon, who is pictured with lightning bolts coming out of his angry lizard eyes). We passed smaller simulator buildings, where some guys step into a cockpit for the first time and other guys do their best to mess up the ride. Just beyond these dreary beige boxes, the coastline was ragged and beautiful—waves crashing onto dark sand, salt wind moving through the evergreens. Joe told me that a lot of people like getting stationed here: the work isn't bad, and the island itself is pretty stunning. Outside the officers' club, men in flight suits were drinking cocktails on a wooden deck.

Joe explained that his team—the team responsible for processing audio data from the hydrophones—was fairly disconnected from the rest of the base. It was a question of security, he said, and when we reached his old building, I saw what he meant: it was surrounded by two fences topped with razor wire. Some of the other servicemen on base, Joe explained, used to think his building was some kind of prison. They never knew quite what it was for; its machinations were mysterious. The only contact Joe's division had with the rest of the base was passing along whatever information it had gathered about subs.

Joe stressed the intensity and secrecy of his old work, everything that happened past the razor wire. I asked him what he had thought the strange sounds were, before he realized they were whale calls—back in 1992, with Second Petty Officer Ronquille. "I can't tell you that," he told me. "It's classified."

THREE

July 2007: Harlem, New York. Leonora knew she was going to die. Not just someday, but soon. She'd been suffering from fibroids and bleeding for years, sometimes so heavily that she was afraid to leave her apartment, heavily enough that she grew obsessed with blood: thinking about blood, dreaming about blood, writing poems about blood. She'd grown increasingly reclusive. She'd stopped working as a case supervisor for the city, a job she'd held for more than a decade.

Leonora was forty-eight years old. She had always been a self-sufficient person; she'd been working since she was fourteen. She'd never been married, though she'd had offers. She liked to know that she could support herself, but this was a new level of isolation. She'd grown obsessively focused on a self-directed exploration of embryonic stem cell research and increasingly distant from everyone in her life. One family member had told her, "You are in a very dark place," and said she no longer wanted to see her.

By summer things had gotten worse. Leonora felt truly ill: relentless nausea, severe constipation, aches across her whole body. Her wrists were swollen, her stomach bloated, her vision blurred with jagged spirals of color. She could hardly breathe when she was lying down, so she barely slept. When she did sleep, her dreams were strange. One night she dreamed about a horse-drawn hearse moving across the cobblestone streets of another century's Harlem. She picked up the horse's reins, looked it straight in the eye, and knew it had come for her.

She unlocked her apartment door so that her neighbors wouldn't have trouble removing her body before it "stank up the place." She called her doctor to tell her as much—*I'm pretty sure I'm going to die*—and her doctor got pissed, said she needed to call the paramedics, said she was going to live. So Leonora called the paramedics. When they were wheeling her off on a gurney, she asked them to turn around and take her back so she could lock the door again. This was how she knew she'd regained faith in her own life: if she wasn't going to die, she didn't want to leave her door unlocked.

That request, asking the paramedics to turn around, is the last thing Leonora can remember before two months of darkness. That night in July was the beginning of a medical odyssey—five days of surgery, seven weeks in a coma, six months in the hospital—that would eventually deliver her, in her own time and her own way, to the story of 52 Blue.

FOUR

Back at his house, Joe showed me how he'd been spending his time since retiring from the navy. In addition to a job restoring salmon habitats—putting in the right plants and taking out the wrong ones—he was regularly participating in eighteenth-century fur-trapper-rendezvous reenactments. He kept an impressive collection of carnivorous plants and raised bees to feed them. He showed me the cobra lilies, his favorites, and explained how their translucent hoods coaxed trapped flies to exhaust themselves by flying for the light.

Certain patterns emerged across Joe's various vocations: evident care and conscientiousness, a desire to be accurate and meticulous. He fixed a frost cloth over his cobra lilies right after he showed me their elegant green-veined hoods, and it was with conspicuous pride that he showed me the eighteenth-century musket he'd built from a kit. I saw the same sense of pleasure at precision when he explained the sheaf of papers he'd pulled out from his old days tracking 52 Blue. They were computer maps documenting nearly a decade of migratory patterns, 52 Blue's journey each season marked by a different color—yellow, orange, purple—in the crude lines of mid-1990s computer graphics. He showed me charts of 52's song and explained the lines and metrics so I could compare its signature to more typical whale noise: the lower frequencies of regular blues, the much higher frequencies of humpbacks.

Blue whale songs hold various kinds of sounds—long purrs and moans, constant or modulated—and 52 Blue's vocalizations showed these same distinctive patterns, only on a wildly different frequency, one just above the lowest note on a tuba. The brief recorded clip of 52 I listened to, sped up for human hearing, sounded ghostly—a reedy, pulsing, searching sound, the aural equivalent of a beam of light murkily visible through thick fog on a moonlit night.

Joe clearly enjoyed explaining his charts and maps. They took him back to the days when the story of 52 was still unfolding, still a mystery—this inexplicable whale and his singular sound. At the time Joe had recently arrived at Whidbey after several years of what was technically classified as "arduous duty" on a base in Iceland, though he explained that those years weren't particularly arduous at all; his kids built snowmen by the Blue Lagoon. Joe was a good candidate for Whidbey. He was already trained as an acoustic tech-

nician, already prepared for the work that happened in his squat little bunker behind the razor-wire fence.

SOSUS, Joe told me, was a "bastard child": it had bounced from
one navy division to another over the years and was treated differently depending on where it was housed at any given time. It got a
lot of funding when it was in the submarine division, headed by an
admiral. But after it was moved to surface fleets, which had less pull,
there was less money to go around. And then the Cold War ended.

Without Soviet submarines to listen to, the navy started thinking about how else the expensive hydrophone array might earn its
keep. That's when it decided to offer the array to science, so it could
listen to everything else. Dennis Conlon—a civilian navy scientist
with the Space and Naval Warfare Systems Command—invited an
acoustics expert from Woods Hole Oceanographic Institution in
Massachusetts named Bill Watkins out to Whidbey. Watkins, who'd
worked with the navy in the past, realized he could use the equipment to track blues, fins, and humpbacks—their migration patterns
and areas of seasonal density.

Now navy guys who'd spent years tracking subs were suddenly
tracking songs. They were accountable for making sense of something other than threats. The sounds they gathered were processed
and examined by Watkins's team back at Woods Hole.

Joe spoke of Watkins—who died of cancer in 2004—with evident
respect. This was a pattern in the various accounts of Watkins I
heard, this reverence: he was honest and passionate and kind. He
could talk to anyone. He spoke a bunch of languages, the precise
number changing each time I heard it: Twelve. Six. Thirteen. Nancy
DiMarzio, one of his former research assistants, claimed it was
twenty. She also said he once fled an African country in the middle of a war. Darel Martin, another naval acoustic technician who
worked with Joe at Whidbey, told me the story of Watkins's Ph.D.:
how he'd learned enough Japanese to defend a doctoral dissertation
at the University of Tokyo.

Watkins was born in 1926 to Christian missionaries stationed in

French Guinea. According to Darel, he hunted elephants with his father when he was a kid. He could hear the elephants from farther off than anyone else: "He found out that he could actually hear twenty hertz, which is extremely low for any human," Darel told me. "You and I can't hear that—twenty's pretty low—but he could actually hear the elephants in the distance. And he would tell his dad which way to go."

Watkins studied broadcast technology at a Christian college in the United States and then returned to Africa to work in radio. He spent most of the 1950s operating a station in Monrovia, Liberia. When he first started working at Woods Hole, in 1958, he was hired not as a biologist but as an electronics assistant—it was the recording he excelled at. He didn't know much about whales then, and he wouldn't earn his Ph.D. in biology until he was in his fifties. By the time he did, however, he had already made profound contributions to the field, developing much of the technology and methodology that made it possible to record and analyze whale songs: whale tags, underwater playback experiments, location methods. He developed the first tape recorder capable of recording whale vocalizations, which opened up new frontiers of fieldwork.

During the years the Whidbey Island team tracked 52 Blue, Watkins came out to the base every few months during migration season, and Joe and Darel would show him the vocalizations they'd picked up. The three men enjoyed working together. While some of the other navy guys didn't like going from tracking subs to tracking creatures—the stakes of intelligence work felt more palpable—Joe and Darel loved eavesdropping on marine life. "It's just endless what you can hear out of the ocean," Darel told me. "We went from being experts on sharks of steel to tracking living, breathing animals."

For Joe and Darel, 52 Blue's unusual frequency was interesting for largely practical reasons: his singularity made him easy to track. Because you could always distinguish his call from others, you always knew where he was traveling. Other whales were harder to tell apart, their patterns of motion harder to discern. The possibility of particularity—*this* whale, among all whales—was unusual: it allowed for an abiding relationship to 52 as an individual creature, while other whales blurred into a more anonymous collective body.

52's particularity, as well as his apparent isolation, lent him—they figured it was a him, as only males sang during mating season—a certain kind of personality. "We always laughed when we were tracking him," Darel told me. "'Maybe heading to Baja for the lady blues.'" His jokes echoed the way frat brothers might talk about the runt of a pledge class, the one who never had much luck with chicks: *52 was ugly. 52 struck out, looked again, tried again. 52 never let up with that song.* It was something more than a job. Darel bought his wife a whale necklace during the years he spent tracking 52; she still wears it whenever they go to Hawaii.

Joe had his own fixations. "One time he disappeared for over a *month*," he told me, his inflection registering the mystery; it clearly still engaged him. At the end of the month, they finally picked him up—farther out in the Pacific than he'd ever been. "Why was there that gap?" Joe wondered. "What happened during that time? You just wonder about stuff like that. What happens in that month? You always kinda wonder."

Watkins was the driving force behind the whale tracking, and he fought hard to maintain the funding, but he couldn't keep it running forever. The Twin Towers happened, and everything changed. Just as the end of the Cold War had signaled the beginning of a new era, so did the onset of another war signal the beginning of the end. "When 9/11 came around, it was a couple of weeks after that, Bill told me all the funding was gone," Joe explained. "Everything."

The whale-tracking team hunted around for other jobs on the base or within the navy. Joe tried the marine-acoustics field but didn't have much luck. So he went back for an associate's degree in environmental sciences, which paved the way for his current job restoring salmon habitats.

Now the records of 52 are just reams and reams of data taking up space in filing cabinets at Woods Hole. The mystery survives in splinters: just a man sitting at his kitchen table, pulling out old folders to point out the ordinary-looking graph lines of an extraordinary song.

FIVE

Leonora grew up in Harlem near Bradhurst Avenue. She was raised mostly by her grandmother, who was four foot eleven and blind from diabetes, a determined and resourceful woman who'd come to the United States from Chennai by way of Trinidad. She always said people back home in India thought America was full of golden sidewalks. It was the flecks of silica in the pavement, she said, their sparkle. Word had spread.

Leonora's grandmother was a woman who felt blessed by an extraordinary second sight—she got a strong sense about people, could feel the energy coming off them. If she didn't want to get to know you, she'd tell you. If she did want to get to know you, she'd run her hands over your face and body to get a better sense of the spirit inside. She could describe your clothing without seeing you. She could sense the energy of different colors: the calm of blue, the heated intensity of red.

During the mid-1970s, when Leonora was in high school, Bradhurst was something of an urban war zone, with its own police task force and sky-high murder rates. One summer when Leonora got interested in photography, taking pictures of friends and folks in the neighborhood, people started calling her Death Photographer because so many of her subjects ended up becoming victims of violence.

She worked hard to find a way out, started City College and made good money bartending at the Red Rooster and Broadway International. One day she was walking along the Hudson and had a vision: it started looking like another river entirely. This was how she realized she needed to get to Paris. She needed to get even farther away from home.

She kept bartending until she had enough money saved, then got herself across the Atlantic as an exchange student. She found a place on the Boulevard Saint-Michel and spent the next year in a happy blur: walked around with a corkscrew in her hand, took a trip to Capri, where she and her friend met a pair of amorous lifeguards, broke into an abandoned villa and ate bread and jam off the dusty kitchen table.

It was tough coming back to New York. Her friends resented the fact that she'd been somewhere—done something—that they hadn't. She lived in New Jersey for six months, which she hated, then returned to the city to be with a man she almost married. They went to the courthouse, and she got such terrible cramps that she had to go to the bathroom. She realized it was her body telling her: *Don't do this*. She listened. She stayed in the bathroom until the offices closed; a police officer had to tell her to come out.

She eventually started working for the city as a case manager for clients on food stamps or welfare. It was emotionally draining work: dealing with families in states of desperate need, hungry kids, a mother who'd scored a little money in the lottery but still dressed her kids in rags and wanted her own mom's share of food stamps. For a while in the 1990s, Leonora worked for a city program helping Russian immigrants. They got off the plane at La Guardia with visas and apartment leases and not much else; she helped them figure it out from there.

She was dedicated to her clients, respected their courage and determination, but by the mid-2000s her health was in decline. She was holed up in her apartment and bleeding all the time. Home was a refuge but also a container for her increasing isolation. By the time she was hospitalized, in July 2007, she'd retreated from the world so much that her time in the hospital felt less like an absolute rupture and more like the continuation of a descent that was already well under way.

SIX

In 2004, three years after the funding dried up, the Woods Hole researchers published a paper about 52 Blue in a journal called *Deep Sea Research*. The paper explained how the audio data had been recorded—gathered by more than ten arrays of hydrophones and analyzed by acoustic technicians familiar with whale calls—but gave few details about the process, for security reasons: "These Navy facilities, hydrophone arrays, their characteristics, and associated data processing techniques have remained classified." The paper described the units of noise recorded from the whale ("calls," "groups," "series," and "bouts") as well as patterns in his motion: "The tracks for the 52-Hz whale indicated relatively slow, continuous movement" across "the deep waters of the central and eastern portion of the North Pacific basin," where he "roamed widely" and "spent relatively little time in any particular area," and—of course—never seemed to cross paths with any other whales.

The article was accepted in August 2004. Bill Watkins died in September. Though he was listed as the lead author on the article, another member of the team—Mary Ann Daher, his former research assistant—was listed as its corresponding author. Soon Daher started getting notes about the whale. They weren't just typical pieces of professional correspondence. They came, as *New York Times* reporter Andrew Revkin wrote at the time, "from whale lovers lamenting the notion of a lonely heart of the cetacean world"; others were "from deaf people speculating that the whale might share their disability."

After Revkin's story ran that December, headlined "Song of the Sea, a Cappella and Unanswered," more letters flooded Woods Hole. (One marine mammal researcher quoted in the story, Kate Stafford, may have inadvertently fanned the flames: "He's saying, 'Hey, I'm out here,'" she told Revkin. "Well, nobody is phoning home.") These letters came from the heartbroken and the deaf, from the lovelorn and the single; the once bitten, twice shy and the twice bitten, forever shy—people who identified with the whale or hurt for him, hurt for whatever set of feelings they'd projected onto him.

A legend was born: the loneliest whale in the world.

In the years since, 52 Blue—or 52 Hertz, as he is known to many of his devotees—has inspired numerous sob-story headlines: not just "The Loneliest Whale in the World" but "The Whale Whose Unique Call Has Stopped Him Finding Love"; "A Lonely Whale's Unrequited Love Song"; "There Is One Whale That Zero Other Whales Can Hear and It's Very Alone. It's the Saddest Thing Ever and Science Should Try to Talk to It." There have been imaginative accounts of a solitary bachelor headed down to the Mexican Riviera to troll haplessly for the biggest mammal babes alive, "his musical mating calls ringing for hours through the darkness of the deepest seas, broadcasting a wide repertory of heartfelt tunes."

A singer in New Mexico, unhappy at his day job in tech, wrote an entire album dedicated to 52; another singer in Michigan wrote a kids' song about the whale's plight; an artist in upstate New York made a sculpture out of old plastic bottles and called it *52 Hertz*. A music producer in Los Angeles started buying cassette tapes at garage sales and recording over them with 52's song, the song that was quickly becoming a kind of sentimental seismograph suggesting multiple storylines: alienation and determination, autonomy and longing, not only a failure to communicate but also a dogged persistence in the face of this failure.

People have set up Twitter accounts to speak for him, like @52_Hz_Whale, who gets right to the point:

Hellooooooo?! Yooohoooooo! Is anyone out there? #SadLife
I'm so lonely. :'(#lonely #ForeverAlone

SEVEN

Leonora woke up in St. Luke's–Roosevelt Hospital in September
2007. What had happened in the previous two months—after the
paramedics wheeled her out of her apartment—was only explained
to her long after it was over, once she'd recovered enough to process
it. The doctors had discovered that a severe intestinal blockage was
making her ill, and she'd had major surgery over the course of five
days. The surgeons removed everything the blockage had rotted;
the more they looked, the more necrotic tissue and gangrene they
found. They kept cutting out portions of her intestines—seven
inches, nine inches, three inches—until they'd gotten it all. By the
time they were finished, nearly three feet of her guts were gone. The
remaining incision was huge.

Leonora was put into a seven-week coma so she could recover
more efficiently, and after she awoke, she remained hospitalized for
several months to keep the open wound from becoming infected.
She was on an IV. She hardly knew how to speak. She thought it was
1997. Her father came to visit once, and she vomited when she saw
him. She could barely make herself understood, barely convey how
much she wanted him to leave.

At one point, she sensed an incredible stench around her. She
didn't know where it was coming from. She said "smell," and someone understood; eventually they realized it was her hair, which was
matted with blood. She asked one of her doctors to cut it. The doctor said that wasn't her job. Leonora said, "If you don't do that, I
will start screaming now and I will not stop." The doctor did it. It
turned out looking pretty good. Weeks later they joked that the doctor might have a second career as a hairdresser.

For Leonora, the hardest part of recovery was losing her self-sufficiency. "Feeling that I could no longer be independent," she said, "that I could no longer take care of myself. Ever since I was fourteen, I've been doing that." In the aftermath of her coma, Leonora couldn't walk. She had trouble remembering words. She couldn't count past ten. She couldn't even quite count *to* ten. But she pretended. She didn't let on. She didn't want other people to see her struggling. The hospital offered decent physical rehab but nothing to help her reinhabit her own mind.

Leonora had been wheeled into the hospital on July 6, 2007, and wasn't home again until 2008. She went to a rehabilitation facility in November, then had a bad fall—she still wasn't walking well—and returned to the hospital, then to another rehab in December. During those months at various institutions she had visitors, but generally she felt abandoned—as if everyone in her life were fleeing her damage, pushing her away for a simple, primal reason: the healthy don't like to be around the sick. Her illness made them uncomfortable, because it reminded them of their own mortality—or the fact of mortality itself.

When people did come to visit, she perceived a dark energy coming from them; it made her feel nauseous. When her father visited, he told her over and over that she looked like her mother—a woman he hadn't spoken about in many years. She felt that her illness raised long-buried emotions in him, feelings of anger and loss.

During much of her recovery, Leonora couldn't even watch television. It gave her headaches. So she turned to the Internet. It was a way to find interest and beauty in the world. And it was then—alone and late at night, once again, searching for something that might offer a sense of meaning—that she came upon the story of 52 Blue.

By then the story of the whale had been floating around the Internet for several years. But it spoke to Leonora with a particular urgency. It resonated. "He was speaking a language that no one else could speak," she told me recently. "And here I was without a language. I had no more language to describe what had happened

to me. So I too . . . I was like him. I had nothing. No one to communicate with. No one was hearing. No one was hearing him. And I
thought: *I hear you. I wish you could hear me."*

She identified with his plight. She felt that her own language was
adrift. She was struggling to come back to any sense of self, much
less find the words for what this self was thinking or feeling. It was
hard to speak, because her trachea was so scarred from all the tubes
that had been thrust down it during her coma. She felt the world
pulling away. When she found the whale, she found an echo of this
difficulty.

She remembers thinking: *I wish I could speak whale.* She found a
strange kind of hope, a sense of certainty that he must know he
wasn't alone. "I was like: Here he is. He's talking. He's saying something. He's singing. And nobody's really understanding, but there
are people listening. I bet he knows people are listening. He must
feel it."

EIGHT

When I first began looking into the story of 52 Blue, I reached out to
Mary Ann Daher at Woods Hole. Her role in the story was curious:
she'd become the unwitting confessor for a growing flock of devotees simply because her name was on a paper recounting work for
which she'd been a research assistant years before. "I get all sorts
of emails," she'd told one reporter, "some of them very touching—
genuinely; it just breaks your heart to read some of them—asking
why I can't go out there and help this animal."

I wanted to see those letters and to hear from her what it had
been like to read them. But she declined to speak to me on several
occasions; it became clear that all the media attention had started
to grate on her nerves. "It's been pretty painful," she told a reporter

in 2013. "You name the country, and I've had a phone call, wanting to get information. And I haven't worked on this since 2006 or so. . . . And . . . oh God, [Watkins would] be dismayed, to put it mildly, to know of the attention."

Research can quickly grow tiresome to its own researchers once it's been distorted by the funhouse mirrors of public fancy. For Mary Ann Daher, I came to realize, I represented little more than the persistence of that distortion: *It's been pretty painful. It's been worldwide.* The phenomenon itself was a reproach to Watkins's legacy: *He'd be dismayed.*

I thought I understood why she was finished, why she was sick of it, why she was tired. This was part of the story, too: the way a phenomenon could alienate its own midwives. The last journalist Daher agreed to talk to was a writer named Kieran Mulvaney. He sent me the transcript of their conversation from 2013. It gives a sense of her wariness and aggravation about the phenomenon 52 had become. "We don't know what the heck it is," she said of the cause of 52's odd song. "We don't know if it's a malformation. . . . Is he alone? I don't know. People like to imagine this creature just out there swimming by his lonesome, just singing away and nobody's listening. But I can't say that. . . . Is he successful reproductively? I haven't the vaguest idea. Nobody can answer those questions. Is he lonely? I hate to attach human emotions like that. Do whales get lonely? I don't know. I don't even want to touch that topic."

She never sent me the letters she'd received from people who loved the whale. So I went looking for them on my own.

NINE

They were voices out of the digital ether at first, emails appearing in my inbox. I found them on a Facebook page devoted to the whale. They were union leaders, artists, programmers. Juliana was a nineteen-year-old English major at the University of Toronto who felt that 52 Blue was "the epitome of every person who's ever felt too weird to love." Zbigniew—a twenty-six-year-old photo editor at the biggest daily tabloid in Poland—decided to get the outline of 52 Blue tattooed across his back after a bad breakup, the end of a six-year relationship:

> i was deeply in love. but as it came out she was treating me like a second category person in relationship. . . . i was devas-tadem mainy becose i have given her everything i could, and i thought she would do the same for me. [Because] of her i lost connection with important friends. View of the wasted time made me sad. . . . Story of 52 hz whale made me happy. For me he is symbol of being alone in a positive way. . . . He is like a steatement, that despite being alone he lives on.

For Zee, as he calls himself, 52 came to represent the lonely days after the breakup, watching sad movies alone at home with his two cats, Puma and Fuga: "for long time i was 'singing' in other frequency then everybody around." But the whale also represented resilience: "this is what my life looks like for last 2 years. im swimming slowly through my part of ocean, trying to find poeple like me, Patient, going past life being sure that im not crippled but special in positive way."

The tattoo was a way for Zee to honor what the whale had meant to him and to communicate that meaning—to sing at a frequency that might be understood. It stretches across his upper back, the "only place on body huge enough to make it look awesome." Rather than offering a visual representation of 52, the tattoo is actually an artful evocation of the fact that 52 hasn't ever been seen and might never be seen: behind a detailed rendering of Moby Dick—another one of Zee's fixations—there is a second whale, a ghost whale, just a negative space of bare skin defined by an outline of ink.

TEN

In 1894 a wealthy amateur astronomer named Percival Lowell built a telescope in Flagstaff, Arizona. He spent the next twenty years looking through it and finding things no one else could see: a series of canals extending from the poles of Mars, a network of spokes radiating from a hub on Venus. He took both as signs of extraterrestrial civilization. He was mocked. He kept seeing the canals, kept seeing the spokes. He kept insisting. Years later an optometrist solved the puzzle: the settings on Lowell's telescope—its magnification and narrow aperture—meant that it was essentially projecting the interior of his eye onto the planets he was watching. The spokes of Venus were the shadows of his blood vessels, swollen from hypertension. He wasn't seeing other life; he was seeing the imprint of his own gaze.

The natural world has always offered itself as a screen for human projection. The Romantics called this the pathetic fallacy. Ralph Waldo Emerson called it "intercourse with heaven and Earth." We project our fears and longings onto everything we're not—every beast, every mountain—and in this way we make them somehow kin. It's an act of humbling and longing and claiming all at once.

"Every natural fact is a symbol of some spiritual fact," Emerson wrote. "Every appearance in nature corresponds to some state of the mind."

For Emerson, these correspondences offered a kind of completion: "All the facts in natural history taken by themselves have no value but are barren, like a single sex." Put crudely: Human projection fertilizes the egg. It not only brings meaning to the "barren" body of natural history; it also offers sustenance to man. "His intercourse with heaven and earth," Emerson wrote, "becomes part of his daily food."

Emerson's celebration of this process was not without interrogations. "We are thus assisted by natural objects in the expression of particular meanings," he wrote. "But how great a language to convey such pepper-corn informations! . . . We are like travellers using the cinders of a volcano to roast their eggs. . . . Have mountains, and waves, and skies, no significance but what we consciously give them, when we employ them as emblems of our thoughts?"

Roasting our eggs on volcano cinders: this is like asking the splendid form of an elusive whale to embody dorm-room homesickness or post-breakup ennui. We offer animals and mountains as ritual sacrifices at the altar of metaphor. *Is he lonely? I hate to attach human emotions like that. I don't even want to touch that topic.*

ELEVEN

Shorna, a twenty-two-year-old in Kent, England, told me she relates to 52 Blue because she's always felt "on a different wave length to other people . . . like I don't fit no where." The feeling grew particularly acute after her brother was killed when she was thirteen: "I felt I couldn't talk to no one. That no one understood or cared enough."

Years later learning about 52 gave her a way to understand the isolation of that time—a sense that her grief was nothing anyone else could understand. Her family didn't want to talk about it; no one at school understood. Therapists were telling her what she should feel. The whale never told her what to feel; it just gave a shape to what she'd already felt: "I felt withdrawn and it made it worse along with the pain of his death." She felt she couldn't connect with anyone.

Sakina, a twenty-eight-year-old medical actor living in Michigan, associates 52 with a different kind of loss—a more spiritual struggle. I first saw her in a YouTube video, wearing a hijab, describing how the story of 52 immediately made her think of the prophet Yunus, who was swallowed by a whale. "It makes sense that the loneliest whale feels lonely," she says. "Because he had a prophet with him, inside of him, and now he doesn't."

I met Sakina in a coffee shop in downtown Ann Arbor, where she told me what happened after she read about the whale online: she started crying and needed to lie down. He evoked certain lonely periods of her childhood—she grew up Muslim in New Mexico—and reminded her of the first time she'd ever learned about the prophet Yunus in religious school, when she was six: "I was frustrated with my teacher for not recognizing that, you know, she can be straight with me and just say this is an allegory." She said, "I found it hard to believe in miracles."

She wondered if 52 Blue came back into her life to finish the lesson that had begun when she was a child. She was being told, *Take it literally. It's more than metaphor.* She didn't imagine 52 seeking love so much as purpose, wanting a prophet to swallow or a prophecy to fulfill. She found herself wondering, *Is he aching for the divinity again?*

TWELVE

There used to be a name for the kind of people who tell tall tales about animals: *nature fakers*. The phrase emerged from a turn-of-the-century debate between a coterie of nature writers and the naturalists who hated their sentimental tales of animal communities, a genre they dubbed "yellow journalism of the woods."

"I know as President I ought not do this," wrote Teddy Roosevelt, but he went on to do it anyway: offered a scathing public condemnation of these nature fakers for their syrupy accounts of the natural world—tales of wildfowl setting their own legs in mud-made casts and crows convening schoolrooms for their young: "He is not a student of nature at all who sees not keenly but falsely, who writes interestingly and untruthfully, and whose imagination is used not to interpret facts but to invent them."

Roosevelt was especially concerned about what he called "fact-blindness," the possibility that telling fake stories about nature might blind us to the true ones. This is the danger of nature faking, making the whale lonely or prophet-hungry, asking the duck to set a mud cast for his own broken leg—the possibility that feeling too much awe about the nature we've invented will make us unable to see the nature in which we actually live.

Roosevelt's argument finds a strange modern echo in one of 52's twitter accounts, @52Hurts, which actually imagines the whale protesting his own symbolic status: *I am no symbol, no metaphor. I am not the metaphysics you feel stirring in you, no stand-in for your obsessions. I am a whale.* Some of his tweets are just nonsense, as if protesting the projection of language in the first place: *Ivdhggv ahijhd ajhlkjhds jhljhh ajlj dljl 52 skjhdsnlkn* and then, a few hours later: *Tjhgdaskj agjgd ahgjhs kjslhsljhs.* These are the tweets of a whale that *doesn't know why it's on Twitter.* Something about them feels weirdly honest, gibberish that's more interested in what *isn't* legible than what we force into hollow legibility, more interested in acknowledging the gap than in voicing the projections we hurl across it.

THIRTEEN

I first found David, an Irish father of two, through a YouTube video he'd made of himself singing a song he'd written: "I've followed sorrow like Whale 52 Hertz—it doesn't have to be this way." When I reached out by email, he told me he'd written the song after losing his job at Waterford Crystal, where he'd been working for more than twenty years. But he'd identified with the whale even earlier— "another being similarly living in parallel"—even when his life appeared to have all the external trappings of belonging: marriage, family, stable job. David insisted he'd always felt alone. It was his wife who first told him about 52, invoking the whale as his echo. "That's you, that is," she'd said.

After the layoff, David and his wife moved to Galway and began forging a new life. In a letter he wrote to me last year, during his first autumn there, he described himself at the cusp of change: "I am told by everyone that Galway will be good for me and that I need to do something 'arty.' I'm starting tonight with a singing group. It's my first day at school again. And I'm forty-seven." He felt the whale as inspiration and assurance in this sense of beginning again: "I have taken the discovery of the Whale as a signal from the depths that I am close to discovery. . . . All I really know is that the 52 Hertz Whale is out there singing and that makes me feel less alone."

When I checked in with David in the spring, he said things in Galway had been a mixed bag. He'd found a job he loved—as head of IT for a farmers' cooperative in a little village called Tubbercurry—and was enjoying the new folks he met in Galway on the weekends. There was a sense of being in a new city full of unexpected kindred spirits. But the singing group, he wrote, had been "a bust. Lots of hugs from pig-tailed sixty-somethings."

Struck by the fact that his wife had been the person to show him the story of 52 in the first place, I asked David if she'd always thought of him as an isolated person. "My wife does think I am someone who has always felt alone," he said. And in fact, just after he'd started his new job, he told me, his wife said she couldn't live with him anymore. "Our twenty-fifth wedding anniversary is in August," he wrote. "Communications have broken down. I am, to quote an old song, 'seething and bewildered like a din-deafened army.'"

But the whale still held something for him, despite the fact that things in Galway hadn't turned out as he'd planned. "I *do* still think that I am close to discovery," he said. "I still don't know what I am watching out for. When I hear 'Whale 52 Hertz,' I feel at peace. I know that I am still heading in generally the right direction. I often think of the whale. I know that she's still out there. I see others searching. Maybe I won't be alone for much longer."

FOURTEEN

I found Leonora on the same Facebook page where I found Juliana and Zee. After I wrote to her, she responded immediately to welcome me into the "vast vibrational pool" of 52 devotees and then told me pieces of her own story over the phone. Before we met in person, she wanted to know more about what kind of story I was telling about this whale and how she might fit into it. But eventually she agreed to meet at Riverbank State Park, in upper Harlem, where she was working as a volunteer and taking art classes four days a week: beginner and intermediate at once.

We met one afternoon in early March, a day caught between winter and spring, wind still chilly off the Hudson. She wore a purple wool cap, a sweater, and slacks. She moved carefully and deliberately and chose her words with the same care. Riverbank was clearly a special place for her. She said it was built on top of a sewage treatment facility and seemed eager to tell me that—proud of how it had turned ugly necessity into possibility.

The park had also been an important part of her rehabilitation process: it was where she went once she had relearned how to walk after coming out of her coma. She had called her sister on the phone after the first time she successfully crossed "the big street," which is what she called Broadway then—her language was still fumbling at that point, grasping at whatever it could hold. She felt embarrassed at the thought of having her home care aide see her practicing how to walk, watching her stumble at every step. So she went to the park instead. The park never judged. It just let her practice.

Now that it was almost spring, Leonora told me she was proud of herself for not getting a cold all winter. She knew it was because of her vitamins—she'd been taking a "barrage" of them ever since she died. That's how she described her illness and coma: a process of dying and coming back to life.

"My ticket back came with conditions," she said. She had to learn to take care of herself—hence the vitamins, the art classes, and the desire to start growing her own vegetables this spring. She was hoping to get one of the small gardens that the park association was going to auction off before summer. The plots were down by the running track, full of the residue of winter: shriveled stalks, leaves withered to a crisp, bent lattices that had once held tomatoes and would hold them again. Leonora said she wanted to plant peppers and parsley, a small crop perched above a sewage plant—a way of saying, *We do what we can with what we have.* She'd come back from her coma in pieces. She was still putting these pieces back together into a life.

A red-bellied robin hopped across one of the garden plots—just across the fence from us—and Leonora couldn't believe we were seeing it when it was still so cold. She told me we needed to wish on it. She told me about her three-day rule. When she asks the universe a question, she always gets an answer in three days—in a dream or a visitation: maybe an animal or something as simple as the smell of lavender. She is open to messages from everything, all the time, in languages that aren't even recognizable as languages at all.

We walked inside and settled at the snack bar—the last place in New York, Leonora assured me, where you could get coffee for a dollar. We sat by the ice rink, where some of the younger hockey players—the Squirts—were practicing. It was Leonora's home turf. The guys behind the counter knew her order before she ordered it. The guy riding by in a motorized wheelchair said hello. The guy lurking by the register wanted her to sign a petition for a candidate for parks superintendent.

At our table, Leonora pulled out a large notebook to show me some of her pen and pencil sketches of 52 Blue. She'd also painted him in acrylic on a scrap of canvas. These were the materials she was using in her current art class, but she'd been drawing him for years already. "He obsesses me," she explained. "I was trying to get a sense of what he looks like."

Her early drawings were "muddled," she told me. So she started looking at photographs of whales to get a better sense of him. "But I still wasn't finding *him*. He's so elusive." She kept sketching him anyway. I saw his colored-pencil body curving under lists of relevant websites she'd gathered. She told me she was working on a painting of 52 for her class's final exhibition, to be displayed in one of the recreation center hallways.

As we spoke, it became increasingly clear that Leonora's sense of connection to 52—from that first online encounter onward—had always been twofold. It was about communication, and it was about autonomy. He represented the struggle to be heard and also the ability to live alone. He represented her difficulties in recovery—the failed attempts to speak—but also the independence that these difficulties had taken away. Others saw the whale as heartbroken, because he couldn't find a companion; she saw him as a creature that didn't need one. She cherished the capacity to live alone, and this capacity was precisely what her illness had imperiled.

Apropos of very little, she told me suddenly, "I haven't been in a relationship since the last century. I haven't been on a date." She said it bothered other people in her life: "It's like a woman is not a whole person until she has a man." But it didn't bother her: "I've never felt lonely. There is not this lonely factor. I am *alone*. But I am not lonely, okay? I go over to a friend's, I buy cases of wine, I have people over, I cook. I'm a very good cook." It bothered her that people conflated 52's aloneness with loneliness. It bothered her that people conflated *her* aloneness with loneliness.

It was hard not to feel a hint of *doth protest too much* in her distinction, but it also felt like a sincere call for a certain kind of legitimate humility: *Don't assume*. Don't assume the contours of another person's heart. Don't assume its desires. Don't assume that being alone means being lonely. The scientists would say of 52, of course: Don't assume the whale is either one.

The first time Leonora ever listened to 52's song, she told me, she felt skeptical of the clip available online. It was short and had been sped up for audibility. She felt sure 52 had "more to say." But she kept listening. "I think I played it back at least fifty times, just trying to get a sense of it." And the listening did something: "As I listened to it over and over, it helped me meditate into him. That was a key."

She told me she believes we could locate 52 this way. "If you want to really find him," she said, "all you need is five people, ten people, to concentrate hard enough, and to send that request out."

She once traveled with 52 in a dream. He was in a pod of whales, no longer alone, and she was swimming with them, maybe carried in their wake—moving just as quickly, her head huge, her body sleek and hairless. Her coma recovery was full of dreams about water. She'd felt a particular connection to water ever since falling over the side of a waterfall at the edge of seventeen—when a voice inside her told her to hold her breath, assured her that she wouldn't die. In her recovery dreams, she swam everywhere: "In the ocean, in the river. I didn't do any lakes or ponds—no stagnant, no still." In the dream with 52:

> We were traveling at speeds that were, I don't know, maybe a hundred miles per hour? You don't even see anything when you're traveling that fast. What you see—it's not that you see it, you just feel it there. I don't know—you just throw something out, and then something comes back, so you know there's something there. You could feel it all over your body. When I woke up, I was moved by it, all I could do was just lay there and think: *What was that? What was that?*

She couldn't make sense of it. She kept drawing him anyway. She kept drawing him *because*. Not seeing the whale kept him infinite. His elusive form echoed her insistence on motion: *no stagnant, no still*. She told me that she hopes that they never find him—whoever *they* might be. "I hope they don't," she said. "I pray they don't. I like to believe that I'll see him in my dreams."

FIFTEEN

The hunt for an elusive whale is—of course—the most famous narrative in the history of American literature. *Hast thou seen the white whale?* The whiteness of Moby Dick is "a dumb blankness, full of meaning," full of many meanings: divinity or its absence, primal power or its refusal, the possibility of revenge or the possibility of annihilation. "Of all these things the Albino whale was the symbol," Ishmael explains. "Wonder ye then at the fiery hunt?"

No one has ever conducted a physical search for 52 Blue. If anyone ever actually finds him, it will probably be Josh Zeman, a filmmaker currently working on a documentary called *52: The Search for the Loneliest Whale in the World*. Zeman first heard the story of 52 at an artists' colony in the summer of 2012, and it struck him immediately. He was in the aftermath of a breakup. He's been working on the project ever since; he described his relationship to the movie as "Ahabian." He's trying to plan a fifty-day research voyage onto the Pacific—a physical search for the whale—but figuring out how to make the trip work "is fucking complicated," he told me. He plans to have a research vessel staffed with five scientists and three crew, using sonar and old migration routes to locate 52. Joe George told Zeman his search was like looking for a needle in a haystack.

I asked Zeman what he made of folks who didn't want the whale found at all—who preferred it mysterious, elusive, unknown. He said he felt like this resistance to finding 52 was actually a way of speaking *for* him—obstructing the possibility of interspecies communication, making him more precious. Zeman doesn't want to follow the whale, he explained, or find him a mate. He just wants to make contact: "Do we want to help him? No. Do we want to say hi? Sure."

SIXTEEN

It was late spring the second time I visited Leonora up at Riverbank Park. The air was full of promise, balmy without making you feel trapped under the armpit of an entire city. Leonora told me she didn't get a garden plot after all. Her allergies had gotten so bad, she didn't even bother entering the lottery; she wouldn't have been able to use the plot anyway. She told me she thinks about me whenever she sees a robin. I told her that two weeks after we saw that robin, I'd met the man I wanted to spend my life with. It wasn't three days, but still. It was something. We headed straight to the community snack bar, got our dollar coffees, and sat in the corner, in the shadow of a wall of lockers.

During our conversation that day, I started to understand better that Leonora's connection to 52 wasn't just a product of recovering from a particular medical trauma, struggling for language or self-sufficiency, but an accumulation of feelings from decades earlier—her youth, her childhood. Even when we weren't talking about the whale, we were talking about the whale. It was under everything. Her whole life suggested what he might mean to her.

She thought of her medical crisis in similar terms: as an accumulation, the intestinal blockage as an accretion of traumas from all across her life, experiences she endured but never let herself cry or talk about. They cluttered her insides and finally made her ill.

The whale offered another kind of gathering: a vessel in which a lifetime's worth of longings might reside. Even while I struggled to make sense of Leonora's fixation on signs and voices, her desire to find the patterns woven through her life felt deeply intuitive—the search for a logic that might structure everything.

At the snack bar, she shared a new angle of resonance with 52: the possibility of extinction. The whale might be the last of his kind, she told me—that was part of how she understood him—and in a way, she will be the last of hers: she doesn't have any kids. She said she hated how people think of this as a kind of insufficiency—an absence. She thought of her artwork as the closest thing she had to progeny.

After the snack bar filled up with a flock of boys, we moved someplace quieter, a long hallway with cinder-block walls where the art would be displayed for her class's final exhibition. In the quiet of that hallway, she told me about the darker years that followed her coma recovery. She was questioning her own purpose: what did her life mean? She wasn't working. She started living on disability and workman's comp.

I was aware that any cynic could have a field day with her brand of New Age mysticism, but the more I heard about her life, everything that led up to her encounter with the story of 52 Blue, the more I started to respect the incredible gravity of what she'd built him up to be—and what she'd rebuilt *herself* to be, under the sign of his story. He had become the mascot and fuel of her own reinvention.

I remembered all the ways she had described her coma and its aftermath—"resurrection," "rebirth," "second birth"—and couldn't help thinking it was no accident that she used these words, that we kept coming back to the subject of babies, having them or not having them, that "birth" was such a big part of how she thought about all this. *I bled for years.* And at the end of all that blood, when she came back from death, she gave birth to herself.

SEVENTEEN

"I just don't know what it is, the fascination with this whale," Joe George told me, sitting at his dining room table. "To me it's just science."

Which made it even more charming, the tray of cookies that

sat between us—all shaped like whales, with frosted tails, various pastel shades of green and pink and periwinkle, and 52 written in matching shades of icing. Joe's daughter had made them for us. He was pleased to offer them but also seemed a bit sheepish; they were complicit in the whimsy of a phenomenon he couldn't quite wrap his mind around.

It felt odd, he told me, to have funding for the whale tracking cut so suddenly and unequivocally—to feel like no one cared about what they were doing—and then to see his whale resurface so many years later in such a strange, refracted form. Suddenly *everyone* cared, but for reasons that didn't really make sense to Joe—a man more worried about doing a job right than mining it for metaphor. *To me it's just science.* And it wasn't just science—it was *great* science. The singular signal made the whale a godsend.

Joe told me that at a certain point, the whale called 52 Hertz stopped coming in at 52 hertz. The last time they tracked him, his call was more like 49.6 hertz. It could have been age—a kind of delayed puberty—or else a function of size, his growing form pulling his vocalizations down into lower frequencies.

There's something nice in the idea that an elusive animal might stop flashing its old calling card—that the physical creature wouldn't even match the statistics of its own mythology. We have tuned our hearts to a signal that no longer exists. Which means there is no way to find what we've been looking for, only—perhaps—to find what that thing has become.

EIGHTEEN

I went back to Riverbank for the art show. It was early summer, a day of celebration: art hanging on the cinder-block walls, dance and music classes performing in the gym. Leonora was taking photos, wearing lavender pants and a pink scrunchie, rolling around the shopping cart in which she'd carried all her paintings. The beginning keyboard class played "When the Saints Go Marching In" under giant beige industrial fans.

Leonora took me to the hallway, where at last I got to see her vision of 52: a whale painted in flat acrylics, flying over a rainbow, over an ocean. The decoupaged figure of a woman was riding him— or flying with him—and Leonora said it was a photograph of herself, taken years ago, though she obscured the face so it wouldn't just be *her*. The woman's head was ducked low in the painting, down to the whale, as if she were listening to something he was saying. "Someone asked me, 'Is the whale kissing you?'" Leonora told me. "And I said, 'Maybe he is.'"

A park employee walked by—a young Latina woman wearing the green shirt of park staff—and Leonora explained to her, without apology or introduction, "This is 52 Hertz. Just how I imagined him." As if everyone would know the whale, or should—as if the project of imagining his distant body should be familiar to us all.

Leonora didn't seem perturbed by how much the whale meant— all those vectors, some of them contradictory. "He's everything and anything," she told me. "Anything you want him to be. He's the dream you could never attain. He's the million-dollar lottery. He's Shangri-La. He's all these things that you aspire to. He's God, even. How do you know that he wasn't sent here to heal us, and his song is a healing song?"

Sometimes we need to be heard so badly, we hear ourselves in every song the world sings, every single noise it makes: *I will start screaming now and I will not stop.* Maybe desire and demand are just the same song played at different frequencies. Maybe every song is a healing song if we hear it in the right mood—on the heels of the right seven weeks, or the worst ones, the ones lost to us forever.

On our way out, Leonora carefully wrapped the whale in paper and packed him into her shopping cart. When we parted ways at the park bus stop, she handed me a FedEx envelope, cut and folded and taped to make a small flat package. Just a little something, she said. I pulled out a small painting of a robin—red breast, tiny claws, a single beady eye. It was the robin we'd seen together, the one she'd taken as an omen and came to believe was my totem. She said the red on his breast meant *activation*.

I thought, *This return ticket came with conditions.* I thought of the man I'd met after I saw that robin, the man I knew I wanted to marry. I felt the contagion of magical thinking: life becomes a series of omens. I wanted them to imply the presence of some organizing spirit, or at least compose a story.

"*Vaya con Dios*," Leonora told me. "You should have a baby someday."

NINETEEN

"The material is degraded before the spiritual," Emerson wrote. He thought we'd "transferred nature into the mind, and left matter like an outcast corpse." *He's everything and anything. Anything you want him to be.*

The actual body of 52 Blue has become the outcast corpse, the matter left over once our machinations are finished. There is some violence in this alchemy, and also some beauty. Emerson understood both sides of that dilemma:

"Every spirit builds itself a house, and beyond its house a world; and beyond its world, a heaven. Know then, that the world exists for you. For you is the phenomenon perfect. What we are, that only can we see."

52 Blue suggests not just one single whale as metaphor for loneliness, but metaphor *itself* as salve for loneliness. Metaphor always connects two disparate points; it suggests that no pathos exists in

isolation, no plight exists apart from the plights of others. Many fans of 52 were lonely even before their lives gave this loneliness a reason: David was lonely in his stable marriage; Zee was lonely before his breakup and after it. Loneliness seeks out metaphors not just for definition but for the companionship of resonance, the promise of kinship in comparison. Now there's an entire coterie gathered around this kinship—people trained to the same pulse of a minivan-sized heart.

You might say it's a community formed around an empty center. When we pour our sympathy onto 52 Blue, we aren't feeling for a whale; we're only feeling for what we've built in his likeness. But that feeling still exists. It still matters. It mattered enough to help a woman come back from seven weeks at the edge of death.

At one point during our conversation on Whidbey Island, I mentioned Leonora to Joe George. At first I wasn't even sure he'd heard me, but near the end of our visit, he turned to me and said, "That woman you mentioned, the one who was in the coma." He paused. I nodded. "That's really something," he said.

Joe was right when he said the whale is just a whale. And so was Leonora when she said the whale is everything. Happiness is a kind of truth. Feeling is a kind of fact. What if we grant the whale his whaleness, grant him furlough from our metaphoric employ, but still grant the contours of his second self—the one we've made— and admit what he's done for us? *That's really something.* If we let the whale cleave in two—into his actual form and the apparition of what we needed him to become—then we let these twins swim apart. We free each figure from the other's shadow. We watch them cut two paths across the sea.

THE
FORT OF
YOUNG
SAPLINGS

VANESSA VESELKA

ONE

In 1972 in Juneau, Alaska, my father was adopted into the Kiks.ádi clan of a native Alaskan people called the Tlingit.* This made me a clan child of the Kiks.ádi, a relationship that would bewilder me for years.

To be clear, the Kiks.ádi didn't take me home to live with them. In fact, I'm sure they weren't particularly interested in me at all. I was tangential to an honor conferred on my father, and none of this would be my story to tell except that when they adopted him they also got me, and all my earliest memories are of totem poles and Native faces, of wandering in the constant rain at beach picnics listening to the Tlingit language, and of the Raven and the Eagle, icons of the primary cultural divisions of the Tlingit, which I saw everywhere—on coffee mugs and ritual drums, on tourist T-shirts and the regalia of Tlingit dancers at the Alaska Native Brotherhood Hall—and were the first representations I knew of a larger, ineffable world.

My father was a community organizer for the Model Cities Pro-

---

* Written Tlingit uses an alphabet developed by scholars in the 1970s and includes diacritical marks that have no direct analogue in written English. A few rough pronunciation guidelines: 1. A period falling within a word, as in *Kiks.ádi*, indicates a glottal stop, similar to the *t* in *cat* in Cockney English. 2. An underlined *x* is pronounced like the *ch* in *Bach*. 3. In Tlingit, the "el" sound is made by placing the tongue against the upper teeth and blowing sharply out both sides of the mouth. 4. The accented *í*, as in *Shxaastí*, places the stress at the end of the word and is pronounced "eh."

gram, one of LBJ's War on Poverty initiatives, and had built friend-
ships among the Tlingit while working alongside them on the
Citizens Participation Committee in Juneau. A former marine from
Texas, who had spent time as a laborer in Brazil and cowboyed in the
panhandle, he probably shared a rural sensibility with his Tlingit
friends. They certainly shared a distaste for pacifism. The Kiks.ádi
were renowned fighters. They had defeated the Russians in 1804
at the Battle of Sitka, a fact quickly raised once in their company,
so bonded were they to the battle. It belonged to them, and they
belonged to it. These things are inextricable.

There was never a reality, though, in which I would be Kiks.ádi.
Tlingit are matrilineal and my mother was not adopted. My parents split up and my mom took my brother and me back to Houston.
Whereas my Tlingit grandmother's house had been full of bric-a-
brac and stuffed frogs, my maternal grandmother's house was full of
plastic-covered furniture and large wooden lamps shaped like pine-
apples. Nana had a three-inch-thick harvest-gold rug that she raked
in one direction daily. I lay in it like in a field of wheat and watched
Ultra Man. My own clan, it appeared, was the Rug Raking Plastic
Sofa Bridge-Players. We had locusts instead of Ravens.

The year my dad left Alaska, my mom moved to New York. By
then I was nine and had already lived in seven different states. I
knew what kids who move a lot know: try to be invisible or try to be
impressive, which is why on day one of my new fourth-grade class
I loudly proclaimed myself the sort-of-daughter of a proud Tlingit
warrior tribe that no one ever beat. Sadly, we did not move again.

By now it was the late 1970s in Greenwich Village. Boys at my
school were grabbing girls and pulling them into unseen corners of
the playground, pushing them down and dry-humping them in a
game called "rape." Half our parents were dealing or doing cocaine.
The rest seemed to be drunk. The vigil flame of syndicated television burned, for many of us, around the clock.

But I could not let the Tlingit go. Even though I was mercilessly teased as an "Indian princess," even though my father had stopped talking about the Tlingit and my mother got uncomfortable when I spoke of the adoption, I remained faithful in the belief that I belonged to a family of great and unbeaten warriors who would someday welcome my return. In the summers, when my brother and I went back to Alaska and he played with friends, I attended adult-education classes at the Alaska State Museum. I was not the only white person in the Intro to Tlingit Culture and Language course, but I was the only eight-year-old. I had been imprinted at just the right age. Like the Velveteen Rabbit, I wanted to be real.

Still, eventually I had to admit that I probably was a delusional liar and a troubled child. Even at eleven, I could see the telltale signs. I was living amid the wreckage of a fourth marriage and a fifth school. My classmates were right. Real Indians rode horses, and we had already killed them all. If there were any left, I wasn't one of them.

TWO

The Tlingit don't fit the common stereotypes of Native Americans. Primarily sea hunters, they're more like Vikings or Maori. A fiercely martial people, terrifying in their samurai-like slat armor, their bird-beak helmets, and their raven masks, they never surrendered to a colonial power, never ceded territory. When Russia sold Alaska to the United States in 1867, the Tlingit argued that the Russians held only trading posts and that the rest was not theirs to sell. The protest was unsuccessful, but it was the beginning of a narrative: the Tlingit had never signed away their land, had never sold it, had never moved.

It was an argument the Tlingit would make, nearly a century later, in the courtroom. In 1959 they sued the federal government in *Tlingit and Haida Indians of Alaska v. United States* and demanded fair compensation for their stolen land. The Tlingit turned out to be as strategically brilliant in the courtroom as they were on the battlefield. They won a pittance but kept their claims alive, navigating difficult legislative waters and, in the 1960s, joining a statewide Native movement seeking a settlement. The Alaska Native Claims Settlement Act of 1971 would award the state's indigenous people nearly $1 billion and recognize Native ownership of 44 million acres of prime forest, 22 million acres of mineral rights, and 16 million acres of subsurface mineral rights. At the time it was signed, the bill was the gold standard of indigenous settlements.

The huge infusion of cash lessened the economic pressure for Alaska Natives to abandon tribal lands. As a result, Tlingit still live today where they lived before European contact and make decisions with little or no interference from the Bureau of Indian Affairs. A friend of mine told me once of a Tlingit elder no more than five feet tall who was unpopular at powwows because she liked to walk up to the biggest Lakota or Crow she saw, jab her fingers in his or her chest, and say, "You lost! We won!" It was terrible diplomacy—the Tlingit are not famous among other tribes for their modesty—but she was not necessarily wrong.

It was true, of course, that the Tlingit could not escape the profound suffering that came from European colonialism. Epidemics devastated the population, and those who remained suffered from all too familiar oppression. But economically and culturally, one could argue that no tribe fared better. If, as historian Shelby Foote once said, the psychology of the American South holds within itself the identity of a defeated nation, then perhaps the Tlingit psyche holds within it the opposite—faith in its ability to fight and win. It was easy to see why my dad was drawn to them.

THREE

I went back to Juneau in 1991. One of the first things I did was look up my Tlingit uncle, Andy Ebona. He and my dad had lost touch but they had been close, and it was Andy who had asked his mother, Amy Nelson, to adopt my father. She agreed but didn't say when. Then one day my father got a call from Andy saying he should get down to the Alaska Native Brotherhood Hall right away—that Amy was going to do it. He rushed over there, but nothing happened. Later he found out that he hadn't been dressed right. He was in jeans.

In the end, the ceremony was simple and quick. Amy asked him to stand. In front of witnesses, she held a dollar bill to his head and gave him his name, Aak'wtaatseen, which means "swimming or moving frog" and comes from a story about a man from another culture who brings something needed to the people. Like all great honors, the name was part recognition, part threat. Promise that you will live up to this, it said. But it did not make clear how.

Waiting on the corner to meet Andy, part of me expected a middle-aged Tlingit man. Another part of me expected a Miyazaki-like apparition, a giant frog with garnet eyes and pockets full of gold nuggets and salmonberries—so vivid and unsorted were my child-hood memories, and so disorienting was it to be back there again as an adult.

That afternoon I ate grilled salmon in Andy's apartment. When I asked about the Kiks.ádi, he brought up the Battle of Sitka, then handed me a book on the Tlingit written by a German explorer in the 1850s. There weren't any good books yet, he said, but one was on the way.

Now, I had planned all along to make a grand statement of loy-alty. I never forgot about the family, I wanted to say, and I never took off my frog ring—it just vanished in a lake when I was ten, and I can still say *raven* and *shaman* and *thank you* in Tlingit, just in case you

were wondering. Yet I didn't want to appear entitled. Nor did I want
to come off like an anthropologist, turning my uncle into an exotic
object. Lost in a fog of cultural sensitivity, I said nothing.

We went to a family gathering later that evening, and I ate her-
ring roe on hemlock and gumboot for the first time. After a few
hours I slipped out, convinced I'd done everything wrong. At this
point in my life, I know it's the way twenty-two-year-olds often
leave parties, under a shroud of inarticulate failure, but at the time I
assigned it to other things. I assigned it to being a collateral relative.

I didn't see Andy again for over twenty years. Then in 2011 he
sent me a Facebook friend request. There was no message, and it
wasn't a particularly intimate gesture, but it was the first gesture
I had received from him that was meant for me directly. Over the
following months, a few more requests trickled in from people who
knew me as a child, and soon a stream of images began to appear
onscreen: snapshots of the Citizens Participation Committee meetings, of my parents and me as a two-year-old, of Andy and other
friends picnicking on a rocky beach.

I decided to go to Juneau. My trip had one purpose only: to connect with my Tlingit family. I wouldn't tell this to any of them,
though; it would be too pathetic. I would be casual. I would pretend
I was dropping by the coastal mountain range fifteen hundred miles
to the north of my home.

Wanting to be prepared, I returned to my fallback: study. I started
with the Kiks.ádi victory at the Battle of Sitka. I went first to Wiki-
pedia, our era's greatest repository of received wisdom, where I was
stunned to find an account that confidently stated that the Russians, not the Tlingit, had won:

> Though the Russians' initial assault (in which Alexandr
> Baranov, head of the Russian expedition, sustained serious
> injuries) was repelled, their naval escorts bombarded the
> Tlingit fort Shís'gi Noow mercilessly, driving the natives into

the surrounding forest after only a few days. The Russian victory was decisive, and resulted in the Sheet'ká Ḵwáan being permanently displaced from their ancestral lands. They fled north and reestablished an old settlement on the neighboring Chichagof Island to enforce a trade embargo against the Russians.

The word *fled* hit me first, then *decisive*. If the battle was such a clearcut Russian victory, why had the Kiks.ádi been bragging about it for the past two centuries? I paused for a moment between the two stories. Then, like any thinker with the slightest leaning toward postcolonial critique, I set aside the dead old white man account. If the Kiks.ádi claimed to have beaten the Russians, I would take it as gospel. Instead of asking if it was true, I would ask how it was true. I would prove my loyalty at last.

FOUR

Cursory reading on the subject only made the claim of a decisive Russian victory shakier. The battle was not followed by an influx of Russian trading posts. The Tlingit did not become slaves, as had other tribes. Although the Kiks.ádi abandoned their position at Shís'ghi Noow (Fort of Young Saplings), they did not exactly flee, but made an organized retreat, covering their people with a rear guard and taking up a new position on the straits. From this position, they began to cut off the transport of Russian fur. The following year another Russian trading post fell to the Tlingit in Yakutat and was permanently abandoned.

The retrospective logic seems to be that since the Kiks.ádi do not run the United States, they must have lost to the Russians in 1804. Native wins are irrelevant, and Native defeats are final. The Russians would inevitably prevail, and if not, it didn't matter anyway, because the Battle of Sitka, the lost posts, the trade embargo on the straits were peripheral skirmishes on the edge of an empire that barely noticed. This last point, I discovered, was far from true.

The Russian-American Company, which led the fight against the Tlingit, was modeled on the Dutch East India Company. It was an empire-building machine funded by the aristocracy and backed by the Imperial Russian Navy. The geopolitical jockeying for control in the Pacific Northwest was intensifying, and British and American ships were already in the area. Russia, who had the been colonizing Alaska since the 1740s, was in danger of losing her foothold in the "New World."

In 1799 the Russians sent Alexandr Baranov to Sitka. Sailing along a dark and dense rain forest of cedar, spruce, and hemlock that rose from the water, trees over two hundred feet tall with crowns disappearing into the mist (which was everywhere) and the drizzle (ever present), he passed beneath the shadow of Noow Tlein, the ancient fortified settlement, inhabited by the Tlingit for at least a thousand years. Built atop an outcrop of rock that climbed sixty feet from shore to shoulder, it was surrounded on three sides by water. Baranov, upon seeing it, wisely chose to keep going. Shipwrecking (something he did a lot) seven miles north, however, he was forced to make land and trade his prized chain-mail shirt to the Tlingit in exchange for his life.

The Kiks.ádi, smart middlemen that they were, struck a deal allowing Baranov to build a trading post. But three years later, in 1802, the Tlingit rose up. K̲'alyaán, a great Kiks.ádi warrior, struck the initial blow, killing a blacksmith and taking his hammer. (Later he would wield it in the Battle of Sitka.)

Now, imagine you're a rube like Baranov, a former Siberian glass-factory manager turned company man. You've been hacking away in the bloody business of colonization for years. Suddenly, you land a job as the head of Russia's first joint-stock entity. It's going to be big, the tsar and his brothers have put their personal funds into the venture, sea otter is going through the roof, and you're no longer in the sticks but on the vanguard of imperial expansion.

And now you, Baranov, have lost Sitka—the only harbor in southeastern Alaska with access to both the sea and the straits leading to the Inside Passage. And your former business partners are now trading their precious fur pelts to the Americans for arms and gunpowder, which they intend to use against you. As Lenin would later say, what is to be done?

If you are the tsar, you send Imperial Navy warships. If you are the Russian-American Company, you send mercenaries and slaves to fight. If you are Alexandr Baranov, you muster your backwoods gumption, put on a fresh chain-mail shirt—because nothing says fealty like chafing beneath twenty pounds of wrought-iron rings— and get yourself down to Sitka and take that post from the Tlingit however you can.

On the afternoon of September 19, 1804, Baranov, chief manager of the Russian-American Company, sailed into the Sitka Sound on his ship the *Ermak*. With him were three smaller armed ships, a flotilla of several hundred sea kayaks, and the Russian Imperial Navy's sloop-of-war, the *Neva*. The twelve hundred men Baranov brought with him were mostly mercenaries—former navy sailors and fur traders moonlighting as hired guns—some Aleuts, and a handful of company employees. They were there to send a message to the Tlingit: Sitka belongs to Russia.

FIVE

The only written eyewitness account of the Battle of Sitka comes from the journals of a Russian naval officer, Lieutenant Yury Lisiansky. In 1802 Lisiansky had been sent to England to buy ships for the Russian-American Company. Using a combination of corporate credit and imperial gold, he made a shady deal for two overpriced secondhand vessels, the *Leander* (soon rechristened the *Nadezhda*) and the *Thames* (soon rechristened the *Neva*).

Taking command of the *Neva*, a square-rigged tall ship with two hundred feet of deck length and fourteen cannons, Lisiansky set out to circumnavigate the globe on what became known as the Krusenstern Expedition. The *Neva* and the *Nadezhda* had already rounded Cape Horn, visited the Galápagos, and completed their circuit of the oceans when, in Hawaii, Lisiansky received new orders: Leave the *Nadezhda*. Forget going to Canton. Forget going to Japan. Head straight to Sitka. Help Baranov win back his fort.

"From the moment we entered Sitka Sound and until we dropped anchor," Lisiansky later wrote in *A Voyage Around the World in the Years 1803–1806*, "not a human being was to be seen anywhere, nay not even any sign that hereabouts was any settlement. Before our eyes were forests, covering the shores totally everywhere. How many uninhabited places have I seen, but none can compare in wilderness and emptiness with these."

On the first day of combat, the Russians were soundly defeated. Caught in a pincer move on the beach by Tlingit warriors led by K̲'alyaán with his blacksmith's hammer, the Russians took casualties, broke ranks, and ran for the woods and water. They lost five cannons, and Baranov himself was seriously wounded.

For the next four days, the Tlingit fort was bombarded from the sea by the *Neva* as emissaries went back and forth. Both sides raised white flags, sometimes simultaneously. At the end of the sixth day, the Russians were in the fort and the Tlingit were in the forest. On these facts everyone agrees.

Baranov himself never wrote of the Battle of Sitka. Many years later, he told the story to a financial auditor for the company; that was the extent of it. Company documents refer to the halo effect of the battle on trade but little else. For almost two hundred years, nothing was published from the Tlingit perspective. I assumed no one cared to ask. This was, after all, typical of battles in the colonies. It never occurred to me that the Tlingit themselves *refused* to give their version because it ran against deeply held cultural beliefs. First, talking about a conflict where peace now existed was considered rude and dangerous. Second, stories were considered property, tied to certain places and certain people. If it wasn't your dead, it wasn't your story. The Battle of Sitka could not be discussed because it was owned by the Kiks.ádi.

There is almost no way to describe the Tlingit concept of ownership without distorting or reducing its complexities. Clans "own" their regalia and their crests, but they also own their ancestral relationships to a place, their songs and dances, their stories and the images that came from those stories. If branding and intellectual property rights were taken to an extreme and merged with the Marxist ideal that people must not be alienated from the objects of their labor—nor from the collective identity arising from that labor—then we might approach the Tlingit sense of ownership. The word for this is *at.óow*, which has been translated as "a purchased thing." The Battle of Sitka was a purchased thing. It was paid for by those who lived it, and must not be sold out.

SIX

"Even those who bought us should hear what happened." —*Sally Hopkins*

For many years the Kiks.ádi, though reluctant to make their stories public, had been recording their elders telling them for the clan's own purposes. Sometimes it was little more than a tape machine brought down to the ANB Hall, turned on at a potlatch. In 1958 a Tlingit man recorded a retelling of the events of 1802–4 for the National Park Service, including an account of the Battle of Sitka.

The woman he recorded was Shx̱aastí, a Kiks.ádi tradition bearer. Her English name was Sally Hopkins, and she was born in Sitka in 1877. Her dialect alone was a treasure for linguistic anthropologists: containing transition markers between ancient and modern Tlingit, it had the echo of precontact speech. Hopkins heard the stories as a girl, from elders who were contemporaries of Baranov. She believed passionately in documenting and publishing the stories before they vanished, a belief she passed on to her Kiks.ádi children.

My copy of *Russians in Tlingit America* arrived several weeks before I was scheduled to leave for Juneau. Somewhere between the size of a hotel Bible and Jung's *Red Book*, it was five hundred pages of dense type. Wanting to be better prepared, I postponed my trip and began to read. No one was waiting for me anyway.

Although the Russian and Tlingit versions diverged in perspective, they agreed on much of the basic flow of events. The battle had never gone as planned for the Russians. They expected to meet the Kiks.ádi at Noow Tlein, the ancient fort overlooking the harbor, which was, according to the commander of the *Neva*, a near impregnable redoubt. But when Baranov and his men arrived, they encountered only a small party of Tlingit. The settlement had been abandoned.

Baranov's men raised Russian flags inside the empty village, slept in Kiks.ádi houses that were occupied without fight or ceremony. This alone should have given the Russians pause. If nothing else, Tlingit are a people of ritual. Their social etiquette rivals the *DSM-5* for coding and complexity. They make geisha look slovenly. If they were really intending to give up the fort they'd held for a thousand years, they would have danced for days, exchanged gifts, and sung. Instead, there was only silence.

According to the Tlingit account, Noow Tlein was a decoy to draw the enemy out of their ships so the Tlingit could gauge their strength. They knew the Russians would rely on naval power and so had constructed Shís'g̱hi Noow—Fort of Young Saplings—specifically to withstand naval bombardment. Built at the high-water line of a gently sloping beach, gunships could barely get near it, and then only during certain tides. If a ship did get in range, the fort's structure was designed to deflect cannon fire.

The Kiks.ádi had studied the way a cannonball's direct hit shattered seasoned wood and built Shís'ghi Noow of saplings whose green and pliant wood offered a certain amount of give. The timbers were also angled and braced to disperse shock down and away, redirecting balls into pits dug to catch them. Lisiansky's journal records Baranov complaining about this very thing, that he couldn't get close, and when he did, his cannonballs bounced off. Coming ashore after the battle, Lisiansky wrote that he gathered at least 150 cannonballs from around the fort walls.

It was never a given that the Russians would win the battle. Lisiansky acknowledged this himself at various points in his account. What neither Baranov nor Lisiansky knew was that the Tlingit had already lost the fort before the Russians ever fired on it.

On the eve of the battle, a Tlingit canoe was blown up as it passed between islands just off the coast. Both sides record the event, though with discrepancies. Some say it was a Russian shot that caused the explosion, others that it was carelessness among the young Tlingit men in the boat. Some say there were survivors, others that the entire crew was killed. The incident earns only a few lines from Lisiansky. Later, however, the Russian commander would come to realize its importance: The canoe carried the entire stockpile of Tlingit gunpowder.

The explosion was the moment the Tlingit lost the fort. All their deft evasions and defensive tactics had been in the service of an offensive, prepared over the course of years, which the Kiks.ádi now knew would never come. And the canoe held more than gunpowder. Also inside were the future clan leaders of each Kiks.ádi house. All of them were killed.

The story became a song, "Sooxsaan," which is one of the two

anthems of the Kiks.ádi. The story in "Sooxsaan" is told through the
eyes of a mother who loses her child when the canoe he is sleeping
in drifts away. She sings out her grief for him to his uncles, those
who were lost in that other canoe. It is a song that marks the passing of different futures. Even reading about it, I worried that I was
treading on forbidden terrain. This, more than anything, was a purchased thing.

SEVEN

The Fort of Young Saplings was empty when the Russians walked in.
They had expected people, negotiations, but there was no one. It was
not the victory they had imagined. It didn't say: *You've won.* It said:
We are not done yet. That winter in Sitka, without goods to trade—or
anyone to trade with—and afraid to hunt in the forest, the Russians
sent delegations across the snow to the Tlingit asking them to make
peace and come back. The emissaries were turned away.

The Russians eventually abandoned the Fort of Young Saplings,
decamping to Noow Tlein, which was vulnerable from the sea but
less so from the land. Obviously, it was not the ships of rival colonial
powers the Russians feared but Tlingit incursions by land and long-
boat. In *Glorious Misadventures: Nikolai Rezanov and the Dream of a Russian America,* Owen Matthews describes the colony at Noow Tlein as
having two towers and a stockade "ringed with cannon—pointing
not at the sea, but towards the endless threatening forest around."

Nothing in the details of the battle and its aftermath showed it to be
anything but a strategic withdrawal by the Tlingit. The Kiks.ádi tested
the Russians at one fort while they moved their people to another;
when the munitions were blown, they dragged out the surrender,
faked a chain-of-command breakdown to create diplomatic chaos, and
got their people safely into the woods. The Russians couldn't follow
because the Tlingit rear guard kept them engaged near the fort. Over

time they were effectively trapped behind the palisade of Noow Tlein, sending envoys out into the snow.

Something in the story of the Battle of Sitka struck me as curiously familiar. It took me a few days before I realized what it was; it was Napoleon. Perhaps, if I hadn't read so much Tolstoy in my early twenties—particularly if I hadn't read *War and Peace* five times—I wouldn't even have looked at the Battle of Sitka and thought about the burning of Moscow. But I had and I did. The Tlingit strategy was really no different than what the tsar's forces would do eight years later when facing Napoleon on Russian soil.

After the Battle of Borodino in September 1812—that valiant last stand where the Russian army suffered horrendous losses—Field Marshal Mikhail Kutuzov did the unimaginable, the un-European thing, stepping aside and letting Napoleon have Moscow. Moscow! Why, the Russians had been there almost as long as the Tlingit had lived at Noow Tlein. How could they abandon it? Yet in the era of saber rattling and charges, amid emerging virulent nationalism, this is exactly what Kutuzov did. And what did he say as Napoleon marched toward Moscow? "I aim not to defeat, but I'm hoping to deceive him." What deception could he have meant?

L'Empereur marched into the metropolis expecting dignitaries, expecting rituals. He got none. Despite wanting to be gracious, he could find no object for his magnanimity. Napoleon in Moscow, like Baranov in Sitka, alone and far from home on the edge of winter, waited for a surrender that would never come. *I have Russia*, said Napoleon. *No*, said the tsar from St. Petersburg, *you have Moscow. I have Sitka*, said Baranov. *No*, the Tlingit said, *you have the fort*.

Both the Tlingit in 1804 and the Russians in 1812 withdrew from the field when they were unable to defeat the invaders, and they regrouped elsewhere. Both created confusion through diplomacy and sent mixed messages to stall the enemy's approach. Both evacuated their people without surrender, leaving the enemy no one to negotiate with. And to this day, both the Tlingit and the Russians inhabit their ancestral homelands. Yet somehow, what Kutuzov did is remembered as a brilliant strategy that saved a nation, while what the Tlingit did is considered, by nearly everyone but the Tlingit, an unequivocal defeat.

I began to wonder how Russian Kutuzov's strategy really was. How great was the psychological distance between 1804 and 1812, between St. Petersburg and Sitka, Kutuzov and the Kiks.ádi? I also thought: *What a gift to bring back.*

EIGHT

The line between passionate curiosity and total fixation is thin. At first I had hoped simply to acquire some conversational fluency on the Battle of Sitka, but now I could think of little else. It seemed at first like historical heresy, but really, why couldn't Kutuzov's response to Napoleon have been inspired by a battle in the colonies? I knew I couldn't prove a connection between the strategies. I was after the possibility.

The obvious first thing to establish was how Kutuzov could have heard about the Battle of Sitka. Lisiansky had published a memoir. I looked up its publication date: 1812, the same year that Kutuzov abandoned Moscow. But both men lived in St. Petersburg; their social circles could easily have overlapped. I considered it equally likely that there was some connection through the Russian-American Company. The tsar and the aristocracy had all invested in the venture, and it seemed plausible that Kutuzov—who had served three successive Romanov monarchs—would have as well. That would have given him a direct interest in the happenings in Sitka, if nothing else. A list of early investors in the Russian-American Company should show his name.

What I needed was a Russian-speaking researcher I could afford. Impoverished, unemployed, and with time on their hands, they're not so hard to find. The Russian department at my former college suggested a young man named Auden, and I gave him two hundred dollars and sent him out into the Internet to look for social ties between Kutuzov, Lisiansky, and Baranov—anything that would make a conversation about the Battle of Sitka a reasonable proposition.

Soon Auden began sending updates. While he wasn't able to find a list of investors, he had come across some kind of company ladies' auxiliary, of which both Kutuzov's wife and her half-sister were members. The company also had a ship called the *Kutuzov*. Ships, like buildings, are often named for war heroes—but just as often for investors. Perhaps the field marshal was both.

Finding a reputable military historian willing to entertain the notion was much harder. The idea that the Tlingit might have saved Russia from Napoleon didn't exactly open doors; it was more the kind of wild postulation used by middle-aged professors to pick up undergrad girls at coffee shops. But I didn't care. I was opening the imagination to new possibilities, and the imperial myopia surrounding the Battle of Sitka deserved to be corrected. Didn't it?

In an attempt at rigor, I refined my questions. How unusual was what Kutuzov did? Were there examples of Native tactics making their way back into European warfare? What exactly constitutes a victory? These were safe questions. My real theories I kept to myself.

Growing inside, though, was another uneasiness. The more I spoke of the Battle of Sitka, the less sure I was that I had a right to the story in which I was entangling myself. We tend to think of a story as personal property: *I own it because I heard it.* This strikes me now as a very colonial way to view the world, though also a human one. And as much as I promised myself I would confine my speech on the subject to what the Kiks.ádi allowed to be published, I found I couldn't stop my imagination. I could not help but explore the story and open it up. When I did, it changed. Something I read in *Russians in Tlingit America* came back to me—"An unauthorized telling constitutes stealing."

NINE

Military historian Dr. Niall Barr, a senior reader in European military history at King's College London, is engaged by the British Ministry of Defense to teach tactical history to officers. The Joint Services Command and Staff College where Barr teaches is an hour outside London by rail. By sheer random luck, I was to be in England the following week.

It was Armistice Day, and at eleven a.m. sharp the train car fell silent. Texting stopped, pens were laid down, and the cart coming through the aisle with juice and coffee paused to commemorate the dead. In contrast to Veterans Day in the United States, there wasn't a flag in sight, only red poppies pinned to coats and collars.

I was nervous about meeting Barr. I had not told him of my theories regarding Kutuzov, only that I was doing some work on the Battle of Sitka and needed help understanding Napoleonic-era field tactics. There were many ways to eviscerate my idea—I was coming up with quite a list on my own—and I didn't want to chase him away before the conversation even began.

We met at the train station and walked to a nearby pub. A tall man in his forties with a poppy affixed to his black wool coat, Barr had gentle manners and an elegant mind. He had looked into the Battle of Sitka and was intrigued by the construction of the Fort of Young Saplings, something I hadn't thought too much about. "Artillery fortification is a highly skilled business," he said. "You're working out the angles. People train for years. It's all about math and geometry, but you really can't discount native intelligence."

I told him what I knew of the battle, the abandonment of the fort, and accounts of the peace ceremonies. I asked Barr if that sounded like a victory.

"There are laws of war," he said, "conventions, some formal and some informal. Professional soldiers know that. By 1812 these conventions in Europe are well understood. When you place a fort under siege, you have certain rights and responsibilities, and the besieged have certain rights and responsibilities. Once a practicable breach has been made—meaning that soldiers can actually get through your fortifications—the governor of the town or fort is to surrender. If he doesn't, the breach will be stormed. If it is stormed, the assaulting troops are at liberty to offer no quarter. They can kill everybody. So once there's a practicable breach, that's when you surrender."

"But the Tlingit didn't surrender."

Barr paused. "It's a powerful idea, how wars end. Who decides who has won and lost? These are eternal questions. You see"—he leaned in—"it's this absurd situation. If a garrison commander surrenders, it's all lovely and nice and everybody marches off. But if the garrison refuses to surrender, it leads to bloodshed and brutality. The very act of surrendering tells you which code is going to be active."

But the Tlingit didn't surrender, I repeated. The Russians had to ask for the deal, bring gifts, and go through a four-day ceremony wearing Tlingit adornments. How was that a Russian victory?

"Baranov sued for peace?" Barr considered a moment. "Still, the fort was vacated, and that would have meant victory."

At this point I rolled out some of my more subversive ideas about Kutuzov and the defense of Moscow. Barr didn't scoff. Rather, he seemed a little delighted. I asked him how atypical the field marshal's strategy had been. "At the time, if you occupied somebody's capital, then it was game over," Barr said. "You can't protect your capital, therefore you should surrender. This is where the Russians did something different—something traumatic, because due to the Orthodox Church, there is something special about Moscow in the Russian psyche. They consider it to be the new Rome. The idea that Moscow would be occupied by a heretic like Bonaparte was beyond the pale."

I asked Barr if he knew of European commanders using tactics in Europe learned in the course of colonial warfare. He did. During the French and Indian War of the 1750s, he explained, the British general Edward Braddock was attacked in the woods near what is now Pittsburgh. As usual, he kept his men in tight formation and had them fire carefully timed volleys at their opponents—a disastrous tactic for wilderness combat. Most of Braddock's expedition was slaughtered, and the remaining troops were routed. Yet over the years, the regiment that emerged from the experience, called the 60th Royal American, employed the Native skirmish tactics learned in America and used them to great effect in the Battle of Waterloo in 1815.

So maybe Baranov did consider himself victorious when he inherited his empty fort. Everyone has the prerogative to be wrong. But here was a concrete example of Native tactics finding their way onto European battlefields. Barr also confirmed my sense that the abandonment of Moscow was a radical move. On these two rails, I traveled closer to all possibilities.

On my way back to London, I got another message from my researcher, Auden. He had found a possible social tie between Kutuzov and Lisiansky: a naval officer who was close to both men. It was a complex net of relationships, said my researcher, but he had sketched out a kind of diagram and attached a scan.

Excited and unable to wind down as the landscape streamed by outside, I slipped a DVD lecture on the Greco-Persian Wars into my laptop. Maybe this would put most people to sleep, but for me it's a minor obsession: I have watched all forty-eight episodes the Great Courses has to offer on ancient Egypt, their thirty-six lectures on Medieval Europe and the Tudor Conquest, and twenty-four lectures on the Age of Pericles. By now I was on to the Persian Empire, and as the train rolled through suburban London, I listened as the professor dissected the ancient Battle of Cunaxa.

TEN

"Be brave, my son. This is where things fail." —*Sally Hopkins*

My father didn't talk much about the Tlingit adoption after he left Alaska. He didn't know how to handle it. He said he never did anything to earn it, and he wasn't sure what was expected of him afterward. Not wanting to be yet another white man claiming what wasn't his, he waited for a signal nobody knew he was waiting for— and over time the adoption, which was meant to create a bond, carved out a gap instead.

When he left Alaska, he let the relationships slip. He didn't bring up the adoption back in the Lower 48 because he didn't want to get lumped in with all the *Dances with Wolves* New Agers. Recently, he admitted to me that he'd missed the point entirely. "It's not whether you deserve it," he said. "It's what you make of it."

For my stay in Juneau, I booked a room on Starr Hill, a place I had known well as a child. The neighborhood's clapboard houses and metal stairs negotiating steep hillsides had not changed. I had once seen a salmon fall from the sky there and hit the ground a few feet away from me. The eagles fighting for it overhead had let it slip, and one swooped down, snatched the fish in its talons, and climbed, leaving behind just a few silver scales.

Now, under a bank of mist moving down Mount Robert was the grim little playground next to what was once my school. On the other side of the governor's mansion was the neighborhood where my Tlingit grandmother had lived. Not far from there was the Alaska State Museum, where I had taken classes as a child, and the State Office Building, near where my father once worked—a tombstone for urban renewal, square as a child's building block.

In the little rented room, I spread out my papers. Since I wouldn't be meeting my uncle until the next day, I had some time. I covered the floor with my notes, legal pads, and printouts with circles and arrows highlighting connections. It didn't look like historical research. It looked like the hotel scene from *The Wall*.

Baranov had turned out to be a dead end. My researcher had found nothing to connect the lowly company man with anyone in the aristocracy, much less the illustrious Kutuzov. It wasn't unthinkable that a man like the field marshal, with a deep financial interest in the fur trade and a military strategist's mind, would have had enough curiosity to ask, if given the chance—"What happened in Sitka, anyway? Open another bottle of vodka, and bring me a fresh cigar!"—but there was no evidence that such a chance had ever arisen. Baranov was simply too low on the food chain, and his family had no meaningful power to bridge that gap. In Russia he was a nobody. Even the Order of St. Vladimir medal presented to him got his name wrong.

Kutuzov, however, did seem to have a connection with Lisiansky. As a young man, Kutuzov had grown up in and around the house of his relative Ivan Golenishev-Kutuzov, whose son Loggin Ivanovich was in the navy and fought in the Russo-Swedish War like Lisiansky. Loggin wrote a book on circumnavigation and is mentioned in a biography of Lisiansky. As navy men with such shared interests, proximity, and experiences, they probably knew each other well, and Loggin was close with his father, who was close with Kutuzov. It was a plausible social avenue.

But something else had begun to trouble me. My problem was proving that what Kutuzov did was special at all. My problem was Cunaxa.

In 401 B.C.E. a Greek mercenary force invaded Persia. The armies clashed near Cunaxa (now the city of Hillah in Iraq), where the Greeks routed their opponents—but their leader, Cyrus the Younger, who had intended to claim the Persian throne, was killed. Even worse, the army was now deep in enemy territory, with dwindling supplies and no means of getting home. They headed north, hoping to reach the Black Sea and build a fleet. And since the Persians were unable to defeat the Greeks in a frontal assault, they drew them into the snowy mountains as winter set in, harassing them without ever making a direct attack. What the Persians had done—redefining victory and fighting on—was no different from what Kutuzov would do.

"If you occupied somebody's capital, then it was game over," Barr had told me. "This is where the Russians did something different." I clung to that. But it was only the first half of his statement. The second was, "But it's also about the conditions you find yourself in." What bound the strategies in Sitka and Moscow was desperation. These were people fighting for their ancestral homeland, and they did what people in that position do. They changed their definition of victory so they could fight on. Who lets their capital burn while their army still stands? The answer is: anyone who must. We did. In the War of 1812, Americans at Bladensburg let the British raze Washington so they could come back against them in Baltimore.

Cunaxa was the spoon tap that cracked the egg. Over the next twelve hours, sitting in my Juneau Airbnb, my whole theory fell apart. I hadn't wanted to arrive empty-handed. I had wanted to bring victory. And beneath the debris was only my desire to belong.

Something I had dismissed as ephemeral now came to mind. The *Neva* was one of two Russian ships that circumnavigated the globe. The other was the *Nadezhda*. Aboard the *Nadezhda* was a man named Fyodor Ivanovich Tolstoy, Leo Tolstoy's older cousin. Leo grew up listening to Fyodor Ivanovich's stories of duels and sailing around the world, and many believe he was the basis for the character of Dolokhov in *War and Peace*. And who can say if Fyodor Ivanovich then repeated a tale told to him by his compatriots on the *Neva*, a story about a great tribe of warriors in the colonies. And who can say if the way he told that story seeded in the child Leo ideas that would surface years later when he imagined the invasion of his own country? It is impossible to gauge what children make of what they hear. Often things come to mean much more than ever intended.

ELEVEN

Down the hill from the house where I stayed in Juneau is the pretty little blue-and-white Russian Orthodox Church that appears in so many paintings and postcards of the city. Dedicated to Saint Nicholas, it was built in 1894 to serve the Tlingit, who were converting in large numbers, just as their relatives in Sitka had done.

The parish is poor, and as I approached the building, I saw that it was in disrepair. There was scaffolding on one side, but the work looked abandoned, and the twine securing a tarp had come loose, allowing it to whip in the wind. I entered late and without a headscarf into the small octagonal room, its vermilion-and-gold icons lit by candlelight. The heat was off and it was cold. A young Russian woman wearing a leopard-print scarf and white knee-high boots ushered her children past me, genuflected, and stepped out of my way. The man leading the service, a tonsured reader in a floor-length black robe, was my uncle Andy.

The Ebonas have been Russian Orthodox for many generations, something they take great pride in. I wasn't sure if Andy would recognize me, but he did. During a momentary pause in the liturgy, he came over and gave me a big hug—I was touched that he had slipped out of the ceremony to do that. "I'll make us dinner tonight," he whispered, then returned to his place near the icons.

Listening to the service, which alternated between Russian and Tlingit, I saw something else I had missed in my postcolonial analysis. I'd left no room for the potential graciousness of peacemaking and its role in the cessation of violence. My assumption had been that if the fighting stopped, either the Tlingit or the Russians had to be subjugated. Nowhere in this narrative was the possibility of a peace that recognized equality rather than domination.

Andy lives in his mother's house, which he and his siblings inherited in 2002 when Amy Nelson, clan mother of the Sitka Kiks.ádi, "walked into the woods," as the Tlingit say. Amy had been taught songs and dances by her mother, and she embraced the culture and passed it on to her children with steadfast commitment. Her obituary said she had been a cannery worker, a housekeeper, and a nurse's aide—and Andy, who is known to be a fantastic cook, told me she taught him how to use the kitchen so he could take care of the other kids while she worked.

Walking into Amy's living room for the first time in many years, I was pleased to see stuffed frogs still hiding in various places. Over the sofa in the sitting room was a print showing the first day of the Battle of Sitka. It captures the moment when K̲'alyaán, brandishing his blacksmith's hammer, led his warriors to the beachhead and took the enemy by surprise. In the picture, Baranov is gravely wounded, and the remaining Russians are fleeing toward their ships. It is a day of victory.

In the kitchen, Andy had a large pot of venison marinara going on the stove. He added some spices, then turned it to simmer. Standing by while he stirred the sauce and set water to boil, I talked about the Battle of Sitka and told him my crazy theory about Kutuzov and the Tlingit.

Andy smiled patiently. "That's interesting," he said. "Maybe."

I waited for more, but he just kept stirring.

"Don't you think it's good to question these things?" I asked.

"Sure," he said and handed me a plate of venison pasta.

In the living room we set up TV trays and ate. I asked him about "Sooxsaan," the traditional lament for the lost canoe. I wasn't sure if it was polite to ask to hear something like that—the exact nature of *at.óow* is still beyond my grasp—but Andy was kind enough to find a recording from a Kiks.ádi party in the 1940s. He put the CD on, and a few seconds later a woman began to sing. The song was profoundly sad, but the woman's voice was astonishingly sweet and agile. It was high but also warm, without a hint of shrillness. She sounded like a young Ella Fitzgerald.

"That's my grandmother," Andy said quietly.

The singer was Sally Hopkins, whose vanished dialect had so fascinated the linguists. When "Sooxsaan" ended, another song began, and Hopkins's voice, which had been full of sorrow, turned darting and honeyed. She started to skip around the melody as if she were only flirting with each of the notes.

"What is that?" I asked with a laugh.

"That," said Andy, "is a love song."

We finished listening, and then Andy suggested we watch something on TV. We settled on an episode of *Game of Thrones*, both of us marveling at King Joffrey's atrocities, and an hour later I went home with homemade bilberry jelly and smoked salmon in a mason jar. The last thing I saw was Andy in the doorway with the print of K'alyaán and his hammer behind him.

The Kiks.ádi cannot be separated from the Battle of Sitka. In some ways, I will never be separate from the Kiks.ádi. I had heard Sally Hopkins sing because my father was adopted. It was not something I earned. It was more than enough.

TWELVE

Accounts of the Peace of 1805 say that the Tlingit "made the Russians their relatives," which probably means they adopted them. It's reasonable to assume that Baranov was also adopted. Besides my father, Amy Nelson also adopted a man named Peter. An old family friend, he is greatly respected within the community, and eighty-five-year-old Tlingit women sometimes call him Uncle, but more often he is known by a nickname they gave him, Bushkaa.

I asked Peter how he saw his adoption. "Well, a lot of people are adopted," he told me. "It's what you do with it. I'm in pretty deep, but I know where I stand. You know how they say everything can be brought back to *The Godfather*? I'm like Tom Hagen—a loyal and trusted servant. Of the family, not of the blood. There is a difference. You can see the people who take it too far and go around calling everybody brother."

I'd been taught to say Uncle and Grandmother. Maybe I was someone who took it too far. All along I'd wondered if I was really following my father's story and not mine. Yet I had been there, too. And if the Battle of Sitka was a Kiks.ádi story exclusively, then what about their Eagle and Wolf wives and children, their husbands? And what about the Russians? Winners or losers, they had also been there. They had paid with their ancestors.

In 2004, exactly two centuries after the Battle of Sitka, the Kiks.ádi invited a descendant of Baranov to participate in a Cry Ceremony—a ritual laying away any remaining grief regarding a conflict. The ceremony was held on Castle Hill, where Noow Tlein once stood and which is now a state park. It is also the site where, in 1867, the Russian flag was lowered and the U.S. flag was raised for the first time over Sitka.

The forts are gone now, the site grown over with grass. These four acres comprise the only land the Tlingit ever agreed to forfeit. The Russians had a right to sell Castle Hill but nothing else. This was the inextinguishable claim the Tlingit would push through the courts until the 1971 Alaska Native Claims Settlement Act, which was, perhaps, the true end of the Battle of Sitka.

The *Neva* sunk off the coast of Sitka, and its ship's bell hangs today in the town museum. Baranov himself never made it back to Russia but died at sea in 1819 from an illness and was thrown overboard somewhere near the Philippines. In an odd coincidence, he died on the same day as General Kutuzov, though several years apart. Stranger still, the Russian-American Company ship Baranov died on was the *Kutuzov*. It was probably as close as he and the great general ever got.

On the Forest Service tape from 1958, just before Sally Hopkins begins to speak, is the voice of her son. He is inviting her in the proper Tlingit way to tell the story of "how we became human." And she recounts the Battle of Sitka. It is not the story of a lost homeland but the story of lost ancestors. And in her story, Sitka is larger than the fort on the hill or at the river's mouth. It is the ancestral Sitka, which emanates deep into the woods and well out to sea.

This is an idea strangely reflected in modern Sitka, which is the largest incorporated city borough in the United States. At 4,800 square miles in size, it includes all of Baranov Island, as well as Chichagof Island, where the Kiks.ádi spent the winter of 1804.

Unromantic evidence like fish traps and basket-weaving techniques place the Tlingit on Baranov Island for at least 6,000 years and at Noow Tlein for a millennium. The earliest dates put their appearance in the Alaskan panhandle at 10,000 to 12,000 years ago. Many clans have stories about rising waters and where they went to avoid them, stories that match the sea-level rise in the rock record and, much to the excitement of anthropologists, new discoveries based on paleo-shoreline models. The stories cannot be truly collected or cataloged, though. They are not extinct, just unavailable. They are *at.óow*.

Along the southeastern coastline, the names—Yakutat, Klukwan, Hoonah, Auke Bay, Klawock, Angoon, Kake, Sitka—are as they were when Baranov first shipwrecked on those shores. The European definition of victory is perfectly comprehensible: whoever vacates the fort at the end of the day has lost. But then how big is that fort? And how long is that day?

AMERICAN HIPPOPOTAMUS

JON MOOALLEM

This is a true story, and a very serious one, even though it's composed of many details that will seem ludicrous and impossible. Most of those details are indisputable, though. And while I worked hard to verify the rest, doing so occasionally proved futile. I'd like to try and explain why.

This is a story about hippopotamuses, as advertised, but it's also a story about two very complicated and exceptional men. These men were spies. They were also bitter enemies. Each wanted to kill the other and fully expected to feel really good about himself after doing so. Eccentric circumstances—circumstances having to do with hippopotamuses—would join these men together as allies and even dear friends. But then, eventually, they'd be driven into opposition again.

Whatever strange bond these two men had, they were loyal to it. They were like repulsive magnets: Some fundamental property of each was perfectly opposed to the core of the other. And yet somehow throughout their long lives—as several volatile phases of American history tumbled along in the background—they also had a way of continually snapping back together. One of these men was a humble patriot, known for his impeccable integrity. He tried to leave detailed, reliable accounts of what he did and thought and felt. The other, I discovered, was a megalomaniac and a pathological liar.

These two men will seem larger than life, but they lived at a time, a hundred years ago, when, I would argue, *life* in America seemed larger than life—when what was unimaginable still felt feasible and ideas that looked ridiculous could still come true.

That said, this is the story of one idea that looked ridiculous and didn't come true. The idea *was* ridiculous. But it was completely reasonable, too.

All I can say is, try to keep that in mind.

PART ONE

I

THE MOST COMPLETE HUMAN BEING WHO EVER LIVED

Frederick Russell Burnham didn't like public speaking, but he arrived at the Maryland Hotel, in Pasadena, California, on the night of September 19, 1910, determined to communicate a few clear and uncontroversial truths.

Burnham was forty-nine years old—a frontiersman and soldier of fortune who'd spent his life leaping into conflicts with American Indians and colonial wars in Africa. He looked bronzed and weather-beaten, like a living monument to those campaigns, and though small—he was only about five foot four—his presence was imposing. He was a compact strongbox of a man. One admirer would describe him as "emphatically a man's man: able, active, alert." The impression he gave was immediately one of "force and self-control."

Burnham had risen to fame as a scout—an esteemed breed of solitary wayfinder and spy with no exact analog in contemporary warfare. Scouts slinked into enemy territory to gather intelligence or cut supply lines, or roamed the no-man's-land around camp to keep watch. They were disciplined, self-sufficient, and preternaturally competent. Their proficiency in the wilderness seemed almost magical at times, and Burnham, who'd earned the nickname King of Scouts, exemplified their character and prowess.

People who met Burnham tended to comment on the same dis-
arming quality of his eyes. The novelist H. Rider Haggard called
them "steady, grey blue eyes that have in them a far-away look such
as those acquire whose occupation has caused them to watch continually at sea or on great plains." They were eyes that absorbed
every inch of the periphery, even as they bored deep into your own—
eyes, one woman noted, "of startling keenness and brilliancy, eyes
that see everything without seeming to see." He was "a man whose
senses and abilities approached that of a wild predator," one writer
explained. He could go two and a half days without sleep. It was
said he could smell water from afar, and very seldom drank alcohol
and never smoked, for fear it would dull his senses. Commanding
officers described him as half jackrabbit and half wolf, or as "a man
totally without fear."

Burnham had come to the hotel in Pasadena to address the
Humane Association of California at its second annual convention,
a banquet hall full of do-gooders, dedicated to the prevention of cruelty to animals. The Humane Association had quickly become one
of California's most powerful civic organizations, and Burnham—
now part of an eccentric brain trust that was getting its own inno-
vative project off the ground—knew that the philanthropists in the
room might be valuable allies. He didn't necessarily respect them,
though. Privately, he mocked humane societies as small-minded
and sentimental—full of romantics who'd rush to save flies from
murderous spiders. It was foolish, he felt, to "fritter away our money
and time on silly, emotional things as proposed by so-called animal lovers" at a time when America roiled with so many substantial
opportunities and terrors.

Burnham was here at the Maryland Hotel to call these animal
lovers to a higher purpose, to gather them behind an idea. It was a
grand and sparkling idea, an idea with momentum. The idea was
already making its way through the U.S. House of Representatives
in the form of a bill, introduced by one of Burnham's partners,

the Louisiana congressman Robert Broussard. Theodore Roosevelt, a friend of Burnham's, had been so impressed with the idea a few years earlier that, newspapers reported, he'd pledged "his hearty approval and promise of cooperation." Days before the speech in Pasadena, Burnham had gone to Denver to meet with the former president and secured his endorsement all over again. *The New York Times* called the idea "practical and timely." Editorials around the country claimed that the idea's time had come, or that it couldn't come soon enough.

The idea was to import hippopotamuses from Africa, set them in the swamplands along the Gulf Coast, and raise them for food. The idea was to turn America into a nation of hippo ranchers.

II

THE MEAT QUESTION

"I do not think this importation idea can be laughed down," Congressman Broussard had insisted to the press. And truly, to anyone who appreciated common sense—who loved to see logic, like a bicycle chain, pushing a wheel smoothly forward—the idea was nothing short of gorgeous. Hippopotamuses, it turned out, could solve a number of problems for the country, all at once. For starters, they constituted a blubbery, elegant fix to what newspapers had taken to calling the Meat Question.

America was withering under a serious meat shortage at the time. Beef prices had soared as rangeland was ruined by overgrazing, and a crippled industry struggled to satisfy America's explosively growing cities, an unceasing wave of immigrants, and a surging demand for meat abroad. There were more mouths to feed than ever, but the number of cows in the country had been dropping by millions of head a year. People whispered about the prospect of eating dogs. The seriousness of the Meat Question, and the failure to whip together some brave and industrious solution to it, was jarring the nation's self-confidence and self-image. It was a troubling sign that maybe the country couldn't keep growing as fast and recklessly as it had been. Maybe there were limits after all.

Now, though, someone had an answer. The answer was hippopotamuses. One Agricultural Department official estimated that an armada of free-range hippos, set moping through the bayous of Florida, Mississippi, and Louisiana, would easily yield a million tons of meat a year. Already Congressman Broussard had dispatched a field agent on a fact-finding mission. The man, a native of southern Africa, found the Louisiana swamps "wildly dismal and forbidding." (The "silence strike[s] one with an almost unforgettable horror," he wrote in his report, titled "Why and How to Place Hippopotamus in the Louisiana Lowlands.") Still, the place was perfect for hippos. His conclusion: "The hippopotamus would find no difficulty living in Louisiana."

Apparently, the animals tasted pretty good, too, especially the fatty brisket part, which could be cured into a delicacy that a supportive *New York Times* editorial was calling, euphemistically, "lake cow bacon." ("Toughness is only skin deep," another reporter noted.) Congressman Broussard's office was receiving laudatory letters from ordinary citizens, commending his initiative taking and ingenuity. Several volunteered to be part of the expedition to bring the great beasts back.

In other words, in the encroaching malaise of 1910, it was easy to be gripped by the brilliance of the hippopotamus scheme, to feel hippopotamuses resonating not just as a way of sidestepping famine but as a symbol of American greatness being renewed. Burnham's generation had seen the railroad get synched across the wild landscape like a bridle and the near solid swarms of buffalo and passenger pigeons get erased. America had dynamited fish out of rivers, dredged waterways, felled and burned forests, and peeled silver from the raw wreckage of what had once been mountains. The frontier was now closed. So much had been accomplished and so much taken. It was clear that a once-boundless-seeming land *did* have boundaries, and with those limits revealed, you couldn't help but feel as if you were drifting listlessly between them. There was a sense in the country of *Now what*? And lurking beneath that: *What have we done*?

For Burnham, though, this moment was a chance for the country to pause and regather itself, then start over, with more wisdom this time. "Let us not make the same mistakes again," he would tell the Humane Association that night in Pasadena. "This nation has reached a stage in its development where we should take stock of our assets and make full use of them in an intelligent manner."

The same industriousness that had allowed America to snatch up the continent's natural resources and snuff out its beauty could be deployed now, more pragmatically, to restock it. Yes, the hippo idea sounded crazy. But as *The Washington Post* noted, "Proposals which at first may look odd and chimerical to the mass of our readers will be seen to be matter-of-fact propositions when they become familiar." And if we'd learned to swallow raw oysters and suck the meat out of crabs, the paper argued, why couldn't we also embrace "that plump and pulchritudinous beast which has a smile like an old-fashioned fireplace?" The reasons it might look impossible were fickle and foolish. Burnham understood that the real boundary America was running up against was psychological—a scarcity of courage and imagination, and not really just meat.

The master of ceremonies at the Maryland Hotel that night was the Reverend Robert Jones Burdette, an avuncular Baptist minister known nationally for his early career as a newspaper humorist and touring performer. (Burdette, it was said, had delivered his comedic lecture "The Rise and Fall of the Mustache" more than three thousand times.) All night he introduced speakers with poems and little jokes. But when announcing Burnham, all of Burdette's corniness fell away. The reverend seemed suddenly stiffened, stilled—like the air before an electrical storm.

"I am going to introduce to you a man who knows the cruel edges of war," he began. "Who has seen the keen blades sweep together as they clashed like the grim shears of Atropos, severing the throbbing threads of human life, smearing the golden sands and the emerald grasses with the darkest stains that ever discolored the pain-distorted face of God's beautiful world. A soldier. A scout whose name has filled both hemispheres with stories of his daring and loyal service. . . . . I am honored in being permitted to present, as our next speaker, the only man in America who [knows] the darkest shades of darkest Africa . . . Major Frederick R. Burnham."

The scout surveyed his audience. He readied himself to speak.

"I am by nature an optimist," he said.

III

GUTS

Frederick Russell Burnham was born in southern Minnesota in 1861. One night the following year, his parents watched from their isolated log cabin as the night sky turned red in the distance. The nearby town of New Ulm was burning. Chief Little Crow was leading the Lakota on a raid, killing hundreds of people, including children, during a conflict known as the Dakota War. Burnham's father, Edwin, a Presbyterian minister, rushed off to the town of Mankato to gather powder and bullets to protect the family.

One evening while Edwin was away, Burnham's mother, Rebecca, was brushing her hair in the doorway when she saw a band of Lakota slip out of the forest. Knowing she wouldn't be able to evade them with her child in tow, she hid the boy—not yet two years old—in a heap of newly shucked corn. She told him to keep perfectly still.

Then she took off, vanishing into the cottonwoods toward a neighbor's house six miles away. At dawn she came back to find that the Indians had burned the cabin, but her son was still alive. He'd stayed motionless in the corn—stashed away, like baby Moses in his basket, as a river of violence rushed past. "I had faithfully carried out my first orders of silent obedience," the scout later wrote.

Seven years later the family relocated to Los Angeles, a town materializing out of the sagebrush and dust. Edwin passed away only a few years after they arrived, and Burnham's mother took out a loan and bought two train tickets, for herself and Burnham's young brother, to return east, where they could be with family. Fred stayed behind, deciding to strike out on his own in California. He got a job delivering telegrams as a mounted messenger for Western Union and excelled at the job, riding hard over precarious terrain day and night, switching to a second horse when he wore out the first, then a third horse, and a fourth. In no time, he'd repaid his mother's loan. He was thirteen years old.

When he was fourteen, religious family members in the small town of Clinton, Iowa, concerned about his soul, summoned Burnham to live with them—to try life as a regular townie kid. But the regularness of Clinton didn't suit him. He wanted to live in a world that unfolded, little by little, on the trail ahead of him. Playing games—ordinary kid games, with sticks and balls—seemed strange to him. "I felt an urge to do bigger things," he said. He lasted a year. Then one night he stole a canoe, slipped off down the Mississippi, and never came back.

Burnham reached Texas, where he encountered the grizzled characters of a fading West. Many of these old frontiersmen had wound up as alone at the end of their lives as Burnham was at the outset of his, and they'd sit with him for hours, unspooling their stories. An old scout named Holmes had lost his family in the Indian Wars and, without any heirs to pass his knowledge on to, began teaching Burnham the old ways of scouting. He led Burnham through the desert for six months, forging the boy's grit and courage into actual skills.

From Holmes and the other scouts he encountered, Burnham learned to read the air like a river and pull the scent of a campfire out of the warmer currents floating along high ridges; how to build up his internal compass and rely on it even in total darkness; how to hone a photographic memory for the tracks of individual horses; how to improvise and conceal booby traps; how to carry a gallon or two of water in a saddle blanket, then wring it out over a concave rock; how never to ride a straight line into camp, in case someone had detected you and was plotting an ambush. More than anything, Burnham learned that, as he later put it, "we should be learning something always, no matter how long we live, or how long we play the game."

The most grueling lessons were psychological—learning to weather the loneliness, fear, and deprivation amid which those physical skills would be deployed. Scouts, after all, worked alone. "The darkness of night is his best friend," Burnham wrote, "for it will hide his secret movements—although it is at night that physical exhaustion is most apt to breed the cowardice that comes creeping into the bones of every man at times." One of the most pernicious forces a scout needed to suppress was hunger. It could be just as powerful a disincentive as exhaustion or fear—often more powerful. In a way, Burnham came to see the stomach as both the weakest and most persuasive part of a man. It messed with you mentally, tried to order you around. A scout couldn't afford to humor his stomach; it was hard enough to make sure his horse was properly fed. So Burnham adapted. He'd hammer deer jerky into a powder, mix the powder with flour, and bake the mixture into a saddlebag-shaped loaf. Then he'd eat off that block of deer cake for the duration of his travels, one pound per day.

This flexibility—the fierce epicurean stoicism that Burnham cultivated—would be a subtle hallmark of all of his future adventures. In East Africa, he'd do as the local tribesmen did, eating no vegetables for months at a time, instead consuming a mixture of three parts milk and one part fresh blood, drawn from a vein in the neck of a living ox the way syrup makers tap the trunk of a maple. During one stakeout, he subsisted wholly on a ration of uncooked corn, grinding away at the stuff until his jaw was sore and his starchy, thickened tongue made his speech unintelligible.

"The man of one diet is hopelessly handicapped," he wrote, "for nature has made it possible for a well organized human being to wrest sustenance out of a thousand foods. . . . Man's stomach, like his hand, can be trained to adapt itself to many strange uses." In other words, the stomach wanted what it wanted, but appetite, like all desire, was a liability. And with enough discipline, you could disregard it and fill the stomach with drab blocks of pure common sense instead.

It was only because Burnham had had this epiphany, and proved his hypothesis in the growling laboratory of his own gut, that he could consider hippopotamus steaks such an obvious solution to America's meat shortage thirty years later.

For all his self-control, Burnham was susceptible to gold fever and spent years during his young adulthood rashly chasing rumors of lost mines around the American Southwest. He had only one small strike, at age twenty-two. It brought him just enough money to send back to the town in Iowa he'd long ago escaped, for a girl he'd met there, Blanche Blick, and make her his wife. He bought them a house in an orange grove in Pasadena and settled into a more conventional life as an upstart Californian citrus grower.

But somehow the man with an alchemical ability to turn crud into food couldn't manage to produce oranges from orange trees. The economics of his operation never came together, and the sedentary lifestyle he'd carved out for himself and Blanche left him restless. The whole project had been a serious miscalculation. He spent his time reading books about Africa and dreaming.

Burnham's infatuation with Africa had started as a child in Minnesota. An older girl had read him adventure stories about young boys trekking into the wilds of a southern territory known as the Orange Free State—one of the republics founded by the descendants of Dutch settlers called Boers. Even as he wandered the Southwest as a young man, he tried to stay up on the developments in the region, following along as long-standing strife between the British and the Boers sparked a brief war in 1881.

Burnham was particularly enthralled by the Cape Colony's prime minister, Cecil John Rhodes. Rhodes was a shrewd and aggressive imperialist—a "superbrain," Burnham called him. Burnham was swept up by Rhodes's vision for remaking the African continent. Like many people of his time, Burnham earnestly believed that the transformation of Africa was a noble and even perversely humanitarian goal, never recognizing the hubris and vile racism that underlay it. "Rhodes saw Africa as a vast unkempt field, calling to him to be cleared," Burnham wrote. He was striving to plant "the flower of civilization" there.

Frontiers like this were Burnham's natural habitat. It was why he'd been drawn to the Southwest in his youth. "It is the constructive side of frontier life that most appeals to me, the building up of a country," he once explained to a friend. "When the place is finally settled I don't seem to enjoy it very long." But the Southwest had been tamed, wrestled from the Indians and demystified. And as deflating as it was to admit, Burnham had truly participated only in the tail end of that conquest.

Now he was transposing all those same boyish ambitions to southern Africa, where the deserts happened to look remarkably like the ones he'd spent a decade traveling. Sitting in his orange grove in Pasadena, something about the blank slate he perceived in Africa and the industriousness of Rhodes seduced him. "I was as one summoned by an irresistible call," he wrote. He figured Rhodes would need a good scout, one who knew how to operate in daunting desert terrain. He left for Africa with his wife and young son, Roderick, on January 1, 1893.

IV

THE HUMAN EPITOME OF SIN AND DECEPTION

In late January 1900 the novelist and war correspondent Richard Harding Davis was sailing from England to Cape Town on a ship called the SS *Scot*. The journey lasted seventeen days, and every night, Davis noticed, the men on deck would gather around the same small, reserved man with piercing blue eyes. The crowd consisted of big-game hunters and career soldiers, many of whom had held command in British wars in India or Sudan—roughneck, capable survivors, in other words, with their own yarns to spin and advice to give. But they all sat like schoolkids, Davis later wrote, pelting the quiet man with questions.

The man explained to them how to tell a column of dust raised by a cavalry from one kicked up by a wagon train; how to read the speed of a horse from its prints; how to conceal a campfire. The crowd was impressed with the quickness and clarity of the man's answers, but more impressed that, in the couple of instances when he wasn't able to answer, he told them so—it was a unique combination of mastery and humility. This man was Frederick Russell Burnham, of course, on his way back to Africa seven years after that first impulsive trip. He had made his name fighting for Rhodes's Cape Colony and gained a reputation as a scout. A series of conflicts had flared up as soon as Burnham and his family arrived in South Africa in 1893. Rhodes's forces were pressing into Matabeleland, in present-day Zimbabwe, and struggling to suppress the Ndebele tribe there. Burnham leaped right into the battle. It felt like the Indian wars of his youth all over again. Before long Matabeleland had been occupied and rechristened Rhodesia.

Three years later, when the Ndebele staged an uprising and the so-called Second Matabele War erupted, Burnham and his family were living outside the city of Bulawayo. There was a second child now, a two-year-old girl named Nada. As the conflict intensified and the Ndebele advanced, the Burnhams were moved into Bulawayo for their protection. The city was being locked down and fortified with homemade defenses; the Burnhams and another family were stuffed into a three-room shack, with their livestock milling outside.

Soon a virus ripped through the colonists' oxen. Thousands of animals died in the course of three weeks. Bulawayo was five hundred miles from the nearest railroad—it was with oxen carts that the colonists brought in food and supplies. Soon thousands of people began dying, too. "For weeks," Burnham wrote, "there was an unremitting stench."

Eventually, Nada came down with a fever. By that point, the remaining livestock had been eaten. Ultimately, Nada was one of many children who could not outlast the siege. Burnham was off fighting when she died, and it was up to Blanche to enlist some friends to bury her daughter in a shallow grave outside town. Burnham was devastated, obsessing over a series of painful and unanswerable questions—questions, he later wrote, that started with *If only*, and even more wrenching questions that started with *Why*.

The following year, at age thirty-six, Burnham left Africa for Alaska. Gold had been discovered, and he was again determined to be part of the beginning of something big. But the gold evaded him. He kept up on the news from South Africa: the antipathy between the British and the Dutch-descended Boers was escalating again.

He was mining quartz north of Juneau when, on January 4, 1900, a telegram arrived from the new British commander in South Africa, who had heard about Burnham's service during the previous conflicts. It read: "Lord Roberts appoints you on his personal staff. All expenses paid if you accept. Start shortest way Cape Town and report yourself to him." Burnham was en route to Africa two and a half hours later, aboard the same ship the telegram had come in on. Once in England, he transferred to the SS *Scot*, where Richard Harding Davis found him, reluctantly mesmerizing his fellow passengers night after night.

The Second Boer War was not going well for the British when Burnham received the call. The Boers had surprised the colonists, shattering their imperial confidence with a string of victories right after combat had started the previous fall.

In truth, the entire conflict was saturated with feelings of bewilderment and disarray. Two modern historians describe the Second Boer War as a clash characterized by a "capacity to produce confusion and ambivalence" and a "wide variety of half-truths." (Even the war's immediate causes are hard to pull from the slop of competing propaganda; in part, the British were seeking control of the Transvaal, a Boer territory rich in gold.) By December 1899 England was determined to change tactics. Lord Frederick Sleigh Roberts of Kandahar was installed as the new commander in South Africa. Roberts began assembling his team, summoning Burnham as his chief of scouts and Major-General Lord Herbert Kitchener of Khartoum and Aspall as his chief of staff. Kitchener was a particularly merciless strategist, and within months the tide turned completely. Soon the Boer government in the Transvaal would be shattered, and its leadership would flee to Europe. But the Boers kept fighting tenaciously as guerrillas—a decentralized, lethal swarm. Burnham's job was to gallop around inside this fractured conflict, undetected.

Like a lot of freelance adventurers involved in the war, and even many British citizens, Burnham felt great respect for the other side. He was awed by the Boers, in fact. He believed that they were uniquely menacing adversaries because, like the best scouts of the American Southwest, they'd somehow retained the instincts and senses of more primitive men. For years after the war was over, he would carry on about the virtuosity of one of his enemies in particular: an enigmatic scout known as the Black Panther of the Veld. "He was one of the craftiest men I ever met," Burnham would tell an interviewer thirty years later. He was "a man of extraordinary power."

The Black Panther's name was Fritz Duquesne. Burnham had heard that he'd adopted the nom de guerre as a boy, after watching a wild panther stalk its prey at a watering hole. Duquesne noticed how efficient the animal was—how it always waited to attack, intent and totally untroubled, until the other animal was compromised. The boy vowed to emulate the panther and made it his totem. The panther, Burnham wrote, was a wild predator that no one had ever succeeded in taming. By the Second Boer War, Duquesne had become just as cunning.

Duquesne would spend the conflict trying to kill Burnham, and Burnham was assigned to kill Duquesne. Burnham called him the "human epitome of sin and deception." Another writer described him as a "walking living breathing searing killing destroying torch of hate."

Duquesne was only one of countless threats Burnham had to dodge during the war, as his commanders sent him to infiltrate and sabotage the scurrying, deadly remnants of the Boer army. Burnham's exploits were numerous and bizarre. Once he hid for two days and nights inside an aardvark hole. Another time he floated down a river disguised as a dead cow, drifting under a fresh, fleshy hide with two eyeholes cut out of it, to size up an enemy camp downstream.

In the spring of 1900 he was captured by Boer scouts but managed to conceal his identity. The Boers had been given index cards describing the famous Frederick Russell Burnham—a supposedly ruthless, godless, illiterate rogue from the American West. Realizing this, Burnham sparked an erudite theological debate with one of his captors—was baptism by immersion the one true route to salvation, or was it baptism by sprinkling?—then followed that up by reciting some poetry. Eventually, he slipped away from the Boers' wagon train in the dark. He spent his thirty-ninth birthday, in May 1900, hiding in enemy territory, preparing to blow up some bridges, feasting on a ration of chocolate and condensed soup. Then in early June, he was given twenty-five pounds of explosives and sent to cut the railway connecting Pretoria to the Indian Ocean.

After setting out, Burnham encountered a group of Boers in the distance, and his horse, Stembok, was shot. The animal fell on him. Burnham's spine burned. He assumed his back was broken. But he managed to reach his target anyway—a specific point on the railway, beside a distillery—traveling the rest of the way on foot, vomiting blood and compressing his abdomen with both hands to lessen the pain slightly. (At one point, he wrote a farewell note to his wife, Blanche, and dropped it on the ground, hoping British soldiers would eventually pass by and find it.) Then, after rigging his explosives and detonating them, he hauled his busted body into a grove of eucalyptus and hid, trying to make himself invisible yet again as a unit of Boers fired systematically into the trees to flush him out. Eventually, the troops gave up and moved on.

Hours later Burnham heard the voices of British soldiers approaching. He was rushed to a field hospital, where doctors determined that, though his spine was not damaged, his internal injuries were severe. Lord Roberts promoted him to major and sent him to recuperate in England. On the ship back, he chatted with a young British newspaperman named Winston Churchill who had also been captured by the Boers and escaped. The two men swapped stories, and though Churchill's involved taking many risks that Burnham, as a scout, could not condone, the scout ultimately understood that the writer had done the best he could. "His moves were restricted by the handicap of physical weakness," Burnham wrote, "which made a twenty mile run at night"—what Burnham judged to be the most straightforward move in those circumstances—"entirely beyond his power."

In England, Burnham was invited to dine with Queen Victoria and decorated with the Distinguished Service Order, a high honor for heroism during wartime, by King Edward VII. Burnham, with his characteristic stoicism, described the award as so humbling and unnecessary that it was "almost humiliating." "I felt of no more importance than a grain of sand on the shore of the mighty sea," he wrote.

———————

Slowly, Burnham's injuries healed. The darkness of Nada's death was dissipating, too. Blanche had given birth to another child—a son named Bruce—and they joined Fred in England. By 1905 the couple was hatching a plan to return their family to Rhodesia and restart their lives.

The Burnhams' oldest child, Roderick, was now nineteen years old and in school back in California, living with his grandmother. One night that October he awoke and ran to her, shrieking from a nightmare. He claimed that he had watched his little brother chase a toy boat into deep water and sink to his death. The next day a telegram arrived from England. It was from Blanche and Fred, and it read: "Bruce drowned. Coming soon." Bruce was seven years old. He'd been swept away in the Thames.

The Burnhams returned to California, wrecked. They spent a lot of their time at home, overlooking a picturesque arroyo, in a secluded area of Pasadena called San Rafael Heights. Burnham tried his best to console his wife.

It was during this time that Burnham started to think seriously, and ambitiously, about an idea he'd had many years earlier. Maybe it was because Bruce's death had made the horror of Nada's slow starvation feel fresh again. Or maybe it was because Burnham was marooned at home, glaring at the arid and relatively lifeless landscape around him—a place, he knew, that had already been drained of so much of its wild, edible game by shortsighted hunters. Eventually, he sat down to write an article about this idea of his, hoping one of the major magazines back east might be talked into publishing it.

"There is in Africa a wonderfully varied range of interesting animals," he wrote. "Most of the desirable ones could easily be introduced into our own Southwest."

PART TWO
Four Years Later

V

WE OUGHT TO HAVE MORE CREATURES

"Transplanting African Animals," by Major Frederick Russell Burnham, was published in New York's *Independent* magazine in January
1910. Before long a chain of serendipitous connections was made,
and Burnham was invited to share his ideas in a hearing before
the House Committee on Agriculture. It would be a long afternoon of testimony, but at the very start a federal researcher named
W. N. Irwin summed up the matter nicely: "Mr. Chairman and
gentlemen of the committee," he told the congressmen, "in studying the resources of our country for a good many years, I was led
to the conclusion that we ought to have more creatures than we are
raising here."

It was March 24, 1910. Under discussion was H.R. 23261, a bill to
appropriate $250,000 for the importation of useful new animals
into the United States—the hippo bill, as the public would come to
understand it. H.R. 23261 had been introduced by the Louisiana congressman Robert Broussard, who had limited himself to a very short
statement at the start of the hearing, not wanting to detract from
the impressive roster of experts he'd assembled—"three gentlemen,"
he explained, "who probably have devoted more time than almost
anyone else to this matter."

Ceding the spotlight was not in Broussard's nature. Then forty-
five years old, Robert Foligny Broussard was a raucous and charismatic Democrat from New Iberia, Louisiana. He was the son of a
Cajun planter and had lived in the district he represented for most
of his life. He loved speechifying and glad-handing and generally
addressed himself to the job of campaigning the way a gourmand
addresses himself to a platter of oysters—despite having never

encountered any real opposition in his seven successive reelections. He claimed to be related to a quarter of the voters in Iberia Parish— sometimes to a full half of them. Louisianans knew him affectionately as Cousin Bob.

Broussard had met Burnham for the first time that morning. Launching a national effort to import foreign animals that could benefit American society, especially hippos, had been percolating on Broussard's legislative agenda for some time, and mutual friends in Washington had referred him to Burnham. He and Broussard were like Darwinian finches—the same species of capable specialist evolved to thrive within two parallel environments. As adeptly as Burnham maneuvered through the African desert, Broussard seemed to maneuver through the disorienting wilderness of Washington, reading the landscape, performing what could only seem like sorcery to outsiders. In Broussard, Burnham saw new hope that his gorgeous idea for America might actually become a reality. He called the congressman "a tower of strength for the movement."

Broussard, for his part, had locked onto the potential of African animals for his own idiosyncratic reasons. Cousin Bob had actually set out to solve a different crisis for his constituents. The crisis was a flower.

Water hyacinths had been brought to New Orleans in 1884, distributed as gifts by the Japanese delegation to an international cotton exposition. New Orleanians loved the frilly, pale lavender flowers and gradually planted them as decorations around the city in garden ponds. The hyacinths multiplied rapidly. (The plant reproduces asexually.) Soon they were spreading through local waterways, clotting into impenetrable mats, then drifting toward the mouth of the Mississippi like big, menacing hairballs toward a drain.

By 1910, when Broussard introduced his bill, the flowers had been plaguing his state for at least a decade. They'd clogged up streams and made shipping routes that had previously moved millions of tons of freight unnavigable. They'd blanketed rivers and wetlands, hogging the oxygen and killing fish. The War Department was staging an all-out offensive against the flower, "[b]ut they have only been partially successful," Broussard said. "They clean a stream today, and in a month it is covered all over again with the same plant."

Broussard was not the sort of man who could abide such defeat. He liked to plug up problems with big solutions; he was "a large operator," one reporter wrote, who "goes in for broad effects." It occurred to him that perhaps some animal could be brought to Louisiana to swallow this particular problem up, and he seems to have hit on the hippopotamus after encountering the curious, aging bureaucrat he'd now called to brief the House Agricultural Committee just before Burnham.

William Newton "W. N." Irwin was a veteran researcher at the pomological branch of the Bureau of Plant Industry at the U.S. Department of Agriculture. He was an apple guy, basically—"one of the foremost fruit experts in the country," according to *The Washington Post*. Irwin appears to have spent his career championing ideas that were simultaneously perfectly logical and extravagantly bizarre. (Another of his crusades was trying to convert Americans from eating chicken eggs to eating turkey eggs, which Irwin insisted were richer, larger, and more nutritious.) He had first laid out the case for hippopotamuses while delivering a paper at a conference in Missouri the previous year. He reviewed the causes of America's gathering meat crisis and noted that, in the past, the country had sidestepped these kinds of Malthusian forecasts by expanding just a little farther west. There had always been more land to put into production. But now there was little suitable rangeland left to occupy. The only way forward, Irwin concluded, was to find ways of wringing nourishment out of land that now seemed barren or worthless—for example, the vast marshes along the Gulf Coast. Extracting the energy embedded there would require assembling a new set of tools—new technologies. The hippopotamus was one such technology.

Hippopotamuses eat aquatic vegetation—loads of it, Irwin learned. Deposit some hippos in a hyacinth-choked stream, he argued, and they'd suck it clean in no time. That is, hippos could solve Louisiana's problem with the flower while simultaneously converting that problem into the solution to another—an answer to the Meat Question. The hippopotamus was a perversely elegant win-win.

Of course, it could be hard to see that logic through all the lavish weirdness of the proposal. But for Irwin—and Burnham—any resistance to their idea came down to simple small-mindedness. The only reason Americans didn't already eat hippopotamuses, Irwin claimed, was "because their neighbors don't, or because nobody ever told them it was the proper thing to do." Like Burnham, he saw the Meat Question as a test of American ingenuity and resolve: to defend our freedom and way of life, some generations of Americans are called to go to war; this generation was being called to import hippopotamuses and eat them. And, also like Burnham, Irwin seemed incapable, or at least unwilling, to let any emotional objections or queasiness detract from the divine common sense of their plan. A few months earlier, Irwin had invited a *Washington Post* reporter to his office, fed him a stick of hippo jerky while showing him a photograph of five East African men skinning the very beast he was now digesting, and whined: "I am at a loss to understand why anybody should protest against the hippopotamus as a food animal. Everyone seems to hate to go out and blaze a trail." In one scientific paper, Irwin compared himself to Christopher Columbus, being laughed at as he sailed toward what looked like the edge of the earth but was, in reality, a new and nutritionally superior world of turkey eggs and hippopotamus brisket.

When it was Burnham's turn to testify, he echoed Irwin's arguments but tried to imbue the bureaucrat's geeky reasoning with his own firsthand experiences and gravitas. Burnham challenged the committee to consider how strange it is that we eat only cows, pigs, sheep, and poultry—just four types of animals, all of which had themselves been imported by Europeans centuries ago. Why, somewhere along the line, had we stopped feeling entitled to improve our country's food stocks by infusing them with animals from the great global pantry abroad? "I think we are allowing one of our greatest assets to lie idle," Burnham told the committee. It was only the passage of time that had made a pork chop or a bowl of chicken soup feel American—not its actual origin. Time would make hippo roasts just as familiar.

It was an impressive testimony. But Congressman Broussard had invited another speaker that afternoon, one who would wind up being the star attraction. Broussard introduced this man to the committee as a "hunter of great note" in Africa who happened to be touring America now, lecturing on the African continent's wild animals. "I now desire to present to the committee," Broussard announced, "Captain Fritz Duquesne."

It was he, the Black Panther of the Veld. Two of Broussard's three expert witnesses—these men seated in the hearing room, graciously educating the 61st Congress of the United States about the usefulness and deliciousness of hippopotamuses—were, in fact, arch enemies who had vowed to assassinate each other.

Duquesne took the floor and sought immediately to establish his singular credibility on the subject at hand. "I am as much one of the African animals as the hippopotamus," he began.

VI

A UNIT OF HATE

The details of Fritz Duquesne's life dart around in a deep pool of uncertainty. Partly this is because the journalists of his day who assembled them were unscrupulous, but mainly it's because Duquesne would reinvent himself again and again.

Frederick L'Huguenot Joubert Duquesne (pronounced du-*cain*) was born in the Cape Colony on December 21, 1877—according to one suspect source, at least; friends would claim that even Duquesne did not know his own age. He was lean and alluring with a youthful, clean-shaven look—a champion womanizer, it was said. His hair was black, or else it was brown. His eyes were brown, hazel, or blue. He spoke with a clipped British accent, which may have been fake.

Duquesne grew up on a farm among other Boer families. His father was a hunter and trader who was constantly traveling, and so Fritz was raised by his mother and his uncle Jan, who'd been blinded when an elephant gun backfired on him during a hunt. As a boy, Duquesne would watch the adults return from the river with a hippopotamus—they were among the easiest animals to hunt— then butcher its massive carcass and divide the meat among their families.

As a teenager, he was sent to school in Europe. He was studying at a military academy in Belgium, learning about weaponry and explosives, when a letter arrived from his father, calling him back to fight for his people against the overbearing British. It was 1899; the Second Boer War was under way.

Duquesne arrived at Boer headquarters in Pretoria, a city in the Transvaal republic, northeast of the Cape Colony, just before the British aggressively revised their strategy and the war turned uglier and more unruly. Over the next year, Lords Roberts and Kitchener would funnel the Boers into concentration camps and scorch the earth behind them. There were as many as 160,000 Boer prisoners in the camps at one time; 25,000 would die there by the end of the conflict in 1902.

Boer soldiers like Duquesne began roving the land in small guerrilla squadrons, without the security or support of a formal army. Duquesne was captured and escaped at least twice. At one point he was shipped all the way to a prison in Lisbon. But he escaped easily, first finding the time to seduce his jailer's daughter. He then made his way to England, claimed to be a Boer defector, enlisted as a British soldier, hitched a ride back to the front in Africa, and took off on his own again.

Duquesne became a military courier, delivering messages between Boer commandos. Traveling around, he saw the devastation of Kitchener's scorched-earth policy—the fires, the horses sprayed with bullets so the Boers could not use them, the crops burned, and the livestock shot up and clubbed. He was sickened by how much the British had obliterated, how desolate they'd left the land.

During this time, Duquesne found an opportunity to visit his family's homestead, north of Pretoria, after eleven years away— according to the writer Clement Wood, who in 1932 published a detailed but extremely romanticized and journalistically tenuous account of Duquesne's life. Duquesne knew that his father had died shortly after calling him back to fight but had no other news of his family. Wood writes that it wasn't until Duquesne got off his horse, and touched the blackened stone that had once been the corner of his house's foundation, that he knew where he was; the British had so totally destroyed the place, it was unrecognizable. Duquesne found a servant there who had worked for his family since he was a child. The old man, Kanya, was living in a primitive shelter he'd dug for himself in the ruins. Hunched over and demoralized, Kanya explained that the British soldiers had hung Duquesne's blind uncle Jan from a telegraph pole with a cow rope, then jabbed at his body with their bayonets. They'd taken turns raping Duquesne's sister Elsbet, then shot her. Then they'd tied his mother's hands, raped her, and carried her off.

Duquesne assumed that his mother had been taken to the nearest concentration camp, a few days away on horseback. He sped there and, disguising himself in the British uniform he'd been given as a supposed defector, entered the camp and tried to track her down. He found her in a barbed-wire paddock clutching a seven-month-old baby, both of them starving and dying of syphilis—essentially dead already.

Before leaving, Duquesne pledged to his mother that he would kill one hundred Englishmen for every drop of blood in her body. But he felt nothing for the baby—it was his half-sibling, but it was also half-British, the evidence of his mother's rape. Riding away from the camp, still in uniform, Duquesne saw two captains in the British Army approaching. He saluted them. Once they'd passed, he turned in his saddle and shot both men in the back. Then he got off his horse and kicked each in the face.

Any number of these details that Wood relays could be wrong—possibly all of them. But at the very least, the story was as an attempt to explain one unmistakably true thing about Fritz Duquesne: that at some point in Africa, he became radicalized, consumed with searing rage for the British and for Lord Kitchener personally.

"Something happened inside of him that had fused him into a unit," Wood wrote, "a unit of hate."

Duquesne was captured one last time, late in the Boer War, while plotting a sensational symphony of explosions around Cape Town. The British shipped him to a prison camp on Tucker's Island, in Bermuda, with his wrists and ankles bound so tightly that he'd be scarred for the rest of his life.

He wasted no time in escaping. In one version of the story, Duquesne coordinated a jailbreak with two other prisoners, banging out their plans in Morse code from their cells. They slipped past the guards and dove into the sea with their clothes and boots tied to their bodies as bullets whizzed around them. They spent three weeks on the lam. Eventually, Duquesne reached the port town of Hamilton, where, according to a 1995 biography by Art Ronnie, *Counterfeit Hero*, he established himself as a pimp for a mulatto prostitute named Vera.

It was a strategic job placement; in the course of her nightly business, Vera acquired detailed information about the ships moving in and out of the port. Duquesne managed to get one of Vera's clients drunk and learned he was a crew member on a private yacht about to sail for Baltimore. While Vera serviced the sailor, Duquesne stole his uniform and sneaked onto the ship in his place. He was eventually discovered, but he hit it off so well with the yacht's owner, a middle-aged inventor of a powdered headache remedy, that he was ultimately invited to ride along. Duquesne set foot on American soil on July 4, 1902. Unless, according to another account, it was on December 16.

There was peace now in southern Africa—the Boer territories had been subdued and claimed by the British. But given his machinations during the war, Duquesne believed he would not be welcome there. He was on his own now. With the help of a network of Boer sympathizers on the East Coast, he slowly began constructing a life for himself in America. He went to New York and got a job selling subscriptions for the *New York Sun*. Soon he was bumped up to reporter. He was an immigrant, in other words, living his own lonely version of the classic American immigrant story—remaking himself, hustling. And it was working. Seven years later Fritz Duquesne found himself sitting in the White House with the president of the United States.

President Theodore Roosevelt, preparing to leave office in early 1909, began enthusiastically plotting a stunning first act to his retirement: a big-game-hunting expedition to East Africa, undertaken in conjunction with the Smithsonian. Roosevelt spent months studying up, writing letters to men who'd hunted in the region for advice. Somehow Duquesne, with his native's knowledge of the continent and its wildlife, had inserted himself into this informal committee of experts and was invited to meet with the president that January. They talked for more than two hours. Duquesne was impressed with the president. He told the press, "He seems to have mastered all the details."

Over the next year, Roosevelt's journey through Africa would unfold in the newspapers back home in daily, time-delayed dispatches. It became a national fascination. Duquesne had been dropped into the center of that excitement, briefly, during their meeting at the White House. Now he'd do his best to capitalize on it.

He wrote a series of syndicated columns called "Hunting Ahead of Roosevelt," in which he drew on his own adventures in Africa to speculate about the kinds of animals and adventures the president was now encountering. When that momentum seemed exhausted, Duquesne went negative, keeping his name in the papers by mocking Roosevelt, denigrating him as nothing more than a dandy tourist blustering across the continent with a team of Africans to do the real hunting for him. And as Roosevelt readied to return in early 1910, Duquesne announced that he believed the former president might have contracted a deadly, still-dormant disease and should not be allowed back into the country.

By then Duquesne had adapted his hunting stories into a theatrical lecture called "East Africa—the Wonderland of Roosevelt's Hunt" and taken the show on tour. It featured moving pictures and stereopticon slides of "hunting scenes and savage life in darkest Africa," all narrated by "Captain Fritz Duquesne," as he'd taken to calling himself. As it happened, he was booked for two shows at the Columbia Theatre, in Washington, just as Broussard was gathering experts for his hippo hearing.

In a sense, then, Duquesne's appearance at the committee hearing was both an advertisement for his performances and performance in itself. The man wanted attention, and he knew how to work his audience when he got it.

Duquesne affably walked the congressmen through his knowledge of hippos and parried their skeptical questions with composed and charming assurances. He described how easy it was to domesticate a hippo; how you can feed a young one milk from a bottle "like a baby" and lead it on a leash. "It is absolutely not dangerous," he said of the animal and described the meat—especially from young, castrated males—as a delicious, satisfying, and sustaining meal. ("Splendid food," Duquesne insisted, "excellent food.") As proof, he pointed proudly to how well his own people, the Boers, had performed in the recent imperial wars, despite being outnumbered. "There was nothing mentally or physically defective about them," he explained, "and they lived on hippopotamus."

Duquesne was not finished, however. He recommended elands, a kind of brutish antelope, as another phenomenal addition to American wildlife. Also giraffes. And what about elephants? Hannibal's army crossed the Pyrenees on elephants, Duquesne reminded the congressmen, so this should give us all some inkling of the animal's usefulness and stamina. "It went right around the Pyrenees," he said, "backward and forward."

It was a fetching, whip-smart whirlwind of a performance, and it seemed to sweep up everyone. Before it was over, one congressman had invited him out to Bethesda to have a look at some captive zebras being bred there and offer an expert opinion.

"I think I have about exhausted the proposition," Duquesne finally told the committee. "I have finished." Although, he added, if the congressmen wanted him to perform his lecture right then and there, he'd be glad to. He happened to have all his materials with him.

VII

THE NEW FOOD SUPPLY SOCIETY

The hearing was followed by a surge of excited publicity. "Hippopotami for Dixie," one headline read. The *Chicago Tribune* covered the proceedings right above news that Delmonico's, the famous steakhouse, had been forced to raise prices due to dwindling meat supplies. Most newspapers led their coverage with splashy quotes from Fritz Duquesne, but even the torturously uncharismatic W. N. Irwin got called on occasionally. ("I like to say 'hippo' instead of the full name, because it is shorter and somewhat more euphonious," Irwin paused to explain to one reporter.) The momentum felt unstoppable. According to *The Washington Post*, it was "a question of only a very few years now when large shipments of hippos will be made to America."

It wasn't likely that Congress would be able to act on Broussard's appropriation bill before the end of its session, but Broussard, Burnham, and Duquesne believed that, with the right legwork, a reintroduced version would breeze through the next session. And so they decided to build a new organization to leverage their position and keep the pressure on—a lobbying firm, essentially, called the New Food Supply Society. Shortly after the hearing, the congressman invited Duquesne and Burnham down to his plantation in Louisiana to hash out some preliminary plans.

It's unclear what, if any, contact the two enemies had had in the nine years since they'd fought against each other in Africa. The evidence suggests that Burnham and Duquesne never actually crossed paths during the war—just loomed heavily, and terribly, in each other's minds. Theirs was an old-fashioned kind of rivalry. What adhered them to one another was a fearful and unshakable respect, nothing as vulgar as hatred. It involved a kind of perverse honor; Duquesne remembered that he had once "tossed coins with a brother scout for the privilege of having first shot [at Burnham,] of splitting his body with a bullet," but had never managed to track the great scout down. Now their inadvertent partnership on the hippopotamus project gave them an opportunity to finally know one another at close range.

Burnham was impressed by his old rival. "Duquesne was clever, educated and resourceful," he would recall. Burnham knew all about the sins in Duquesne's past but chose to force them out of his mind.

He wanted to help the Boer. Duquesne was free-floating in permanent exile and, nearly a decade after being cast out of Africa, still struggling to set a new trajectory for himself in the United States. Burnham believed that this noble attempt they were making to answer the nation's Meat Question would show his former adversary, firsthand, the sort of hard work, imagination, and values that made America great. It might finally steer his talents in a productive direction, cleanse him.

Burnham was ambivalent about playing the reformer. He remembered his own experience as a kid, suffering through life with his pious relatives in Iowa. But he believed that if he could understand what "had transformed this strong and remarkable man into a being abnormal and terrible" and "conquer the cruel darkness" that had infected Duquesne somewhere along the way, there was a chance that the wily Boer could "become one of the world's noblest figures." And so, Burnham later wrote, "I set out to win over to genuine Americanism one of the most remarkable men I had ever met." Duquesne could be assimilated, made useful—just like the hippopotamus.

As Broussard, Duquesne, and Burnham began plotting the formation of the New Food Supply Society in the spring of 1910, each man was being driven by different levels of idealism and opportunism and by different semisecret motives. Letters began flying among the three men. Duquesne, however, seems to have been the only one doing any concrete work. Not long after the hearing, the society had sent him on a fact-finding mission to Louisiana, and he hoped that his role as freelance hippo expert might soon turn into a legitimate job. He made it clear that he was doing this work at his own expense and that the newspapers seldom paid him for the articles he penned to promote the society's goals. In a letter to Burnham, he described writing African animal essays all day until his hand cramped and his handwriting became illegible, at which point he'd switch to using a typewriter, which carried its own costs—ribbons, maintenance, and so on. Burnham tried to buck him up. ("My dear Captain," he wrote. "You certainly are pushing your part of the society in advance of the rest of us.") He told him he would try to hammer out some financial arrangement and employ Duquesne properly. Duquesne replied to Burnham that he didn't appreciate being left in the dark. "I do not want this movement to die through undue satisfaction or dry rot," he said.

Months passed like this. Burnham tried to keep his optimism up, writing to pitch new acquaintances about the idea and scheduling public appearances, including his speech to the Humane Association of California in Pasadena that fall. But the time between the three men's letters grew longer and longer. In September 1910 Duquesne wrote to Broussard: "What have you that is new or valuable in the way of suggestion? If any make them and I shall act." Broussard replied: "There is no news to communicate."

The following month, the *New York World* published an article about the importation of African animals that apparently credited the idea to Charles Frederick Holder of Santa Catalina Island in California, a well-known fisherman of exceptionally large tuna. Duquesne was irate. He sent copies of the article to both Burnham and Broussard, seething, and demanded that Broussard issue some sort of universal correction to the press.

It was a momentary outburst; soon the slow and painful birthing process of the New Food Supply Society would quietly resume. But something in Duquesne had snapped. He may have believed deep in his gut, as Burnham did, that importing hippopotamuses was the right and necessary thing for America—that the animal, if transplanted properly, would thrive here. But it was clear by now that he was working primarily for the prosperity of his favorite transplanted African animal: himself.

"It seems every day I hear of someone else, not Duquesne, being the man who brought this matter before the people," he wrote to

Broussard. "I am working day in and day out to keep this matter before the people, at some expense too. The thing was never heard of in DC till *I* spoke to you," Duquesne insisted. "No one else, mind you. Only Duquesne."

PART THREE
Seven Years Later

VIII

CAPTAIN CLAUDE STOUGHTON

Around Thanksgiving in 1917, the head of the New York City Police Department's bomb squad, Thomas J. Tunney, asked two of his detectives to begin investigating a certain Captain Claude Stoughton, a British officer who had served in the West Australian Light Horse division and was now stationed for a time in New York.

It's unclear why exactly Tunney had taken an interest in Stoughton, though his suspicions seem to have grown out of an investigation of a warehouse explosion in Brooklyn. City authorities had also been approached about Captain Stoughton by a widow on Riverside Drive. America had entered World War I that April, and the woman was troubled by sympathetic comments about the Germans that she'd heard a slightly inebriated Stoughton make at parties, and even more so by the style of his mustache. He wore it "trained upward in imitation of the well known style affected by the German emperor," she explained.

Tunney's detectives began digging up what they could on the man. They obtained a photograph of him in uniform and learned that he lived in a second-floor apartment at 137 West 75th Street. But a search of the apartment produced photos of Stoughton dressed in other countries' uniforms, too. Another photograph identified him as a war correspondent for a Belgian newspaper and showed him wearing his hair in florid curls. Another pictured him with ammunition slung over his torso, standing over a dead white rhinoceros. (Clearly, Tunney wrote, the man "fancied photographs of himself, as he made up rather dashingly.")

The trove of paperwork the detectives recovered was similarly fragmented and irreconcilable. There was an insurance policy for a staggering $80,000 worth of motion picture film, taken out five years earlier. There were newspaper articles—piles of them, which, according to *The New York Times*, detailed "practically every bomb explosion since the war began," with a special focus on a ship called the SS *Tennyson*, which had blown up a year earlier, after leaving Brazil for New York. One of the clippings described an investigation into the Tennyson explosion that had led to a British safe-deposit box, where police seized $6,740 in cash in an envelope addressed to someone with the virtually unpronounceable name Piet Niacud.

The men had also obtained a program for a theatrical lecture staged seven years earlier. The cover featured a very small circular photograph of President Theodore Roosevelt in safari gear, and a much larger studio portrait of Captain Stoughton. He was identified here by another name, one that had appeared in several other documents as well—including, most troublingly, a letter of introduction from a diplomat in Nicaragua, describing him as a man who had "in many circumstances rendered notable services to our good German cause." The name was Fritz Duquesne.

"A thousand questions sprang up in our minds about the man," Tunney remembered. They started following whatever leads they had. At some point they reached out to a well-known adventurer in California who, according to a magazine clipping they'd found, had once appeared alongside Duquesne at a congressional hearing about hippopotamuses in March 1910.

IX

PREPAREDNESS

In 1917 Frederick Burnham was living in relative seclusion. Shortly before the First World War started, he'd sold the house in Pasadena and moved his family and in-laws to a ranch in Tulare County, California, backed up against Sequoia National Park. He felt that Pasadena had swollen into a stifling suburb. The ranch, which the Burnhams called La Cuesta, offered them privacy, space, and some very well-deserved peace.

The phase of Burnham's life that had included the hippo hearing, seven years earlier, had been busy and stressful. While the New Food Supply Society was struggling to get off the ground, he was also traveling back and forth between California and Mexico, establishing copper mines and irrigation projects in the Yaqui Valley for a number of financiers, including the Guggenheim family and J. P. Morgan. The move to La Cuesta ranch presented him with yet another empty frontier to master and improve—but a tranquil one, on a smaller scale, far removed from any geopolitical violence. He imported white-tailed deer from Mexico and took pride in how they prospered. He introduced wild turkeys, peccaries, pheasants, and game bantams. The Burnhams were part of a small community of settlers living deep in the Sierras, widely dispersed—people who worked hard and made do on their own. Burnham thought of them as a "lost white tribe."

"When the World War broke," he remembered, "it was some time before the reality of it penetrated into our deep canyon." But when it did, the lost tribe sprang into action. Young men filed out of the mountains to enlist and fight. "Elderly women walked four miles in the heat of summer over dusty mountain roads to knit and sew for soldiers over seas," he wrote. This determination reassured Burnham. Otherwise, he was unsettled by the war. The new technological mode of warfare—the gassing, machine guns, and trenches—had "turned us all into military robots," he wrote. He argued that the traditional skills and ethos of self-reliance that those old scouts had taught him as a boy remained as important as ever, and he worried that they were being lost.

Self-reliance was becoming an obsession of Burnham's—the only sensible response to the growing disorder of the world. In the run-up to the war, he became part of the so-called Preparedness Movement in America, which believed that conflict was inevitable and that President Woodrow Wilson wasn't building a sufficiently large and capable military to handle it. In early 1917 he even enlisted as a lieutenant in a battalion of aging, able-bodied men from around the West that his friend Theodore Roosevelt had begun organizing, threatening to lead them into battle himself if President Wilson continued to keep America's actual armed forces on the sidelines. By now American writers had related Burnham's feats in Africa, making him a famous war hero. But it gnawed at him that he'd never actually fought for his own country. He thought, at age fifty-five, that he'd finally get his chance. But Roosevelt's army never shipped out. It wasn't until America finally joined the Great War in April 1917 that Burnham found an idiosyncratic opportunity to serve.

Manganese, a mineral used to make steel, had suddenly become invaluable during the war: a scarcity developed after shipments that the United States relied on, including German exports, were compromised or cut off. America scrambled after new exports from Brazil and other South American countries but also took a hard look at its own potential reserves. The mineral had not been worth much during the gold and silver rushes, and engineers now began poring over old U.S. Geological Survey documents and historical maps, looking for any sign of deposits that the miners had skipped over.

Burnham attacked the problem differently. He began rounding up prospectors he'd encountered in his youth. They were wizened old nomads now, but, Burnham would remember, they'd retained an "indescribable spiritual quality" and "perennial optimism" that allowed them to "wander vaguely over the desert wastes with the patience of the burro and the imperturbability of the Sphinx." Burnham began roaming the desert with these men, hunting for manganese, returning to deposits they remembered stumbling across years ago. Soon they were pulling manganese out of the hills in Nevada, from the sides of Mount Diablo, outside San Francisco, and from the belly of southwestern deserts, and sending it off to be bolted into the flanks of the modern war machine. For Burnham, it was reassuring proof that old skills could still contribute in a new kind of war.

In other words, Burnham spent the years after Broussard's congressional hearing essentially championing the same ideals he'd fought for in Washington: self-sufficiency and industriousness powered by an underlying optimism. As a young scout, he'd taught himself to stay awake for longer than seemed humanly possible by thwacking the back of his head with his fist if he started to nod off. Now, at the outset of the twentieth century, America clearly had problems—horrible and frightening ones. But they seemed solvable to Burnham if the nation would only rap itself on the head with enough determination and force, if it would shout at itself to wake the hell up. His loyalty to this belief was unwavering. And in this way he was the perfect foil to his old nemesis, Fritz Duquesne—who during those same years, the New York City police detectives were now learning, had been slowly shedding his belief in everything.

X

CAPTAIN FRITZ DUQUESNE'S SOUTH
AMERICAN EXPEDITION

Duquesne had worked hard to cobble together a small amount of notoriety and influence by the time he appeared at Broussard's hippopotamus hearing, and as the New Food Supply Society bumped along, he was determined not to let any of it go. He branched off on his own, marshaling all his entrepreneurial energy to stay in the limelight. He wound up spiraling into darkness instead.

At first, Duquesne simply took the hippopotamus idea and built on it, eccentrically. In the spring of 1911 he organized a series of banquets in Washington and New York, likely as showcases for a potential animal-importing venture he was considering launching on his own. He served guests a menu of imported African springbok soup, dik-dik, and hippo croquettes. Next, he explored bringing elephants to Central and South America and selling them as beasts of burden.

In 1913, however, Duquesne began planning a more promising business venture—one that apparently had started in earnest but would gradually contort into a deadly con. Theodore Roosevelt was now organizing a follow-up to his African expedition: a long, daring journey to trace one of the Amazon's tributaries through the Brazilian jungle. Duquesne saw another chance to capitalize on the public's fascination with Roosevelt's adventures, just as he'd done with his lectures during Roosevelt's safari.

He started canvassing acquaintances, then acquaintances of acquaintances, for money to produce *Captain Fritz Duquesne's South American Expedition*. It would be part movie, part lecture; he'd travel through the jungle filming the same sorts of things that Roosevelt would encounter, then narrate his footage live on stage. Duquesne eventually secured funding from the Thanhouser film corporation and the Goodyear tire company—he'd apparently agreed to do some rubber hunting in South America on the side—and promised to deliver the finished travelogue in time for the Panama-Pacific International Exposition in San Francisco in 1915. He bought twenty thousand feet of film, at four dollars a foot, and insured the lot of it before sailing out of New York, thereby generating the policy that Tunney's detectives would discover in his apartment four years later.

Apparently, not one foot of the film was ever used. World War I began shortly after the Duquesnes left New York, in the summer of

1914. The details are foggy, but President Wilson's insistence that the United States initially remain neutral seems to have disillusioned and enraged the Black Panther. Duquesne's contempt for England, forged during the Second Boer War, was so overpowering that, in his mind, the only conscionable response to the outbreak of the Great War was for America to team up with Germany and crush the British Empire. In short, he hated Britain so much that he would hate any nation that refused to hate it, too. According to his biographer Clement Wood, Duquesne's attitude became: "There are no good Americans except the anti-English ones."

Duquesne abandoned his film project and went straight to the German consulate in Brazil and offered up his services as a spy and saboteur. He started hanging around the docks in disguise. From then on, he would move through life in a cloud of aliases. These included Frederick Barron, Colonel Bezin, F. Crabbs, Colonel Marquis Duquesne, Fred Buquesne, J. Q. Farn, Berthold Szabo, Von Goutard, Vam Dam, Fritters, Worthy, and Jim. Some people knew him as the Handsomest Man in Europe.

But now, on the docks, Duquesne morphed into a frumpy and feeble middle-aged botanist from the Netherlands who walked wrenched over in a stoop and wore thick, unflattering glasses. He called himself Frederick Fredericks.

As Fredericks, Duquesne hung out in bars, sidling up to drunk English sailors and offering them bribes to carry rare orchid bulbs to his friends and relatives abroad. But the packages contained explosives; Duquesne would later claim to have sunk twenty-two ships and started one hundred dock fires during this time.

Most famously, Duquesne would claim responsibility for the destruction of the HMS *Hampshire,* a British ship that sank west of Scotland in 1916, killing more than six hundred men aboard, including Duquesne's old nemesis Lord Kitchener, now Britain's secretary of war. But as Frederick Burnham later pointed out, most of what Duquesne actually accomplished during his time in South America was likely to disrupt outgoing shipments of manganese—exacerbating the problem that Burnham and his tribe of prospectors would file into the desert to solve. That is, the two adversaries still somehow managed to lock themselves in an oblique, intercontinental standoff—Frederick Burnham versus Frederick Fredericks, with one man racing to rebuild what the other was breaking apart.

In February 1916 Duquesne packed the film from his aborted motion picture project into a trunk and registered it as cargo aboard the SS *Tennyson,* a British ship heading for New York. Then he went about engineering the ship's destruction.

Maybe there was no film in the trunk; maybe it was filled with explosives instead. Or maybe they were in the six boxes labeled "Minerals," which, investigators came to believe, Duquesne had also stashed aboard the *Tennyson.* But something on the ship exploded as it approached the equator. Three sailors were killed in the fire. Before long a clerk who claimed to be a co-conspirator was captured by British intelligence and gave up Duquesne's name. He also led authorities to the safe-deposit box and the envelope full of money waiting for "Piet Niacud." *Niacud* was *Duquesne* spelled backward phonetically.

Duquesne was now wanted for murder by the British. But before long, on April 27, word came in *The New York Times* that Duquesne had himself been murdered. He was traveling through the Bolivian frontier when his party was raided by "hostile Indians." Then two weeks after that, a second dispatch in the *Times* reported that he was, in fact, alive—that though badly wounded, he'd heroically fought off the vicious Bolivian raiders and escaped. The world, it seemed, had underestimated the tenacity of Fritz Duquesne.

But the truth was, there were no Bolivians and there was no attack. Duquesne seems to have faked his own death, then regretted the decision and miraculously resurrected himself. According to

Inspector Tunney's account, police eventually discovered that the
first wire report from Buenos Aires, telling the *Times* of Duquesne's
death, had been filed with the byline "Frederick Fredericks."

XI

FRAUDS

By the beginning of 1917, Duquesne was a suspected murderer and
a fugitive, a fake film producer and a formerly dead botanist, and
likely still a German spy. But it was taking American authorities
time to piece all this together, and Duquesne was either audacious
or reckless enough not to care if they did. That summer he resur-
faced in Washington, D.C., and was very quietly puttering around
under his own name, trying desperately to latch on to some kind
of living.

Duquesne connected with Horace Ashton, an old friend whose
photographs had illustrated some of his hunting articles. Ashton
did his best to help Duquesne, even putting him up for a job as a U.S.
censor and propagandist for the war effort. Apparently, Duquesne
reached out to Congressman Broussard, his old comrade from the
New Food Supply Society, too. Broussard, presumably in the dark
about Duquesne's recent activities, had also tried to help, coming
close to getting him hired as a low-level clerk for the U.S. Army.

After a while, however, Duquesne must have started to seem like
a lost cause—broke and unemployable. Ashton brought him back to
New York and let him crash at his apartment—the second-floor flat
on West 75th Street. There Duquesne attempted to get back on the
lecture circuit. But the zeitgeist had changed. His old material was
irrelevant now—the public wasn't interested in learning about African safaris, only in hearing Allied war heroes tell battle yarns. And
so Duquesne transformed himself into Captain Claude Stoughton, a
nervy and debonair military man who had, his promotional materials claimed, "perhaps seen more of the war than any man at pres-

ent before the public." Stoughton had been bayoneted three times, gassed four times, and stuck once with a hook.

Captain Stoughton's speaking career took off. His talks made decent money, his heroism earned him respect, and ladies found him alluring. Duquesne was wrenching his way back into society. His invented persona had such magnetism and such possibility, in fact, that he began deploying his alter ego in a wide variety of personal appearances. Claude Stoughton was a gifted booster, brimming with pep and dynamism, and he seemed willing to promote any cause if it kept the admiration and affection flowing. This even included making speeches to pull in donations for the Red Cross and to sell Liberty Bonds. Stoughton would appear uniformed, before crowds of devoted American patriots, and belt out slogans like, "We must have dollars as well as men in the fight for freedom!" The irascible Black Panther, whose contempt for England had metastasized so completely that he'd gone to work blowing up ships for the Germans, was now raising money for the Allied war machine.

The biographer Art Ronnie writes, "It is difficult to explain the paradox of Fritz Duquesne at this time." This is an almost preposterous understatement, but also, ultimately, as truthful and illuminating as one can be. There's a cynical way to read Duquesne's activities in New York: that he was up to no good, running some diabolical con that would eventually throw the world he'd infiltrated into chaos, just as it always did. But it's also possible that Duquesne simply liked the attention, the performance. And maybe he liked it so much that he wouldn't allow even his deepest and most sinister principles to break him out of character—because his character's life was so much more gratifying than the remnants of his own.

Ronnie describes him as "an arrogant prisoner of his own ego." He had stopped caring about anything except his own glorification. The Black Panther was an adrenaline junkie and a nihilist now. There was nothing he wouldn't get behind, and there was nothing he wouldn't destroy.

————————

Duquesne was arrested in New York on December 8, 1917, charged with insurance fraud. Investigators alleged that, aside from orchestrating a scheme to claim the insurance money for the film he blew up on the *Tennyson,* he was also running a similar, parallel fraud— one that accounted for Inspector Tunney's original arson case in Brooklyn. While in South America, Duquesne had apparently agreed to produce educational movies for an Argentine board of education, bought $24,000 worth of film on his return to New York, insured it, stashed it in the Brooklyn warehouse, then set off an explosion that burned the building down.

Duquesne was held in a city jail for months as the fraud charges knotted into complicated legal cases, and the British haggled for his extradition for the explosion aboard the *Tennyson.* He started behaving erratically. His appearance changed. The alluring glint in his eye turned into something wilder. He started blathering nonsensically. In May 1918 a judge ordered a three-person "lunacy commission" to assess his condition and issue a "lunacy report." Duquesne appeared at the commission's hearing ranting and unhinged, shouting orders at the doctors who'd come to testify as though he were commanding them in battle. The lunacy commission sent him to a state mental hospital in Beacon, New York.

Soon Duquesne's body stopped working as well. In court one day, he collapsed and claimed to be suddenly paralyzed from the waist down. This elicited skepticism from the government, but when doctors stuck pins in his legs and under his toenails—torturing him, in short, to prove he was malingering—Duquesne never once wriggled or winced.

And so he was transferred to Bellevue Hospital on a stretcher and installed in the very last bed of a long, secure ward. He had a view of First Avenue through a window with three iron bars. He slept with his blanket over his face and every day asked to be set by the window in a wheelchair so he could watch the birds. The nurses adored him and would lift his slack body wherever it needed to go. He got lighter and lighter. He read the newspaper with a pair of pinhole glasses he crafted out of cardboard. The birds started eating out of his hand. He wasn't an old man, but he seemed like one. Then one night he escaped.

Duquesne had managed to acquire two small hacksaw blades and had been quietly going at the window bars day after day as he sat in his wheelchair. Eventually, he got all the way through two of them, and just past midnight on Tuesday, May 27, 1919, four days before he would finally have been extradited to England, he squeezed out.

He'd been faking paralysis for seven months. (Later he claimed to have been vigorously massaging his legs, to keep his muscles conditioned, during his twice-daily visits to the bathroom.) After wiggling through the window, he leaped six feet onto the roof of a neighboring icehouse, or perhaps shimmied down using a blanket as a rope. Then he leaped again from there to the ground. And still "even this display of agility," reported *The New York Times*, "did not give him his liberty." From there, Duquesne was "forced to climb a brick wall about six feet high and an iron fence with menacing spikes, about eight feet high." Then after he'd done all that, he lurched down 27th Street toward the Hudson River, hopped a ferry to Hoboken, New Jersey, and disappeared.

The wiliness and determination of it all was jaw-dropping. Duquesne had waited patiently until he'd receded to near invisibility, then pounced. It was a classic Black Panther performance. It must have killed him that no one was around to see it.

A month later, in fact, Duquesne messengered a letter to a friend in New York, purporting to lay out the dramatic mechanics of his escape. The operation had involved two swashbuckling, fictitious accomplices and a foreign sports car zooming away in the night. The letter was a kind of press release; Duquesne wanted his friend to get the story published. "Nota bene," he wrote. "As many [newspapers] as possible. Keep clippings."

XII

TAKING CHANCES

There are no herds of hippopotamuses in Louisiana. As far as I can tell, not one ever set foot in the bayous of the Gulf Coast. The idea was never exactly defeated but seems merely to have evaporated over a very long period of time.

In March 1911, a full year after the congressional hearing, Frederick Russell Burnham traveled to Washington to meet with Congressman Broussard again about the hippo idea. They decided that Broussard would reintroduce his bill that spring, and in the meantime Burnham would lead an exploratory trip to Africa, scouting out other good candidate species for importation to strengthen their case. He would leave as soon as possible.

"We are serious in the movement, and I am confident of the success of the project," Burnham told the *Washington Herald*. A year earlier the New Food Supply Society had seemed awash in goodwill from the public and the press. But America had apparently turned more skeptical now; as Burnham gave interviews around Washington and New York that week, he sounded increasingly pained to stress the sincerity and value of their vision. Finally, he just told one reporter: "I have spent 11 years in Africa, and I have had two years of experience in British East Africa and have traveled about and led expeditions into the interior, so I know the lay of the land pretty well, and I think I know what we are doing," and left it at that.

Burnham never sailed for Africa, however. He was forced to cancel his expedition at the last minute, when the revolution in Mexico escalated and his business partners called on him to protect their investments along the Yaqui River. Even so, he kept sending Broussard encouragement and information: tips he'd elicited from a famous German circus master for shipping wild animals long distances; photos of the ostriches at an ostrich farm in Pasadena, with an assurance that "if that strange and erratic bird can be handled and domesticated," then the other "magnificent animals of Africa" could be, too. Broussard, meanwhile, made one set of meticulous political calculations after another about the society's next move, postponing the introduction of his bill from one upcoming session of Congress to the next. But he'd soon leave the House for the Senate. Then in 1918 he passed away.

W. N. Irwin, the Agriculture Department bureaucrat, died within a year of his appearance at Broussard's congressional hearing. Scientific papers that Irwin had written continued to appear long after his death, drifting into journals like whispers from a particularly petulant ghost. One, published in 1914, proposed importing a breed of pygmy hippo instead of the larger variety, because it would be easier to control.

Eventually, officials at the Department of Agriculture contradicted Irwin's reasoning in the press, insisting that hippos were a terrible idea and that America ought to work instead to turn those useless-seeming marshes into grassy pastures, then give the South beef cattle to raise on that reclaimed land. Because people ate beef. Because beef was a normal meat to eat.

And that's essentially how America *did* choose to break through the Malthusian barrier that the New Food Supply Society saw coming in 1910. Rather than diversify and expand our stock of animals, we developed ways to raise more of the same animals in more places. Gradually, that process led to the factory farms and mass-confinement operations we have today—a mammoth industry whose everyday practices and waste products are linked to all kinds of dystopian mayhem, including the rise of antibiotic-resistant bacteria and a spate of spontaneous abortions in Indiana. Runoff from feedlots sloshes down the Mississippi River to its mouth, pooling into one of the world's biggest aquatic dead zones, seven or eight thousand square miles large at times—an overblown, reeking grotesque of the exact conditions the water hyacinth was creating there, far

more modestly, in Broussard's time. Meanwhile, the flower continues to cause problems. The state of Louisiana alone spends $2 mil-
lion a year spraying herbicides at it.

These aren't problems that America created so much as ones
we've watched happen—consequences of our having ducked other,
earlier problems by rigging together relatively unambitious solutions that seemed safe enough. We answered the Meat Question.
But there were more meat questions ahead.

I'm not arguing that America would be a better place if it had
imported hippopotamuses in 1910. But there is something beautiful about the America that considered importing them—an America so intent on facing down its problems, and solving them, that
even an idea like this could get a fair hearing; where the political
system and the culture felt so alive with possibility, and so confident in its own virtue and ingenuity, that elected officials could sit
around and contemplate the merits of hippo ranching without wor-
rying too much about how it sounded; where people felt free enough
to imagine putting hippopotamuses in places where there were no
hippopotamuses.

Who knows how we became so guarded? And maybe it's naïve to
think that we weren't back then. But the fact is, Robert Broussard's
bill did exist. It was discussed and debated. There was a window
when anything was possible. Then the window closed. In retrospect,
it's hard to even pinpoint a moment when America said no to hippopotamuses. There were just too many moments when it failed to
say yes.

In the end, Frederick Burnham and Fritz Duquesne stood at
either end of a spectrum—a spectrum where optimism shaded
slowly into cynicism. The petering out of the hippo scheme, and the
horrible reality of world war that arose on its heels, may have been
a point when America took a step away from Burnham and toward
Duquesne; when we became just a little more convinced that modern life would be governed by the sinister logic of a Black Panther

and not by the lucid vision of a scout. Some orchid bulbs are actually explosives. Some paralyzed people can secretly walk.

Summarizing the whole episode at the end of his life, Burnham wrote that, in his memory, the difficulty with the animal-importation plan started with one particular congressman's objection. The man had argued that, if exotic species like the hippo were introduced for the common good, wealthy, self-interested hunters would simply sneak in and kill the animals for trophies. It was inevitable, the congressman said—betraying a conviction that people are basically sly and opportunistic and should never be trusted.

You can call that cynicism, or you can call it realism. But it's the attitude that's given us a hundred years of hippopotamuslessness in America.

In the summer of 1943 a man named Mart Bushnell visited Frederick Burnham at his home in California. Burnham was eighty-two, still four years away from his death, and accustomed to visitors. Men who had read about his exploits as boys kept turning up to meet the old scout before he died. They were never disappointed. Bushnell, after his own pilgrimage, wrote of Burnham, "He surpassed even the highly colorful adventurer he has become in my own imagination." He still had a thick head of hair, nearly all his teeth, and a mind that was as quick and focused as ever. Most of all, Bushnell was taken by the same enduring quality of Burnham's eyes: "clear, steady, and almost magnetic in their probing," he called them.

Bushnell was visiting on business from the Boy Scouts of America. Burnham was not only a longtime member of the group's national council but a model for the entire organization—the original Boy Scout. The group's founder, the Englishman Lord Robert Baden-Powell, had been one of Burnham's commanders in Africa and was so impressed by his friend's integrity and ability that he aspired to build an institution to raise generations of similarly capable men. The Boy Scouts wore neckerchiefs because Burnham had always worn one in the desert. Their motto, "Be Prepared," couldn't have been a clearer distillation of his beliefs.

Bushnell had come to discuss the creation of a Major Frederick Burnham Medal for Frontiering and Scouting Skills. And he'd learn, Burnham had very strong opinions about what should be required to earn such an honor. Boys, he felt, should demonstrate mastery of everything from "stalking and evasion" to "axemanship" and should have to hike in isolation for two days and nights with almost no food, foraging for wild vegetables. Major Burnham, Bushnell explained, was "vitally concerned with the virility of the country's future man power."

America was now in the throes of a second, gruesome world war—"war to the *nth* degree," Burnham called it. And yet, he argued, "not even the world-wide harvest of death need dismay us. . . . In spite of war's present black-out, the future is certain to be brighter than all the ages past." Somehow his optimism was still unflinching, and he projected it, almost tangibly, into the space around him. Bushnell told his superiors that his visit with Burnham was "one of the most stirring experiences of my life. How I wish every boy in America could feel the impact of this wonderful fellow's personality!"

Burnham was also a wealthy man now. Twenty-five years earlier he and his son Roderick had struck oil on an overlooked piece of land near Long Beach. He used the money to buy three adjacent houses in a new neighborhood being built on the bucolic fringes of Los Angeles. Roderick and his oldest daughter's family moved into two of the houses, and Burnham and Blanche took the third. Directly above it, on a scrubby, mostly desolate hillside that Burnham said reminded him of the landscapes of Rhodesia, was propped a tremendous white O—part of a sign to advertise the new real estate. The developers were calling the area "Hollywoodland."

Burnham built a study for himself on the first floor and filled one wall with dozens of framed portraits of the friends and men-tors who had influenced his life: Lord Roberts and Lord Kitchener, Cecil Rhodes with his dog, Theodore Roosevelt and Gifford Pinchot, Roosevelt's chief forester who'd championed Burnham's animal-importation scheme from inside the administration. *The New York Times* had once claimed that Burnham's story was one "no novelist could write because of its seeming incredibility." (Ernest Hemingway and Cecil B. DeMille, however, would later both be working on screenplays about Burnham at the time of their deaths.) But now Burnham committed to setting it all down himself and would spend much of his last years at his desk, a large map of Africa behind him, writing simple essays and remembrances. In 1943 he collected them into a book, printed a few hundred copies, inscribed each, and distributed them personally to friends. "Dear Pinchot," he wrote in one. "Once upon a time we took an active part in trying to save this nation from starvation. Hippo meat would now be welcome."

Burnham called the book *Taking Chances*. (The title came from an Ohio senator who had said, "It is the spirit of venture, of taking chances, that has built America. Without it we cannot go forward, with it we cannot fail.") One of the chapters, "The Totem of the Black Panther," was about Fritz Duquesne. Duquesne was now in his late sixties and had just begun serving a twenty-year sentence at Leavenworth Federal Penitentiary in Kansas. The Black Panther had reappeared briefly after his hospital escape, posing as a New York City vaudeville critic named Major Fred Craven, but subsequently disappeared again. Then in 1941, after two years of FBI surveillance and staged meetings in a bugged office in Times Square, the government arrested Duquesne as the alleged leader of a thirty-three-person Nazi spy syndicate. The so-called Duquesne Spy Ring included a thuggish Gestapo operative trying to foment strikes among American workers, an aging male librarian, and a seductive figure skater named Lilly Barbara Carola Stein. The bureau accused Duquesne of coordinating the syndicate's communications with Germany, sending the Third Reich technical information about military equipment and munitions. Prosecutors produced his communiqués as evidence: the Black Panther had stamped each with an inky, attacking cat.

J. Edgar Hoover bragged that the operation that led to Duquesne's arrest was the most ambitious and well-executed spy roundup in American history, and it produced what is still considered the nation's largest espionage case. In the arc of Duquesne's life, however, it amounted to just another con—a final, eccentric, and ham-fisted epic. His FBI file described him this way: "Excellent talker with captivating personality. Inveterate liar. Sexual pervert."

"His doom fills me with sadness," Burnham wrote of his old adversary in *Taking Chances*. He had tried to redeem Duquesne and was still hopeful that some empathetic and perceptive historian might one day absolve the Boer by showing he was merely "a product of the extreme hate to which we have all contributed, and for which we continue to pay the price." Burnham still kept a letter from Duquesne in his desk in the Hollywoodland study. "To my friendly enemy," it read, "the greatest scout in the world, whose eyes were the vision of an empire. I craved the honour of killing him, but failing that, I extend my heartiest admiration." And among those portraits on the wall, he'd hung an old, framed picture of the Panther, too—just a reedy, awkward boy in his first military uniform, looking sideways.

Burnham was organizing his papers as well—preparing them, and the singular life they chronicled, for posterity in archives at Stanford and Yale. One day in 1944 he came across a typescript of the speech he had given to the Humane Association at the hotel in Pasadena, thirty-four years earlier, while advocating for Broussard's bill. There in the text was his younger self, ardently challenging his audience to recognize that the "complacent belief in the unending plenty of our natural wealth" had now been obviously disproven, but also unveiling an idea that could restore that feeling of promise in America—one that just made so much sense but would require working against "overwhelming difficulties and the loud guffaws of the ignorant" to make a reality.

Burnham read the speech over. His hand shook with age, but he pressed hard and scrawled a note across the top:

"The facts are still unrefuted," signed, "FRB—1944."

MOTHER, STRANGER

CRIS BEAM

CHAPTER 1

Three years ago I got the phone call. I had always wondered about her death, how long it would take to find out about it, and who would track her children down to tell them. Now I knew. Fifty-three days, and a lawyer.

I had left my mother's house when I was fourteen years old, and I never saw her again. I was thirty-six when I found out she was dead. In the early years of my separation from her, I tried not to think about her. For high school I moved into my father's house, where my mother's name had always been a bad and angry word—then I went to college and got jobs and lovers like everyone else I knew. After the rise of the Web, I tried to spy on her from afar, but I never turned up much aside from memories that came kicking up at me like startled bats.

Ours was a family of two realities: the one we lived through and the one that had formed in my mother's mind. She was often convinced that we were going to starve because we didn't have enough money for food. When I was growing up, she talked endlessly about not being able to cover the mortgage on the house and how we could end up homeless and living in a box. It took me years to realize that these were fantasies. As a child, I tallied the cans in the cupboard and ticked off the days until Daddy's check would come. But despite what my mother said, there was always enough. Sometimes we ate at the restaurant in the strip mall that smelled more like carpet than like meals or filled the car with greasy bags from

Taco Bell. Still, my mother's whispery laments were like chalk on a window: they didn't leave a mark, but the sound stayed with me for days.

"We're going to die in here," she said, darting her eyes around our living room walls. "We just don't have enough to make it."

She always claimed to be working five jobs, though I only counted one, sometimes two. She said she was a prostitute.

When the air would become electric and I knew I should run and hide, my mother told me that her grandfather had raped her every night. "Every night," she seethed, and I was probably ten, the walls seeming to melt away. Her shoulders squared, and her eyes blazed with cruelty. "And you think you're better than me?"

My ears folded when she said these things. The floor was stairs, and I was falling but also standing. I wouldn't meet her gaze. She would forget these moments of madness by morning, or whenever her shoulders went back to their regular submissive hunch. She would forget partly because she said she had no memory of her childhood or that grandfather; everything between kindergarten and sixth grade for her was one black, impenetrable wall. And she would forget because she really was a different person then, split off from everything she knew.

She died of brain cancer, aggressive glioblastoma multiforme, diagnosed two years prior. Her obituary told other stories about her than the dark ones I remembered. I learned she had a great sense of direction, liked to hike alone in Yosemite, dealt poker at frat houses to pay for college, and had two surviving aunts. I already knew she loved cats and the mountains, had taught high school Spanish and math, and liked to eat hamburgers. I remember all this from my fourteen years in her house. I didn't know she considered herself a "Breck Girl," and I had no idea what that meant. Also that she "had such a great love for everyone, and never met or knew anyone she could not forgive." I don't know if she forgave me.

After I left my mother, I could never explain to myself why I didn't go back. I knew that I was terrified of her, yet I was scared of the guilt I felt for leaving her. These opposing terrors seemed to cancel one another out, turning me into a burned-out husk of inaction.

I didn't have a language for my mother, probably because she didn't have a cohesive language for herself. She could snap herself into a mom I couldn't recognize, a mom I wished I could forget. Sometimes I thought my muteness meant that nothing of significance happened, and I would doubt the fear that gripped me through adulthood. I would later learn that a telltale sign of trauma is that it doesn't have language at all.

After she died, though, the larger memories of her came rushing back, and I wanted to find the vocabulary. I wanted to pull my mother out of the hole that occupied the center of her story and listen for a voice. I wanted to find the reason for her madness. I wanted to see if life with her was bad enough to warrant my disappearance—or hers, depending on the perspective; I wanted to tease our existence apart and see if I had a self, still standing. "If it wasn't anything," as William Faulkner once wrote, "what was I?"

But first I'd have to come back from the dead.

When I left my mother's house at age fourteen, she quietly killed me off. She took a trip to Kansas with my brother, who was ten. One day my grandfather asked her about me.

"Cris died," my mother told him. My brother, Andrew, panicked, but she pulled him into another room and told him to play along. I don't know if she told the aunts and cousins and everybody else this same story. Did I die in a crash or of some disease? I never heard from anyone on her side of the family again.

Andrew followed a path similar to mine. He also moved out of our mother's house when he was fourteen and went to live with our father. Unlike me, when he was still in high school he sneaked back into our old home. He wanted to retrieve some of his baby pictures, along with his old teddy bear, Charlie. He found the key to the front door in its usual hiding place; he calmed the dogs and tiptoed into the empty house. My old bedroom, he said, had been transformed into an amateur taxidermy studio for my mother's boyfriend, with glass eyeballs and animal pelts scattered about. My brother's bedroom hadn't been touched. Three years of dust had accumulated on his old action figures and video games; too-small pajamas still lay crumpled in the hamper.

My brother was freaked out by the dead animals and by his former self, preserved behind our closed bedroom doors. He snatched his teddy bear and rushed downstairs, blindly grabbing a handful of photographs that my mother kept in a box in the living room.

He drove a safe distance away and then stopped and looked at the pictures. They were mostly of me: baby snaps and Christmas shots from when I was around three years old. There were a few of us together, when he was a baby and at Halloween when we were dressed as clowns, and none of our mom. He was too scared to return unless he knew that Mom had moved away.

The next time he went back, Andrew was in college. He drove across the Bay Bridge to look one last time at the place where we grew up. He parked outside and stared for a while. The house looked different; it had a paint job, and the shrubs were trimmed.

Eventually, a woman opened the door. "Can I help you?" she asked.

Andrew told her he had lived there as a child, and the woman's face went white. She asked him for his name. Andrew told her and said that he was Candy Beam's son. The woman took a long breath. She had bought the house from Candy, she explained. "But she said both of her children were dead."

CHAPTER 2

My mother and father met in a high school chemistry class in Wichita, Kansas, or this was the story I heard. It was the year the Beatles released "I Want to Hold Your Hand." My mom was smart and pretty and had a great figure from teaching swimming all summer long to neighborhood kids. I imagine she was a catch.

My parents both attended the University of Kansas; my mom was in a sorority. They dated all through college and then got married and had me. Fairly standard stuff, except it was the war, and everybody was busy trying to avoid going to Vietnam. My father, luckily, was stationed in Mesa, Arizona.

Many years later my mother told me stories about these early days. She said I was born on a reservation, in an army tent. She also told me, in one of her stranger moments, that she delivered me after riding on a camel, maybe in Arizona. The truth was this: I was born in a veterans' hospital, a breech baby, with my father waiting right outside the door.

When the war ended, we moved to Minnesota, where my father got a job as a buyer for a department store and my mother stayed home to take care of me. These were good years, as I remember them; I can go back to the way I saw my world, to my kindergartner's mind and words.

We lived in a white house with a red roof. In that white house, I watched my mom get fat; she was helping me read, and there was less and less room on her lap. Pushed to the edge of her knees, I was working on chapter books when my mom told me to sit next to her instead. There wasn't room for me anymore.

She said there was a brother growing in there, like a doll but better, because I would be able to teach him things. I went to the neighbors' house on the night my dad drove my mom to the hospital. The lady was named Robin, and the man looked like Jesus, and we watched Benji movies together under a quilt that smelled like dogs. My mom didn't come home for three days because she was bleeding, but my dad said that was okay because I had a brother who was also at the hospital. My dad gave me a game called Operation: with tiny tweezers, you removed the organs from a fat man. The man looked very alarmed, and his nose buzzed if you made a mistake, but he didn't bleed.

One day a year or so after his difficult birth, when my brother was a toddler, my dad told me we were moving to California. My mom didn't cry, not at first. Apparently, California was too far to walk to; we would drive in the silver car, and later Archie the cat would fly in a plane.

I began writing a book about it, adding more every day. I had read about Chinatown, where the money had holes, and also about the Golden Gate Bridge. I knew about the curvy streets and giant hills. So I wrote chapters about each neighborhood where we might live. The book was long, the longest thing I had ever made.

I sat on our yellow couch for a surprise revelation one night after dinner, with my book tucked up under my T-shirt. I made my dad sit down on one side of me, my mom on the other. I pulled the book out and held it up for them to see the cover. "San Francisco," it said. "A Book by Cristie Beam." I turned the page and read.

I started with the 1906 earthquake, because that was exciting. I felt my mom start to get small beside me and my dad sit up straighter. My mom started sobbing and ran from the room.

"Why are you crying?" I asked her. She was sitting on the bed.

"Because you want to go to California like Daddy."

I knew then that she would make me choose between them.

CHAPTER 3

My family's breakdown began when we arrived in California, in the spring of 1979. We had driven from a fading white winter into a sunshine suburb where kids wore flip-flops and terrycloth shorts and girls my age had hair like horses' manes. The town was called Concord, and it was the last stop on the commuter train from San

Francisco, a place of tract houses and scrubby front lawns and the hard racial tensions of the working and middle classes entwined together.

We pulled up in front of a tract house painted a dusty sage green. The moving van's doors yawned open, and our entire Minnesota life poured out. I quietly found my books while my dad bought navy blue loveseats and shiny end tables for the living room. My mom bought a porch swing that reminded her of her childhood in Kansas and swung alone in the backyard.

I started first grade, and my teacher was boring, but I liked my crossing guard; she remembered my cat's name and asked me lots of questions.

Before California my dad came home for dinner, but once we moved, we waited. My brother would eat, but my mom and I watched *M*A*S*H* while our food slowly dried out in the oven. I tried to snuggle in close to where my mom smelled the best, but she was distracted and didn't hug back. It was about four months after we'd moved that my mom started her muttering. "He's with her," she'd say, staring hard at the television.

I didn't know who "she" was. I stared away from my mother, at the white telephone that hung from the wall: I was willing my dad to call.

In my Holly Hobby diary, I was a diligent recorder of daily minutiae; every dated page is filled. But in the way of seven-year-olds, I was less careful about my narrative links. I often wrote things like "I made a circus. Mommy hit me." The line "Mommy hit me" is followed the next day by "I hit Kim." Poor Kim, a childhood friend, is a running character in the diary, and she unknowingly bore the blunt end of my mother's instability. There were lines like "Mommy hit me" or "Mommy pulled my hair" or "Mommy diddent love me today" a lot that year, but the funny thing is, I don't remember any real physical violence. I remember her muttering about my dad and drifting away, deeper into her television and her migraine headaches. The sentences about my father were about absence, especially as the year progressed: "Daddy left for work at five p.m." or "Daddy diddent come home tonight."

Some months later, when I was eight years old, my father moved out. (This is all, unfortunately, I can say about my father. He asked not to be included in this story. I went to live with him after I left my mother at fourteen. He loves me, and we have a relationship, but we couldn't reconcile our understandings of the past. So from this point on, I must leave out any part of my story that concerns my dad.)

After that, my mother fragmented. I used to blame my father more, suspecting that his leaving was what snapped the delicate thread between her head and her heart. Later I would come to believe that my father only strummed the string that had really broken long before, launching her back into a madness she had tried so long to block.

CHAPTER 4

After my father left, men streamed in and out of our house. There was the carpenter, who had a retarded son I was supposed to play with and one day flashed me from his bathrobe. There was the man who fixed toilets and swore. There was that dancing guy, and the man with the gun rack on his truck, and the one who sat on the edge of the chair staring when I played the piano.

Maybe my mom really was a prostitute. She said she was. She claimed to work on Wednesday nights from a bar near the BART station. That was her shift. This she told me calmly when she said she was already working five jobs and couldn't possibly work any harder, right before she shuffled upstairs with one of her migraines.

The memories of my mother's prostitution are among my most

confusing recollections. They clash wildly with the persona my
mother presented most of the time, to most people. Usually she was
shy, with the voice and demeanor of a nervous young girl. She wore
fuzzy sweaters and tennis shoes, her hair clipped back in barrettes,
and she got me to pay the men in the gas station or to ask the neighbors for butter. Her eyes easily filled when confronted with strangers, especially in those early years: she was skittish, with an overlay
of sweetness.

But then, at night, the men would come, between the regulars. I
would hear them clomping up the stairs, and I would hear her, too,
in the room across the hall. The sound of sex, the smell, seemed to
be everywhere. Sometimes I'd see them in the morning: dark-haired,
mustachioed, '70s men, buckling their Sansabelt pants or lacing up
their work boots before they shut the door. My mom would shuffle down later in a rose-colored nightie, her breasts low and heavy,
making instant coffee in the microwave. She didn't talk about the
men, didn't introduce us, and mostly they didn't say anything to my
brother or me, either. We just ate our cereal and left for school.

When I was nine, my mom bought me a deadbolt for my bedroom
door and told me to use it.

I was scared of the lock, actually. I was scared there would be a
fire and nobody would be able to break down the door and save me.
But when I asked my mom why I had to shut the bolt at night, she
wouldn't explain.

And in this way, I was less afraid of the men than I was of my
mom. I don't know if she was exchanging sex for money or just
exchanging a lot of sex. What I do know is that talking about the
men could make her split into her "bad mom" self, the one she
wouldn't remember. Or maybe it was the other way around: when
my mom was normal, she was quiet and shy and good; when she
split, she was a whore.

"Why do you think you're better than me?" she once shouted,
apropos of nothing. When my mother shouted and accused, I knew

she had changed; when she was her normal self, guilt was her weapon, not rage. This particular day she was holding a plate; I thought she was going to throw it at me.

"You're not a whore—you've never had to be a whore!"

My mother laughed, and this is how she was when she shifted: she stood up straighter, her shoulders went back; she seemed taller, electric, charged. Her grin was tighter, her eyes brighter; even her hair seemed to rise. She wielded the plate in the air. "I have to be a whore to put food in your body! And you think you're too good for me. You think you're better than everybody!" She leaned in, the spit from her screaming landing on my cheeks. "How do you think I paid for my college? I was a whore! A whore! I've always been a whore!"

Beyond her hulking form, I saw my toddler brother hiding behind the couch. I calculated the timing. Could I duck beneath her arm, grab my brother, carry him up the stairs, and lock him in my room with me without her catching us? Impossible. My mom was big, but she could be fast.

She gave me an opportunity to save my brother when she stomped into the kitchen and broke the plate in the sink: I grabbed him and made it to my room. I knew if we waited, this bad mom would go away, and I wished hard on all my stuffed animals for her to go driving, because she would come back from those drives, normal and tired and knowing nothing at all about the terrible things she'd said.

I didn't know it then, but there was a diagnosis that was popular at the time that my mother seemed to conform to: multiple personality disorder, mocked and demonized after Hollywood's Sybil. Thirty years later the diagnosis would still be controversial, and I would still be embarrassed and afraid to stick my mom with such a label. Like prostitution, the very idea is salacious and sensationalized, rarely capturing the lived experience of those with the condition. It's now called dissociative identity disorder (DID), and people who suffer from it have disrupted identities and can't recall significant personal information. Almost always they've been deeply traumatized in childhood, often through repeated and prolonged sexual abuse. People with DID have two or more distinct personality states.

But I knew little about mental illness when I was ten.

When I turned eleven, the men stopped coming around, and my mom stopped talking about her five jobs. She seemed to get a little better, likely because she had settled with a boyfriend named Ron, who was a firefighter. My mother always wanted a protector.

CHAPTER 5

It was during a time when she seemed saner that I decided to throw a birthday party for my mother. I was eleven, and I wanted to show her that I loved her; I thought I had the power to keep the good mom going strong—that, like the moon, I could control her tides. Of course, I was a child; of course, I was wrong.

Birthdays so far had been memorable in a good way. At one Miss America–themed party, I invited several girls over to dress up, pageant style, and walk the runway across our living room floor. My mom took our pictures with the Polaroid, and we made frames out of cardboard, adorning each with phrases like "Number One!" and "Winner!" At another birthday party, my mom created a scavenger hunt, and we ran around looking for sparkly rocks or asking neighbors for a slice of cheese. My mom was intensely shy and repeatedly told us that "you shouldn't stick your head above the crowd, or someone could chop it off." But on our birthdays she allowed us to be special. For one day, my brother and I could wear the paper crown from Burger King and be the center of attention.

All these parties required forethought, and kindness, so these memories are the most painful and awkward to revive. They're like the gels they slide over the lights at a theater, suddenly casting everything in a reddish or greenish tone. If my mom was so achingly normal on my birthday, so generous, so present, what did that say about the ghost who faded away most nights? The spliced-in mom who threw plates and slapped and screamed? Or the mom who was like a baby, crying when my dad came to pick us up and take us away from her?

But it was at the birthday party for my mother that I threw myself that the isolated version of her reemerged, with full force.

I planned the party in cahoots with her boyfriend Ron. He wore polyester pants and zip-up ankle boots, and he and my mom drank pink wine from the box that perched on the top shelf of our refrigerator and listened to Barbra Streisand albums while filling in crosswords. My mom could complete the puzzles faster by herself, but she liked to coo in admiration when Ron held the pencil.

I asked Ron to pretend to take my mom to dinner and then to turn the car around twenty minutes later so everybody could jump out and yell "Surprise!" The only sticking point in the fantasy was who "everybody" was. My mother had no friends, so I didn't know whom to invite. I called my friend Heather's mom, a lady named Lucile, who had known my mom back when my parents were married. And I called my mom's job, a place I knew as a boring room by the freeway where she worked with a chain smoker named Elaine doing "the books." Elaine and Lucile said they'd come, but that made only two guests.

Should I ask some of the men to the party? I didn't have their phone numbers, so I started inviting the neighbors. I went door to door, explaining that her birthday was coming up and would they please come to a party and hide in our closets and jump out and yell "Surprise!" These people, dragged away from their sitcoms and their Swanson dinners, looked bewildered: they didn't know her. I told them to come over at seven; there would be cake.

I canvassed several blocks, but in the end maybe six people showed, plus Lucile and Elaine from work. They still wore the same confused expressions as they buzzed the doorbell, and I pushed them into closets or down below the couch. I was shaking with excitement as I turned out the lights and watched at the front window for Ron's headlights to appear in the driveway; I had to shush someone's whispered "What the hell are we doing here?" lest he blow the surprise.

Finally the car pulled up. I heard my mother giggling to Ron about his forgetfulness and having to come back home so soon as the door handle turned. I flicked on the lights, and all the strangers, on cue, leaped up and shouted.

"Surprise!"

She was framed in the doorway and reached backward for Ron's arm. Her mouth opened and closed like a fish. I had forgotten that the confetti I had made from construction paper was still stuffed in my hand, so I threw it, in a sweaty clump, at her face. She batted it away.

Slowly, the neighbors came forward.

"I'm Donna," a woman said, extending her hand. "Happy birthday."

My mom looked like she was going to cry, and I realized, like a sudden kick to the throat, what a terrible mistake I had made. This was worse than sticking your head above the crowd. It was assembling a crowd for her beheading.

"Why would you do this to me?" my mom whispered as I pulled out the cake Ron had bought from the grocery store. Everybody sang "Happy Birthday," but it was awkward when some people didn't remember her name. A few neighbors had brought presents like stationery or jars of peanuts wrapped in tissue, but it was clear my mom wouldn't open them, since she kept saying "Thank you for coming!" after her first nibbles at the frosting.

She was swaying strangely in her beige flats. I tried to make grown-up party talk like I'd seen on TV, but nobody was interested in me, and I was distracted by my mom's voice, which was that of a little girl, with too much breath and fear and pitch. I didn't want anyone to see her like this; she usually stayed indoors when she was her tiniest self; *the voice* was a precursor to one of her marathon migraines. I had forgotten about getting anything to drink, so there was only the pink wine, and people drank tap water out of our mugs, and the walls were getting too close and almost sweaty, and the people seemed to want to leave but I couldn't go home with them.

In the morning my mother thanked me for the party; she had spent the night getting soothed by Ron, and I had spent it counting and recounting my stuffed animals, touching their noses and tapping their heads in my special code, so I could face my mom again.

CHAPTER 6

When I left my mother's house at fourteen, I took only four things: a big bag of clothes, her dime-store eyelash curler, a photograph of my crossing guard, and my Holly Hobby diary from 1979. I had only wanted to grab quick and unnoticeable things from the house.

A judge had informed my father that kids could shift custody arrangements on their own as soon as they turned fourteen. This had always been my plan, to get away. I wanted it, but I also feared it, feared what it would do to my mother. Over Christmas break, at my father's apartment, I secretly applied to private schools in San Francisco. The timing slipped up beneath me like a sheet of ice. And then I had to tell my mother.

I chose a moment when her back was to me, her arms full of laundry, as she was climbing the stairs.

"Mom?" I said, looking up at her wide back. I held the banister for support. "I applied to some high schools in San Francisco."

She stopped. She didn't put the laundry down.

Slowly my mom climbed the rest of the stairs and disappeared into her room. She emerged a few seconds later, breathing heavily. "It's your decision," she said.

I started to climb up to her, but she motioned me to stop. "Your father can give you things I can't. I knew you'd choose him one day."

"It's not about Dad," I protested. "It's about the school. There are some really good schools!"

My mom sighed, and her eyes filled with tears. "If you go to live with him, I'll never see you again."

I knew this was true. She would never come see me, and she wouldn't call because I'd be living with my father. After I left, any connection would be up to me.

Because she had always relied on me. It had been my role to retrieve her from her months of sobbing after my father left and to interrupt the hours she'd spend in the tub in the dark. When she'd whisper "It's just too hard to be here," I'd rush around like a dog on ice to distract her: "Let's watch a movie, let's make popcorn, let's look at my new dance! I'm making it up right now!"

It had been my role to shield her from the glances at the grocery store when she talked like a five-year-old, counting the money that didn't add up. It had been my role to shake her to go back to the store when she'd drive away without my brother, when he was a toddler left screaming in the parking lot, waiting to be strapped in. It had been my role to keep my mom tethered—to me and to everything else. Somewhere deep and unspeakable inside me, I knew I had to get away.

It was after that that I got sick. My fever spiked to 102, then 103, and the pains in my belly were unbearable. My mom drove me to the hospital, where a kind nurse stroked my head and called me poor baby, and then there was a needle in my arm and a doctor and a mask on my face, and I was being sped down a hallway on a gurney.

The doctor thought my appendix had ruptured, which was the reason for the rush. When they cut me open, though, they found nothing wrong at all. Later, the surgical reports from the hospital indicated that they removed a perfectly healthy appendix and discovered some light endometriosis around my uterus. (They cut over to my right ovary, which was healthy and fine, and discovered only "streak tissue" where my left ovary should be: a birth defect, apparently, a missing piece.)

I think now that my body was merely marking another kind of pain. When I got better, I packed a suitcase. I layered my clothes and the diary, her eyelash curler, and the photo of the crossing guard. I then waited for the right moment. It arrived when one of my mother's old boyfriends came by to fix something under the sink. He was a burly, sweaty kind of guy with a truck full of tools. I asked if he could drive me to San Francisco.

We lobbed my heavy bag into the back of his truck with all the hammers and old toilets. I didn't know then that I would write about this day some twenty-five years later from a bright apartment in New York City and still be looking for the mom who watched me from the window. I didn't know then that her premonition, or her curse, would come true.

What I did know, as my mother's errant boyfriend and I pulled up in front of my dad's apartment building, country music blaring from the truck's windows, was that I wanted some kind of ceremony to make sense of leaving her. I knew, somewhere in my stitched-together gut, that I had just made a choice that would haunt me forever—I had chosen to amputate my mom, and without my life-blood, she would be too sick to love me again.

Over the next four years, the pains came at night, when the lowing of the foghorns would fold me to sleep. Then I would dream myself back into my old green house. In the dreams, my mother wouldn't be there. I was alone and terrified. Somebody or something was coming to kill me, and I was afraid I was already dead, because I couldn't move: my whole sleep self was a phantom limb, locked into the person I had left behind.

CHAPTER 7

Throughout my twenties, I wrote to my mom every four years or so, just to prove that I could. Every time I wrote, a card or a letter would arrive a few weeks later. "I can tell every word was written with the intention to hurt me," she wrote more than once. When she replied around the time of my birthday, she sent me a card with a clown and balloons meant for a three-year-old. Twice she misspelled my name. When I sent her a letter to tell her I had graduated from college, she sent me a note on scrap paper saying only "Congratulations. I wish you the best." The longest letter she wrote was in response to a query I had sent her, asking her what she thought had transpired in her life to make us so distant and estranged.

She wrote back about her cats and dogs, and about the ghosts who lived in her house—she told me not to worry, as the ghosts were friendly and her yard was pretty. Aside from the graduation note, she always signed off with a warning: I had chosen to leave her, she said, and there was nothing she could do to change that.

After each letter, I simply shut off the mom switch I had briefly toggled on. I didn't think about her, didn't talk about her, forced her image back down each time something—a song on the radio, a certain shade of yellow—would sweep me back to childhood, and my blood would seem to rush in reverse. Aside from the spontaneous letters, I did everything I could to forget.

But madness has no logic, and it has terrible timing. One morning, after I decided at age thirty to have a baby, I cracked. I couldn't leave the bathroom floor. I clung to the toilet and scraped my fingernails against the floor tiles. I leaned my head against the cool porcelain of the bathtub for relief. I was flooded with the smells from my childhood, of frozen Salisbury steak bubbling in the microwave and cut grass from outside. I was terrified that if I left the bathroom, my California hometown, Concord, would be right out the door. I could smell it that clearly. And yet I knew this was crazy. I was terrified I was going crazy.

I didn't resist a hospital rescue. I knew I was unraveling.

A doctor gave me medicine right away. And then, after I waited for a while in a small room, a tall woman with blond hair walked in. She sat in a chair in front of me and met my eyes. She took my hands.

"Why?" I asked, and started to sob.

The therapist's grip was steady.

"Why?" I cried harder, gasping. "Why did my mother molest me?"

It was the first time I'd said it out loud.

CHAPTER 8

After my psychic break, I spent a year in Los Angeles in the lower swells of a serious, occasionally suicidal, anxious depression. This yearlong darkness was much more than fallout from articulating a singular abuse. It came from arousing the suspicion of it and wishing my agonies could coalesce around a moment, then finding that they could not.

As a child I was pliant with my mother, skinless for years, and then I left. In my depression, I realized I'd left a still soft self behind, with her. For a long time, I didn't have language for what had happened in her house.

She had moved away from my childhood home, but her phone number was easy to find. I called her for the second time in a decade.

Mom sounded exactly the same. She was breathy, girlish, distracted. "Where are you?" she said. "Oh, if you were right outside my door, I would give you a hug."

I told her I was five hundred miles away, living in Los Angeles.

"Oh Crissie," she said, using my childhood name. "I remember what your head smelled like when you were a baby. You smelled so good. So good."

I knew this was a strange thing to say. I knew it right then.

"I'm thirty now," I said.

"That's so hard to believe," my mom answered, and she laughed. "Because I'm only twenty-five!"

I told my mom I had gone through a depression, sparked by my decision to have a baby, although I hadn't gone through with it. I asked about the genetic links to depression in our family, but despite her months of sleeping in the daytime, bathing in the dark, and ceaseless tears, she didn't know of any. You should be happy, she said. What on earth was there to be sad about?

"Well, you," I told her. "I don't have a relationship with you."

My mom was quiet for a minute. "That was your decision," she said, her voice flat. "You're the one who wouldn't have anything to do with me. There was nothing I could do about that."

My mother made me dead before my time, but it was she who was the ghost. I wanted to confront her with the things she'd done. I wanted to ask questions, and I wanted her to forgive me for leaving when I was young and scared, so I could have the chance to forgive her, too. I wanted her to change that old song on the radio that she insisted was our story the story that left her jilted by a lover. Because, really, I was her child, and I couldn't have left her if I tried.

She had checkmated us both. In her eyes, I was still the person who moved to my father's apartment at fourteen; she was powerless against my father, and she was powerless against me. I had moved on some, and I couldn't be that girl again—the girl with no edges, the girl who blotted her mother's madness and still went to school and smiled and swallowed it down. I also couldn't be my mother's monster. I couldn't be the one without the love inside to come back.

But these thoughts would only come long after I hung up the phone. Right then a familiar guilt had coated my throat, and I was silent. So my mom asked after my brother. Unlike me, he hadn't contacted her even once after he moved away. I gave her the briefest of reports, and she said she was happy because he sounded happy.

Everything was so "happy," I wondered if she was on some drug; I had always sort of wished I could attribute her behavior to an external substance. At this point in the call, I was starting to feel robotic, so it was surprisingly easy to ask her if she'd ever been addicted to anything.

She sounded shocked. "No!" she squealed. "Not even cigarettes. I haven't had any problems ever. Knock wood. But you, with trying to have this baby . . ." She paused.

"What?" I asked.

"Well, the doctors said you'd probably never be able to have children."

She was referring to the surgery when I was fourteen, when the doctors found nothing wrong.

"I don't know how much you remember about that surgery," my mom continued, "but it was very serious. The doctors had to remove one of your ovaries, and all of your female parts were inflamed and infected. They said you probably wouldn't be able to have babies from all of the scar tissue."

And there we were. Her trauma had seeped out again and foisted itself on me. But this time I knew the story wasn't true. I had a medical report. And this time I could see the lie casting its glance back onto all her other stories—the desert birth, her almost starving, the daughter she claimed had stopped loving her. Nothing about my mother was solid but this: she had created her loss through my image, and I would careen forever if I couldn't let her go.

I lay on the grass outside my Los Angeles apartment for a long time after that talk and looked at the stars. I wouldn't call her again.

CHAPTER 9

When I found out that my mother was dead, I was enraged. Not because she was gone—for that I felt a slight uptick of relief. I was angry because nobody had told me earlier. I hadn't known she was sick, hadn't known there was a funeral, hadn't been able to say good-bye. I had never known how to talk to my mother, but I wanted to say good-bye.

A lawyer had found my brother first to broach the news, and my brother had called me. This lawyer wanted us to sign some papers, but I called him directly to ask why no one in her family—in my family—had reached out to us.

The lawyer turned out to be a friend of my mother's. She had done his bookkeeping for years. He told me that the family didn't know how to find us, his tone cool and professional. This, I said, was impossible. I am an author and a professor at three universities; a Google search of my name yields plenty of hits. My brother has a Web site with an address and phone number on it. After all, the lawyer himself tracked us down.

The lawyer then said that my mother had written us letters to tell us she was dying and we didn't write her back.

"Oh," I said, stunned. "She wrote to us?"

I didn't tell him that the few letters she had sent me over the years had been in direct response to mine, that she'd never mustered the courage to make contact on her own.

"The family didn't think you cared," the lawyer continued. "You didn't write back to her letters, so why would you go to her funeral?"

"But I never got a letter," I protested, sounding every bit the five-year-old I felt like inside.

The lawyer knew her husband, Clem, and her sister. "Well, honestly, I think Clem and Phyllis thought you had already caused your mother enough grief in her life, why should you be allowed to cause any more?" he said.

In my mother's will, I discovered, she had left the house for Clem to maintain his "health and standard of living." After he passes, half the sale of the house will be distributed to her relatives: Mom's sister and her sister's two children are to receive a quarter, and my brother and I will collect an eighth apiece. In twenty years I may get a hundred bucks out of the deal. The only other bits in the will were two diamond rings, which she bequeathed to my cousin Kathy.

After hanging up with the lawyer, I decided to track down Clem. I had never met him. I discovered that he lived in a house he had shared with my mom for eighteen years in Benicia, a town eleven miles from where I grew up. I saw a picture of it on Google Maps: it was a one-story clapboard house, painted blue with white trim. Clem was seventy-two, but when he answered the phone, he sounded younger. Your mother, he said, was the nicest person he had ever known.

CHAPTER 10

"Your mother loved you," Clem said. "She cried over you all the time. She never understood why you never came and saw her. Birthdays especially."

Clem confirmed the letters she supposedly wrote when she was sick, though he never saw them. He said she cried when she didn't hear back from us. He said he didn't know how to find us for the funeral. In fact, he said, "I didn't know if you was even alive."

I had done a real bad thing, leaving her like that, he continued, but she was never angry—just the rest of the family was, for treating her so bad.

I remembered the way my mother had told her family that I was dead and wondered if they ever believed it. I thought how strange it was to be a ghost: solid enough for everyone's projections to land and stick but too ephemeral to fight back. I also felt that Clem didn't like talking to me.

She was the smartest person in town, he said. "You really missed a lot not knowing your mother."

I asked him if she had been afraid of dying.

"No, because she'd already died twice before," he said. "With you and your brother, giving birth. She died both times, in childbirth, but then she came back."

Clem told me someone was waiting for him at the store. But I wanted to hear more.

What about our report cards and stories and drawings and photographs from when we were kids? I asked him. I had been an avid journaler as a child, and my brother drew tons of pictures back then. My mother kept all these things in boxes labeled with dates. When I left her house, I took only the diary and the eyelash curler and the picture of my crossing guard. I didn't have school photos or birthday pictures. There was nothing to prove our childhoods with our mother, only the scattering of pictures of the visits with our dad that marked us growing up.

"No, no, we threw all that stuff away," Clem said. His voice was rushed. "She didn't want it anymore."

The depth of this loss stopped me cold. "Um, could I have a picture of her, something of hers?"

"The only pictures I got are the pictures of her and me, and they're up on the wall."

"Could I get a copy of that picture, just to see what she looks like?"

"No," Clem answered, his voice firm. "I don't got nothing." He hung up the phone.

A week after I got the news of my mother's death, I called my aunt Phyllis, her only sister. Clem had told me she had remarried and was living in a retirement community in Texas, just enough information for me to find her phone number. Despite Clem's promise of the family's anger, Phyl spoke with me for an hour and a half.

"Your mom loved you kids so much," Phyl told me. "She loved you more than she loved herself."

Phyl told me mom tried to reach me many times. My aunt was seventy-three, but she too sounded younger, the Kansas accent flattening her tones. Your mother even went to your dad's house in San Francisco to try to see you, she said. She said someone who worked for him answered the door (my mother thought it was a butler or a maid) and told my mom to never set foot in the vicinity again. Of course, this was a fantasy: my father lording over a batch of servants.

Supposedly my mom called repeatedly. Phyl's assurance made me doubt myself. Had she ever really called me? Why hadn't I answered the phone? She went to your high school graduation, Phyl said. "You looked right at her," she claimed. "But you wouldn't speak to her, so she left."

This story, at least, I had heard. When I was set to graduate from high school, I sent an invitation to my mother but didn't receive a reply. I gave a speech, but there were hundreds in the audience. My brother said later that he saw her there, phantom-like, hovering in the back. When I went to look for her, she was already gone.

My aunt said my mom wanted us to have the things my father could provide—private school, those imaginary butlers and maids— that she herself could not. And then she wanted us to make our own decisions about him. She never wanted us to hate our father the way she did.

Phyllis remembered the trip my mom and brother and I made to Kansas more than a year after the divorce. My mom hadn't told anyone the news for many months, so it wasn't surprising that she hadn't spoken about her fantasies of suicide, her fears of starvation, or the way she would crack up at night. Nevertheless, my aunt said my mom was in a state of shock during the visit, withdrawn and barely speaking. I wish someone had known to help her more.

Later, Phyllis sent me a few things from my mother: two tiny paintings my mom had liked and probably picked up from the weekend garage sales she used to troll, as well as a few pictures of her in college, looking surprisingly young and pretty. She didn't have pictures of me or my brother, save for some silhouettes she rescued from my mom's attic. I remember these silhouettes: we had them made during a trip to Disneyland, and I find it somehow fitting that this final keepsake is but an outline.

After I got off the phone with Phyllis, I decided to call Kathy, the cousin to whom my mother was closest.

Kathy, too, told me how much my mom loved me, and said she used to have pictures of my brother and me all over the walls in her house. She said my mother told her that she had tried to be in touch with me but that I "wanted nothing to do with her."

I think about the reasons a mother would need to believe her children betrayed her. The simplest answer is the sympathy such a story garnered, the wall of warm bodies it built around her, soothing her. Maybe she just couldn't endure the idea that she had caused pain; there simply wasn't room in her psyche to stand up and be accountable, as she'd been curled up in a little ball, ready for blows, for so long. And perhaps my mother needed a betrayer because she had been betrayed. Maybe the pictures on her walls weren't really of us but of herself, the little girl she couldn't remember.

Kathy wondered out loud whether her brain cancer had been around much earlier than anybody knew, whether maybe cancer kept her from living in reality sometimes and she just learned to hide it.

Kathy described the day of my mother's diagnosis. My mom had been to her local gym, but after her workout she just sat in a chair staring into space. The gym was closing, and an employee urged her to go home. She didn't respond. The employee tried again; she seemed catatonic. Finally, my mother got up and walked away.

According to Kathy, Clem found her later, at home and in bed. When he walked into the bedroom, my mother started yelling, "Who are you? Get out of my house!" Clem ran for the neighbors, and she yelled at them, too. They called an ambulance, and at the hospital doctors ran scans and discovered the tumor. She later told Kathy that she didn't remember a thing; she had no idea how she even drove home from the gym.

This, I told Kathy, sounded exactly like the alternate personality

I knew from my childhood. Her spaciness. Her yelling nonsensical,
dangerous things and then forgetting that she had screamed at all.
My mom could snap into another self, and she did. And whether
the tumor caused it or was merely a parallel discovery, nobody will
ever know.

CHAPTER 11

If I wasn't going to get confirmation of my mom's mental illness,
from Clem or Phyl or anyone else, I wanted proof of how it might
have begun. I wanted the truth about the grandfather. And I got
that truth when I spoke with one woman who knew my mom when
she was young. This person unfurled her story like a balled-up blanket, and suddenly it was all before me.

My mother had been severely abused.

In 1953, she said, my maternal great-grandfather began molest-
ing my then-five-year-old mother. The assaults went on for years.
This person knew because she had grown up around the grandfather, and he had raped her, too.

She had never told another soul about her own abuse, this person
on the phone, and she sounded relieved to have it out. She made
some excuses for James Falkner, said he had once owned a granary
in the small town of Belvue, Kansas, and had been one of the richest
men in town. But then the Depression hit, and he lost it all. Maybe
this was why he abused young girls, she reasoned; maybe it was
repression, frustration, or rage. And then she asked me not to reveal
her identity. James Falkner had long been dead, but she had her own
family to protect.

This person was in touch with my mom in the last years of her
life, when, she said, my mom finally started to remember.

"Your mother, she carried a lot of pain," the woman said. "She didn't remember the abuse until a few years ago, just before she got the brain tumor. But then she started having nightmares."

She said my mother called her when the nightmares began; she was having night flashes of someone, a man, coming to her at night and assaulting her, but at first she didn't know who it was.

"I didn't want her to think it was her father, because it wasn't," she said. "The grandfather moved in with the family when your mother was about five. Your mom thought her mother knew it was happening, and it happened all the time. For years."

I cried when I got off the phone, with sadness for my mom but mostly with relief. The singular darkness lifted from her and landed on a person I had never known but had heard about in snatches of her madness. My mother's grandfather stories were sequestered away in the part of her brain that lashed and screamed and called me a whore, the same part of her brain that marched her up the stairs and into my bed on a night I wish I could forget. Language fails to reach the experience, the twinned despondence and terror of *molest*, but I remember it like I remember her words *he raped me every night*. And when I learned it was true—that my memory of her blocked memory was solid and valid and real—I felt a thin kind of hope. At the end of her life, it seemed, a light had cracked through the blockage; there was a bridge. The mom everyone said was so nice, the mom who "loved everybody, forgave everybody," was beginning to remember the unforgivable grandfather. And maybe, at the end of her life, there could have been a bridge to me.

I remembered the story of the grandfather that my mother told me. Even when I was a kid, I felt he was part of the mystery, and sometimes when I was brave I would tiptoe into asking her about him.

"I don't remember anything about my childhood," she would say. "From about six through sixth grade, it's all black. I remember dressing up as someone called Mrs. Jones when I was really little, but maybe that's because there was a picture."

"And your grandfather?" I asked her.

"I don't remember him, either," she said. "There are the stories about him burying his eyeglasses in the garden, but you already know those."

CHAPTER 12

I'd been afraid, all these years, to diagnose my mother with a mental illness, especially because the disease I thought she had had been so stigmatized. In the 1990s a scandal erupted around recovered memories; experts and laypeople were suddenly claiming that experiences like hers were impossible. The fashion turned, and people suddenly were supposed to never be able to forget serious abuse: the therapists were accused of suggesting stories and foisting memories on their impressionable patients.

My mother, of course, never went to therapy. In fact, she hated the very idea of psychiatry; I remember her telling me once that there was likely a reason she didn't remember her childhood, and she didn't want anybody digging into what she had effectively suppressed.

But if people didn't believe in the memory blocking, then you can't have dissociative identity disorder, or multiple personalities, because it is the repression of memories that causes the self to split. And some people don't believe DID even exists. This is why, despite my mother hitting all its hallmark signs, I'd been scared to label her that way.

I decided to call up one of the most respected figures in the joint fields of psychiatry and trauma, Judith Herman, who wrote the groundbreaking book *Trauma and Recovery*. Herman believes DID is real. "DID is controversial among academics who don't know anything about psychiatry," she told me, "but within psychiatry it's a well-established diagnosis. It's a controversy that lives on quite irrespective of actual clinical experience or research experience." She noted that several new books had been published in the past year about treatment of DID, and that seminal research conducted in the 1980s by Frank Putnam had been replicated many times. This research showed that about 95 percent of people with multiple personalities experienced significant trauma in childhood and that incest was among the most common forms of that trauma. "DID is almost always related to very severe, early-onset, prolonged, repeated child abuse."

Then I talked about DID with my partner, Lo Charlap. Lo teaches psychopathology and trauma at New York University, and she thinks the memory debate may be rooted in a problem with language. Basically, the people who study memory and say that repressed memories don't exist and the people who study psychology and say they do may both be right. It's common, Lo says, for a person to not be able to talk about her abuse for many years after it happened. "If you don't have words for an experience, you can't make it a memory," she says, "because we communicate memory through words." But that doesn't mean people like my mother have no recollection at all. "It's more of an unsymbolized sense or a diffuse knowing. If your mom didn't have any knowledge of what happened to her at all, she wouldn't have been living in response to it all the time."

In other words, a "recovered memory" can be this: after therapy or years of a safe and protected life, a person can suddenly give language to what was once only sensory terror. That's what happened with my mom.

My mother also, in her way, remembered her abuse all her life; she remembered it enough to know that she couldn't think about her childhood. Possibly she remembered it in her migraines and in her frightened and depressed ways and, alternately, in her prostitution. This, too, is a kind of remembering.

She said her grandfather died when she was in seventh grade, and that's when her memory came back. And there was most certainly no connection. She loved the phrase "most certainly." She tried to kill herself shortly after her grandfather died, and she spent some time in a hospital. This she remembered and my aunt verified. Her parents told her that her suicide attempt was because her school-work was too hard, and she believed them.

I still don't know what makes a person crazy. Was it when her grandfather raped her or when she knew her mother was in the bedroom next door pretending not to hear? I don't know if it makes a person crazy to remember and to forget at the same time.

I don't know if it makes a person crazy to leave her mother's house or to never go home again.

CHAPTER 13

Writing my way through to my mother sometimes feels like a Faulkner story: There's no linear narrative to keep me steady. Just like his character Caddy Compson in *The Sound and the Fury*, my mom didn't have a voice; she was a gaping hole at the center of her story. William Faulkner considered *The Sound and the Fury* his favorite work but also his biggest failure: he could never get her right.

While I was looking for the mother I had lost, I discovered by accident that the Faulknerian feel of my family was no coincidence: the great Southern novelist Faulkner was my maternal great-uncle several generations back. (I was the first person in my immediate family to discover this.)

My mother's mother was a Falkner, without the *u*. I remember her from childhood and our family trips to Kansas: a stern, plain woman who kept tiny ceramic animals in a glass terrarium in her kitchen.

It was easy to work backward along the Falkner line, as I had some stories, and the author's historians and enthusiasts cleared the genealogical path. I easily found that her maternal grandfather, another Falkner, lived with the family until Mom was a young teenager, and this I could verify with address records and death indexes.

In all of Faulkner's stories, the once grand Southern dame is hobbled; her wig is askew and her slip is showing; she's haughty and confused toward the blacks who live in cabins on her crumbling property, and her shame has soured her speech. This is partly because the famous Colonel's son—Faulkner's grandfather, who features heavily in his fiction—was a rascal and a drunk; he sold his father's railroads to fund his years of alcoholism. His son, Faulkner's father, was forever trying to restore the lost fortune and prestige. In Faulkner's lineage, there was great promise and a fall from grace. In mine there was only the fall. And for William Faulkner, race was a sharp, particular pain embedded in the Southern side: foreign, to be sure, but also familiar, because the Faulkners had black slaves. In my family line, the racism was more intimate and the hate more precise, because the Falkners had black spouses.

I wonder at the racism that Faulkner himself writes so much about, about swallowing a public rage and shame and then passing it privately on.

My story catches another reflective gleam of Faulkner, as incest, real or fabricated, is a major theme in his work. I don't know what really happened in Faulkner's life or how far back along our joint tree the abuse coils and springs, but I do know that the author thought about it a lot. Caddy Compson's brother only imagines the incest in *The Sound and the Fury*, but he also shows that even fabrications have the power to drive one to mania.

After all, when I was nine years old, my mother gave me a lock for my bedroom door and told me to use it, forcing me to imagine my way into the demons only she could see. Around the same time, she yelled out the story about her grandfather raping her. Back then I couldn't confirm the story, and later she forgot she had even told me about it.

I learned then that there wasn't much distance between a myth and its validation.

CHAPTER 14

I hadn't seen my brother for almost a year before we learned our mother had died. After all, estrangement runs in our family. But after we discovered our mother had passed away, he invited me to his apartment in Brooklyn. Despite my misgivings, I went.

For two years before our mother's death, I'd been trying to connect with my brother, unsuccessfully. He'd been very angry with me, he said. One of the problems was that he felt I didn't respect his boundaries. I had mothered him as a child, he said. Now I had to let him grow up. One of the problems was that I talked about our mother to him after my breakdown at thirty, when I was looking for validation of my memories, and he didn't like talking about her. I had invaded his psyche, so he shut down. Still, we agreed then on the big pieces of our history, on the way she acted and the way she cut us out. But he was done with Mom, he said then. He didn't think about her anymore.

Mom's death changed things. We decided we'd spend some time together, mourning in our own way. I met my brother on Bedford Avenue in Williamsburg, two blocks from his apartment. We walked to the river. As we walked, we talked about our work, looking at the Canadian geese pecking at snow behind a wire fence. He'd taken a few days off from his job as a designer at an advertising agency, though he felt strange, as I did, telling people why. The standard gush of compassion felt unwarranted, undeserved: we weren't like other people with dead mothers, and no, we weren't leaving town for the funeral.

We went back to his apartment: it was filled with his wooden carvings and paintings and stringed instruments of all types. Andrew is an artist and musician. Ever since he was a young child, his imagination was wild and bright; he's since parlayed that into a successful career. He made tea. His cat, Mothra, was in heat and gurgling on the floor. She tried to hump his dog.

We tried to talk about Mom again as we sat in his place, but we didn't know how. I played with the rim of my teacup and watched the animals, and my brother posited a theory. "I think Candy had a lot of pain in her life, especially in utero," he said, and then paused, getting me to meet his eyes. "I think she wasn't wanted when Gwen"— our grandmother—"got pregnant with her. In fact, she was hated."

My brother, like me, was looking for answers. He was looking for a singular reason, a starting place for her strangeness, a wounding that preceded and absolved us. I told him how sad I felt that we didn't say good-bye, that nothing had been resolved.

"It is sad," he continued. "But I think for Mom it's all okay now. All of this doesn't matter anymore."

I felt suddenly, utterly alone. I picked up the cat, but I didn't have what she needed either: she clawed her way out of my arms to look for the dog.

While my brother and I agreed on our past, we couldn't find the same present. Andrew felt a kind of spiritual connection to our mother in her passing, while I couldn't feel her at all. "I believe Mom still loves Dad," he said. "And he—he still loves her."

I flashed to a childhood memory: our father dropping us off after a weekend visit. We would return home to find our mother hiding behind her bed, crying, and refusing to come out until she was sure he had driven several miles away.

There was no love between them, as far as I could remember.

"Are you sure that's not a wish?" I asked him.

My brother didn't think so; now he wanted peace, whereas I still wanted answers. He could say good-bye. After our talk, my brother remembered my mom's fondness for the Mamas and the Papas, so he played a rendition of "Dream a Little Dream of Me" on his ukulele for my mother and recorded it. It's a very sweet version, high-pitched and twangy. I cried as I listened to it, for the yearning and the gentleness. It's this softness I love in my brother, and he seemed especially so right then, longing for a mom and dad to love each other.

With her death, my brother could close his chapter on our mom. But not me. I still reread her letters. I can't help it. It's as if I'm waiting for her voice to rise from the page. And I still look for more clues. Several months ago I called the hospital where my mother was treated for her final illness and was told that I could access her records, but first I'd have to fill out forms proving my relationship as her daughter. The medical secretary warned me that if we were talking about a brain tumor, this could number in the hundreds of pages, and I would have to pay.

I didn't write in for the records. Maybe it was because I was afraid to look. But also maybe it was because there was nothing more to find. Even if I discovered the tumor was located in the temporal lobe, which is associated with psychosis, or in the frontal lobe, linked to depression, where would I be? Maybe I could understand more of her medical history, but nothing would clear my psychic inheritance or give me back a good-bye.

I also realized that, in the end, I didn't want the records. I didn't want her stack of sickness and death to overcome the few small things I have from her life.

As I sat with Andrew, I thought about the six letters I have from my mom and the eyelash curler I stole from her twenty-five years ago, sitting next to a huge pile of paper chronicling the months of my mother's dying. I thought about the boxes of photos, report cards, and diaries that Clem threw away. I wished I had taken the photographs of her, and of me as a kid. I wished I had my school reports, the stories I wrote, my drawings, my letters, my baby pictures, my grades: anything to teach me who I am. Could there ever be a proper memorial for such a loss?

Perhaps the memorial is this search, which will probably last, in some way, forever. Still, I think, as I write from my bright apartment with my dogs and books scattered about, that Caddy Compson may have been the hole at the center of her own story, but her life gave form to the voices around her.

WHEN WE ARE CALLED TO PART

BROOKE JARVIS

S peeding down the street is a car that I love. A Toyota station wagon—probably from the 1980s, but who can say?—that used to be red or maroon but is now mostly gaping, rust-lined holes and sun-bleached swatches of gray and white. The windshield is cracked; since I last saw the car, someone has patched a hole with plywood and covered the top with roofing paper. For a second my breath catches, and I stop in my tracks. Dumb as it is, I hope. But the car is moving too fast, too purposefully down the center of the road. And instead of a pair of sunglasses, white hair sticking out of a visor, and a small, hunched figure with her hand held up to block the sun, in the driver's seat is a much younger, black-haired woman I don't know.

I should have realized that the car would still be here. In Kalaupapa plenty of vehicles keep rolling for years after the salt air and the ingenuity of isolation have left them more plywood than metal. But it's still a shock. The car is driving, and Gertie is not.

Gertie—Gertrude Kaauwai—hated that station wagon. She'd had to switch to it once her remaining foot deteriorated to the point that, even with her stubbornness and the dexterity gained by more than four decades on crutches, she could no longer climb into her big gray truck. On my first day in the settlement, before I met her, my new boss pointed the truck out to me on the street and explained that I should get as far out of the road as possible when I saw it coming—usually in the morning, during Gertrude's food run for her dozens of cats, or in the late afternoon, when she was driving to the bar and would have to squint into the western sun. The disease had gotten to Gertrude's eyes, and she couldn't see well at all. If she'd lived anywhere else, she would have been forced to stop driving long before. But Kalaupapa has its own rules.

The settlement, as everyone who lives here calls it, is the only town on an isolated peninsula on a sparsely populated Hawaiian island. Its history began a century and a half ago, when the first boatload of leprosy sufferers arrived—the unwilling founders of what in different times was known as a leper colony, or a leprosarium. Decades after modern medicine neutralized the disease, Kalaupapa is the largest remaining settlement of its victims in the United States.

I'm back visiting for the first time in more than four years, but nearly everyone guesses much less: "How long's it been? A year? A year and a half?" Time's passage always feels more uncertain here, more uneven. When I lived in Kalaupapa, I got used to hearing frequent references to patients who had died many decades before, often as if they were still alive. When I was new and still putting faces to names, I assumed several of them were.

Now I know all too well who's missing. During the twelve months I lived here, in 2008 and 2009, we lost nine patients, almost a third of those who remained; since I left, three have died. I heard about them over the phone or by email: Uncle Henry first. Gertrude a year later, on Christmas Eve. Auntie Kay just a few months back. Her things are now boxed up in plywood crates in her side yard, waiting to be shipped to her family on the once-a-year barge.

And someone else is driving Gertrude's car; someone else is living in her house. No one plays cribbage anymore in the settlement bar, where she used to hold court until the eight o'clock closing time every night. The bar's owner, a patient named Gloria, tried to ease the transition, rearranging the tables so that no one would have to sit in Gertrude's old seat. People appreciated the effort, but it was basically futile; her absence was inescapable all the same. These days, with so few patients left, there's no moving forward after a death in Kalaupapa. There's really not much moving forward at all.

I used to love to explore the woods outside the settlement, which are filled with evidence of a much bigger town: concrete walkways and front steps that now lead nowhere, glass medicine jars and ceramic doorknobs shining in the mud. Once a friend and I set out to capture a wild beehive and found our target not far into the forest, inside an overturned, overgrown cast-iron bathtub.

At first I found these discoveries quaint or charming. Like the settlement's isolation, like its peculiar history, they were half-abstractions, stories to tell when I returned to the outside world. But in time I began to see them as the remaining patients did: relics not just of people they had known but of a community that had dwindled to just them and that would not last beyond them. No new patients, and no children, have come in decades; every death is one step closer to the end of Kalaupapa as they have known it.

In a settlement defined by tragedies—parents and children torn apart, years of forced isolation, funeral bells that once rang every day—this is the one that no one expected. The place that no one wanted to create, the place where no one wanted to go, is coming to an end. And even a prison eventually becomes a home, becomes something you mourn.

"Molokai?" the shuttle driver at the Honolulu airport asked. "Why would you go there? They don't even have a McDonald's!"

This was true, I knew. Molokai—a thirty-eight-mile-long island situated between Oahu and Maui—also had no stoplights, barely a handful of restaurants, and a population holding steady at around 7,400 people. Major roads crossed rivers via fords, not bridges. When the rivers ran high, whole sections of the island would be cut off. The local paper would sometimes quote "Uncle Merv" or "Aunty

Paula" without giving a last name. It was known as the last Hawaiian island, still home to a majority native Hawaiian population. When I arrived at the open-air airport the next day, a hand-painted sign greeted me. ALOHA, it read. SLOW DOWN. THIS IS MOLOKAI.

A year earlier, during my final months of college in Virginia, I had discovered an ad for work in Kalaupapa National Historical Park, which coadministered an unusual settlement on the Kalaupapa Peninsula, on the north side of Molokai. It was home to twenty-eight leprosy patients—the peninsula's only permanent legal residents and the last remnants of a 140-year-old community that at its peak had housed more than eleven hundred people. For months I held up the job to my graduating friends as proof that it was crazy to apply for desk jobs when we were so young and there were so many strange adventures out there, but it was more rhetorical device than plan. I never really believed I'd actually end up on Molokai, boarding the little nine-seat Cessna for a flight over the edge of the earth.

Residents sometimes explain Molokai's geography by comparing it to a shark. The southern shore, with its low beaches and shallow reefs, is the belly. Halawa Valley, at its eastern tip, is the nose, and the long beach of Papohaku in the west is the inner curve of the tail. In between are grasslands, farms, and a rainforest cut by deep valleys. Protruding from the island's north shore—the shark's dorsal fin—is the Kalaupapa Peninsula.

Looming over the peninsula is a cliff, known to locals as the *pali*. It formed more than a million years ago, when a landslide sent a third of Molokai crashing into the sea. The break left the island's north shore a sheer, impassable wall, three thousand feet high in places—the tallest sea cliffs in the world. Much later the eruption of a small volcano formed a flat peninsula at the base of the cliff. Only incidentally connected to the larger island—"topside" Molokai, as it's known locally—the peninsula is five square miles of land surrounded on three sides by deep ocean and on the fourth by the chiseled face of the *pali*. In the winter, storms swell rivers and stir surf, cutting off all ocean access and, periodically, trail and air access as well. The peninsula is an island within an island, a tiny, solitary world of its own.

The plane skimmed briefly over houses and fields, and then the land simply stopped. The earth turned ninety degrees, from flat cow pasture to sheer cliff, and there was nothing below us but crashing waves, thousands of feet down. For a moment, it seemed that the plane would drop, too, simply fall out of the sky. Instead, we flew along the western coast of a low peninsula, rising subtly to the lip of a deep crater in its center. I registered a forested interior, a jagged, rocky coast on the far side, and close at hand, a small grid of roads and buildings extending from the beach. We landed on a thin airstrip at the very tip of the peninsula, the plane pulling off the tarmac and parking on the grass in front of a one-room airport and a lighthouse. A few miles to the south, the cliffs we had just crossed faced us, deep green, furrowed, and imposing. Of topside I could see nothing—just a few distant trees at the cliff's edge. We were sealed in: the tropical paradise version of a snow globe.

In the 1860s the peninsula's unique geography caught the eye of the Hawaiian government. A series of newly introduced diseases—measles, influenza, smallpox, whooping cough—had ravaged the islands, and now leprosy, an even less-understood scourge, had arrived. A chronic bacterial infection, leprosy is rarely fatal, but the disfigurement and pain it causes have long made it one of humanity's most feared and misunderstood diseases. The bacterium that causes it fares poorly in the body's warm core, so it primarily attacks hands, feet, faces, eyes, and skin. Numbness and paralysis lead to unnoticed and untreated burns or cuts and sometimes to infection and amputation. Hands begin to "crab," or close up, and bones and tissue break down and are absorbed by the body. Victims may lose nasal cartilage, gum tissue and teeth, even eyelashes and eyebrows. Blindness, too, is common.

Terrified officials looked to the peninsula as a natural prison, a place to quarantine sufferers from the general population. The peninsula's milder western coast, known as Kalaupapa, was already occupied by a native village, so the first boatload of patients who arrived in 1866 was deposited at Kalawao, the barren, windy eastern coast. (By some accounts, early patients were made to swim to shore, so great was the ship captain's fear of infection.) The patients were dropped off with few provisions and no medicine and were expected to grow their own food in spite of their health and the harsh environment. Ten of the first twelve to arrive died within two years. The peninsula earned dire nicknames: the painful shore, the living grave.

Change came slowly. Help arrived first in the form of family and friends of the condemned, then religious workers, and much later, government employees. They were known as *kokua*—"helper" in Hawaiian, but a word that eventually came to refer to anyone who lived in the settlement but wasn't a patient. The most famous *kokua* was a young Belgian priest known as Father Damien, who came to minister to the patients in 1873. He made a point of sharing bowls and pipes with patients and counting himself as one of them. "We lepers," he would write. Damien eventually contracted the disease himself and died sixteen years after he arrived in Kalawao. Gandhi later claimed him as an inspiration; in 2009, the Vatican canonized him as a saint.

Gradually, the settlement was relocated to the calmer Kalaupapa side of the peninsula, replacing the village, and the state began to take a more active role in its management. Supplies and care dramatically improved, but dehumanizing treatment continued. Many houses still have wooden boxes on their porches, built there so *kokua* could leave meals for patients—then called inmates, as those accused of having leprosy were arrested and put on trial—without having to go near them. Fences separated the patient and staff areas of the settlement, and endless rules governed when, where, and how those afflicted with the disease could interact with others. The building where families could visit their incarcerated loved ones had a chain-link fence running down its center.

Some patients underwent involuntary tests of experimental medicines; some were sterilized. Those who had children were separated from them. Newly arrived patients, even young children, were told that they would never leave Kalaupapa—that they would die there. "This is your last place," one patient recalled being told.

I stepped off the little Cessna that first morning, sweaty and conspicuous in the winter clothes and pallor I had carried with me from the mainland. My new boss, Steve, met me in his truck to drive me back to the settlement. My job was to prepare for the mandated closure of the peninsula's only landfill by setting up composting, recycling, and waste-prevention programs. Everything we couldn't figure out how to deal with would have to be flown out at high prices or trekked out on the back of a mule. Trash lady, essentially, but like everything here, made much more complicated by separation from the outside world.

Living in Kalaupapa, I'd been warned, meant knowing the math and measurement of isolation. One bar, one post office, one store, to which bread was delivered by plane from topside on Mondays, vegetables on Wednesday mornings, and milk on Wednesday afternoons. (Don't buy too much, or people will talk about it; don't be late, or you won't get any.) A care home for the patients, a cafeteria for workers. No children under sixteen allowed, even for a visit. Twenty-eight patients still living, and no more to come. And one barge a year, a lifeline celebrated like a holiday. It offloaded food, gas, cars, lumber, and other supplies onto the tractor-tire-lined pier that jutted into the bay and left carrying old appliances and junked cars that were finally beyond saving.

Besides the barge and the expensive Cessna flight, the only other reliable way in or out of Kalaupapa was a brutally steep three-mile trail that led to topside Molokai. Its twenty-six switchbacks zig-zagged up the cliff face like a scar, sun-beaten and dusty in the summer and pitted with thick mud in the winter. Once a bridge around a vertical section of cliff was washed away in a landslide, leaving the settlement inaccessible except by plane for nearly seven months.

Steve took a road that led away from the airport along the beach toward the settlement, rumbling over the cattle guards meant to control the goats, boar, and axis deer that overran the island. The strip of land between the road and the ocean was filled with graves—field after field of them. Headstones were wildly tilted in the sandy soil, some collapsed into rubble piles or reduced to jagged fragments of metal rusting in the salt air.

Many of the graves had no headstones at all, just white wooden crosses with names stenciled in black paint. These were clearly among the most recent memorials. The earth beneath them was still heaped up, still decorated with bedraggled stuffed animals and faded plastic flowers, unopened beers with rusty caps. Behind the wheel, Steve caught me gaping. These, he pointed out, weren't even all the marked graves—there were large and small cemeteries all over the peninsula, some only recently reclaimed from the forest. And the known graves accounted for only a small percentage of what the settlement's induction numbers suggested must be here.

A few small wooden cottages started to appear along the road, trucks or ATVs parked in their yards. As we pulled into the center of town, Steve pointed out the churches, the administrative offices, the one-pump gas station, the curving concrete pier. Homes fanned out from the tiny downtown in a loose grid—one-story cottages on short stilts, most built from the same handful of blueprints.

Steve dropped me off at Bay View Home, a complex of long, pale yellow buildings whose porches looked west over a row of palm trees, Kalaupapa's shallow bay, and the receding face of the *pali*. Bay View had once been a dormitory for blind patients but now housed park workers and the occasional volunteer. On my new porch were a couple of wheelchairs, covered in spiderwebs like the rest of the building. There was also an oddly shaped platform that I later learned was a chair for patients to sit on while sores on their feet were treated and dressed.

Bay View sat near the edge of the settlement, one of the last buildings on the way to the trail. From the center of town, it would have been easiest to walk home by cutting through a field next to the care home than to stick to the more circuitous road. But in the center of the field lay the rubble and twisted metal remnants of a hospital—it had been destroyed in a fire when both of the settlement's fire trucks malfunctioned at the same time. Remembering the unmarked graves, I stuck to the road and didn't cut corners. For weeks I wouldn't walk anywhere that wasn't paved.

The Hawaiian word for "taboo" is *kapu*. Unlike its English counterpart, the term hasn't had its ominous religious connotations washed away by overuse: it means the kind of disrespectful behavior that can follow you for the rest of your life, and beyond. I didn't learn the word for weeks or months, but I felt it right away, on my first day in Kalaupapa. I knew enough of the settlement's history to understand that there were invisible rules governing everything around me, but not enough to know what they were or how to avoid breaking them.

On Steve's advice, my first act as a new resident of the settlement was to go to the bar, a tiny place with a few folding chairs and a single refrigerator. I found the place packed; a cow in the pasture above the *pali* had chewed through the settlement's TV cable. A tiny white-haired woman in dark sunglasses, a visor, and a knitted cardigan pulled over a polyester button-down was sitting with her back to a slatted window, presiding over a game of cribbage. She had a bandage on one leg, which had been amputated at the shin, and an orthopedic walking cast on the other. A pair of crutches leaned against the wall by her chair. Her fingers were almost entirely gone.

When it was her turn to shuffle, she spread the cards across the table and stirred them around with an eraser-tipped stick grasped between the nubs of her fingers and her palm before gathering them back up. This, I knew, was Gertrude.

Gertrude drove her gray truck to the bar at four o'clock in the afternoon every day. She never drank, but she was still the place's best customer, the one whose presence kept things hopping. A few years earlier she had stopped coming to the bar at night because she could no longer see well enough to drive home in the dark. Without company or a game to count on, other people stopped coming as regularly, just drifted through or got beer to go. Finally, Gertrude's neighbor, a historical preservationist for the park named Richard, agreed to ride his bike to the bar every night at eight and drive her home in her truck. Cribbage became a nightly ritual and the bar an axis of the settlement's social life.

The bar had been owned by several patients over the years and had operated under a number of names; now a handsaw with FUESAINA BAR painted on it hung outside. In the back room was a counter where Gloria Marks, the current owner, leaned over a ledger, tallying items sold. There were postcards for sale, a whole stack of them featuring a cloud formation that looked vaguely like the face of Father Damien. As in most of Kalaupapa, there were also cats by the dozen, chasing geckos, fighting each other, reclining on the unoccupied chairs. The cats "belonged" to Gertrude, if the word can be used to describe the naming and regular feeding of otherwise feral animals. There was Crooked Tail, named for obvious reasons, and a thin, mustachioed cat she called Hitler.

Gertrude walked me through the rules of cribbage, banging her shuffling stick on the table when I made mistakes in counting points. When it was my turn to shuffle, I shyly told the table I wasn't very good at it. "You got hands!" Gertrude yelled. I shut up and shuffled.

Gertrude's nickname when she was younger was Spitfire. She refused to go to school after seventh grade and would take off on horseback to "the backside"—the wild, uninhabited part of the peninsula east of the settlement, including the jungle that had grown over most of Kalawao—any chance she got. After losing her foot in her thirties, she used her crutches to do things that made the doctors furious, climbing the trail—it was fenced off at the top in those days—and navigating the boulder-strewn beach that led to a deep valley carved into the cliffs. She siphoned gas out of people's cars and hid it in drums in the woods, for no other reason than to do it. She was angry a lot. Much of her anger had to do with her first two husbands, both of whom, she told me, became abusive. She cursed people out, broke up relationships. She freely owned up to having been a general pain in the ass.

Gertrude told these stories readily, matter-of-factly, not long after we met, before I had seen much of her stubborn side myself. Of all the patients, she was perhaps the most open to new people, the easiest to get to know. Anyone, no matter how temporary their stay in the settlement, was welcome to join her for cards, to call her Auntie and ask her about her life. You'd find out right away if she thought you were being rude or an idiot—rolled eyes, slow head-shaking and muttering as she focused intently on her cards—but you'd get plenty of chances to do better. And once she got to liking you, she'd rib you mercilessly about your cribbage playing, shriek at your comebacks—in the right mood, she especially loved jokes about her disability—and add your little bottles of bad wine to her bar tab. But heaven help you if you failed to show up for cards for a few days.

Gertrude would often cover her mouth with her hand while she talked, hiding the effects of the disease. She'd sometimes refer to herself as an ugly old lady, but even into her seventies, she was also an enormous flirt. She was convinced that there were rumors around town—I never heard them from anyone but her—about her "going around" with several young male workers in the settlement.

When Richard, her neighbor and close friend, then in his fifties, had a fight with his girlfriend, Gertrude asked both of them, "Is it me?"

Gertrude first came to Kalaupapa in the early 1940s, when she was eleven years old. The doctor didn't tell her she had leprosy—she insisted that she contracted it only after arriving there. Instead, she told me, the doctor said she was going to live with her mother, who had been sent to Kalaupapa some six years earlier, leaving her family behind on Maui. Gertrude had been told only that her mother was sick and in a hospital; she didn't remember hearing the words *leprosy* or *Kalaupapa*. Her father had remarried, to a woman Gertrude said abused her, including by burning her with a hot iron. She welcomed the move but had little notion of where she was going.

When Gertrude arrived, she met a young woman and embraced her, convinced it was her mother. But Gertrude's mother was already dead. The woman was a patient named Sarah Benjamin who took it upon herself to mentor the young girls who were sent to the settlement. "I could be your mother," she told Gertrude.

In Gertrude's recollection, after a few months in Kalaupapa, the doctors decided she wasn't sick after all and tried to send her home. She was so terrified of returning to her stepmother that she prayed for what she called "the sick." Eventually, it came. "I started to get lumps all over my face, in my mouth, all over my belly," she told me. "Lumps that hurt so much. Nobody can touch you. It was so painful."

She prayed again: "Jesus, I asked you to give me leprosy. But not like this!" And she believed she heard a voice in response: "You asked for it, my child." From that time on, she said, "I came sick, sick, sick. I was all, they called it, bust up." For several years, she was frequently bedridden with pain.

At the time, doctors were still treating leprosy sufferers by injecting them with oil extracted from the seeds of the chaulmoogra tree, a remedy for skin conditions used for centuries in Asia. The injections were painful but arguably a lesser evil than the nausea-inducing practice of taking the oil orally; one doctor wrote in his autobiography that more than one patient told him they'd rather have leprosy.

In 1941 doctors at a leprosarium in Louisiana discovered that a recently synthesized drug could actually cure the disease. The drug required frequent, painful injections, but it marked the beginning of leprosy's gradual retreat from the fearsome place it had occupied in the popular imagination since biblical times. In the 1950s a pill treatment became available, and by the 1970s drug trials were under way for the treatment still used today, a multidrug regimen that can cure leprosy on an outpatient basis. Today those who begin taking medication early on may not experience any noticeable effects at all.

But for those who came to the settlement before the arrival of effective drugs, it was a wringer. Patients who had arrived as children would later describe their terror upon first seeing the settlement's residents, their faces and hands and feet ravaged by the same disease they had contracted. I once asked Gertrude what was the biggest change she'd seen the settlement undergo in her years there. "The patients," she said. "They look more clean."

After the medicine arrived, it took years before state authorities were convinced that it was safe to shut down the quarantine and allow the settlement's residents to return to the world that had expelled them. When they did, they considered closing Kalaupapa altogether. But there were the current patients to consider—many of them were disfigured or disabled and unused to the outside world, where the stigma attached to their disease had not been erased by its cure. So in 1969 the state decided that patients could choose to leave or to stay—to live out their lives in the only home many had known since childhood, protected from prying eyes and supported by the state, free to travel as they wished. Embracing the isolation that had once been imposed on them, hundreds stayed. But no one new would come.

And so Kalaupapa became a place frozen in time. The community continued to exist, but it could not grow, only slowly erode away. Support staff came and went, and small-town life went on, with gossip and grudges and parties and romance. But year by year the population of patients—to whose lives Kalaupapa's current reality is unyieldingly tied—grew older and ever smaller.

The first thing that every patient I met asked me was how long I'd be staying. Many of them found it hard to keep up with the revolving door of temporary workers, forever making friends only to have them leave; some had lodged complaints with administrators to ask for less frequent turnover. I set out to prove that I was serious about being a part of the settlement community, helping plan dinners and parties and an Easter coconut hunt, showing up regularly for cribbage and craft nights and volleyball games. I joined a group that cleaned out the old social hall, scrubbing the ancient movie screen until decades of grime ran off in thick brown drips. The old system of reels carried down the trail by mule was easily replaced with an LED projector and a Netflix subscription, and suddenly we had the only active movie theater on the entire island.

And I started going to church. I wasn't religious; I was just checking out one of the settlement's main activities. But when a church's entire congregation consists of seven people, attendance can't politely be a one-time thing.

Kalaupapa had two active congregations, one Catholic and one Protestant. The Catholic church, St. Francis, had the more robust membership—perhaps not surprising for a place whose most famous former residents are a priest and a nun. (Both Father Damien and Mother Marianne, a nun who ran a hospital for leprosy patients in Honolulu before coming to Kalaupapa in 1888, were sainted in the years after I left.) Unlike the Protestant church, it also had a full-time clergyman, a tiny Belgian octogenarian priest named Father Felix.

But I was raised Presbyterian and never quite figured out when to stand or kneel during Mass, so that first Sunday morning I joined the handful of congregants at Kanaana Hou, a yellow building whose churchyard was ringed with a stone wall and overgrown bougainvillea. We gathered on the church stoop, facing the *hale kahu*, or minister's house, which had stood empty for years. Once every few months a visiting minister would come to preach at Kanaana Hou, but usually it was up to the congregants to run things.

When everyone was gathered, someone pulled the rope to ring the heavy bell in the steeple. We entered together, singing along as Richard played "When the Saints Go Marching In" on his recorder. That week it was up to Pali, an eighty-one-year-old patient and the church's de facto deacon, to lead the service. He chose songs on the fly from the church's English and Hawaiian hymnals, challenging Richard to accompany us or strumming and drumming along himself—he was missing fingers on his right hand—on his perpetually out-of-tune guitar.

Pali, short for Edwin Lelepali, was the life force of the church. Born in Honolulu, he'd been diagnosed with leprosy at ten and sent to Kalihi Hospital on Oahu. He was transferred to Kalaupapa shortly after the Pearl Harbor bombing, sent in a cattle boat along with a large group of mostly child patients—the state figured Kalaupapa would be safer. Like the others, he'd been sent there against his will, but when his father visited a few years later, he told him that he'd fallen in love with the place. Instead of the crowded streets of Honolulu, there was hunting, fishing, camping. He wouldn't go back to Honolulu if he could.

By the time I met him, Pali had buried two wives and countless friends in the graveyard by the beach. He had also buried a series of dogs beneath a row of elegant headstones. AKAMAI: THE BEST WATCH DOG AND LOVED, read one of them. At Kanaana Hou he oversaw the offerings, the annual bingo game, and the meals after funerals.

When it came time for the sermon, Pali stood up, put his hands in his pockets, and spoke briefly and obliquely about struggling with temptation. We closed, as the congregation always did, by singing the first verse of "Blest Be the Tie That Binds," the same hymn that punctuates Thornton Wilder's *Our Town:*

> Blest be the tie that binds
> Our hearts in Christian love.
> The fellowship of kindred minds
> Is like to that above.

After the service, Pali stopped me. "You'll be here next week, yeah?" he asked. The next week he asked the same thing. A few weeks later he told me that the following Sunday it would be my turn to lead the service.

On the last Sunday of each month, we drove across the peninsula to hold an unusually solemn service inside Siloama, the church's predecessor from the days when the settlement was on the Kalawao side. The congregation was formed in 1866, the same year the first patients arrived. The building—a white one-room chapel with a narrow steeple that stood out against the dark green cliffs—had been rebuilt or restored more than once, but it was a reminder that our current congregation was the latest, and perhaps the last, in a direct line that began with some of the first patients to be sent there. There were large tombs in the churchyard, a thick Hawaiian-language Bible on the altar, and an outhouse with the PATIENT and KOKUA signs left intact from the days of strict segregation. On the wall behind the altar was a plaque, installed in the 1950s by another Kanaana Hou congregation. It read:

THRUST OUT BY MANKIND
THESE 12 WOMEN AND 23 MEN
CRYING ALOUD TO GOD
THEIR ONLY REFUGE

FORMED A CHURCH
THE FIRST IN THE DESOLATION
THAT WAS KALAWAO.

One Sunday morning that spring, a tiny dark-haired woman in glasses, a visor, and a colorful muumuu got up to speak. Catherine Puahala was one of Kanaana Hou's most dedicated congregants, but she had lately been sick and unable to attend church; she now stood with help. Catherine was eighty-one. She couldn't keep on weight and was always cold. She spoke that morning about how delicious the warmer air felt, how glad she was not to have to wear a sweater, how blessed we all were that God made the world so good.

Like Pali, Catherine had lived in Kalaupapa since just after Pearl Harbor. She'd had a happy marriage to a man named Jubilee, one of the long-deceased patients I'd at first assumed was still alive, so often did I hear people talk about him. I saw her mostly at church or at community parties, a visor pulled low over her face, her arm almost always intertwined with someone else's. Once someone asked if she and a pretty young nurse were sisters. "Different mothers!" Catherine quipped.

Earlier in life, Catherine had worked with leprosy-patient advocacy groups both on and off the island. The disease had not been kind to her; of all the patients I knew, she had perhaps the most noticeable damage to her face and hands. Her smile might not have been recognizably happy to people who didn't know her, but you could hear her pleasure when she spoke. Her voice was somehow both slurred and precise, her enunciation exaggerated to make up for the effects of lost tissue and numbness. But the kindness and happiness that suffused her words were obvious. We called her Catherine the Great.

———

For decades there was no firm plan for what would happen to Kalaupapa once the last patient was gone. The National Park Service, which started operating on the peninsula in 1980, at the behest of patients who wanted the settlement's history preserved, began formally drafting one only in 2009. Crafting the plan required striking a delicate balance: preserving the peninsula's historical seclusion and sacred status while gradually opening it up to the outside world.

Kalaupapa and its residents had been a source of international fascination for the better part of a century—largely on account of Father Damien, whose story was the subject of books and films as early as the 1930s. As the process of canonizing Damien and Sister Marianne advanced in Rome, reporters and miracle seekers alike began to make pilgrimages to Kalaupapa. Over the course of a few decades, the settlement's patients went from having their outgoing mail fumigated to receiving audiences with Pope John Paul II.

Ever since the patients of Kalaupapa had begun determining their own future in the late 1960s, however, they had carefully guarded their privacy. Many of the modern rules that keep Kalaupapa so isolated—the ban on children, the limits on outside visitors, even the prohibition against surfing (for fear that if residents could surf, outsiders would be tempted to sneak down the trail) had come not from administrators but from the patients themselves. Now the residents of the changeless town found themselves asked to face—and weigh in on—the imminent end of their world. Many simply wished that it would not end, that nothing would change. No development or commercialization, no hotels or camping. Many of them opposed the idea of unescorted visitors, or of visitors staying overnight; a few wanted to maintain the ban on children.

But the end was coming in any case. One of my Bay View Home neighbors was a park employee named JJ, whose job was to tag and organize items that would one day be displayed in a Kalaupapa museum—likely after the patients were gone and more visitors allowed to come. He was cataloging aloha shirts and orthopedic shoes, rosaries and photographs and wheelchairs, musical instruments and specialized tools designed by patients to make everyday tasks easier: opening a soda can, holding a spoon, turning a key, cutting with scissors. Eventually, the curatorial project claimed the foot-dressing chair from the Bay View porch, the one we used to sit on to watch the sunset. It was strange to see it years later, tagged, filed, and de-spidered in a temperature-controlled room filled with furniture and shelves of old prostheses, one of them with a shoe and sock still on it.

It's an odd thing to preserve history as it's still being lived, and surely odder to be a living, breathing character in that history. Early on, I'd expected the patients to be eager to share their stories of the past, their opinions about the way they'd been treated. But they preferred the small-town gossip of the present, what we called the coconut wireless: who was annoyed with whom, who was getting hired or fired, who drank too much at a party, whether the grass was being mowed often enough, whose visitors caught too many fish.

The community meetings that were held monthly by the Patient Advisory Council, the park superintendent, and administrators from the state Department of Health tended to run toward similar matters. Once we spent at least ten minutes gravely discussing eggs: Why did the store run out last week, and what could we do to keep that from happening again? We spent another fifteen minutes debating which dogs were well behaved, which were in heat, and which should be kept on leashes. One week administrators sent around an official memo reminding everyone not to park their car in the middle of the street just because they'd run into someone they wanted to talk to.

One day in July, Auntie Catherine the Great announced that she didn't think she'd be making it until Christmas that year. To the

rest of us, her health seemed no worse than usual, but she was adamant. Christmas was her favorite holiday, and she wanted to have
one more. So one sunny summer day a group of patients and *kokua*
gathered at her house to eat a Christmas feast of turkey, dressing, and cranberry sauce. We hung twinkling lights, and a worker
dressed as Santa. Catherine grinned as we sang our way through her
favorite carols.

A week later Catherine died after being medevaced to a hospital
in Honolulu. She wanted, like so many patients before her, to be buried in Kalaupapa, her last place.

The tropical weather and the absence of a morgue meant that
there was usually little time for mourning before everyone swung
into action, dropping the day's work for the familiar tasks that
follow a death. Maintenance workers took the old backhoe out to
the field by the beach and dug a grave. They assembled the simple wooden coffin from a supply that administrators had ordered
long before. Nurses dressed the deceased in the outfit that, while
living, he or she picked out, packed in a bag, and stored in prepara-
tion: burying clothes. They applied makeup, maybe placed a favorite
stuffed animal in the coffin. In death as in life, Kalaupapa residents
often wore sunglasses, to cover drooping eyelids.

I'd worn black to my first funeral in Kalaupapa—for a patient
named Elaine, who'd once owned the bar and who chose to be buried
in a sequined dress—and stood out ridiculously in the sea of aloha
shirts. The next time I was out of the settlement, I bought my own,
knowing that there would be more occasions to wear it. By the time
I left the next spring, seven more patients would die; Catherine was
the first of them I was close to. It was shocking to see her in Kanaana
Hou, the place where I'd known her best, lying in an open coffin and
somehow looking nothing like herself. We sang "Blest Be the Tie
That Binds," the same hymn we sang at the end of church services
every Sunday, but this time we sang the later verses, too:

We share each other's woes,
Our mutual burdens bear.
And often for each other flows
The sympathizing tear.
When we are called to part
It gives us inward pain
But we shall still be joined in heart
And hope to meet again.

Electric drills emerged to screw the lid onto the coffin. Men hoisted it into the settlement ambulance, a hand-me-down from another island still labeled "Johnson Atoll." Everyone headed out to the cemetery by the beach, where the backhoe stood ready to scoop the dirt back into its place: a grave in front of Catherine's husband, Jubilee.

We were engrossed in the graveside service when one of the settlement's fire trucks rolled up. Without asking anyone else's permission, Kalawaia, a park carpenter, had decided to borrow it to pay tribute. He sent an arc of water over the grave toward the ocean. The sun turned it into rainbows.

Gertrude hated going to the care home to get the dressings changed on the end of her leg and her remaining foot, so she often avoided it. But the disease had left her with little feeling in her extremities, so she didn't notice when her foot became infected late that summer, straining against her bandages. By the time anyone discovered what had happened, her whole lower leg had turned black.

She was sent to the hospital in Honolulu, where doctors wanted to amputate. Losing one foot, however, had been quite enough for her. "You send me back!" she told the doctor once she found out the plan. He warned her that she was likely to die. "Well," she said, "if I die, I die in my house, and in my place, where I love. That's all right with me."

Back at the settlement, Gertrude treated herself with a plant she called "Hawaiian medicine," the precise nature of which she kept a secret from everyone but the settlement cook she trusted to gather it for her. Amazingly, her leg got better. While it healed, she stayed away from the bar—she couldn't use her crutches and hated to be seen in a wheelchair. Instead, I'd visit her little green-trimmed house in the afternoons. We'd look at old pictures and watch TV, and I'd help her cut up steak and open cans of food for her cats. Without the distraction of cribbage, she was free to talk, and I took the chance to ask her about some of the things the patients rarely seemed to want to discuss.

Not long before, a state senator had come to the peninsula to deliver a resolution passed by the legislature, 142 years after the first patients came to Kalaupapa: a formal apology for the way they had been treated. The resolution recognized the patients and their families "for their sacrifices, for thinking more of the public than of themselves, for giving up freedom and opportunities the rest of society takes for granted, for rebuilding their lives with pride and dignity, for overcoming prejudice and discrimination, and for consistently reaching out to others in need."

I asked Gertrude what she thought of the resolution. She said she didn't need an apology—if patients hadn't been quarantined, she said, "people like you folks that don't have the sick" would have gotten it. I considered debating this point with her. In fact, when the Hawaiian government decided to exile leprosy sufferers to Kalaupapa, the risk was lower than anyone knew: leprosy is far less contagious than was once believed, and an estimated 95 percent of people are genetically immune (though the percentage is lower among native Hawaiians and some other ethnic groups). But I didn't. Instead, I asked Gertrude about the part of the apology that said the people of Kalaupapa had "been remarkably resilient and have responded to their situations with kindness, generosity, and for-giveness rather than anger, bitterness, and despair." This seemed like a pretty good summary of what I found most impressive about the patients, I said. Gertrude replied that the legislators must not have talked to the bitter ones.

To explain her own lack of bitterness, Gertrude would often talk about her third husband. When Gertrude's second husband was dying, he asked his cousin Barney to look out for her. Before long Barney asked Gertrude to marry him. She said no; he wasn't a patient, and she couldn't believe he could really want her. But he kept asking, over and over again, for more than fifteen years. In 1995, at sixty-three, she relented. "He didn't wait even a few minutes," Ger-trude told me. "He just went to the priest and told him he's going to marry me." They were married in Father Damien's church in Kala-wao. Barney taught her not to be ashamed of how she looked, to have patience with those who stared on their visits to the mainland. Most of all, she said, he was kind to her and taught her to be kinder to other people. Though he'd been dead for years, she still credited him with her wide circle of friends, the joy of her current life.

There was a big turnout for Gertrude's first night back at the bar. Good news is so rare in the settlement that it demands celebration, and we'd all been worried about how the crumbling edifice of Kalau-papa would withstand a Gertrude-sized hole.

Gloria's husband, Richard, died in December. In February Kuulei Bell, a patient and Kalaupapa's former postmistress, who'd once hung a lei around Pope John Paul II's neck despite being instructed to hand it to an aide, passed away in a Honolulu hospital. We learned of her death at church on a Sunday. Pali, as I'd often heard him do, began counting the remaining patients—who was in Kalaupapa and who was in the hospital, who might be the next to go. Earlier that day he'd gotten upset when I told him I'd be leaving the settlement in a month's time. The familiarity of the news didn't make it easier. I squirmed with the guilt of being the latest person to leave him behind.

In my last few weeks, I hiked to the deep lake inside the crater at the center of the peninsula—a trip I had saved, thinking that leaving something unseen would make the insular peninsula seem bigger than it was. I let the little shrimp that live in the water nibble my toes, thinking of the patients' tales of diving in the lake in their younger days. When I left, I told everyone I'd be back—probably the next winter, I said. I told Gertrude that I'd see her again soon.

But once I was gone from Kalaupapa, time started speeding up again. Soon nearly two years had passed. Then one gray winter day, I got a phone call.

Gertrude died on Christmas Eve in a Honolulu hospital, not in her home after all. But she would be buried in Kalaupapa. She had been adamant that she didn't want a funeral, and my friends who went told me it was a strange, spare graveside vigil. People started telling stories about Gertrude, until a *kokua* interrupted. This wasn't what Gertrude wanted, she said. So people dispersed. I'm sure some of them ended up back at the bar, sure that it seemed empty and wrong without her.

It was a common observation that *kokua* were the only ones who cried at funerals. Patients were stoic; they had already been to so many. In the 1940s, Gertrude used to say, there were sometimes two or three a day; she went to every one. I once asked her how she felt about the eventual end of the patient community in Kalaupapa, the end of the world in which she had lived nearly her entire life. She told me she couldn't imagine Kalaupapa without the patients. "If God gon' bless me to live yet, in those years," she said quietly, "it's going to be very sad for me."

I didn't manage to visit Kalaupapa again until last summer, more than two years after Gertrude's death. Seventeen patients were still living then, but only eight of them were in Kalaupapa. The rest were mostly in the hospital; Norbert Palea, the youngest at age seventy-two, was in prison for smuggling methamphetamine back to Kalau-papa after going to Honolulu for medical treatment. Kanaana Hou's regular congregation was down to four people. Richard had become an official registered member: concerned that the church that had been started in 1866 would end with her and Pali, Auntie Kay, another dedicated patient member, had asked him to join before she died.

Pali was still running things, though somewhat less ebulliently than I remembered, and was still counting patients. "You think they'd keep this place open for just one?" he asked one day as we went riding in his truck. He'd been repeatedly assured that Kalau-papa could be his home as long as he lived, but lately he'd been asking this question. He was still refereeing volleyball games on Wednes-days and Saturdays. People had started to call the game Paliball, and I heard a *kokua* compare it to cribbage and Gertrude: it was hard to imagine it continuing without him.

There was a new effort under way to sterilize the cats, and while you still saw them sleeping most everywhere, including all over the warm, silent streets after dark, they were noticeably fewer and even seemed less mangy. High-speed Internet had finally arrived in Kalau-papa, via a very long cable that snaked over the cliff and down along the trail. The bar was quieter at night than I remembered it.

One day I hitched a ride to the airport and walked back to town through the graveyards along the beach. Nearly five years after Cath-erine's funeral, the sand was still heaped up on her grave. The name on her wooden cross was faded and partially obscured by dozens of leis made of beads, yarn, and fake flowers; unopened Heineken bottles sat at its base. Nearby I found the new graves of Auntie Kay and Uncle Henry.

On the edge of the beach, I found Gertrude's grave, surrounded by its own little rock wall. Her cross, too, was piled with leis, and a forest of plastic flowers populated by ceramic figurines and seashells crowded around it. The cribbage board we used to keep score was sticking halfway out of the sand, its bright paint worn away to bare gray wood.

I didn't think I'd cry, but the wholly expected shock of finding a cross with Gertrude underneath it overwhelmed me, and I did. I sat for a while and watched the waves, the ironwood trees swaying in the trade winds, the afternoon light on the *pali*. It hadn't occurred to me to bring anything to put on the graves, and now I was sorry.

The graveyard was nicer than it used to be: Richard had found some money to repair the headstones that had fallen over or been split apart by rusting metal. As usual, the beach by the graveyard was empty of people, though a few monk seal pups had hauled out on the sand—a highly endangered species enjoying a recent renaissance, taking up residence on the quiet beaches of Kalaupapa. Watching them reminded me of my first hike up the trail to the top of the *pali*. From high up the cliffside, I watched a humpback whale float, still, on the surface of the bay. After a time, she began to thrash about so violently, she disappeared in the roiling water. Then something that looked from a distance like a small gray bullet shot out of the waves: a whale calf taking its first breaths.

My last morning in the settlement, I went around hugging people and promising, once again, to be back soon. Finally, I put on my pack and headed for the trail. There's an overlook at the top, just before it cuts away from the *pali* and toward the topside road. The view of the peninsula from there is a common image on postcards and in books and brochures about Kalaupapa. In person, though, you can see the movement: a truck headed to the salt pools on the lava cliffs north of Kalawao, a tiny, unidentifiable person walking on the black sand beach. I tried to guess by the location and color of the cars who was home, who was visiting the store, who was taking their dogs out for a ride. I needed to get going, but I kept turning back for one last look.

MY
MOTHER'S
LOVER

DAVID DOBBS

TWENTY QUESTIONS

The February after my mother died, my brother, Allen, left his New Mexico home and boarded a plane for Honolulu. He carried aboard a backpack that carried a rosewood box that carried our mother's ashes. The next day, on Maui, he bought six leis and rented a sea kayak. With the leis in a shopping bag at his feet and our mother's ashes in his pack, he paddled into the Pacific.

That day nine years ago was the sort one hopes for in the tropics: warm and balmy, with a breeze that pushed cat's paws over the water. Beyond the mouth of the bay, he could see rising plumes, the spouts of humpback whales gathered to breed. He paddled toward them. When he was closer to the whales than to the shore, he shipped his oar, opened his pack, pulled out the box of ashes, and set it on his lap. He let the boat drift and watched the distant spouts. At one point he was startled when, without any prelude, a whale surfaced about thirty yards away and released a gush of air. It bobbed, noisily breathed, and dove.

Allen wouldn't get a better cue. From the bag at his feet he pulled the leis, one at a time, and set them on the water. They drifted apart to form a loose, expanding circle.

Then he turned the latch on the box and opened it. The ash looked denser and darker than he expected. When he rocked the box back and forth a bit, they shished and gently rattled. Mom. He had traveled a long way to bring her here, but there wasn't much to return. Five pounds of hard ash. He lifted the box, tilted it, and poured her into the sea. Evelyn Jane Hawkins Preston Dobbs, not one to dawdle, dove straight for the bottom.

Four months earlier she had been lying in a bed in Houston's Methodist Hospital, where decades before she and my father had trained as physicians and where she had given birth to four of her six children. She had long been fearsomely strong. *Tough?* we used to joke. *Our mama's so hard you can roller-skate on her.* Now she struggled to breathe. Her hair, once wondrously thick, lay thin and dank. Tubes fed and drained her. Purpura stained her skin. She was eighty years old and had been sick for most of the previous decade. She'd had enough. "A stroke," she said. "Why can't I just have a stroke and die?"

Allen, an emergency room doctor, stood at the head of the bed holding her hand. "Mom, I hate to say it. But a fatal stroke is about the only thing you don't seem at risk of."

"Damn it, Allen, I'm a doctor, too," she said.

"I'm quite aware of that." Allen looked at us helplessly.

Until then it had seemed as if the world would need her permission to finish her. Now she had given it. She closed her eyes.

After a while she said, "Children, I want to talk about later."

"Okay, Mother," said Sarah. Sarah was the fourth of the six children, the one who lived nearest to her and had done the most to look after her. "What about later?"

"When I'm gone," she said, "I'd like to be cremated."

This was new. In the past, she had talked about getting buried next to her father, who was in a leafy cemetery in Austin.

"Okay," said Sarah.

"And I want you to spread my ashes off Hawaii. In the Pacific. Will you do that for me?"

"Sure, Mom," said Allen. "We can do that."

My mother smiled at him and squeezed his hand.

"Mother?" Sarah asked. "May we ask why the Pacific?"

She closed her eyes. "I want to be with Angus."

We children exchanged glances: Had anyone seen this coming? Heads shook, shoulders shrugged.

What we knew of Angus was this: Angus—the only name we had for him—was a flight surgeon our mother had fallen in love with during World War II, planned to marry after the war, but lost when the Japanese shot him down over the Pacific. Once, long ago, she had mentioned to me that he was part of the reason she decided to be a doctor. That was all we knew. She had confided those things in the 1970s, in the years just after she and my father divorced. I can remember sitting in a big easy chair my dad had left behind in her bedroom, listening to her reminisce about Angus as she sat with her knitting. I remember being embarrassed and not terribly interested.

I was interested now. Even thirty years before, her affair with Angus had been three decades old. Now, sixty years after he had fallen into the sea, she wanted to follow him.

"Of course," said my brother. "We'll do that for you, Mom."

A week later, seemingly on the mend, she went home to the elder center where she lived. For a week or so she continued to gain strength. But then she started to have trouble breathing, was admitted to the home's care center, and on her second day there, suddenly stopped breathing. Despite a standing do-not-resuscitate order, the staff tried three times to revive her, to no avail. The doorman told me later that when the ambulance arrived and the medics rolled her out, she was "blue as can be, Mr. Dobbs. Blue as can be." The hospital, too, tried to bring her back, and they were still trying when Sarah arrived. By that time our mother was brain dead and could breathe only with a tube—precisely the situation she had sought to avoid. Sarah gathered her strength and told the nurses that this was against her mother's wishes and she must insist they remove the breathing tube. "It was like jumping off a cliff," she told me later. "It was the hardest thing I've ever done. It was harder than pushing out a kid." The nurses called the doctors.

As they pulled out the breathing tube, my mother bit down on it.

Sarah screamed, "Oh, my God, she's fighting for life!" The doctors, assuring Sarah that this was a common reflex, tugged the tube free. Then they left.

Sarah sat next to the bed and laid her head next to our mother's and held her hand. With the tube gone, my mother's breathing slowed. Sarah cried against her neck. It took about ten minutes.

An hour later my brother, sitting in his car on the side of a highway in New Mexico, called me to tell me she had died.

"So it wasn't a stroke," he said after we'd talked a while. "But at least it was fast."

"Have to admire it," I said, laughing. "Mom always got pretty much what she wanted."

Or so a child likes to think.

By the time Allen got her to Hawaii, three months had passed. In the meantime we'd held two memorial services in Texas, after which I returned to my home in Vermont, where the coldest winter in a generation had the place in a lock. When I opened Allen's email describing the ceremony he had fashioned, I was sitting at my office desk overlooking the North Branch of the Winooski River, which was frozen three feet deep and topped by three feet of snow. I read Allen's email twice, looked at the pictures, looked out my window, read his email again. I wondered how much you could discover about a person sixty years dead when all you knew about him was his name was Angus, likely a nickname. I'd had three weeks—three decades, actually—to ask my mother such things before she died, but had not. Now, with ice and snow outside and Hawaiian light sparkling in my head, I picked up the phone and called my mother's cousin Betty Lou.

"What do I know about Angus?" said Betty Lou, repeating my question. Betty Lou has a beautifully soft North Texas accent. She was down in Wichita Falls, Texas, where she and my mother had grown up together, sometimes in the same house, much as sisters. It was cold there too.

She took a deep breath. "Well, there's not a whole lot I knew about Angus. But I knew his real name was Norman, I'm pretty sure it was, and he came from Iowa. He was divorced. They met in San Antonio when he was stationed there awhile. During the war. She was out of her head with that man. When he got stationed to Hawaii, she followed him clear out there. He ended up getting sent way out in the Pacific—Guam, Iwo Jima, somewhere like that—and got killed right near the end of the war."

"How'd she find out?"

"She got a letter from somebody in his outfit. Letter actually reached her *after* the war ended. And that letter, David, just about destroyed your mama. She could not be consoled. Weeks. I've never seen anybody grieve like that. Before or since. She did eventually pick herself up and go on, because you knew her, David—your mama was a strong woman. She even scared me sometimes. But I'm not sure she ever got over losing Angus."

"You remember his last name?"

"Best I recollect, was Z-something. Zert, Zaret, Zart. Something like that."

"You sure it started with a *Z?*" I asked. "That could make things a lot simpler."

"I hope so, David. Because beyond that it gets pretty dang complicated."

It took me about twenty minutes online to find a copy of the *World War II Honor List of the Dead and Missing, State of Iowa.* The book was just scanned pages, not digitized, with the names listed alphabetically by county. All I had to do was scroll to the end of each county's listings, past the Adamses and Joneses and Moores and Smiths and Thompsons, and look for Zs. There were not many. I found him about halfway through the book, in Johnson County:

ZAHRT NORMAN E 01700383 CAPT M

The *M* meant he was missing.

I began searching genealogy sites for anyone in Iowa named Zahrt. Every time I found someone, I sent an email saying I was seeking information about a Captain Norman E. Zahrt, who was a close friend of my mother—sometimes I phrased it as "a dear friend of my mother"—who according to a letter she received was either killed or went missing in action toward the end of the war. I sent about a dozen of these emails and got a few replies, all negative. After a couple of weeks, I opened my email one morning and found a new response:

> *David,*
> *What a surprise to get an email from you. Yes, my father is Norman Zahrt. My mother is Luella. Norman and Luella had two children: David born Sep 37 and Christy born Jan 40. I have attached a file which I presume you can open. It is Norman's graduating medical school class. Please let me know whether or not you can identify Norman.*
>
> *I don't have words to describe the mixed emotions that come to me when I revisit this issue. I've come to learn that in the process of growing up one accumulates scars. And that the challenge is learning to own your scars, and live them.*
>
> *You can imagine that this inquiry fills me with questions.*

I didn't have to imagine the questions. He listed nineteen of them:

1. *What prompted this search?*
2. *How long has the notion of this search been "brewing"?*
3. *What brings you to the point of finding Norman's descendants and asking these questions?*
4. *What is your mother's name?*
5. *What was your mother's occupation?*

6. *Do you have a picture of her you could share with us?*

7. *Are you certain that Norman and your mother met in San Antonio?*

8. *If so what was your mother doing at the time in San Antonio?*

9. *Was your mother in the military?*

10. *Was she assigned to Hawaii?*

11. *Did she travel to Hawaii with the express purpose of seeing Norman?*

12. *Did your mother affirm that Norman was divorced, or did you receive that information from a secondary source?*

13. *Who was Norman's friend who wrote to your mother after the war?*

14. *Is Norman's friend still alive?*

15. *Can we reach Norman's friend?*

16. *Is your father still alive?*

17. *Can you tell us a little bit about your father?*

18. *Did he know that his wife wanted to be with Norman?*

19. *What else can you tell us about your mother?*

As you can imagine this is, to say the least, an interesting surprise. My sister and I would like to entertain a continuing exchange with you, but this is probably enough to begin with.
david

I had never seen a note at once so prosecutorial and generous. For days I dithered. Finally I wrote and answered all nineteen of his questions as best I could.

When David, along with his sister, Christy, responded, they did so with an openness that showed they really did want to own their scars. My mother posed as big a mystery to them as their father did to me. We began a long collaborative search—dusty records, strained recollections, tree-shaded graveyards—that ends, for lack of a better marker, with the story I'm about to tell you.

SAN ANTONIO

For years my mother wore a gold locket. When I was a boy, I liked to pull it up from inside her blouse on its chain so I could squeeze the curved button that ran along one edge and make the curlicued gold cover, heavily sprung, pop open to reveal a photograph of my mother's grandparents. On an elegant chair sat my grandmother and my mother's namesake, Ivy Evelyn Stone, a formidable-looking woman wearing a full skirt, a fuller blouse, and an immensely confident expression. Next to her chair stood her husband, Gene, a railroad engineer in their hometown of Wichita Falls. Especially in Wichita Falls, a railroad town, this was a high-status position then, like that of an airline pilot fifty years later. He is dressed in suit and tie, hair slicked, with his hand on the back of the chair.

I viewed this portrait as a fair representation of the distant world from which my mother came: a stable, solid existence full of aunts and uncles and her mother and father and grandparents all living toughly but carefully in the high bright sunstruck towns of North Texas. The picture agreed with the steady, accomplished, morally sturdy person I and many others knew my mother to be. But it hid the fact that she came from a world that moved violently beneath her feet.

When my mother was young, her grandmother Ivy Evelyn, the one in the locket, was about the only person in her life who moved steadily, trainlike, along predictable lines. My mother's own mother, Clara Lee—Ivy Evelyn's daughter—ran fast and wobbly. In Wichita Falls, she earned a reputation as a rounder, meaning she got around. Soon after finishing high school, Clara Lee moved to Dallas. There she met and married George Hawkins, an eighteen-year-old busboy who shared her notion of a good time. This notion quickly produced my mother, Evelyn Jane, but it did not produce a steady marriage. They split within a year. Clara Lee took my mother back home to

Wichita Falls, and Ivy Evelyn soon found herself tending young Evelyn Jane, first occasionally, while Clara Lee went out, and then full time, when Clara Lee fled, alone, back to Dallas. Ivy had barely finished raising Clara Lee to adulthood. Now she was raising Clara Lee's two-year-old.

My mother proved a cheerful, obedient girl—an ardent student popular with her schoolmates and lively and memorable enough to appear in a novel (*If Wishes Were Horses*, now long out of print and unobtainable) that a childhood friend wrote a couple of decades later. She grew up keenly aware of what constituted proper behavior. Dark remarks about her mother stung. Yet soon after she graduated high school, she got serious with a local man named Carroll Preston, and within a year she married him. She was nineteen, and he was only twenty. In some ways, this marriage seemed to reject Clara Lee's errant path for Ivy's straighter track. The story about my mother's wedding on the society page of the *Wichita Record News*, October 8, 1940, mentions her mother only at the very end. Still, soon after the wedding, my mother became pregnant. Preston tried to make a go of it, working at a restaurant. But there are hints she found him boring, and they soon divorced.

And so at twenty-two, Evelyn Jane Hawkins Preston found herself in a position remarkably similar to the one her own mother had occupied two decades prior: she had a high school degree, a young daughter, a divorce, no husband, and few work prospects, and she lived with her parents—who, after an interval of almost twenty years, had remarried each other. This was actually Clara Lee's sixth marriage and George's fifth, for they had both married promiscuously since their divorce. This marriage, however, would last almost twenty-five years, until George died in 1967.

That my mother's parents steadied only after letting others raise her must have chafed. Yet my mother made the most of it, letting Clara Lee help raise Lynn and, in an elegant Oedipal coup, enjoying some time with her father, whom she adored.

It was about this time, in 1943 or early 1944, that my mother took a job at one of the cafeterias at Kelly Air Force Base, just outside San Antonio. The war was in full roar, and the base was growing rapidly, with pilots and crews training for the Army Air Forces.

Sometime in 1943 one of those crews brought Norman Eldridge Zahrt to Kelly. Norman had arrived in Texas the year before, bringing his own overstuffed baggage. Born January 5, 1915, he was almost six years older than my mother. He had lived a fairly ordinary boyhood in Marengo, Iowa, where his parents farmed corn. He did his share of farmwork, fished, and shot photographs, publishing at least one, of a tornado spout, while in high school. He was strikingly handsome and known for surprises. He surprised his family, for instance, by becoming the first Zahrt to attend college, at the University of Iowa in Iowa City, thirty miles southeast of Marengo.

He surprised them again in the middle of his senior year by eloping with Luella Sprague, who had graduated as valedictorian at Marengo's only high school and was attending a teachers college in Iowa City. During their Christmas vacation in 1936, Norman and Luella drove two hundred miles west to Elk Point, South Dakota, a border town suited to a quick wedding. David, their first child, arrived nine months later. Luella dropped out of teachers college. Norman finished his bachelor's and then startled everyone further by entering the University of Iowa medical school. Christy, David's sister, was born the year Norman got his M.D., 1940.

In the fall of 1942, when Norman was starting an obstetrics residency, he was drafted by the U.S. Army Air Forces. He went to Florida for basic training and then, over a fourteen-month stretch beginning in January 1943, to several Texas air bases. He fetched Luella, David, and Christy from Iowa, and they settled in Houston, where he sometimes worked at Ellington Air Force Base. David and Christy remember the house being on Houston's western outskirts so Norman could easily travel west to San Antonio. Sometime that year, in San Antonio, he met my mother.

Any foreboding Luella felt at all this change would have been hard to separate from a wariness natural to her experience. Her father died two weeks before she was born. Her mother died when she was three years old. When she was nine, her adoptive mother died.

Now, in January or February 1944, when she and Norman and the kids had been in Texas for just over a year, Norman informed Luella that he was going to Mississippi, where he would train as a flight surgeon for the Air Forces' Fourth Emergency Rescue Squadron, or 4th ERS—a new sort of outfit that would specialize in rescuing pilots shot down over water. It was hazardous duty and would pay accordingly. He would train for three months in Gulfport, Mississippi, then head for the Pacific.

In March he put Luella and the kids on a train to Iowa and moved east. About that time, he wrote his best friend from college, Don Reese, that he was trying to arrange for his lover, a woman named Evelyn Jane whom he had met in San Antonio, to follow him to Gulfport. When they could not pull that together, they turned their focus to Hawaii. My mother, aided by an acquaintance of her father's who was in the Army Air Forces, secured a job in Oahu, where the 4th ERS was to move in July. To get the job, she had to sign a contract promising to stay for a year. She left for Hawaii that summer, probably June, by way of Seattle.

She was chasing a man with two small children. And she was leaving her own three-year-old, my half-sister, Lynn, with the very parents who had abandoned her twenty years prior.

HAWAII

Of their time in Hawaii no letters survive, nor diaries, and Angus's military records are skeletal. But there are pictures, and the pictures tell a tale.

Angus had time to take a lot of them. The 4th ERS found themselves mostly idle in Hawaii, waiting for planes coming from the West Coast and then for the Allies to take and secure the bases in Guam, Saipan, and Iwo Jima that were the 4th's ultimate destinations. Angus performed physicals on the men and taught swimming—something, as a fellow medical officer in the unit later said, it seemed it might be useful to know.

Dozens of his photos now occupy an album my mother left in a box full of other things so varied and trivial that my sister almost tossed the whole lot. The leather cover is crumbling, the thick pages have browned, but the photos, corner-mounted, remain sharp and clear. Amid pictures of buddies in flight suits, of Angus smoking in the bubble of a gunner's window on an army plane, of men playing cards, of a tired-looking Angus reclining bare-chested in a plywood easy chair, are pages and pages of Angus and Evelyn Jane.

In the pictures of them together, they often look like newly-weds. One photo appears as if it could be a snapshot of the day my mother came off the boat. It bears no date, yet carries a distinct air of arrival. She and Angus are walking down a sidewalk still patchily wet in the Hawaiian sunshine, as if a shower has just passed over. My mother, who liked to dress well, looks sharp in a tailored trench coat and sunglasses. She carries a newspaper under one arm and smiles cheerfully but with a slight wariness, as if the picture is a bit more than she would like on the record. Close beside her—there isn't an inch between them—walks Angus. He wears his khaki uniform and leather jacket. He beams.

If my mother looks a bit recalcitrant in that photo, she seems to have lost all such reservations by October, the date on the back of a series of ten photographs of her and Angus playing with a half-dozen puppies on the front lawn of a ranch house, which stands conspicuously behind them. While it's possible that this was someone else's house and someone else's puppies, no one looking at these pictures would think so. They reek of an effort to record a happy domesticity. They are family portraits. Of course, they probably were not living together; it's hard to see how Angus would have been allowed to live off base. Yet the two of them seem, to use a phrase of delicacy my mother would later favor, familiar with each other.

Yet in many of the photos, an anxiety seems to pervade. They had to know that their time together would end in war. And they had left kids behind. You can't find a single photograph here that looks the same when you view it with that in mind.

Around the time these photos were taken, Angus wrote Luella asking for a divorce.

One later photograph looks very much like the one of her arrival, yet different in its subtleties. Again they walk down the street. Again a sailor passes behind. Palm trees rise in the background. Angus wears his summer khakis with no jacket, his tie tucked into his shirt placket, and a soft garrison cap has replaced the billed crusher he wears in the earlier picture. My mother also wears a khaki suit, skirted, and it bears above her left breast an insignia that seems to include wings. She has got herself into something, some auxiliary outfit supporting the USAAF. She's doing her part.

So what's different? For starters, they look hot and tired. And where before perhaps an inch separated them, now a foot of tense space stands between. Angus, hidden behind aviator sunglasses, walks slightly in front and to one side. He manages a defiant dignity by looking straight at the camera. But my mother turns an ashen face away from both Angus and the camera. She looks as if she wishes she were somewhere else. Was she suddenly feeling ashamed? Had she and Angus been fighting? Had the regrets latent in the earlier photographs broken into the open? Or had the rolled-up papers in Angus's front pants pocket—awkward to carry but apparently too important to discard—brought bad news?

Bad news found them at least twice in Hawaii. The first bad news came in late November that year, 1944, when Luella wrote Angus refusing the divorce he'd requested. No one knows whether Norman ever told my mother about this.

The other ill tidings arrived in December, when the Army Air Forces ordered the 4th ERS to Saipan. Angus would ship out in

January. Evelyn Jane, having signed on for a year, would remain in Hawaii—her lover three thousand miles west, her daughter three thousand miles east—another six months.

TO WAR

The Fourth Emergency Rescue Squadron sailed from Oahu on January 19, 1945, aboard the USS *President Johnson*, a transport ship that had been around since 1903. It stopped at Midway, then, dodging Japanese subs on the way, reached Saipan, in the Mariana Islands in the far western Pacific, on February 6.

If Norman craved adventure, the deployment almost surely answered. The Emergency Rescue Squadrons had been formed in the summer of 1943 to consolidate the Army Air Forces' prior efforts to rescue aircrews shot down or forced to ditch. In Europe the ERS units worked out of the United Kingdom and, later, Italy. In the Pacific, they hopscotched west and then north along the long curve of coral archipelagos—New Guinea, the Philippines, the Marshalls, the Marianas, and finally Iwo Jima—that the Allies took to secure bases in their slow, bloody push toward Japan. Taking these islands required some of the war's most horrific battles. Hundreds of thousands died. The fight for Iwo Jima alone killed almost 7,000 American servicemen and some 19,000 Japanese. The ERS units played a small but critical role in this push toward Japan. Before their arrival, 80 percent of Allied pilots shot down in the Pacific theater died or were taken prisoner. Once the Emergency Rescue Squadrons began working out of their far Pacific bases in 1944, they rescued more than half of the downed pilots. They saved several thousand men. Angus's unit alone, in the roughly two hundred days it operated from Saipan and then Iwo Jima, flying 862 missions, rescued 577 airmen.

The ERS crews relied heavily on two planes. One was the B-17, the flying fortress that was the war's busiest bomber. The B-17 could fly up to two thousand miles, and crews loved it because it could keep flying even when horribly damaged. Dozens flew home with huge holes torn in them by antiaircraft fire or enemy fighters. One landed with most of its nose torn off. Another had its tail section all but severed in a collision with an enemy fighter yet made it back to base, where the tail collapsed on landing. B-17s also ditched well, floating up to half an hour, whereas the B-29s and B-25s that shared bombing duties in the Pacific usually sank in seconds. The B-17s used by the rescue squadrons were adapted at the factory to leave the bomb-bay area largely empty. Each carried under its belly a twenty-seven-foot lifeboat that could be dropped by parachute to downed aircrews.

The rescue squadrons also flew the Catalina PBY—a flying boat. The Cat's wings and engines sat atop its boat-shaped fuselage, allowing the plane to land and take off in seas with waves as high as six feet. The PBY served well as either patrol plane or light bomber. Several squadrons' worth, the Black Cats, were painted flat black to hide them from radar and antiaircraft gunners when dive-bombing Japanese ships at night. Like the B-17, the PBY had enough range to support distant bombing missions. It carried a crew of eight, some of whom manned heavy machine guns in the plane's nose and sides if the plane encountered fighters.

Rescue could be dangerous, dirty work. In the Pacific, the crews typically flew in support of the endless sorties of heavy bombers and support fighters that were attacking Japan every day. As the warplanes neared their targets and began taking fire, the rescue planes would hang back and circle, monitoring their radios for word of downed planes. If a B-17 found a crew in the water, it would drop its boat, then radio for a ship or submarine to rescue the airmen. A PBY might do the same or attempt a direct rescue.

These attempts were always risky, as the PBY was slow, lightly armed, and not terribly sturdy. Even successful rescues could be harrowing.

By the time the 4th ERS reached Saipan, the Allied advance had taken enough territory from the Japanese that everyone had heard what sorts of horrors might await a crew shot down and captured. One PBY crew had been downed, captured, tortured, and then, as a spectacle to raise morale, dragged one at a time before the assembled Japanese troops, made to kneel, and beheaded with swords. This is why even pilots who didn't know how to swim ditched at sea rather than on land.

Angus and his mates lived first in tents, then in plywood huts. The photos Angus mailed to my mother—most of them two-inch-square prints, a few blown up larger—show him and his buddies first building and then living in these large, open barracks. He sent shots of his mates playing cards and posing in combat garb and flight gear—Angus wearing full leathers with a fur collar, a bulky parachute, and a Mae West life vest, a .45 automatic on his hip.

Angus, perhaps enjoying extra privilege as both a captain and a doctor, received a corner area in the plywood barracks, with room for a plywood writing desk and easy chair. The photo album holds a notable quartet of photos of Angus sitting in that chair. In one he reads. In another he smiles groggily. In a third he appears to sleep. In the last he looks as if he's tiring of either the photos or the photographer or the war or everything. On the wall behind him in these photos, tucked into a strap in his hanging suit bag, is a large print of a brunette in pinup pose. She reclines, apparently on a bed or couch or floor, with her arms up and bent so that they frame her face, her hands gently holding her wrists on the cushion just above her head. Within this tiny two-by-two-inch print, the pinup occupies less than an eighth of an inch square. I had to use a loupe to tell whether the woman was wearing a blouse. I had to use a magnifying glass and a bright flashlight to see that she was my mother.

It's not clear how often they wrote. Mail moved slowly—weeks to clear the censors, miles, chaos, and bureaucracy between Saipan and Oahu. Later, when my mom returned to San Antonio, the letters, three or four weeks old, came every week or two. For six months, though, separated from both lover and daughter, she had only the mail with which to bind what she hoped would be a new family. Apparently, nothing in Angus's letters made her doubt those hopes.

LOST

Pushing the Japanese across the Pacific required enormous savagery and persistence. No amount of firebombing—and the USAAF was incinerating thousands, even tens of thousands of civilians a day now—seemed to weaken Japan's resolve. Almost no one knew about the atomic bombs that would speed the war's end. By June 1945, when my mother sailed back to the States, the Allies' plans called for five more months of heavy bombing followed by a massive ground invasion. Most people expected the war to run into 1946.

On July 22 Angus wrote my mother asking if she had gotten back to San Antonio yet. He complained of heat, dust, bad food, thirst. He bemoaned "the 2–3 inches backwards you slide in this sand with each step, which makes me very tired." All that, he wrote, "coupled with an extreme lethargy from the heat, I guess, left me pretty depressed. There's nothing very good about this letter, I guess. It's about as lifeless as I feel."

Three days later, in the first hours of July 25, Angus was with the 4th ERS detachment at Iwo Jima when a call came in for a B-17 search and drop. Amid especially heavy bombing on the twenty-fourth, with hundreds of bombers igniting firestorms in multiple cities on the Japanese mainland, a fighter pilot flying in support of the bombers had been hit and bailed out near Lake Hamana, a coastal bay 150 miles west of Tokyo. The 4th quickly readied a B-17 to find him.

Angus was not on flight duty that night. He was free to stay on base. B-17s often flew without flight surgeons, since they never picked anyone up. But the commotion either woke him from sleep or rescued him from its pursuit, and he gathered his gear and cameras, donned his flight suit, and joined the crew of nine aboard a B-17 known as *Jukebox 21*. Since he played no functional role on the flight, he was, in technical and bureaucratic terms, a passenger.

The crew aimed to hit the coast near first light, find the pilot, and drop him a lifeboat. A U.S. submarine, the *Peto,* lurked nearby ready to fetch him. *Jukebox 21* cleared the runway at 0245 hours and headed north toward Lake Hamana, 750 miles away. At 225 miles an hour, it would reach the coast in about three and a half hours. Although the crew didn't have to worry about enemy fighters—the Japanese Air Force had already been decimated—they surely expected anti-aircraft fire, and given the bombing the area had suffered lately, they could expect the antiaircraft crews to be inspired. Only a month before, the Allies had firebombed the city of Shizuoka, just east of Lake Hamana, destroying more than half the city and killing over ten thousand.

Yet *Jukebox* was well maintained: a sturdy plane crewed by experienced men and a pilot who'd flown a full tour in Europe before joining the 4th in Iwo Jima. It was a good night to fly, dark but clear. And it was always a relief to climb from the heat of the islands into cooler air.

They called in for their first two hourly radio checks right on schedule, at 0345 and 0445. But at 0545, *Jukebox* neither called nor responded.

When several more hours passed, the 4th ERS sent twelve planes to look for *Jukebox*. For two days, in rotating flights out of Iwo Jima, Angus's squadron mates and other crews systematically worked grids between *Jukebox*'s last radio position and Lake Hamana. They found nothing. Months later the unit's commander, William Lindsey, wrote the father of *Jukebox*'s radio operator, Sergeant Charles Hurn, that "the disappearance of this plane has always been a complete mystery." It was the 4th's worst loss of the war, and its last. Three weeks after *Jukebox* went missing, Japan surrendered.

PERSONAL EFFECTS

In the days just after the war ended, as my mother readjusted to life in San Antonio with her mother, father, cousin, and daughter, two letters reached her from Iwo Jima. The first was Angus's of July 22, lamenting the heat and sand. "I love you very much," he reassured her. "I miss you always, but not acutely, for the demands of my environment haven't given me time to think of it too much."

The second letter, arriving a week or two later, was written by one of Angus's squadron mates. It informed her that Angus's plane had disappeared, that a two-day search had turned up nothing, and that the crew were now presumed dead. With this letter, the last she would ever receive from or about Angus, my mother became a survivor of the unfound.

Luella's notice came through more official channels, and sooner: she received word from the USAAF in early August that Angus was missing in action. Later she seems to have received the sort of letter that Commander Lindsey had written in October to Charles Hurn's father, explaining that the crew were presumed dead. It's clear that in or around October she did receive from Lindsey $500 worth of war bonds that Norman owned and had with him, along with his last paycheck, for $209. Luella, who had moved to Iowa City earlier that year, wrote Lindsey that it was "reasonable, almost a certainty, that my husband had more money than this amount" and that she would like Lindsey to help find it. Conceivably she suspected my mother had it. Lindsey wrote back saying no other funds were found or known of.

Then, around Thanksgiving, the army quartermaster's office sent something more substantial: Angus's footlocker, which contained the personal effects he had left in his bunk area. The accompanying inventory listed four pairs of khaki pants, seven khaki shirts, two ties, one pair of boots, and one pair of eyeglasses; one medical-notes zipper case, one medical manual, and one *Basic History of the United States;* one set of dominoes; one record player (broken); one box of camera attachments (the camera apparently having gone missing with Angus); and one "bundle miscellaneous." Did that bundle include the pinup photo of my mother? Did it include her letters? It seems reasonable, though far from certain, that Angus's cabin mates removed all that before someone packed and sent his things. One hopes so.

By the time Luella received the footlocker, a year had passed since she had refused Norman's request for a divorce. She had refused on the advice of a lawyer who essentially told her, "Not now. He's half a world away. Let another year pass. Let the war end. If he still wants a divorce then, fine. But not now. It's a war. Everybody's crazy." This proved good legal advice. Had they divorced, Luella would have lost substantial death benefits for both herself and her children, who went to college on them. Had Angus lived, it might have proved good marital advice. But her refusal also carried a downside. It allowed him to now leave her yet again. Having been abandoned three times by her parents, Luella had now been thrice abandoned by Norman as well: once when he volunteered for the 4th ERS; a second time when he fell for my mother; and a third when he fell from the sky.

Luella still had David and Christy, now nine and five, to care for. And soon she had a new love, her husband's old college friend Don Reese.

Reese had grown up in Turin, Iowa, and met Norman at the house of a fraternity they both joined at the University of Iowa. Though he did not attend medical school afterward, Don took a pre-med curriculum alongside Angus. Through Angus he met Luella. But he already had a love of his own: a young woman named Nell, whom he'd known since he was a boy.

In Don and Angus's last year at college—the same year Angus married Luella, and perhaps inspired by that union—Nell began to press Don for marriage. When Don's parents objected, he balked. He and Nell remained at this impasse when Don graduated and took a job in Chicago.

A year later, still at odds, he convinced a wary Nell to move to Chicago for the summer so they could be near each other. She did and found a job at the Bon Air Country Club. Family accounts of that summer are vague. According to one, Don and Nell spent a lot of time quarreling over Don's continued fence-sitting. One evening late in August, soon before Nell would have to return to school in Iowa, Don arranged to pick her up after work. He parked across the street from the Bon Air and waited. Eventually Nell emerged and started walking across the street. For whatever reason—distraction; tension; emotional confusion; fatigue; the late hour—she failed to notice an oncoming car. As Don watched, the car ran over Nell, killing her instantly.

Three years later, not long after the attack on Pearl Harbor, Don enlisted in the navy. For four years he served as a medical corpsman on landing craft in the Pacific, undersupplied and overwhelmed, struggling to patch together Marines torn to bits in the beach landings. When the war ended, he was discharged and returned to Iowa City. On arriving, he learned that Norman had died. Not long after, he ran into Luella. That was roughly about the time she received Angus's footlocker. She and Don married the following October.

According to David and Christy, Don and Luella seemed badly haunted by the ghosts of their lovers and by things never said or done. Back in 1944, for instance, it was Don to whom Angus had written to tell of his hopes of bringing my mother with him to Gulfport. Did Don ever tell Luella that he had known this? Whether shared with Luella or held close, his early knowledge of Norman's affair, and the complicity it created, had to prove an awkward weight, and only one among many. Don and Luella were, says Christy, an affectionate couple, but they carried burdens and resentments that rose less from one another other than from the many losses they had suffered. "We grew up in anger soup," Christy later recalled. My mother, of course, was a key ingredient.

In their house, says Christy, the name Norman Zahrt was rarely heard. "We learned," says Christy, "you just didn't bring it up."

Luella was doing the best she could to forget Norman. But unbeknownst to her, someone else was trying to dig him up.

UNTIL THEY COME HOME

Norman was one of tens of thousands of World War II soldiers, sailors, and airmen missing when the fighting ceased. In the months and years after the war ended, a section of the army quartermaster's office called the Graves Registration Services began a relentless effort, which continues even today, to locate them. One of the GRS's first steps was to send crews to Japan to find crash sites. Using local interviews, archaeological excavations, forensic exams, medical and dental records, and Missing Air Crew reports, they sought to find and identify the bodies of those missing. In the early summer of 1946, a GRS team working near Lake Hamana learned that a B-17 had crashed there on July 25 the previous year. Locals told the GRS team that they had buried ten crewmen nearby. But when the team searched the area, they found only a bit of a propeller and a few random parts—enough to know they'd found a B-17 but not to identify it.

A year later another GRS team returned and found more wreckage, including three engines. The engines' serial numbers conclusively identified the plane as *Jukebox 21*.

They also found ten badly decomposed bodies buried in shallow graves. The bodies showed no bullet holes, blade marks, or other signs of attack. Many had crushed ribs and shattered bones in their hands, feet, and lower legs—injuries common in violent crashes. Locals in the area confirmed that the plane crashed on July 25, 1945, amid heavy antiaircraft fire. Graves Registration concluded that

Jukebox had been downed by antiaircraft fire and that the crash killed all aboard.

But the excruciatingly difficult task of identifying the dead remained. GRS could not simply say that the ten bodies found near *Jukebox 21* were those of the ten crewmen listed in the plane's missing aircrew report. They had to definitively identify each.

By this time the GRS had established a large cemetery and forensics center in Yokohama. There they examined the ten bodies found near the *Jukebox* crash site and compared them with medical and other records for the plane's crew members. They quickly identified six of the ten. But they felt enough doubt about the other four that they left them unidentified, and these became Unknown Bodies X-408, X-412, X-415, and X-416. The skeletons of X-408 and X-416 were fairly complete, with a few bones missing from hands, feet, and lower legs. Scavengers or the crash impact had reduced X-412 and X-415 to fragments of skull, jaw, torso, and upper legs.

Graves Registration wrote the families of the six identified airmen and sent their remains home. It did not contact the families of *Jukebox*'s four other crew members' families, which included Norman. For a year the four unidentified bodies lay buried in new graves in Yokohama while the GRS worked through more promising cases.

In autumn 1948, however, someone in the GRS reexamined Norman's file and fixed on two pieces of information that the first examiners had either lacked access to or failed to notice. One was a record of distinctive dental work that Norman had received while in Saipan and that was thus missing from the dental records made at his military induction. The other was a note in his medical history, probably easy to overlook, that as a boy he had broken his collarbone. With these two bits of information foremost, the GRS reexamined the forensic-exam files of the four unknowns remaining from *Jukebox 21*'s crash site. The file showed that Unknown X-408's forensic exam the year before had noted a long-healed break in the left clavicle—and dental work matching that described in Norman's dental record. A series of double-checks, sign-offs, and bureaucratic confirmations made it official: Unknown X-408 was Captain Norman E. Zahrt.

The letter reached Luella during her third Christmas with Don, in 1948:

QMGMF 293
Zahrt, Norman E.
SN 01 700 783
20 December 1948
Mrs. Luella Zahrt
617 Rundell
Iowa City, Iowa

Dear Mrs. Zahrt,
We are desirous that you be furnished information concerning the resting place of the remains of your husband, the late Captain Norman E. Zahrt.

  The official report of burial has been received and discloses that the remains of your husband were originally buried at Yakute, Arai-Machi, Hamana-Gun, Shizuoka Prefecture, Japan, but were later disinterred by our American Graves Registration Personnel, properly identified, and reinterred in Plot USAF, Row 23, Grave 1129, United States Armed Forces Cemetery Yokohama #1, Japan, located at Yokohama on the island of Honshu, Japan.

  The report further indicates that these remains have now been casketed and are being held at the United States Armed Forces Mausoleum, Yokohama #2, Japan, pending disposition instructions from the next of kin, either for return to the United States or for permanent burial in an overseas cemetery.

  There are enclosed informational pamphlets. . . .
James F. Smith
Major, QMC
Memorial Division

Major Smith asked Luella to promptly complete a Request for Disposition of Remains so the quartermaster could send her the body.

Luella, ignoring the many questions raised by this letter, wrote the quartermaster to ask just one: Given that she had remarried, was she still next of kin? The quartermaster replied that she was not: Her remarriage gave Norman's parents the sole right to designate his final disposition.

She would hear no more from the army.

Angus's father, who meanwhile had moved to Long Beach, California, asked that Angus's body be sent to Golden Gate National Cemetery for burial. The casket arrived in early July. On July 18, 1949, almost four years after Norman was killed, Norman's parents stood across from a color guard and a chaplain and buried their son. Perhaps understandably, Don and Luella, once Norman's best friend and wife, did not attend.

"There were any number of reasons not to go," said Christy, decades later. "It was a long way from Iowa, of course, and in those days you didn't just pack up four people and fly. It was probably far beyond our means.

"Besides, my mom was still mad at him. I guess she figured she had already buried him."

HOUSTON

My mother knew nothing of all this. Not being kin, she heard nothing from the government, and Norman's family knew nothing of her identity and likely wouldn't have told her anything if they had. But she was not sitting around waiting for mail. She was studying medicine.

She had enrolled at San Antonio's Trinity College in the fall of 1946, burned through the curriculum in three years, and then entered Houston's Baylor College of Medicine in September 1949.

She was a twenty-eight-year-old single mother with an eight-year-old daughter and no parental support. But she was a far more focused person than she had been five years before. She had become the woman that both her Baylor classmates and everyone who met her later knew: smart, funny, and charming, as always, but also immensely disciplined.

It was during her first year at Baylor that she met my father, who was one class ahead of her. From Hempstead, Texas, a small town west of Houston, and seven years younger than she, he was tall, handsome, shyly funny, and one of Baylor's sharpest students. They fell in together a year after she graduated, in 1953, when they were both interning in St. Louis. Three years later they married and soon had Allen, the first of five children. For a time they must have seemed a couple blessed—two smart, attractive, agreeable young doctors spawning a passel of bright kids.

Yet somewhere my mother's second shot at happiness went awry. My father, while enormously talented and beloved by his patients, lacked any knack for self-promotion or pricing. He stayed busy but was only modestly prosperous compared with his more mercenary peers. My mother, meanwhile, reveled in her rise through Houston's medical culture. She was elated to make the *Who's Who* one year; she kept that dark blue volume prominently shelved among her counseling room reference books. She began to resent my father's seeming lack of ambition even as he grew uneasy with her excess of it. Their fights grew more frequent. With each battle she grew louder and he quieter. Finally, he fell silent: His long work days mashed together so thoroughly that when he moved out, we were so used to not seeing him that my mother actually got away with waiting several days to tell us. They divorced in their seventeenth year.

My mother tried to take this stoically, but it showed. She often looked tired, and she was more likely to cry if one of us acted stubborn or mean. Once, furious at my brother and me for some adolescent idiocy, she hollered us into the car, backed it squealing onto the street, slammed it into gear, and floored it. A few seconds later we reminded her that she had forgotten something—I don't remember what, but it was essential to her mission. She hit the brakes so hard we did a one-eighty. Around us rose the smell of burnt rubber. My brother and I faked smiles of thrilled, cocky pleasure. But we did not speak, lest our voices crack with fear.

There's a danger, amid all the trouble and sadness here, of missing how much fun my mother was, how much she enjoyed life, and how much love she created. She played the piano (moderately well), played bridge (gleefully), punned (ruthlessly), and sang (exuberantly) in the church choir, the kitchen, the shower, the car—at every excuse. She liked to garden. She didn't do it often, but on those occasions when as a boy I would seek her out and find her pruning the rose bushes or planting monkey grass, she seemed at peace. Some of this was the warm relaxation brought by working outside.

But as a father now myself, I suspect that some of the happiness I sensed at these moments was the incomparable pleasure of being sought and found by one's children. I had first to search the big house, nine rooms on two floors, then yell out the back door. On hearing her distant call, I am running. I let the screen door slam and fly through magnolia shade and into the sun to find her weeding her rose garden. She looks up, and with the back of her sleeve, she pushes her black curls from her forehead and gives me a wondrous smile. She delightedly says my name. This smile, which will embarrass me at other times, now completely drives from my head whatever inspired my search. When she asks what brings her the pleasure of this visit, I can't recall what I've come to her for. Clearly this.

My mother's romance with Angus formed a pivot on which her life turned. She credited him with inspiring her to pursue medicine, and with that new focus, she moved from a self-destructive course to one more disciplined, elevated, and rewarding. Her affair with him, even as it indulged her mother's brand of impropriety, lifted her from the gravity of Clara Lee's example. But it took an enormous toll. It undermined the lives of Angus's widow and children for decades. And to my mother, Angus—the one love she lost to bad luck rather than failed effort—remained forever the idealized lost chance. His death took from her not just any happiness she might have found with him but also the ability to find peace with someone as gentle as my father. Angus had opened a door to happiness that, once closed, shut her out forever. The sound of it slamming echoed a long time.

And not just for her. Christy Zahrt once drove all the way from Nevada to visit me in Vermont, and after a long afternoon at my backyard picnic table, excavating our past, she said, "Sometimes it's hard to get your head around this. Everybody ended up married to somebody they wished was somebody else. Don married Luella, but wished he was married to Nell. Luella married Don, but wished she was married to Norman. And your mom married your dad but wished *she* was married to Norman. Your dad was the only one who didn't know about any of this—and he ended up wishing he'd married someone else anyway."

When I stopped laughing, Christy said, "We're obviously not siblings—we can't be, because Norman died way before you were born. Yet I feel as if somehow we are."

I said I was just thinking the same thing.

"Of course, if Norman and Jane had stayed together," she said, "you wouldn't be here."

I had thought of that, too.

Given how different my parents were, their marriage would almost certainly have failed even without Angus in my mother's past. Yet I believe my mother resisted that failure more ferociously and took it more bitterly, and blamed my father all the more, simply because my father was not Angus. My father was and is kind, smart, funny, strong, generous, and handsome. But he was not restless, daring, or self-absorbed. He did not exude the narcissist's glow. After he left, my mother hinted at her resentment by telling us the fragment of the Angus story we possessed at her death. Her tale boiled down to this: She'd known real love once, by God, but lost it.

FINDING ANGUS

One afternoon a few weeks ago, when I was scrolling through the photographs for this story, my nine-year-old son, looking over my shoulder at pictures of Evelyn and Angus in their youth, asked me if I thought that telling this story would be okay with my mom. I said I thought it would. I had once asked David Zahrt how he felt about this story going public. "The past is approved," he said, "and the future is open"—another way of saying we must own our scars, rather than wish them away. And to my mind, my mother had told us twice that she was finally ready to release her past and thereby own it.

The first tell was her request that we bury her in the Pacific. She had to know this amounted to a public declaration. I think that's why she looked so relieved when she asked us to take her to Angus. It's work, hiding these things.

The other tell was the locket that held the picture of her grand-parents. About a year before she died, my mother sent that locket to Betty Lou. Betty Lou found this unsettling. The locket seemed a fitting thing to share, but the timing made Betty Lou worry that my mother was fast fading and that this gift represented a good-bye.

That locket had held the same picture for almost a century. Yet when Betty Lou pressed the button and the locket popped open, it revealed not the photograph of her grandparents, but a photograph of Angus.

Had my mother kept Angus's picture behind that of her grandparents all those years? We agreed she must have. It's not as if she put his picture there just to send to Betty Lou.

It seems Angus had been there right next to her heart all that time. He had been there when as a boy on her lap I tugged the locket up from between her breasts so I could look at it. Instead of Angus, of course, I had seen my mother's grandparents. She had put them there because she loved them. But she had also put them there to cover and protect Angus's memory: one past to cover another, just as she built one life to encase an earlier one.

A decade ago I began chasing Angus as a way to better know my mother. A year ago I went to see him. To make sure he did not slip away yet again, I carried all the information needed to find him: the name of the cemetery and his grid, row, and plot number. I had built an empty half-day into the end of a Bay Area business trip. When I finished my work, I got out my phone, opened Google Maps, and found the big national cemetery at the foot of the Golden Gate Bridge. It would be a two-hour walk across the San Francisco hills.

I found the cemetery down by the water, just as the map showed, at one end of the lovely old fort called the Presidio and walked through the stone gates. Behind me rose the bridge, before me a broad rolling landscape contoured by precisely laid rows of white headstones. A couple of hundred yards up the driveway was a little box that said "Grave Finder." You turned a ratcheted wheel that flipped through last names until you found the one you were looking for, and it gave a code for the grave's location. I turned it to Z— but found no Zahrt. I checked everything and did it again. No Zahrt. I stood there dumb amid thousands of silent headstones and tried to figure what was amiss. Either the Grave Finder had the wrong information or I did. I walked back so I was among the gravestones, sat on the grass, and again opened Google Maps on my phone. Again I checked my coded entry for the grave information. Then I Googled "Golden Gate National Cemetery." And I found that, behold, the Golden Gate National Cemetery is not the national cemetery that lies at the foot of the Golden Gate Bridge. That cemetery, as the sign on the gateposts informed me once I looked at it, is the San Francisco National Cemetery. The Golden Gate Cemetery is eight miles south, in a place called San Bruno.

I looked at my watch. My plane would leave in three hours. I would have to visit Angus another time. For now, surrounded by dead strangers, I could only sit in the grass and laugh. My sister Cynthia laughed, too, when I called her and told her the story.

"That man," she said, "is simply not to be found."

A month later, contriving another business trip and taking another long, warm walk, I finally found Angus, on a bright slope in San Bruno. Norman's stone stands near an oak tree among the graves of others buried in 1949, none of them killed in the war. Many of the stones designated these men as "Son of" or "Husband of." Some had the names of wives, buried there, too, carved into the reverse side. Norman's holds no mention of family.

I sat for an hour, thinking of him lying here for fifty years while my mother thought he was still in the Pacific. When we granted her burial request and took her to Hawaii to join him, we had actually left him far behind. Now she was slowly dispersing in the Pacific while he lay buried neat and deep in San Bruno. It would take a lot of time and rain to bring them together. If we had saved some ashes, I could have sprinkled some on his grave. But we had not, and I did not want to leave a picture that would just get thrown away. My mother would not have liked that. So I took some photographs and walked past thousands of headstones and back to the train.

Later, at home, I printed out a two-inch-square photo of Angus's resting place. I found the photograph my brother had emailed me from Maui years before, showing our leis floating over my mother's

ashes, and I made a two-inch-square print of that. Then I opened my
mother's crumbling photo album and slipped the pictures into the
two remaining empty sets of corner mounts. I considered pulling
those mounts off and pasting the photos closer to one another. But
I thought, No: My mom had glued them in that way, and I shouldn't
change it. This was as close as I could get them.

A
THOUSAND
POUNDS OF
DYNAMITE

ADAM HIGGINBOTHAM

Wednesday, August 27, 1980

12:30 A.M.

The helicopter thundered over the darkened forest, heading west, rising into the mountains beneath an almost full moon. Even for FBI special agent Dell Rowley, a slight five foot nine, the narrow cargo space behind the two front seats was a tight fit. The helmet and Kevlar vest he wore over his black fatigues, and the weapons he carried, did not make it any more comfortable. But the pilot was supposed to be alone, so Rowley had to stay where he was. Besides, the copilot's seat was occupied by three canvas money bags, stuffed with cut-and-bound bundles of newsprint calculated to match the weight and volume of almost $3 million in hundred-dollar bills—and $1,000 in cash, to complete the effect.

By the ambient glow of the instrument panel, Rowley read the second letter from the extortionists whose giant bomb currently sat in the second-floor offices of Harvey's Wagon Wheel Casino, twenty miles away, back in Stateline, Nevada. The bomb was silently counting down to an explosion that the nation's best technicians still had no idea how to prevent. The author of the letters was given to grandiose turns of phrase and idiosyncratic language and had provided complex instructions for the ransom drop: a helicopter, a lone pilot, a flight along Highway 50 into the mountains, a signal from a strobe light, a clearing for a landing zone, the $3 million in used bills. No weapons, no one riding shotgun. The first note had concluded with an ironic flourish. "Happy landing," it read, a subtly misaligned row of letters banged out on an electric typewriter.

But the FBI agents had no patience for such arrangements. They knew that the money drop was the weak point in any extortion attempt. Up in the night sky above Rowley, high enough for the wind to carry away the telltale throb of its rotors until it was too late, was a Huey carrying a six-man SWAT team from the bureau's Sacramento office. In Rowley's hands was an MP5 submachine gun fitted with a silencer. In his head was a simple plan.

As the skids of the Bell Ranger touched down on the mountainside, the pilot would douse the lights and kick open the door, and Rowley would roll unseen to the ground. He would scuttle into the trees, switch on his night-vision goggles, and locate the extortionists.

Then, if necessary, he would kill them.

ONE
Six Months Earlier

Jimmy Birges walked up the steps to the front porch of his older brother's house in Fresno, California, and rang the doorbell. Then he rang it again, and again. On the fifth ring, Johnny Birges reluctantly opened the door. He was high.

A diligent anthropologist seeking the embodiment of a certain kind of California lifestyle at the end of the 1970s would be hard-pressed to find one more potent than Johnny Birges. He was blond and tan—the result of nailing shingles six days a week in the fierce Central Valley sun—with narrow green eyes, a wispy mustache, and shaggy hair down to his shoulders. He moved his tools from job to job in the back of his snub-nosed Dodge Tradesman cargo van, which on Saturday nights he still used to take his bike to races. The van was plain white, but Johnny had fitted it with mag wheels and wide tires. On the driver-side door was a sticker that read, WHEN

THE VAN'S A-ROCKIN', DON'T COME A-KNOCKIN'. On the dashboard was another: ASS, GRASS OR CASH—NOBODY RIDES FOR FREE. Johnny was high every waking moment of the day. His brother couldn't stand him.

As smart and composed as his brother was hazy and unkempt, Jimmy Birges was eighteen but skinnier and taller than Johnny and a student in a high school program for gifted kids. He had grown his dark hair long, too, but it was neatly parted in the middle, and he favored button-down shirts and Top-Siders. He had a smooth charm, which he would later put to use as a car salesman at Fresno Toyota. The stoner and the straight arrow were predictably at odds. After his brother had left home, Jimmy tried sharing an apartment with him, but they couldn't get along. In the end, he moved back in with his father, in the family's house on North Fowler Avenue in Clovis, a quiet northeastern suburb of Fresno. The two boys had barely seen each other in three years.

"How did you know where I live?" Johnny asked.

"I don't want anything from you," Jimmy said. "Big John sent me to tell you he needs your help."

The Birges boys were still bound together by at least one thing: a terror of their father, a cantankerous Hungarian émigré whom they and everyone else called Big John. Johnny hated his father but still yearned for his approval. He waved Jimmy into the house, where he was cooking breakfast for his girlfriend, Kelli Cooper.

Then Jimmy told his brother what their father had in mind.

Big John was going to extort a million dollars from Harvey's Wagon Wheel Casino in Lake Tahoe, and he planned to do it by building a bomb.

The two boys had a good laugh about that. Kelli laughed, too. Another of Big John's crazy schemes.

TWO

Janos Birges arrived in the United States in May 1957 a penniless thirty-five-year-old political refugee. He was dark and handsome then, with an intense gaze, a high forehead, and an aquiline nose; beneath his shirt, a tattooed eagle spread its wings across his chest. He had fled Hungary six months earlier, when Soviet tanks rolled into Budapest, crushing the popular uprising against the country's Communist government.

Born in 1922 in Jászberény, an agricultural town in central Hungary, Janos was the only child of a landowning and farming family; he'd say later that he considered himself upper middle class. But his father was a ferocious drinker and hated having the boy around. He sent Janos to live with his grandparents at the age of three, and Janos spent nine happy years with them. In 1933 they sent him back, and several years later, at fifteen, Janos ran away for good. He went to Budapest, where he was taken in by a butcher and his family.

The stories he told his sons about what happened next are hard to verify. He was always secretive about his past, and the boys never asked too many questions. Knowledge is power, he often said; the more people know about you, the weaker you are. But the account he gave them was by no means unlikely. At first, he told Johnny, he worked as the butcher's apprentice and was soon running the shop. Then in 1941 Hungary entered World War II on the German side and sent troops to support the invasion of Russia. That was the year Janos enrolled in the Royal Hungarian Air Force Military Academy.

By the time he graduated and entered the Royal Hungarian Army Air Force as a pilot, in 1944, the tide of the war had turned: the Nazis had formally occupied Hungary, and the Red Army was approaching its eastern borders. Janos was put at the controls of an Me 109 fighter plane and sent up to fight the Russians. He liked to tell his son that he shot down thirteen Allied planes before being hit by antiaircraft fire over Italy and captured by Allied troops. U.S. records show only that in 1945, a month after the Hungarian capital fell to the Soviets, Birges was arrested by the Gestapo in Austria. He was charged with disobeying orders but escaped; he was arrested again in 1946, by Hungarian military authorities, but released without charge.

Hungary was now entirely under the control of the Soviet Union. It was around this time, Birges would later claim, that he began working for U.S. military intelligence in Austria—though decades later a search of the files of the U.S. Army's 306th Counter Intelligence Corps in Salzburg revealed no mention of a Janos Birges. But in April 1948, he was arrested by Soviet secret police in Hungary and charged with espionage. The trial lasted seven minutes. He was sentenced to twenty-five years of hard labor and sent to a gulag in Siberia. He spent almost eight years there, cutting down trees to make railroad ties and twice contracting jaundice, before he was released—at the same time as thousands of Axis prisoners of war were repatriated from captivity in the Soviet Union—and finally returned to Hungary.

Then one night in 1955 he met Elizabet Nyul in a Jászberény restaurant. A petite twenty-seven-year-old with an elfin face and brooding eyes, she was waiting for her husband, who worked there as a waiter. Janos invited her to dance. They danced together twice, and he asked her to marry him.

Elizabet was the second youngest of a dozen siblings, impulsive and headstrong. The divorce came through quickly, and in January 1956, Elizabet and Janos were married. The early days of the marriage were a brief period of tranquillity for Birges. Less than a year later the Soviet Union moved to suppress the revolution in Budapest, and Janos and Elizabet found themselves among the 200,000 refugees who fled the Soviet crackdown, which left 2,500 Hungarians dead. He and Elizabet escaped into Austria. There Janos worked as a German-Hungarian interpreter for the Red Cross, until, months later, he was granted political asylum in the United States.

———

At first the new lives of John and Elizabeth followed the steep trajectory of immigrant cliché. According to John's account, on arriving in New Jersey they were given three dollars by the Red Cross. His new wife wanted sunglasses, so they spent all the money buying a pair. They made their way to California and got work on a farm, John as a carpenter and Elizabeth in the packing house. Later, John found work with the metal-fabrication company PDM Steel. He spent five years there, learning welding and pipe fitting. Johnny was born in 1960, Jimmy in 1962.

Two years later Big John put $500 into starting his own landscaping company. He worked around the clock seven days a week and never took a vacation. He dressed in work clothes or outfits from the Salvation Army. He was nonunion and a fighter. Johnny once saw him put two men down at once. He was five eleven, fit and powerful, and an imposing presence; other men were afraid of him. He could be charming, but his sense of humor was sometimes cruel. He was often reckless, inclined to cut corners. Years of blasting wells and trenches out of the California hardpan had made him pretty comfortable around dynamite.

By 1972 Big John was a millionaire, with three separate businesses, twenty-six employees, and lucrative contracts with California municipalities and golf courses. He bought three Mercedeses and, when he lost his license after picking up one too many tickets for speeding, his own plane, a Beechcraft. He used it to fly to job sites and liked to pull terrifying low-altitude stunts, sometimes with his sons on board: buzzing water-skiers on a lake to watch them scatter or flying under a freeway overpass. Elizabeth handled the accounts, and eventually Big John bought her a business she could call her own, a restaurant. The Villa Basque, on North Blackstone in Fresno, had two candlelit dining rooms with red-and-white table-cloths and a banquet hall.

At home, Big John was a tinkerer and a would-be inventor, always soldering and wiring. When the family moved to a modest wood-framed ranch house on the rural outskirts of Clovis, with fifteen acres of vineyards, he set up a large workshop out back. His ideas could be inspired, but he often lacked the patience for details and was unlucky with those he did perfect. The labor-saving meatball-making gizmo he built for the Villa Basque never worked quite right; he built his own electric irrigation timer, and developed an automated ditchdigger for laying pipes more quickly, but he was beaten to the patents by other inventors.

And money did not make Big John and Elizabeth happy. They drank and fought, and he suspected her of having affairs. He called her a nymphomaniac and claimed she used the restaurant as a well-spring of sexual encounters. She took to disappearing for days at a time; he always brought her back. Once they argued so furiously that she fell to the kitchen floor and had a seizure right in front of him. They took her away in an ambulance—said she'd had a nervous breakdown.

Johnny and Jimmy enjoyed the trappings of a comfortable life. Their parents bought them motorbikes, go-karts, and three-wheelers with balloon tires. Elizabeth liked to dress them in identical out-fits. One summer she took them on a road trip across Europe. But Big John made them work nights in the restaurant and summers for the landscaping business. They labored at job sites up and down the state, sleeping in trailers with Big John's crew. The only hair-cuts they were given came once a year, at the start of summer vaca-tion, when Big John would take a pair of clippers and shave their heads. Their scalps would blister as they dug ditches in the searing valley heat.

Big John also beat them relentlessly—with belts, electric cables, boots, and coat hangers. At night he would come into their room, pull back the covers, and whale on Johnny while Jimmy lay mute and motionless in bed. When Jimmy was six, his father caught him with his elbow on the table at dinner and punched out four of his teeth to teach him better manners. Johnny hated school, and in first or second grade he was caught jamming glue and toothpicks into the locks so no one could open the doors. At twelve he began drinking beer; he smoked pot for the first time two years later. Johnny tormented his younger brother, and Jimmy would run to his mother and father. Big John would beat Johnny some more, then turn around and berate his younger son for telling tales—he couldn't stomach a stool pigeon.

When Elizabeth finally filed for divorce, in November 1973, she moved into a travel trailer behind the house, where she could keep an eye on her sons. By that time Big John was making plans to retire, and he sold off the landscaping business to his foreman. He began flying up to Lake Tahoe in his plane to gamble. Elizabeth had a boyfriend, but the arguments and her disappearances continued.

At the end of July 1975, Elizabeth vanished again. This time she left behind her Mazda pickup, parked outside the kitchen door with the keys in the ignition, her pocketbook on the passenger seat. Big John didn't seem to notice. Three days later her body was found in a field behind the house. An autopsy showed a lethal combination of alcohol and Valium in her bloodstream; she had choked on her own vomit. The coroner ruled it a suicide, but something never seemed quite right about that. Her stomach was full of whiskey. Jimmy knew that she only ever drank vodka. And they never found the bottle.

Big John changed after Elizabeth died. Not long after the funeral, he went around the house cutting her out of the family photographs with a pair of scissors. He took the urn that held her ashes and emptied it in the yard, in front of his sons. He began spending money like never before. He started dressing well for the first time in his life, in suits and turtlenecks. He wore a pencil mustache, drank mai tais, and dated the waitresses at the Villa Basque. And he began gambling more heavily in the casinos up in Lake Tahoe. His favorite was Harvey's Wagon Wheel in Stateline, Nevada.

THREE

Harvey's Wagon Wheel was one of the first casinos built in State-line, an isolated resort town nestled among the pines and incense cedars at the foot of the mountains on the southeastern shore of Lake Tahoe. Harvey Gross was a wholesale butcher from Sacramento who first arrived in Stateline in 1937, when the place was a handful of buildings without power, water, or telephone lines. What it did have was recently legalized gambling.

In 1944 Gross and his wife, Llewellyn, opened the Wagon Wheel Saloon and Gambling Hall, a single-room casino with three slot machines, two blackjack tables, and a six-stool lunch counter. The western theme—log cabin decor, the wagon wheel and steer's head on the sign—was Llewellyn's idea. The Wagon Wheel sat hard against the Nevada border, which cut east-west across Highway 50, dividing Stateline from the California town of South Lake Tahoe. Outside the casino was the only twenty-four-hour gas pump for sixty miles.

By the 1950s the Wagon Wheel was attracting a fashionable, wealthy crowd up from Sacramento and San Francisco every sum-mer, and Gross had found a local rival in Bill Harrah, who had opened his own casino directly across the street. In 1963 Gross rede-veloped his place into the first modern high-rise hotel casino on the South Shore, a concrete monolith with eleven stories, 197 rooms, and his name up on the roof, curling across a giant wagon wheel and longhorn skull in red neon.

By 1980 Bill Harrah was dead, but Harvey still faced competition from the suits who ran an expanded Harrah's in his rival's name and from the new local outposts of corporate gaming, the Sahara Tahoe and Caesars. In the shadow of these sleek new towers, Harvey's was beginning to show its age. But Gross still had his giant highway bill-boards, his multistory gaming floor, his miniskirted cocktail waitresses delivering cheap drinks. Harvey's Wagon Wheel remained a multimillion-dollar enterprise: a winking, jingling money factory by the lake.

Like all gambling towns, Stateline was a magnet for crime, and Bill Jonkey, one of the two agents in the FBI office in nearby Carson City, was a frequent visitor. In 1980 Jonkey was thirty-five years old, a burly outdoorsman with a thick mustache and the easy confidence of a movie cowboy. He had been in the FBI for nine years and law enforcement for most of his life. Born and raised in Glendale, California, he was a surfer who had traded his longboard for a badge before he even graduated college. As a twenty-one-year-old officer for the Long Beach Police Department, he patrolled downtown and the west side: the docks and the port, the sailors and the riffraff. It was active. Very active. Getting into fights was a good education.

The FBI took him in 1971. At first he was assigned to the Denver office, then Vegas, where he immediately started making plans to get up to the resident agency in Carson City. It was a small office, with only two agents, and most of the time you worked alone. Jonkey's supervisor was all the way back in Vegas. He went to work in jeans and cowboy boots, had a horse and an acre of land. He was a western guy; he didn't do humidity or cities. The place was perfect.

His jurisdiction included the gambling towns around Lake Tahoe, which kept him pretty busy: tracking fugitives, handling some organized crime, the odd phony check. The extortion calls came in once or twice a year. Bomb threats, usually. Always the big casinos: the Sahara, Caesars, Harvey's. A pipe bomb, a paper bag left between two slot machines. Or someone would call security at Harrah's and say they'd left devices everywhere: *Check in the trash in the men's restroom if you don't think I'm serious.* Some wires, no explosives: bullshit stuff. The guy would call back and say, *Did you find it? Well, there's twenty more of those. I want $500,000.*

The feds always got them at the money drop. Jonkey and the other agents would stake out the location in advance. Once they drove out to the desert and spent three days disguised as hunters— camping gear, rifles, dead rabbits, beer—before they saw a guy come sauntering up the track looking for the old water heater where the money was supposed to be hidden. Another time the drop was in a trash can down on the Tahoe shore, miles from anywhere. At ten at night, two men came out of the lake in diving gear. The agents got them just as they got everyone else. They could make the plans as complicated as they liked, but in the end they always had to come for the money.

In 1974 the FBI sent Jonkey to a two-week bomb investigator's course in Quantico, where he learned to read the evidence left behind by an explosion. By the summer of 1980 he'd been out to two or three bomb scenes. But nothing big.

FOUR

Big John liked Harvey's Wagon Wheel. They treated him the way he felt he deserved to be treated: as if he were someone. Blackjack was his game, and pretty soon he was playing often enough that he was regarded as a high roller. He'd come home to Clovis waving stacks of hundred-dollar bills and bragging about how easily he could beat the dealers. At Harvey's they put him up for free, gave him the best rooms, often his favorite, Suite 1017. He got to know his way around the place, befriended the staff. In 1976 he was invited to spend three days at Harvey Gross's ranch in the Carson Valley. One of the pilots who worked for Gross even took him on a trip up to the lake in the boss's helicopter. When the pilot heard Big John was a flier, he let him take the controls for a while. Big John had never flown a helicopter before but took to it quickly; hovering was tricky, but level flight was simple. The pilot let him try a takeoff. It wasn't exactly smooth, but Birges had the machine in the air without much difficulty.

Big John began spending more and more of his time in Tahoe. The boys were left to look after themselves back at the house in Clovis. One day a truck pulled up with a delivery from the Nugget grocery store: $8,000 worth of canned food, everything from Campbell's soup to tuna. The groceries filled the shelves in the garage, floor to ceiling, twenty feet wide and two feet deep. Next came meat and seafood: 2,100 pounds of beef—three whole steers—plus four lambs, pork, lobster, ham, and 200 pounds of hot dogs. Big John stacked all of it in the walk-in freezer at the back of the house and told the boys they had enough food to keep them going for three years. Then he took off to gamble in Tahoe again. He said he'd be back in a month.

In 1978 he started seeing a woman from the restaurant, Joan Williams. Williams was a dark-haired forty-something mother of four, a university graduate with a degree in Spanish literature who liked to bowl and play golf in her spare time. Separated from her husband and children, she worked weekends at the Villa Basque. During the week, she had a job with the Fresno County Probation Department, where she mostly handled DUI cases and misdemeanors.

Joan's parents didn't much like her new boyfriend—they thought he was a slick talker—but that didn't stop her. Within the year, she had moved into the house on North Fowler Avenue. It was just them and Jimmy there now; Johnny had taken his high school proficiency test, quit school, and moved out of the house for good.

It was around that time that Big John first heard from Harvey Gross's debt collector. He came by the restaurant and told Big John that a couple of his checks had bounced. Big John owed Gross $1,000. He settled up quickly. That same year the Villa Basque burned to the ground. The police suspected it wasn't an accident. Big John took the insurance money—all $300,000 of it—and lost it at blackjack. With everything else gone, he sold the house in Clovis to Joan for a fraction of its true value to help pay off his debts. But it wasn't enough.

In 1979 Big John bounced another $15,000 worth of checks at Harvey's. That September the debt collector came to visit him at the house in Clovis. Big John promised he'd be up in Tahoe within a month and that he'd pay off $1,000 of what he owed then.

But he didn't. Instead, the next month he signed a lease on a condo near Harvey's and went straight back to the tables.

By then Big John's health was coming apart, along with the rest of his life. He'd had stomach trouble for years and had two separate ulcer surgeries. He drank Maalox and buttermilk like water. In the spring of 1979, complaining of fatigue, he was diagnosed with abdominal cancer. Later that year he was admitted to the hospital with acute gastrointestinal bleeding. Even that didn't stop him gambling. He spent two or three weeks of every month at the Tahoe condo, trying to make back his losses at the Harvey's blackjack tables. But whatever edge he once felt he had over the dealers there, it had vanished, along with his money.

At the end of the year, Big John showed up unexpectedly at Harvey's Wagon Wheel and demanded a room for the New Year weekend. He had a girl with him. The manager put him in Suite 1017, his old favorite. But before the celebrations could begin, the manager was back, apologetically informing him that another guest needed the suite. Big John protested, but it was no use. He and the girl spent the last night of the 1970s in a room so small they could barely get around the bed. "I thought you were a big shot," she told him.

The next morning John Birges awoke to face the new decade. He was nearly fifty-eight years old, terminally ill, broke, twice divorced, and humiliated. He had nothing left to lose.

FIVE

Johnny Birges didn't hear any more about his father's bomb until one day in June 1980, when Jimmy called to tell him that Big John had found the dynamite he wanted. Now all he had to do was take it. The boys agreed to help.

Late one Friday night, Johnny drove his Dodge van over to the house on Fowler Avenue to pick up Jimmy and Big John. They headed east into the mountains, toward the Helms Creek hydroelectric construction project. A colossal underground engineering scheme to create a new reservoir and build a pumping station in vaults beneath a granite mountain in the Sierra Nevada, the project would ultimately require the excavation of more than a million cubic yards of rock and earth and the blasting of almost four miles of tunnels, each thirty-eight feet in diameter. That called for an extremely large quantity of explosives.

Turning onto the access road to the site, Johnny stopped the van to cover the license plates with fake ones he'd made from blue and yellow construction paper. He drove on through the front gate, then parked in the shadows behind a mound of dirt. Next to the batch machine—a giant concrete mixer that turned constantly—was a small red wooden shack hung with a sign that read, DANGER EXPLOSIVES. The three men pulled on gloves.

Big John crept around the back of the shack, carrying a portable oxyacetylene torch in a backpack. He forced open a window, and he and Johnny climbed inside. With the torch, Big John cut the padlocks off the steel door of the powder magazine. Inside was case after case of Hercules Unigel dynamite and blasting caps. Each case weighed fifty pounds and measured two feet by one foot. Johnny passed them out the window. Big John and Jimmy stacked them in the dirt. The boys got nervous. But Big John kept wanting more.

It took an hour, and by the time they'd finished, the back of the van was almost completely filled with dynamite. Johnny turned the van around, and Big John used a tree branch to scuff out their tire tracks. They pulled through the gates and headed west. No one saw a thing.

The van rolled back into Clovis at around three in the morning. They had stolen eighteen cardboard cases filled with dynamite and blasting caps to go with it—more than a thousand pounds of explosives in all. The dynamite was formed into sticks eighteen inches long and two inches around, wrapped in yellow wax paper and stamped with the manufacturer's name. Used correctly, it was enough to reduce a large building to a pile of rubble. They stacked the boxes in the walk-in freezer, surrounded by the remains of the beef, lamb, and lobster ordered years earlier. Then Big John padlocked it shut.

The following day, the *Fresno Bee* ran a brief news story concerning the mysterious theft of $50,000 worth of dynamite from the hydroelectric project up at Wishon Lake. "Whoever took the explosives left no prints, tracks or clues behind," the paper reported. The county sheriff's office had no suspects.

Johnny was at home when the phone rang.

"You did it, didn't you?" Kelli said.

"What?"

"The dynamite. You stole it."

"I don't know what you're talking about," Johnny said. "What dynamite?"

Johnny and Kelli broke up soon after that.

SIX

The freezer full of dynamite gave Big John a new sense of purpose. In the machine shop behind the house, he did a little work each day, welding and soldering. Slowly, his most ingenious invention began to take shape.

Two weeks after the raid on Helms Creek, Johnny went over to Fowler Avenue to see what his father had been up to. The workshop was well equipped but chaotic. In the middle of it all, covered with a blanket, were two rectangular boxes welded together from sections of quarter-inch steel plate.

Even empty, the larger of the two boxes—26 inches high, 24 inches wide, and 45 inches long—was too heavy to lift. Fitted with recessed casters and a second set of wheels with rubber tires, it was large enough to contain nearly all the dynamite they had stolen. The second box was smaller—just over a foot square and 22.5 inches long—and was designed to be welded to the top of the first. This would house the brain of Big John's bomb: the nerve center for a nest of booby traps and triggers he had devised with the aim of thwarting even the most sophisticated attempts to defuse it.

The bomb, Big John explained to Johnny and Jimmy, had eight separate electromechanical fusing mechanisms. If any one of them was triggered, it would complete a circuit between a battery and detonators attached to the dynamite, and the bomb would explode.

First, the two boxes were lined with aluminum foil sandwiched between two layers of neoprene; if anyone attempted to drill through the outside of the box, the drill bit would make an electrical contact between the steel box and the foil, completing a circuit and detonating the device. Second, Big John had used spring-loaded contacts to booby-trap the screws holding the tops of the boxes in place. Unscrew any of them and the contacts would close, completing a circuit. Third, the lids of both boxes were rigged with pressure switches like those used in car doors to operate dome lights. If either lid were removed, the switches would open, completing a circuit.

Fourth, inside the top box Big John rigged a float from a toilet cistern. If the box was flooded with water or foam, the float would rise, completing a circuit. Fifth, beside the float was a tilt mechanism built from a length of PVC pipe lined with more aluminum foil; inside hung a metal pendulum held under tension from below with a rubber band. Big John took a circuit tester and demonstrated to Johnny: once this was armed, if the bomb was moved in any way, the end of the pendulum would make contact with the foil, completing a circuit. Sixth was a layer of foil running around the seam connecting the two boxes; if a metal object were inserted between the top and bottom boxes to lever them apart, this would complete a circuit.

Finally, Big John had installed a solid-state irrigation timer—designed for greenhouses and sprinkler systems—connected to a six-volt battery. This could be set in time increments from forty-five minutes to eight days. But once it had been activated and all the booby traps had been armed, it would no longer be possible to get inside the bomb to turn it off. As soon as the timer reached zero, it would detonate the device.

Johnny realized what this meant: his father's bomb was impossible to disarm. Big John did not plan to provide Harvey's with instructions on how to turn off the device in exchange for the ransom. Instead, what he would offer was a guide to making the pendulum mechanism safe, so that the bomb could be moved from the casino to another location, where it could be detonated without incident—though even this wouldn't be without its hazards. On the side of the top box, Big John built a panel of twenty-eight steel toggle switches, neatly numbered and arranged in five rows. He told Johnny that three—or perhaps five—of the twenty-eight could be used to switch the pendulum circuit on and off. Many of the others were dummies—but some of them weren't. Flip any one of the live switches, and it would complete a circuit. Then the device would explode instantly.

SEVEN

Throughout the summer, Big John kept working on the bomb. He wired in the firing mechanisms and spot-welded the boxes together. He built a dolly to move it around. Johnny gave the casing a slick finish. He covered the screws with Bondo and gave the boxes a coat of flat gray paint. He and Jimmy were in agreement that they wanted nothing to do with Big John's extortion plot. But they were too afraid of their father to argue.

When Jimmy asked his father how he planned to pick up the extortion money, Big John refused to say. Jimmy had heard him mention a helicopter, and he knew Big John had stolen two strobe lights from airplanes parked at Lake Tahoe Airport. But he wouldn't be drawn out on the details. "Don't worry," he told Jimmy. "You'll see."

Two weeks later Big John unlocked the door of the walk-in freezer. Outside in the sun, he and Joan removed the sticks of dynamite from their paper wrapping and laid them out on the ground. The explosives reeked of turpentine; the fumes gave them both headaches and made them nauseous. They packed the sticks tightly into Hefty bags and put them inside the bomb casing. Eventually, with all the dynamite in place, Big John and Jimmy rigged the explosives with bundles of blasting caps and wired them into the fusing circuitry. The bomb was now complete.

A week after that, Jimmy came into the kitchen to find that the extortion note was finished, too. It was sitting there on the table in a clean white envelope. Joan had typed it up on her electric typewriter, the one she used for the business and creative writing classes she was taking at night.

On Saturday, August 23, Big John summoned his sons to help him practice rolling the device onto the cart he'd built to move it across the Harvey's parking lot. Big John pulled the half-ton bomb up with a block and tackle while Johnny guided it into position. Then the rope snapped and the bomb rolled back. Johnny, who couldn't move fast enough, yelped in agony as the wheel rolled over his left hand. Somehow nothing was broken, but it gave him a way out. "I don't want nothing more to do with it!" he shouted. "I'm out!"

He climbed into his van and left. Jimmy turned to his father. "Well," he said, "if he's not going to do it, I'm not going to do it."

On Sunday, Big John called Johnny. He asked if he could use his son's van again. "Okay," Johnny said. "As long as I don't have nothing to do with it." Out at the house, Big John told the boys that if they wouldn't help with the delivery, they had to help him with the ransom drop.

Inside the bomb, the timer was already running.

EIGHT

Terry Hall and Bill Brown were sitting around the house drinking beer at around one in the afternoon when Big John called. Bill was a redneck pipe fitter from Arkansas. He had a hard-luck past, jailhouse tattoos, and a record to match: car theft, drunk and disorderly, battery, reckless driving, assault with a deadly weapon. At fifty-nine, he was a hard man running to fat, with an ulcer, an ex-wife, and four children to support.

Terry was twenty-four. Muscular. Swarthy. Dark hair set in a close perm. He had a kid with Bill's daughter Juanita, and the four of them lived together in a house on North Jackson Avenue. Bill and Terry were both out of work. Terry had a felony conviction for forgery and had been in and out of trouble since he was a kid. The cops had picked him up a few times for sniffing paint, and at around fourteen or fifteen he used to shoot heroin pretty often, maybe do a little acid, smoke some weed. But mostly he liked to drink. He and Bill were both hard drinkers. They'd get loaded six days a week. Beer, usually. Once in a while, vodka and orange juice.

Bill had worked for Big John for maybe ten or fifteen years but hadn't done anything for him since he sold the landscaping business. Now, on the phone, Big John said he had a job for him, $2,000 for a day's work. "Who I got to kill?" Bill said.

Big John told him he wanted the two of them over at the house right away. Bill and Terry finished their beers and got into Bill's '71 Matador, a great swaying boat of a car with rust spots stippling the blue paint. When they arrived, Bill and Big John went around the back of the house to talk. A couple of minutes later, Bill called Terry over. Beside the garage, Bill told him that Big John wanted them to deliver a machine to Harvey's. He didn't say why, and Terry didn't ask. Terry didn't think there was anything odd about it. The way Big John explained everything, it was just so easy, like they were expected to be there. Big John gave them directions on exactly where to take the machine and handed Bill fifty dollars.

They left for Tahoe at dusk. Big John drove Johnny's Dodge van north up Highway 99. He took it very carefully. They had the radio on and cracked some beers. Big John and Bill talked, mostly about the work they'd done together in the past. They drove all night.

When they got to Harvey's, it was around five in the morning. It was still dark. They walked over to the back door of the casino. Terry went in and looked at the elevator, to check the route. But Big John wanted to wait and get some sleep before delivering the machine. They drove south for a few miles and found a place called the Balahoe Motel, ten rooms set back from the highway in the trees. Big John gave Terry some money and told him to get a room.

But Terry was on parole in California for burglary and probation for a hit-and-run. He told Big John he couldn't register under his own name. He wasn't supposed to be out of the state. So he wrote down "Joey Evetts" on the registration card. Terry's handwriting was small and neat, with copperplate curls. His *s* could look like an *o.* Under the address he wrote "Van Ness Street" and made up a number. Then the desk clerk asked him to read her the license number off the van. She wrote it down on the card.

They stayed in the room all day and most of the night, drinking and watching TV. At two-thirty a.m. on Tuesday, Big John went out. He was carrying a briefcase. He told Terry and Bill to pick him up at Lake Tahoe Airport, a five-minute drive down the highway. They waited until four, and then went out to the van, but it wouldn't start. They called on the manager's intercom to ask for jumper cables, but he didn't have any. When Big John finally came walking back, he said he'd call a tow truck. Bill and Terry put on the blue overalls Big John gave them. The tow truck driver arrived and got the van started. Big John gave him a hundred-dollar bill and told him to keep the change.

On the way to Harvey's, they pulled over in a nearby parking lot and took the license plate off another van. With some rubber bands, Big John used it to cover the plate on the Dodge. They reached the parking lot at Harvey's at around five a.m. They unloaded the machine and towed it across the parking lot behind the van. Bill and Terry took it over to the front doors of Harvey's, under the canopy.

Terry pushed the dolly while Bill pulled. It was hard going. From outside the double doors, Terry could see a man in a cap sitting behind a desk. As they came in, the man got up from behind the desk and walked away. Through the double doors, past the desk, and then to the elevator, no more than fifty feet away. Bill helped get the machine off the dolly and into the elevator. Then he went back to the van. Terry went on alone.

On the second floor, out of the elevator, left and left again. A Harvey's employee passed Terry but paid him no attention. He pushed the machine into a small waiting area outside the casino's telephone exchange and pulled the cover off. He removed his overalls and stuffed them and the cover into a plastic Harvey's bag that Big John had given him, just as he had been told. Then he left, taking

the stairs, and went out the front of the building. It had taken no
more than two minutes.

Outside, the sun had come up. Terry went around the corner
toward a stoplight between Harvey's and Harrah's. He was standing
there waiting for the light to change when Big John came up behind
him. They walked together across the Harvey's parking lot, got in
the van, and drove away toward California. It was only a couple of
minutes before they made a stop at a bait shop. Terry bought some
more beer. Then they stopped at a creek to take a piss. While Bill and
Terry were relieving themselves, Big John took the dolly out of the
back of the van and threw the pieces into the creek.

Bill and Terry looked at Big John. Bill asked him why he was
getting rid of it. Big John told them they'd just delivered a bomb.
Nobody was going to get hurt. He'd left a note telling them to get
everybody out.

Back in the van, Bill and Terry just sat there looking stunned.
Terry couldn't think of anything to say. The plan sounded hope-
less. He figured all he could do was sit back and hope he didn't get
arrested.

On the way back to Fresno, Bill and Terry started drinking
pretty good.

NINE

It was about five-thirty a.m. on Tuesday when Bob Vinson, who
supervised the graveyard shift at Harvey's, realized he was out of
cigarettes. He was on his way down from his second-floor office to
the gift shop to buy a pack when he noticed something odd. The
accordion door leading through to the room that housed the casino's internal telephone exchange was half open. He stepped around
the door and looked inside.

There was a big gray metal object sitting there, right outside the phone exchange. It hadn't been there twenty minutes earlier. It was on metal legs. The legs were all balanced on pieces of plywood. They were pressing into the thick orange carpet. Whatever it was, it was heavy, and he was pretty sure it didn't belong there.

The security supervisor that morning was Simon Caban, a big man who had been a helicopter door gunner in Vietnam. By the time Caban arrived on the second floor, a few janitors and security guards had gathered around the phone exchange; calls had already gone out to the Douglas County sheriff's department and the fire department. When he saw the strange machine, but especially the envelope lying on the carpet next to it, he was alarmed. He'd just taken a training course on letter bombs. "Everybody step back," he said.

Caban and a sheriff's deputy grabbed a pair of the janitors' broomsticks and, taking cover behind the big gray box, used them to poke at the suspect envelope. It was lying face up. It wasn't sealed. It didn't look dangerous. Inside were three pages of type. Caban picked up the one with the least amount of writing on it. The deputy grabbed the other two. They started reading at the same time.

Caban didn't have his glasses with him and found it hard to focus on the page. He was leaning on the box. The deputy was squatting on the floor at his feet. Caban was about to tell the deputy to give him the rest of the letter when he pointed up at the box. "That's a bomb," the deputy said. Slowly Caban lifted his weight off the contraption and backed away.

Bill Jonkey was still at home when the sheriff's dispatcher called. He hit the top of Spooner Summit just after sunrise, and as the highway dropped over the crest of the Carson Range, the eastern shore of the lake was still cool in the shadows. The deputies met him in the parking lot at Harvey's, where the evacuation had already started. The hotel was full to capacity with vacationers in town for Labor

Day weekend, and as Jonkey went up to the second floor, guests were milling around in the parking lot—elderly couples still in their pajamas, kids without shoes—waiting for buses to drive them over to the high school. On the casino floor, Harvey's security guards were emptying the cage of the $2 million or $3 million in cash held there and figuring out how to lock the doors of a building that had been open twenty-four hours a day for seventeen years.

Jonkey met Danny Danihel, captain of the Douglas County fire department's bomb squad, outside the phone exchange. Danihel, a former explosive ordnance disposal specialist in the U.S. Army who had served in Vietnam, was supposed to be off for three days starting that morning. He was packing for a camping trip with his family when he got the call.

Jonkey's first thought was how well made the bomb was. The welding, the seams, the paint job—the thing was beautiful. None of the bomb squad guys had seen anything like it. And there didn't seem to be any way into it. Then they showed Jonkey the letter.

"Stern warning to the management and bomb squad," it began.

> Do not move or tilt this bomb, because the mechanism controlling the detonators will set it off at a movement of less than .01 of the open end Ricter scale. Don't try to flood or gas the bomb. There is a float switch and an atmospheric pressure switch set at 26.00-33.00. Both are attached to detonators. Do not try to take it apart. The flathead screws are also attached to triggers . . .
>
> WARNING:
>
> I repeat do not try to move, disarm, or enter the bomb. It will explode.

This mixture of stentorian threats and technical minutiae continued for three pages. The bomb was filled with a thousand pounds of TNT, the letter explained, enough not just to obliterate Harvey's but also to severely damage Harrah's across the street. It was equipped with three separate timers. The letter advised cordoning off a minimum of twelve hundred feet around the building and evacuating the area. "This bomb can never be dismantled or disarmed without causing an explosion," it said. "Not even by the creator."

The letter's author was demanding $3 million in used hundred-dollar bills, delivered by helicopter to intermediaries, with further details to follow. In exchange, instructions would be provided for how to disconnect two of the automatic timers so the device could be moved to a location where it would explode harmlessly. There was a tight deadline: "There will be no extension or renegotiation. The transaction has to take place within twenty-four hours."

The note concluded with a message for the helicopter pilot making the ransom drop. "We don't want any trouble but we won't run away if you bring it," it said. "Happy landing."

The letter, like the device itself, was unlike anything Jonkey had seen before. Some of the claims were ridiculous; that stuff about the "Ricter scale" was obviously bullshit. And when Danihel's bomb squad took measurements of the device, they concluded that it wasn't quite big enough to contain a thousand pounds of TNT. But when Danihel began shooting X-rays of the box, Jonkey saw evidence of a chilling complexity within.

There were wires connected to the twenty-eight toggle switches and to the screws, just as the letter said. There were also triggers that weren't mentioned in the note: a possible collapsing circuit, a relay and the outline of pressure-release switches, triggers with what looked like crude metal paddles on the lids of the boxes. And whatever was in the bottom box, there was so much of it that it almost filled the space inside, and it was so dense that Danihel's portable X-ray machine couldn't penetrate it. Nobody would go to all the trouble of building a device of such sophistication just to give it a payload of kitty litter. Jonkey and Danihel couldn't be certain, but it seemed entirely possible that they were looking at the largest improvised bomb in U.S. history.

TEN

Jonkey set up a command post in a conference room on the second floor of the Sahara Tahoe, a few hundred yards away across the Harvey's parking lot. By eight a.m. the hotel had brought up twenty or thirty telephones, desks, and copy machines—everything he needed to coordinate the operation. The Douglas County sheriff's office handled the perimeter, setting up a cordon and assisting with the evacuation of Harvey's. More FBI agents arrived from Reno.

At around eight-fifteen a.m., Jonkey called his boss, Joe Yablonsky. The head of the FBI's Las Vegas division, Yablonsky had come from a successful run as an undercover man, mixing with mobsters in New York and Florida. He wore yawning open-necked shirts, amber sunglasses, heavy gold rings, and a medallion. He never met a TV camera he didn't like. Behind his back, his men called him Broadway Joe. He was not Jonkey's kind of guy.

"Boss, I've got this extortion going up here," Jonkey told him. "Stateline, Nevada."

"Oh, okay. Good," Yablonsky said. "You got a handle?"

"It's a huge bomb. They're asking for three million dollars. I'm gonna need some help up here."

"Well, I can probably send you up . . ." Yablonsky paused. "Three guys."

"Well, that would be helpful. Is that all?"

"Yeah, that's all I can spare. We got a lot of things going on down here."

Within two hours, word of the bomb had spread across the country. Rubbernecking crowds filled the Sahara parking lot. News trucks from Reno gathered along Highway 50. Explosives experts were on their way into Tahoe from specialist facilities throughout the United States: an army EOD squad from the nearby depot in Herlong, California; scientists from the Naval Surface Warfare

Center in Indian Head, Maryland, and Lawrence Livermore National Laboratory in northern California; and the Nuclear Emergency Support Team, recently created by the Department of Energy to respond to incidents of nuclear terrorism.

At ten, Jonkey's phone rang. "What the hell are you doing up there, Bill?" Yablonsky said. "I'm watching television. This is on every major news network. This is huge."

"Well, boss, that's what I tried to tell you."

"You need some people up there!"

"Yeah. Sacramento division has been in touch with me, and they're sending up about sixty guys."

"You'll have sixty-five more by tomorrow morning," Yablonsky told him and promptly got on a plane to Tahoe.

By three in the afternoon on Tuesday, the Nevada National Guard was enforcing a quarter-mile cordon around Harvey's. Highway 50 was blocked in both directions. Inside the deserted hotel, Danny Danihel and his men were alone with the bomb. On the casino floor, hands of cards, stacks of chips, and cash lay abandoned on the tables. The food in the buffet was congealing.

The bomb team examined the device every way they could. They photographed it and dusted it for fingerprints, X-rayed it and scraped it for paint samples. They scanned it for radiation with a Geiger counter. And using electronic listening devices and stethoscopes, they strained again and again to hear any sound coming from inside it. Late that night, they were able to pick up something coming from the lower box: an intermittent whirring noise. You had to listen for a minute to hear it, but it was definitely there. Somewhere inside the bomb, something was happening.

At around nine or ten that night, Jonkey and Herb Hawkins, his supervisor from the Vegas FBI office, went to see Harvey Gross up in the temporary office he'd been given at the Sahara Tahoe. They needed him to make a decision about the ransom.

Gross asked them what they thought. They told him that according to the letter, if he paid $3 million, the instructions on moving the device would arrive via general delivery at the post office. They didn't need to explain that that could be a long time coming. And who would risk moving the thing, based on what the extortionist had told them? It would take a minimum of four men. All of them would be killed if something went wrong. No, they told Gross, it was impossible to move. The best place to have it explode was right where it was.

Once he understood all that, Harvey Gross made his decision. "There's no way I'm paying these sons of bitches any money," he said.

ELEVEN

Big John arrived back at the house in Clovis late on Tuesday afternoon and told his boys to get ready for the payoff. Big John ran through the list of equipment they'd need: the two strobe lights he'd stolen from Lake Tahoe Airport, two large green canvas bags for the money, ski masks and jackets, a .357 revolver, a .22 and a .303 rifle, a box of ammunition for the .303, and a twelve-volt motorcycle battery Jimmy had brought from work, which would power one of the strobes. They loaded the gear into the back of Big John's gold Volvo.

Big John and Joan took her car, a little Toyota Celica hatchback. The boys followed in the Volvo. It was early evening. They stayed together, driving north on Highway 99 and then east onto 50. They dropped Joan and her car off near Cameron Park Airport, outside Sacramento. Then the boys went on with their father in the Volvo. Johnny drove. From the back seat, Big John gave directions and finally revealed the rest of the plan.

Following Highway 50 as it wound up into the wooded crags of Eldorado National Forest, they were headed for a remote clearing high in the mountains above Lake Tahoe. There, at four thousand feet, Johnny would drop his father and brother. Big John and Jimmy would take the guns, one of the strobes, and the bags and settle in to wait for the sound of a helicopter sent from Harvey's, less than fifty miles away. When they heard the aircraft approaching, they would turn on the strobe. This would be the signal for the pilot to land.

When the pilot touched down, Big John and Jimmy would over-power him at gunpoint. Big John would take the controls and fly Jimmy and the money to a second clearing he had found, near Ham's Station, forty miles away on the other side of the valley, where Johnny would be waiting with the Volvo. Jimmy and the money would go with Johnny, while Big John landed the helicopter at Cam-eron Park Airport, where Joan would pick him up. The four would then rendezvous back in Clovis. Then Big John and Joan would escape to Europe to launder the cash.

Things started to go wrong almost immediately. The three men were high in the mountains between Placerville and Kyburz, when Big John realized they had left the battery back in Clovis. When they reached Kyburz, a handful of wooden buildings scattered down the incline between the highway and the American River, it was around eleven p.m.

The door at the one-pump gas station was locked and the night bell was taped over. Big John pushed on it anyway. Nothing. He walked over to a wrecked VW parked in front of the gas station; maybe there was a battery in there. He started rummaging around beneath the hood. Inside the station, a couple of dogs began bark-ing. Then their owner, a skinny old man, burst through the door, shouting and cursing and waving a pistol. Big John and the boys dived into the Volvo and fled.

Now Big John was desperate. They turned the Volvo around and headed back the way they had come, toward Placerville, thirty miles down the mountain. At the Placerville Shell station, they found an attendant named Ken Dooley. "I want a battery," Big John told him. The kid sold him a twelve-volt Easycare 40 for forty-five dollars, in cash.

Big John got back in the car, and he and his sons set off up the mountain. Along the river, back through Kyburz. Johnny took a sharp left onto Ice House Road. The turnoff to the drop point was marked with a fluorescent orange cross spray-painted on a tree. It was late. By the time Johnny finally left his father and brother in the clearing with the strobe, the battery, and the guns and took off again in the Volvo, it was approaching midnight. There wasn't much time.

Five more minutes down the highway, Johnny pulled off onto a short gravel frontage road. He saw a restaurant with a neon cocktail glass glowing overhead and a phone booth outside. He dialed the number Big John had given him. It rang once, twice.

TWELVE

The Bell Ranger was running on fumes when FBI agent Joe Cook touched down on the runway at Lake Tahoe airport. The extortion note was very specific: *Land at 2300 hours, wait under the light by the gate in the chain-link fence; further instructions would arrive via taxi or the pay phone near the fence at exactly 0010.*

But Cook was late. He had flown up that night from the FBI office in Los Angeles, navigating for four hundred miles using a Texaco road map. When he landed, he radioed the tower for a gas truck and walked to the fence. The phone rang almost immediately. Cook answered on the second ring. It was eight minutes past midnight.

"Your instructions are under the table in front of you," the caller said. "You have three minutes."

Cook felt something taped to the underside of the shelf in the phone booth: a thin sheet of aluminum and, under that, an envelope.

"To the Pilot," the note said. "I remind you again to strictly follow orders."

Cook hurried back to the helicopter. He handed the piece of paper to Dell Rowley, hunched out of sight behind the seats with his submachine gun. As Cook prepared for takeoff, Rowley read him the instructions: *Follow Highway 50 west in a straight line. Stay below 500 feet. After fifteen minutes, start looking for a strobe light on your right. Land facing south. Two hundred feet away, you'll find further instructions nailed to the trunk of a tree.* Cook took the helicopter up and flew along the highway, following the curves as it wound through the forest. When he reached the fifteen-minute mark, he began circling.

Rowley's orders were simple: protect the pilot. Rowley was a SWAT team leader who had come to the FBI after serving in the U.S. Army and then the Border Patrol down in El Paso, Texas. He was an excellent shot, and he wasn't going to take any chances.

Down in the moonlit clearing, Big John and Jimmy listened for the chop of rotor blades. Once Big John thought he heard something, took the cables, and turned the strobe on for half a minute. But it wasn't a helicopter. No one came. Miles away, in entirely the wrong place, Joe Cook scanned the darkened landscape for more than an hour. He circled wider and wider. Nothing. Eventually, he and Rowley gave up and flew back to Tahoe with the three bags of scrap paper and the thousand dollars. The SWAT team stood down.

On the other side of the valley, Johnny waited for four or five hours in the dark. He kept the car window open, listening for the sound of his father and brother flying in with the money. Finally, he decided something must have gone wrong. He drove the Volvo back to where Joan was waiting, in Cameron Park. She was sitting in her car beside the airport fence, on the right side of the road. She'd heard the governor on the radio. He said there had been some confusion. It sounded like they still intended to pay the ransom.

Johnny drove back up the mountain to find Big John. Joan was close behind him in her Celica. On a right-hand hairpin at the bottom of Ice House Road, Johnny took the bend too fast. In his rearview mirror, he watched Joan skid across the road and slam into the embankment. The car was wrecked. Johnny went back and found Joan bleeding from her nose and head. Together they drove up the road a short distance in the Volvo. Jimmy and Big John were walking down toward him. It was around six a.m. on Wednesday, August 27, 1980. It was light out. They were empty-handed.

Johnny, Jimmy, Big John, and Joan picked up the guns from the drop site, then drove Joan down to the hospital in Placerville. Johnny took her in; he told the receptionist he had just been driving by and saw that she'd crashed. Then the three men took the Volvo down the street to the public phone at a Beacon gas station. Big John told Johnny to call the Douglas County sheriff's office: *Tell them to flip switch number five on the bomb and await further instructions.* Five was a dummy switch, Big John said. But it would buy them some more time.

It was almost seven when they began the three-hour drive back to Fresno. Jimmy was asleep in the passenger seat, Big John passed out in the back. Johnny was already late for work with the roofing company. As the landscape flattened out and the two-lane highway split into freeway, he put his foot down: 40, 50, 65 miles an hour. Then he saw lights in his rearview mirror.

Officer Jim Bergenholtz of the California Highway Patrol was a stickler for details. He had paced Johnny for two miles before finally pulling him over. After he issued him a speeding ticket, he took careful note of the number of men he saw in the gold Volvo and exactly where they were sitting.

THIRTEEN

For the first twenty-four hours, Danny Danihel had felt pretty comfortable with the bomb. A device that big could easily bring the entire building down, but he knew that no sensible extortionist would blow up his target before he'd gotten his money. Since the midnight deadline had come and gone, the situation was different. Now the thing could go off at any moment.

And despite his listening devices and photographs and the patchwork of X-rays stitched together across the wall of the command post across the street, Danihel had no real idea what was inside the device. By Wednesday morning he still had dozens of questions: When had the timer started running? How accurate was it? How reliable were the batteries? Was its creator really an expert or just some nutjob who wanted people to think he was?

At nine-thirty a.m. on Wednesday, the experts gathered in the Sahara command post for a roundtable meeting. They threw out every idea they could come up with. Flood the bomb with liquid nitrogen. Encase it in concrete. Pick it up and carry it to a nearby golf course. Finally Leonard Wolfson, a civilian consultant to the navy, suggested using more explosives to defeat the bomb, with a linear shaped charge. A precisely formed piece of plastic explosive encased in a brass jacket would create two explosive planes of hot gas collapsing on one another to form a fine jet: a pyrotechnic cutting tool. This could disable the bomb by severing the fusing mechanisms the technicians could see in the top box from the explosives they believed filled the lower box. Wolfson explained that the time between the detonation of the charge and the gas jet striking the box would be half a millisecond. If the bomb contained only low-voltage circuitry, it would be decapitated before the electrical impulses from the battery could reach the detonators and trigger the dynamite. It was risky, but it was the best idea they had.

At noon, the men around the table took a vote. It was unanimous: they would follow Wolfson's plan. Using a computer terminal set up in the Sahara to communicate with Lawrence Livermore, Wolfson began making calculations. A defense contractor down in Las Vegas machined the brass components for the shaped charge, which were then flown up to Tahoe by helicopter.

At 3:10 p.m. Danihel walked up to the bomb carrying the shaped charge taped to a two-by-four. He had been awake for thirty hours. He was very tired and very scared.

Standing beside the bomb, he positioned the charge against a stack of Tahoe phone books and a Formica-topped table at the precise angle dictated by the scientists at Lawrence Livermore. He checked the angles using a tape measure and a piece of string. He primed the charge and checked the detonators. He checked the continuity of the firing leads with a galvanometer. He made the connection to the firing leads. Then he checked everything again.

At that moment back in Fresno, Johnny Birges was just leaving work. Big John and Jimmy were on the road again, making the long trip up from Clovis to Placerville in Jimmy's pickup, on their way to collect Joan from the hospital. As they headed north on Highway 88, Big John told Jimmy that it was time for another phone call.

Despite what he had claimed in the extortion note, the irrigation timer in the bomb would run for at least three more days before detonating the explosives. Big John wanted the governor to make good on his promise of a second attempt at the ransom exchange. The highway through the Gold Country plains toward Placerville was remote and deserted. As they approached the old mining town of Ione, Big John told Jimmy to pull over at the pay phone outside Antonio's Italian Restaurant. It was a little after three-thirty in the afternoon.

In Stateline the sheriff's office announced a fifteen-minute warning. Crowds of gawking tourists and reporters craned their necks from behind the barricades. Some of them were already wearing I WAS BOMBED AT HARVEY'S T-shirts. Word went around that gamblers were placing bets on what would happen next.

Danny Danihel walked down the frozen escalator, past the blinking slots, and out into the afternoon sun. Around the corner he met up with Carl Paulson, another member of the bomb squad, who was waiting beside his truck outside Harvey's Pancake Parlor. The empty street rang with the sound of a deputy calling out a final warning over the PA of his patrol car. Then silence, save for the clicking of the stoplights on Stateline Avenue. Danihel's radio crackled with the final okay. Under the hood of Paulson's truck, he touched one of the two strands of firing lead against the truck battery. "Fire in the hole," he said. He touched the second strand to the battery. It was 3:46 p.m.

"Holy shit," Danihel said. But nobody heard him over the roar of the explosion.

FOURTEEN

Danihel and Paulson scrambled beneath the truck. Fragments of concrete and pieces of plaster rained from the sky. On the roof of the Sahara Tahoe, Bill Jonkey sheltered behind a shallow parapet. Shards of wood, metal, and glass sprayed out from both sides of Harvey's as Big John's bomb vaporized in a flash of superheated expanding gases. A pressure wave radiating outward at more than fourteen thousand feet per second tore through the second floor, bursting through doorways, flattening walls, and shattering windows. Behind the barricades, a ragged whoop went up from the crowd.

Danihel and Paulson lay on the warm asphalt, waiting for the patter of debris falling on the roof of the truck to subside. From within the building came sounds of rending and crashing as floors and ceilings collapsed. When they finally stood, the damage wrought by almost a thousand pounds of dynamite was clear. A jagged five-story hole yawned in the middle of the casino. "We lost it," Danihel said. "The whole thing went up."

Five minutes later Wilma Hoppe, answering phones at the Douglas County sheriff substation just north of Stateline in Zephyr Cove, received an operator-assisted call from a pay phone in Ione, California. The operator's voice said, "A dollar seventy-five. There must be some confusion." Then another voice came on the line. Hoppe thought it sounded like a white man of around thirty.

"If you still want the exchange, I'll call back in one hour," he said. Then he hung up.

Big John and Jimmy were back on Highway 88, headed for Placerville, when they heard the news on the radio. "Well, I don't have anything to live for now," Big John said.

Half an hour later they arrived at the hospital to collect Joan. She had a Band-Aid across her nose. They watched as footage of the explosion replayed on a TV in the waiting room. The sight of what he had done—the hurtling debris, the gaping hole in the facade of the casino—briefly lifted Big John's spirits. "It worked pretty good," he said.

Joan said they still had to report the accident to the Highway Patrol. They drove up to Ice House Road to get her car. A tow truck was waiting; Joan had locked the keys inside, and Big John had to force the window open. They followed the tow truck back down Highway 50. It was really quiet all the way back to Clovis. Nobody said anything about the bomb.

When the charge went off, Chris Ronay was standing next to Carl Paulson's truck. He had come straight from the FBI Explosives Operations Center in Washington, where he worked as a bomb analyst. That afternoon the local agents had pulled him off the plane before it even reached the gate at Sacramento Airport and flown him to Tahoe by helicopter.

Ronay heard two explosions in close succession: a hiccup and then a boom. The concussion knocked him to the ground. Beside him the state fire marshal shouted "C'mon!" and took off running toward the hotel lobby entrance. Ronay followed. Plaster dust was still drifting in the air.

The explosion had torn a giant spherical hole through the middle of the hotel. Where the bomb had once sat on the second floor, a hole sixty feet in diameter gaped in the foot-thick concrete. There was a matching hole fifty feet across in the floor above and another thirty feet across in the floor above that. The void reached up to the fifth floor and all the way down into the basement. Around it, webs of twisted rebar were tangled with broken drywall, bedclothes, and pieces of metal window frame. Toilets teetered on the edges of newly calved precipices. TV sets dangled by their cables over the abyss. From somewhere deep inside the darkened carcass of the building came the distant sound of whirring machinery, still drawing power from an auxiliary generator no one had thought to shut off.

Ronay looked down at the dust carpeting the parking lot. His job was just beginning.

FIFTEEN

Once Highway 50 reopened, the investigation—a Bureau Special, Major Case No. 28, designated Wheelbomb—began in earnest. Fifty agents from the FBI's Sacramento and Las Vegas divisions were now installed in Stateline and devoted full time to the hunt for the Harvey's bombers. Bill Jonkey was appointed case agent for Nevada, charged with coordinating the investigation on his side of the line until the culprits were found.

Late on Friday afternoon, two days after the explosion, enough debris had been cleared from around the hotel for Harvey's to reopen part of the casino for gambling. The old Lake Room was small and shopworn, but the symbolism was important—and so was the money. Yablonsky gave a press conference there, on a red-curtained stage behind the bar. He admitted to the press that the FBI had not yet developed a significant lead and had no detailed descriptions of the suspects. He announced a reward for information: $175,000—soon raised to $200,000—put together by Harvey Gross and the management of three other casinos in Stateline. It was the largest bounty Yablonsky had ever heard of in a criminal case.

By Monday Yablonsky was still waiting in vain for a solid lead. "There is not anything I can say I'm panting over," he told reporters. Agents had recovered fingerprints from the bomb and were checking them against their records. More eyewitnesses came forward, including a musician and two friends who had been crossing the street from Harrah's at five-thirty a.m. on Tuesday and had gotten a good look at the two men wheeling the cart across the Harvey's parking lot. But none of the witnesses could agree on what the suspects looked like.

Among the hundreds of tips the bureau had received was a call from Gerald Diminico, the manager of the Balahoe Motel on Emerald Bay Road near the airport. He said that two men driving a white van had checked in there the day before the bomb was discovered. They had made a nuisance of themselves asking for jumper cables at four in the morning and checked out soon afterward.

In Fresno FBI agents checked over the details they read from the registration card at the Balahoe Motel: Joey Evetto, of 4423 Van Ness, Fresno; a white Dodge van, license plate 1A65819. The Fresno Police Department could find no record of that name in their files or those of the sheriff's office, and there was no 4423 Van Ness in the city. A call to the California DMV from an agent in Sacramento revealed that no license had ever been issued to a Joey Evetto. It did, however, return a hit on the license plate. The department had an application for a title transfer on file, but the clerks would have to search the transfer applications by hand. It would take some time.

Within ten days of the bombing, the FBI team in Stateline had its first break. Based on the composite pictures and some telephone tips, the agents had assembled a short list of prime suspects. The focus of the Wheelbomb investigation now settled on five electronic engineers employed at two aircraft factories: the Gates Lear plant in Tucson, Arizona, and the Lear Avia plant in Stead, near Reno. They resembled the men in the composite pictures. They were new to the area, they had a van, and they had been in Tahoe at the time the device was delivered to Harvey's. They had access to strobe lights and had technical and aviation experience. The FBI put them under twenty-four-hour surveillance, including wiretaps on their phones. What the agents heard on the wire only confirmed their suspicions.

Finally, confident that they had the bombers, twenty agents drove up to Reno from Stateline to confront the suspects with the evidence. The interview team was led by Bill O'Reilly, a stocky Angeleno with a mustache and an Afro, who had come to the FBI from the LAPD bomb squad. As the bureau's case agent coordinating the Wheelbomb investigation in California, O'Reilly was Bill Jonkey's counterpart on the other side of the state line.

Once O'Reilly and his team arrived in Stead, the agents divided into pairs to take each of the suspects to separate rooms at the plant for interrogation. Five minutes in, O'Reilly and another agent, Carl Larsen, stepped out to take a break. Something about this felt very wrong. They glanced down the hallway at one another and shook their heads.

They had the same sinking feeling: *Shit. These weren't the guys.*

On September 17 Joe Yablonsky held another press conference and finally released composite pictures of two of the men they were looking for. They were both white. One was said to be five feet seven inches, about twenty years old, with sandy blond hair and a mustache. The other had short dark hair and protruding ears. "A hayseed," Yablonsky said. "A goober type."

Two weeks later there had still been no takers for the reward.

"Under normal conditions, a person would sell his mother down the river for $200,000," Yablonsky told the press in Stateline. The bombers must be part of a particularly tight-knit group, he figured— perhaps a family. It was the only logical explanation.

Jonkey and Ronay were still sifting through the debris in the Harvey's parking lot. Their team recovered casters, twisted fragments of the leveling bolts, and hundreds of pieces of mangled steel plate, the biggest no more than two inches across, folded and deformed by the force of the explosion. Every day they sent packages of what they'd gathered back to the FBI explosives lab in Washington. Blast damage experts surveyed the wreckage, measured evidence of the overpressure wave and scorching. They proved what Jonkey and Ronay already suspected: the concussion of the linear-shaped charge had set off the pendulum mechanism in the bomb, which had then detonated as designed.

But the forensics provided them with no clearer picture of the bomb makers. The world was not short of suspicious characters with a grievance, access to explosives, and a use for $3 million in cash; the investigators now had a list of several hundred suspects. They considered the IRA, Iranian students, the Mafia. They hypnotized witnesses to try to recover details from their subconscious, including one who had seen a Toyota pickup stopped on Highway 50 at the time the "flip switch five" call was made. They interviewed Harvey Gross a dozen times, asking for the names of anyone with a grudge strong enough to warrant destroying his life's work. But Harvey was seventy-six years old. They could ask all they liked. He just couldn't remember.

In the meantime, the FBI office in Sacramento had heard back from the California DMV. The van they had been asking about, the one that had been spotted at the Balahoe Motel, was a white 1975 Dodge Tradesman registered to one John Birges. The registration renewal had been held up because of unpaid parking tickets. The DMV provided a copy of a driver's license in the name of John

Waldo Birges, with the address 5265 North Fowler Avenue, Clovis, California.

One day in October, a Fresno FBI agent came to the door of Big John's house asking about the van. Not me, Big John told him. You want my son.

SIXTEEN

In the weeks after the bombing, Johnny had gone back to his routine. Monday to Saturday with General Roofing, six a.m. to three p.m. High all the time. A few days after the failure of the ransom handoff, he had sold his van, trading it in at Fresno Toyota for a brand new 4x4. He didn't feel that bad about what had happened. Nobody got hurt. And in spite of everything that had gone wrong already, he still had faith in his father. Big John knew what he was doing.

But when Johnny came home from work one day to find an FBI agent's business card wedged into the jamb of his front door, he freaked out. He had sold the van, but he had no alibi to explain why it might have been seen in South Tahoe while the bomb was being delivered. Johnny, Jimmy, and Big John got together in the kitchen on Fowler Avenue that night. They came up with a story.

Johnny would tell the FBI that he'd gone up to the mountains around Placerville by himself, early on the morning of Sunday, August 24, two days before the bomb was delivered. He was looking for a place to grow marijuana. He drove south to Highway 88 and turned off onto a gravel road near Ham's Station. He arrived at nine or ten in the morning, parked the van, and walked around for a few hours. When he got back to the van, it was early evening and the battery was dead; he'd left the stereo on. He'd had to ditch the van and hitchhike back to Fresno. When he got home, he called his brother and arranged to use his pickup to get to work on Monday and Tuesday. Then, in the middle of the night on Tuesday, he and Jimmy drove over to Ham's Station, where they jump-started the van and drove it back to Fresno.

Big John assured Johnny that the investigators had no evidence. All he had to do was stick to his story and he'd be fine. So when the federal agents came around again, one afternoon after work in late October, that's exactly what Johnny did. No, he said, he'd never been to South Lake Tahoe. He hadn't let anyone borrow the van. He had no idea how it could have been spotted outside the motel on Emerald Road early Tuesday. No, he'd never heard of Joe Evetto. No, when he came back to jump-start the van, he didn't think it had been moved or tampered with—although, now that they mentioned it, one of the door locks was open, and maybe some of those tapes in the snack tray had been moved around a bit.

When he finished, the agents told him his story was ridiculous and unbelievable. He was clearly lying to protect whomever he had allowed to use the van. They asked him to take a polygraph. It was entirely voluntary; they just wanted to eliminate him from the investigation. He said he'd think about it. They said they'd be back. They added John Waldo Birges to their list of suspects.

By the beginning of November, the Wheelbomb operation had ballooned into one of the largest and most expensive criminal investigations the FBI had ever conducted—and it still hadn't produced any results. At the end of the month, a teletype went out from the Las Vegas division to the FBI director's office and eight other agency offices around the country, offering a blunt and bleak summary: "Investigation in this case still has not realized even the slightest information which would lead to the perpetrators of this crime, despite thousands of interviews and review of over 123,000 records." On December 1 the Wheelbomb investigation was scaled back sharply. The command post was relocated to Jonkey's small office in Carson City, reducing the bureau's presence in Stateline to a single room with one telephone line in Harvey's Inn, the motel Gross had built down the street from the main casino. Back in Fresno, the local agents still believed Johnny's alibi was riddled with inconsistencies, but they had no way of proving that he wasn't telling the truth. They interviewed Jimmy twice, but he gave them the same elaborate explanation about the marijuana patch and the dead battery. He, too, told them he had mixed feelings about taking a polygraph test. Big John backed up Johnny's story.

Special Agent Norm Lane couldn't help liking Big John. Fresno was a bad town, and Lane and the other agents in the bureau's office there spent most of their time going after bank robbers and gang-bangers from the Aryan Nation or the Mexican Mafia. But this guy was something different: clever, funny, charismatic—always had a little smile on his face, an air about him that suggested he thought he was smarter than you. Big John told Lane his whole life story. He said Johnny used marijuana; that was partly why he threw him out of the house. He said that Johnny certainly didn't have anything to do with the Harvey's bombing.

He said that he himself had been a regular at Harvey's and had become friendly with the staff and with Harvey Gross. He admitted he had been a heavy gambler at times but said that over the years his winnings and losses had pretty much balanced out. The last time he had been up in Tahoe was back in July sometime. He'd slept in his car, in a sleeping bag. He said he'd heard about the bombing, either on TV or in the Fresno newspaper. He said he thought organized crime was behind it.

By the beginning of the new year, four months after the bombing, only Bill O'Reilly, Bill Jonkey, Jonkey's supervisor Herb Hawkins, and three other agents working out of the resident agency in Carson City were still assigned to the investigation full time. By then the bureau had compiled a list of 486 individual suspects worldwide and eliminated 233 of them. If they were lucky, the names of the men they were looking for were somewhere among the remaining 253.

SEVENTEEN

In January 1981 the FBI agents in Fresno, still trying to eliminate Johnny Birges from their investigation, served him with a subpoena. He was called to testify before a grand jury in Reno. Once again Big John told him to just stick to his story. Everything would be fine.

Johnny went alone. When he arrived at the federal courthouse in Reno, he was surprised to find that there wasn't a judge. It was just a regular room with some chairs and some ordinary-looking citizens in it. The whole thing took an hour, maybe an hour and a half. The assistant U.S. attorney asked Johnny about the van and the Bala-hoe Motel. The jurors listened to him, watched his face. Johnny felt pretty nonchalant. He didn't think they could prove he was lying. Still, on the long drive home, he began to wonder what he had gotten himself into.

On May 13, 1981, Harvey's Wagon Wheel held a ribbon-cutting ceremony and formally reopened for business, after repairs and security improvements totaling some $18 million. By then the reward offered for information on the bombers had swollen to $500,000. Half a million dollars—enough to set someone up for life. Harvey and the other gaming kingpins in Stateline were determined to make sure whoever had destroyed his hotel didn't get away with it.

It was a month before the call finally came in. At first the kid was scared shitless that they were going to kill him or something. He called the FBI's Fresno office a couple of times but wouldn't give his name. Eventually, in early June, he agreed to meet a Fresno FBI agent face-to-face. His name was Danny DiPierri. He said he knew who had bombed Harvey's. He'd dated a girl who had told him all about it before it ever happened. Her name was Kelli Cooper.

After that, things started moving quickly. The agents took Danny out to the Holiday Inn by the Fresno Air Terminal and hypnotized him. They wired him and put him on the phone with Kelli. A full background investigation began into John Birges Sr. By late June the Wheelbomb team in Carson City knew a great deal about Big John, and none of it was good. They'd heard about his gambling debts. They'd heard he had once been a high roller at Harvey's and a guest at Gross's ranch. They'd heard he lost half a million dollars. They'd heard about how he'd been moved out of that suite on New Year's Eve, how he'd felt belittled and humiliated in front of his girl-friend. They'd heard that he'd torched his own restaurant for the insurance money.

Agents from Fresno were sent out to locate the new owner of Johnny's van. Chris Ronay and his team flew back from Washington to conduct a microscopic examination of the Dodge, searching for old fingerprints, paint chips from the bomb, and explosive residue. Agents from the Sacramento office went to question personnel at the Helms Creek hydroelectric project about the theft of explosives reported the previous year. By the end of the month, one agent had found a witness placing Big John at the scene of Joan's accident on Ice House Road. Another had tracked down Officer Jim Bergenholtz of the California Highway Patrol and his meticulously kept note-book. By early July forty-four agents were back on the case full time. The Birgeses were designated prime suspects.

Johnny and Jimmy had known something was up for weeks. All summer agents followed the boys everywhere they went, from morning until midnight. They followed them to work and home again. If Jimmy went on a date, they waited until he picked the girl up from her house, then went in and braced her parents. Sometimes the agents just sat outside his house, waiting. Johnny had nick-names for them all: Hair Bear, he called O'Reilly; the lone woman, Sherry Harris, with her auburn hair, was known as Grapehead. They even had a name for him: Kickback. They all knew he liked to get high. Sometimes Johnny wouldn't see them watching him at all, but they'd call him later and tell him where he'd been and what he'd been wearing, who he'd seen, and what he'd been doing: *Up at the lake with that girl, Johnny? Nice.*

Throughout July, Bill Jonkey visited Big John almost every day. He'd go out to the house on Fowler Avenue with one of the agents from the Fresno office—Norm Lane or Tom Oswald. Jonkey just wanted to get Big John talking—sometimes about how his sons were doing, sometimes about nothing much at all. Sometimes he wouldn't even mention Harvey's. Other times he'd take along some of those glossy color eight-by-tens he had of the bomb, feet pressing down into the bright orange carpet outside the telephone exchange.

Sometimes Big John would yell and scream at them through the locked door. Maybe he'd heard that they'd been talking to his neighbors; that could really get him going. Then he'd start yelling about Jonkey and Lane, about the FBI, about all the motherfucking cops out there. They knew Big John kept a loaded .22 rifle beside that door. Jonkey would stand outside in his polo shirt and jeans, turned away just so, his sidearm out of sight behind his right leg. Then sometimes the door would open abruptly, and there he'd be, Big John, ready to talk again. He couldn't help himself. Jonkey would discreetly holster his gun, and they'd start in.

"What the hell do you want to talk to me about today?"

"Well, Mr. Birges, can you help us?" Polite. Plaintive, even. "Here's a picture. Why would a guy put switches on the front like that? And what do you think you could have used to cover up the screw holes in there?"

"Well . . . can I keep this?"

"No, Mr. Birges, you can't keep it, but you can look at it."

"Well, there probably were screw holes. You can use Bondo or something . . ."

He wanted to ask them questions. He was interested in the payoff—what had gone wrong? And the explosion—why had they blown it up themselves? He wanted badly to show them how clever he was, how much he knew about everything. About electronics. About fabrication. About bombs.

By that time the bureau's investigators knew more about Big John than he could ever have imagined. They knew about Elizabeth's strange death, about his experience with explosives, his temper, and his recklessness. They knew about the flying stunts; the FAA had taken his pilot's license away. And they'd been out to the turkey farm his brother-in-law Ferenc Schmidt had, on the outskirts of Fresno.

Ferenc, who was married to Elizabeth's younger sister, Jolan, was only too happy to help the FBI. He and Big John had never liked one another. Ferenc had thousands of birds out there in three open-sided sheds, each a hundred yards long, tin roofs with dozens of automatic feeders beneath them. Jonkey was especially interested in the feeders. They were Big John's work. After Harvey's cut off his credit, Big John hadn't had anything to do, and Ferenc had agreed to give him a few hundred dollars for some work. Big John had built an electric bird-feeding mechanism and a pigpen for him from scratch. The feeding system was operated by electrical pressure plates. When the turkeys ate all the feed in a tray, the release of the weight closed a switch, and more food tumbled out.

The mechanism wasn't sophisticated, but it was clever, built from Plexiglas and black neoprene, with a big brass paddle to make a contact. Jonkey and Chris Ronay agreed that they had both seen this kind of technology before: the ghostly shadows inside the box outside the casino telephone exchange.

Still, they had not yet found a single piece of conclusive evidence placing Big John or the boys at the scene of the explosion. Examining the registration card from the Balahoe Motel for prints, scouring Johnny's van for explosive residue, comparing stationery from Joan's desk at the Fresno County probation office to the paper used for the extortion note—it all came to nothing. They had tracked down a steel supplier in Fresno that stocked all the materials necessary to build the bomb and who counted Big John among his customers. But Big John always paid in cash, and the supplier kept no receipts. The switches at the turkey farm and the ones Jonkey had seen in the X-rays at Harvey's shared an unusual mechanical signature, nothing more.

The agents' best hope of finding the evidence they needed was to prove that Big John might be planning something new. Then they could legally put a wiretap on the house on Fowler Avenue and listen in to everything that happened there. But although they had the paperwork for microphone surveillance ready to go, they could find no one who could conclusively state that Big John was discussing plans for another bomb.

And yet: he was.

EIGHTEEN

Big John had started talking about putting a second bomb in Harvey's almost as soon as the dust from the first one had settled. The day after the explosion, he called Bill Brown and Terry Hall over to his house and told them what he had in mind. When they said they didn't want to have anything to do with it, he told them to keep their mouths shut about what they knew. Otherwise he'd have them killed.

A little less than a month later, Jimmy Birges was asleep on the couch when a noise woke him in the middle of the night. It was around four a.m. Big John had just come home. He'd taken Jimmy's new pickup an hour north to Wishon. He said he'd stolen another dozen cases of dynamite and put them in the freezer.

A few days later Jimmy was in the garage, and Big John brought a stick of it out to show him. It was red jelly wrapped in white plastic, crimped at the ends. Big John asked him if he'd help him move it somewhere else. Big John put the dynamite in the back of Elizabeth's old pickup. Jimmy followed in his Toyota. They drove a few miles out into the blank farmland at the edge of town, near Ferenc's turkey ranch. There, beside two large trees, Big John had already dug a hole. It was big enough for the whole haul of dynamite, around seven hundred pounds in all.

Throughout the winter and spring of 1981, as Johnny testified before the grand jury in Reno and the FBI agents in Carson City and Fresno searched desperately for any scrap of incriminating evidence against the Birges family, the dynamite sat there, buried at the bottom of a flood control ditch. Then Big John got into some kind of fight with Ferenc and his wife. They wouldn't pay him for the work he'd done; they told him his turkey feeders were no good and the gate on the pigpen opened the wrong way. By then the FBI agents were all over Johnny, but Big John didn't care. He was angry. He dug up the dynamite. He rigged a little of it under the wooden bridge Ferenc had over there. The bridge was the only way he had to get in or out of the farm. Johnny heard the explosion all the way across town.

Big John carefully clipped every story printed in the *Fresno Bee* about the theft of the dynamite and the bombing at Harvey's. After the Harvey's explosion, he went back to Tahoe with Joan and dropped by the casino. He might have been casing the place—or he might just have been playing the tables again. Because he also had another target in mind. Early in the summer of 1981, he went over to San Francisco to have a look at the Bank of America building, the monolithic high-rise on California Street. He told Jimmy that maybe he could get a bomb in there.

Whether he chose the bank or the casino, he'd figured out a way of making it easier. The new device would be remote controlled and would drive itself in. At the beginning of August, Big John went to an electrical supply store north of Fresno and bought twenty switches. This time, he told Jimmy, Harvey Gross wouldn't pay three million. He'd pay five.

On August 12, 1981, a typically infernal summer afternoon in the Central Valley, Bill Jonkey knocked on Johnny Birges's door. He asked him yet again to explain his whereabouts on August 26 and 27 the year before. Again, Johnny told his story, but this time Jonkey poked holes in it, and Johnny struggled to fill them. Yes, he said, he had taken an unusually roundabout route home that day, because he didn't know there was a shorter one. Yes, he had gotten a speeding ticket on the way back, and there were two other men in the car with him. They were hitchhikers. Both were young, white men of average build; no, he probably couldn't identify them if he saw them again.

That same day Norm Lane and agent Carl Curtis visited Big John in Clovis. They asked him where he had been those same nights the year before. He wasn't sure, he said, but he was probably right here at home. Then why, the agents asked, had several witnesses seen him on the afternoon of August 27, at the scene of a car accident on Ice House Road, up in the Eldorado National Forest?

Ah, now he remembered—that must have been the day he and his son went up there to collect Joan from the hospital, he told them. She'd wrecked her car. She called and asked them to pick her up. What was she doing up there? Well, she'd driven up to South Tahoe to go gambling the night before. But when she got there, she found some of the casinos were roped off. There was a bomb scare or something. So she'd driven to Reno instead.

Big John readily admitted that he'd been up to Harvey's a lot himself over the years. In fact, he said, he still owed the casino $15,000. He'd probably lost about $700,000 since he started playing the tables there. The agents suggested that would provide ample motive for wanting to extort money from Harvey's by, say, planting a giant bomb in the hotel.

Big John said that he would never do such a thing. He'd once made a lot of money in the landscaping business. But then he'd discovered that his wife was not only having an affair but paying the man for his services, at a rate of $946 a session. It was then that he'd realized that money wasn't a source of happiness. He decided to get rid of all the money he had—by gambling at Harvey's. Now that he'd succeeded, money no longer had any meaning for him. He was much happier.

The agents said they knew that he had all the welding, electronics, and explosives skills necessary to build a bomb like the one that blew up Harvey's. They'd been told he had a lot of dynamite. Big John said he was flattered that the FBI believed he could pull off such a crime. He said that they were probably right; he was skillful enough to build such a complex device. But he certainly didn't have the courage you'd need. He showed them a letter from his eighty-one-year-old mother in Hungary. She wrote that she'd like him to visit her one last time before she died. He said he wasn't quite ready to make the trip yet, but when he was about to leave the country, of course he would notify the Fresno office of the FBI.

The next day Lane and Curtis dropped in on Big John again, this time with Bill Jonkey. They gave him a form to sign to consent to a search of the house. Big John said he couldn't sign, because the house was technically Joan's. But he was more than happy to show them around the workshop. On the way to the garage, he pointed out a big walk-in freezer. He said he used it for food storage. In the workshop, the agents noticed cans of gray spray paint and a small can of White Knight Auto Body Repair Putty. They saw a piece of sheet metal of about the same thickness as the piece found taped beneath the phone booth at Lake Tahoe Airport. They saw a drill press, an arc welder, and an oxyacetylene welding tank set. And they saw a homemade cart with casters for wheels and a T-handle made of welded angle iron.

Big John told the agents that he could never have used his workshop to build a bomb like the one in Harvey's. A sensible technician would need an entirely secret location known only to the individual building the bomb—whoever he was.

NINETEEN

Later on the same day Big John gave him a tour of his workshop, Bill Jonkey put on a jacket and tie and drove over to Reno. The Wheel-bomb team was almost out of options, but they had one remaining card to play: it was time to get a warrant for Johnny Birges's arrest.

At the federal courthouse, Jonkey told the grand jury that everything Johnny had told them eight months earlier had been a lie. Here's what really happened, he said. Johnny was up in the mountains the day the bomb went off; the traffic citation proved as much. He was there with his father. Birges senior's girlfriend had been in an accident nearby; there were witnesses placing them both at the scene. That afternoon the jury returned its decision. John Waldo Birges was indicted for perjury. Jonkey was back in Fresno that night with a warrant.

The next day Jonkey and Carl Larsen drove over to Johnny's house. They found him hiding in the bathroom, holding the door shut from inside, and pulled him out at gunpoint. "This is the big time now, Johnny," Jonkey said. "We've got a federal warrant for your arrest." They cuffed him and put him in the car.

Jimmy came over to the Fresno FBI office on O Street voluntarily; the investigators had nothing on him. Inside, the boys were taken to separate rooms for questioning. They both held tight to their story. The agents were tense. If the boys called their bluff—if they simply asked for a lawyer and stuck to their alibis—the district attorney would never be able to make the case against Big John. Everyone, even Johnny, would walk. In the interrogation rooms on the fourth floor, hours passed. Larsen worked the mother angle: *She didn't raise you to be a liar. She wanted you to be better than this.*

That did it. Johnny didn't want to be the only one going to jail. He knew if he didn't talk, someone else would. He said he'd tell them everything. But first he wanted to speak to his kid brother.

Jimmy had been stonewalling his interrogators for three hours by then. Wouldn't say anything. But then he saw Johnny coming down the hall. The agents had set the scene perfectly: Johnny was shuffling in cuffs and ankle chains. Jimmy turned to one of the FBI men. "We are not going to jail for our father," he said.

He said he wanted to talk to Johnny.

"Did you tell them?" asked Jimmy.

"Yes," said Johnny.

Jimmy came back to the table with tears in his eyes. He said he was ready to tell the truth. Bill O'Reilly read him his Miranda rights.

That was the end of it. After that you couldn't shut them up.

Around three o'clock in the afternoon on Saturday, August 15, Big John and Joan left the house on Fowler Avenue in the gold Volvo. They hadn't heard from Jimmy since he'd left for work at the Toyota showroom the previous morning. That meant trouble. They'd driven only a few hundred yards down the block when they were cut off by a pair of unmarked sedans with whip antennas. Four FBI agents, including Norm Lane and Carl Curtis, pulled them out of the Volvo and cuffed them at gunpoint.

Down in an interview room on O Street, Big John refused to say anything before he'd talked to a lawyer. He asked to speak to Jimmy. When his younger son came in, he told Big John that the FBI knew everything. The agents even knew about Bill Brown and Terry Hall. Big John was furious. If it hadn't been for Johnny, the government would never have found out. If it hadn't been for Johnny, they wouldn't have been able to prove anything in four thousand years.

Joe Yablonsky held a press conference the next day. The FBI kept the boys in protective custody for a while after that, put them up in the Fresno Hilton, told them to order what they liked. Johnny had a blast. It was like an adventure. Later O'Reilly took them on a road trip through California so they could show the agents each of the locations used in the botched ransom drop. On September 9, 1981, Johnny turned twenty-one. The FBI agents gave him a card and signed it with the nicknames he had given them.

There were two trials in the end: a federal proceeding in Las Vegas and a state trial in Minden, just a few miles from the ranch where Harvey Gross's pilot had shown Big John how to fly a helicopter. The boys were phenomenal; they had great memories.

Big John never did come clean. For four years he went through lawyer after lawyer until, finally, he defended himself. He told the prosecutors he'd built the bomb; they were never going to take that away from him. But he said he'd been made to do it. Organized crime: a mysterious hood named Charlie, who told him that if he blew up Harvey's, his debts would be forgiven—and if he didn't do it, they'd cripple him for life.

Big John cross-examined his sons, speaking to them like strangers. He suggested Jimmy put him up to it, because he needed money for college. He said the bomb was never supposed to hurt anybody. When Chris Ronay took the stand, Big John took a car headlamp out of a briefcase and told him they could have used one to drain the battery and make the bomb safe. He suggested Danny Danihel, the leader of the Douglas County fire department bomb squad, had deliberately blown the whole thing up.

The state's prosecutor didn't buy a word of it. "Everything is covered, but it doesn't make sense," he told the jury. "He didn't care what happened to whom or to what. He was getting even, and he was going to get money if it all worked right, and he didn't particularly care about anyone else, the employees, the guests, the players. They could all have been blown up for all he cared."

On March 7, 1985, the jury filed into the state courthouse in Minden and announced that they had found Janos Birges guilty on eight of nine counts, including extortion, making a bomb threat, unlawful possession of an explosive device, and interstate transportation of an explosive device. The judge sentenced him to life in prison. In return for giving evidence against their father, John Waldo and

James Birges pleaded guilty and were granted complete immunity. They never served a day behind bars for their involvement in the bombing. Ella Joan Williams was found guilty of conspiracy and sentenced to seven years in prison, but her conviction was later overturned on appeal.

They locked Big John up in the federal penitentiary in Lompoc, California. After the second trial, the boys never saw him again. But before his final conviction, Jimmy wrote his father a three-page letter. In it, he apologized for what he and his brother had done and asked for his forgiveness. He explained that he had no work and no money. He said that now he and Johnny would have to do whatever they could to stay out of jail. "Dear Big John," he wrote.

> You are the smartest and most remarkable person in the world. I respect you more than anything and I will try to be worthy of you. . . . I often lie awake at night thinking of what I have done to you. I cry often at the thought of what I did. I wish we could have been a happy family from the start. I am glad that you brought me up the way you did because it made me realize how hard life was early on. . . . I will love you always. Your son, Jimmy.

EPILOGUE

Janos Birges finally succumbed to liver cancer in the medical facility at the Federal Correctional Center in Jean, Nevada, on August 27, 1996, almost sixteen years to the day after the device he had built exploded in Harvey's casino. He was seventy-four.

Bill Jonkey stayed in touch with the Birges boys for a few years after Big John went to prison. He thought they were basically good kids. Chris Ronay and Jonkey went on to be involved in the FBI's investigations of later bombings, including Lockerbie, Oklahoma

City, and the first World Trade Center attack in 1993, but they never
encountered another case like the one at Harvey's Wagon Wheel.

Jonkey retired from the bureau in 2000 but sometimes still lectures on what happened at Harvey's. When I met him recently, he
said that if he saw Big John's bomb again today, he still wouldn't
know how to defuse it. His team never saw the inside of the box,
and to this day he can't be certain exactly what was in it. There were
things in there that the boys might not have known about. And he
could never be certain that Big John was telling the truth.

Jimmy Birges never left Fresno. He settled down, eventually
started a welding and fabrication business, had three children, and
began coaching Little League. He did pretty well for himself, well
enough to start racing cars in his spare time. Things didn't work
out so smoothly for Johnny. Having the same name as his father
made life difficult. People didn't want the son of a bomber working
on their roofs. He moved to Bakersfield and started his own contracting business. He made a lot of money, but he also acquired a
cocaine habit.

In 1986 his fiancée was driving back from Avila Beach one day
and fell asleep at the wheel. The car left the road, and she was killed
instantly. Her death seemed to sap Johnny of all motivation; he
moved to Santa Barbara with nothing but a box of clothes, his truck,
and a little coke. He drifted for a while, started surfing, and eventually opened his own board-shaping shop down the coast in Ventura.
But he was a short-tempered drunk and a fighter, and he'd end up in
jail for a few months at a time.

In 2008, after one DUI too many, he was sentenced to 240 days
in the Ventura County Jail, where he got into a fight in the yard and
ended up with a broken jaw. He used the rest of his time inside to
write a book about the bombing. He changed a few things around,
embellished the story here and there, and ended up publishing it
himself, as a novel. When he called his publishers a year later, they
told him they hadn't sold a single copy.

THE OILMAN'S DAUGHTER

EVAN RATLIFF

ONE

I n the summer of 1972 when Judith Adams was sixteen years old, a strange woman knocked on the front door of the shotgun house where she lived with her mother, on the south side of Baxter Springs, Kansas. Judith opened it. The woman was small and thin, a brunette, and Judith detected an angry edge, as if she were in a hurry to get somewhere and the teenager now in front of her were standing in her way. She demanded to see Judith's mother. "Mom!" Judith shouted back to the kitchen. "There is someone here who wants to speak with you."

Sue Adams stepped past Judith onto the front porch, pulling the door closed behind her. It was a small deck, just wide enough to set out a couple of chairs when the weather was nice, looking out over a flat little front yard with a maple tree and a driveway that ran up the side. Judith heard the women raise their voices and tried to peek through the little window in the door. Her mother glanced back at her, then reached her hand up to block the glass. Moving to the living room window, Judith saw three men at the end of the driveway, next to an old black pickup truck. What stuck with her most, remembering the moment decades later, was the way the men stood with their backs to the house.

After a few minutes, the strange woman stormed back to the truck. She and the three men climbed in and drove away. "What was that?" Judith asked when her mother came back inside.

"It was nothing" was all her mother would say. A few days later, however, she sat Judith down for a talk. "If a lady ever pulls up in a car and tells you to get in with her," she told her, "don't go with her."

"Why?" Judith asked.

"That woman that came the other day said she was your mother," Sue Adams said.

"Was she?"

"No."

Judith had known for most of her life that she had been adopted. Sue and George Adams had thought she should hear the truth as soon as she was old enough to understand it. But they'd never said who her birth parents were, and Judith never asked. Her early childhood had been hard; she was born with scoliosis, forced to wear a Milwaukee brace to straighten out her spine. Sue and George had helped her through it, been the only parents she felt she needed, even after they divorced when she was thirteen and she and her younger sister had stayed with her mother.

Judith's friends always laughed about how Sue could be overprotective to the point of paranoia—how she kept Dobermans in the yard and guns in the house and waited for Judith in the parking lot when she attended school dances and went roller skating. Her sister was also adopted, but it was Judith whom Sue seemed to worry about the most.

In 1989 Sue Adams was terminally ill with heart disease. Judith was thirty-three then and working at a collection agency in Joplin, Missouri, just across the state line. She got a call from her father, George. "I need to talk to you about something," he said.

When Judith arrived at his house, her adoptive father told her that he'd just heard from a woman named Ethel Louise Williams. Williams, he told Judith, was her birth mother. "I didn't want to hold this back from you," he said. "I'll give you this number and stand behind you whatever you do." Five days later Sue Adams died.

The timing of Judith's biological mother's appearance was unfortunate, even cruel. Judith couldn't imagine what the woman wanted with her now, three decades after she'd given her up and days before her adoptive mother's death. But after a couple of days, curiosity got the better of her. She called up Williams and agreed to meet at the home Williams shared with her husband in Baxter Springs, just a few blocks from the house where Judith had lived as a child.

She drove over from Joplin the following afternoon. When she knocked on the door, a small woman with graying brown hair opened it. "You look just like your father," she said.

Judith followed Williams inside. "I've got something for you," Williams said. She handed her daughter a clutch of papers. "A lot of people want this transcript, but I told them that nobody gets it but you." It looked like a typed letter and contained, Williams said, the story of Judith's birth. Then she proceeded to tell the story herself.

"Your father is a very important man," she began. His name was M. A. Wright, and he was an oilman in Texas—not just any oilman but a wealthy and prominent one who had run Humble Oil and Exxon, two of the most powerful companies in the world. And he was still alive, down in Houston.

Judith stared at the papers. Though she didn't yet realize it, the woman in front of her had forever divided her life into two parts: the time before she knew, and everything that would come after.

TWO

Five years ago, while visiting New York City from out of town, I sat down for lunch with my literary agent. Or at least he was an agent who allowed me to think of him as my agent, despite the fact that it had been years since I had sold a book to a publisher, a book that was purchased by only a few thousand people. But he'd always made time for me amid his successful clients.

One of them, as it happened, was Dominick Dunne, the well-known writer of sordid crime stories. It was because of this fact that the agent had recently received a phone call from a woman who introduced herself as Judith Wright Patterson. The story of her life, she'd insisted, was the kind of tale that Dunne should write for *Vanity Fair* magazine. As far as the agent could make it out, the woman had discovered in midlife that she was the daughter of a wealthy oilman in Texas, and now she was trying to prove it.

At the time, Dominick Dunne was working on a novel, and my agent thought he was probably too busy to tell her story. Dunne probably heard a dozen stories as crazy-sounding as this one every day.

Over lunch the agent recounted the story to me.

"Actually that sounds kind of interesting," I said.

"Well," he said, "maybe you should call her then."

A few days later I dialed Carthage, Missouri. Judith picked up after the first ring, and I introduced myself as a reporter. I told her that I'd only heard the outlines of her story but it sounded remarkable.

"Evan, I'm going through a living hell," she said. "I need your help."

She then spoke for a half hour, maybe. I typed as she talked; she spoke slowly and carefully, so it wasn't hard to get everything down. Later, when I met her in Missouri, I found that this deliberateness carried over in person. She was a natural storyteller. Her hair was always permed, her eyelashes curled, and her makeup touched up before I arrived. She walked gingerly due to lingering back problems, which only served to enhance her sense of purposefulness. She had almond eyes and a can-you-believe-I'm-telling-you-this smile that exposed a set of prominent canines.

Five years after that first call, I am faced with hundreds of pages of notes describing dozens of hours' worth of conversations with Judith Wright Patterson, in which I have dutifully recorded her telling and retelling a story as complex as it is strange. For most of that time, I wasn't really sure what to make of it. But I kept returning to Judith's tale, I realize now, because I was seduced by the question at the center of it: if a stranger suddenly appeared in your life and offered you the chance to become someone else—to rewrite your own history and possibly your future—would you take it?

THREE

The story that Ethel Louise Williams told Judith began in 1955. That spring Williams—then Ethel Louise Harris—took a Greyhound bus headed south out of Baxter Springs bound for Tulsa, Oklahoma, looking for a new start. Her life so far had been one set of troubles after another. She was twenty-one years old and had three children: two daughters, Diana and Roberta, and a son, Rickey. At seventeen she had married a local man named Robert Harris and moved to California, but he had abused her, and so she'd moved back home, though she had left Roberta with him. Now Louise, as people would later come to call her, was heading south to find a way to support the two children she had left.

Somewhere on the way to Tulsa, she noticed a man asleep in back of the bus. She didn't pay him much attention until there was a commotion, and she looked back to find that he'd rolled off the seat and onto the floor. The passengers around him laughed, realizing that he hadn't been asleep but rather stone drunk and passed out. Something about his expensive-looking suit caught Williams's eye, though, and she took the water bottle and washrag she'd brought for her kids, helped him back into his seat, and started washing his face. He drunkenly introduced himself as one M. A. Wright, told her that he worked in the oil business.

When the bus arrived in downtown Tulsa, she started to take

him over to skid row, thinking that he'd find a place among other down-on-their-luck folks. But Wright insisted that they walk around. When he was on his feet, she noticed how handsome he was in spite of his oversize ears, with olive skin and brown hair just graying at the temples. And he was tall—tall enough that Louise could stand under his arm.

They passed by the Adams Hotel, an art deco building on Cheyenne Avenue downtown. Wright seemed to know it and decided he'd find a room there. Louise, not understanding how he'd pay for it but needing to find a room of her own, took her kids and headed for a boardinghouse.

For Louise, Tulsa was bustling with the opportunity lacking in Baxter Springs, a declining lead-mining town whose primary claim to fame was the historic Route 66 highway that passed through. Within a few days, she had landed a job working as a waitress at the Dutchman's, a steak house on the east side of Tulsa. But she hadn't forgotten the man from the bus.

One afternoon she ran into him again. She was pleased to find that he recognized her.

"I've been thinking about you," he said. "Where have you been?"

They were standing next door to the Mayo Hotel, far and away Tulsa's finest at a time when the city was awash in oil money; industrialists, oil barons, and celebrities regularly crossed its marble floor. Wright told her he'd taken a suite there. "Come on in," he said. "I'll buy you a cup of coffee."

As they sat in the hotel's café, several of Wright's acquaintances happened by: a pair of sisters who said their last name was Phillips, accompanied by two men. It was only when the older of the two introduced himself as Waite Phillips that Louise realized she was in the presence of one of America's great oil families. The Phillips brothers—Frank and L. E.—had built the oil company of the same name that now spanned the globe. From the way the Phillipses joked with Wright, Louise could tell they were friends.

She started spending the evenings with Wright. They would eat at the Mayo and tour around the bars downtown, the forty-four-year-old oilman in his suits, the diminutive twenty-one-year-old beauty wearing the jewelry he'd bought for her at Vandevers department store. He smoked cigarettes out of a little silver case and grabbed nips from a flask he kept in his boot. Then one evening he invited her up to his room, and they kissed. She stayed the night.

They fell into an affair, and he moved her into a room next door at the Adams, paid for her to board Rickey and Diana with a woman in south Tulsa. He bought Diana a fluffy pink dress and put her in a private preschool. He told Louise that he'd been married and also had a daughter. Although she was never quite clear on the details, she was under the impression that he was divorced. Louise herself was still married to Diana, Roberta, and Rickey's father but in name only; she didn't even know where her husband was.

Wright bought her a set of luggage and a mink stole, a diamond watch and a diamond bracelet, pearls and earrings to match. He squired her to dinners and parties with his wealthy friends. At a white tablecloth banquet out at the Tulsa Fairgrounds, she got to meet John Paul "J. P." Getty, a real oil baron, the one of the world's first billionaires. The Phillipses were there, as was Howard Hughes.

Spring edged into summer, and she and Wright remained lovers. She talked about getting their engagement photograph put into the paper; it seemed to her that things were moving in that direction. But Wright hedged. He didn't like to have his picture taken, he said.

He was mysterious with her in other ways she didn't understand. For one thing, he hadn't told her what M. A. stood for. "I want to know who you are," she finally told him one afternoon, walking down the street. "It's not right for you to do me this way."

"Marcus Arrington Wright," he said.

"No, that's not right," she said, "because up there at the Mayo Hotel, I've heard them call you Mike."

Wright started to get agitated. "Call me M. A.," he said.

So she dropped it. And then one night she was in his room at the Mayo. He put his arms around her and then stopped. She was pregnant, and he knew it.

FOUR

What happened after that became all mixed up in Ethel Louise Williams's memory. She later recalled that M. A. Wright became upset. He "couldn't even lay his pants on the bedpost," he told her, without her getting pregnant. It was no good for them to get married, he said, because she'd have a dozen kids.

But he also told her that he would take care of everything. He called someone—she thought it was a lawyer. She later remembered he hung up the phone and told her not to worry. "Go ahead and get your picture in the paper," he'd said. He had business in Houston, had to get out of town in a hurry. He wrote down some numbers and told her to hold on to them.

Something about it all made her feel "like a whore or something," she later said. So she tore up the numbers and threw the scraps in the trash. The day he was supposed to leave they fought again, and he stormed out of the hotel room. At the bottom of the stairs, just above the marble floor of the Mayo Hotel lobby, he looked back at her and told her that he'd never see her again.

"So when he left, you knew he was gone?" she was asked in a deposition forty years later. "I knew he was gone," she said. "I was in a spot. I knew that I was in trouble because I would never ever see him again."

So Louise gathered her things and her kids and moved home to Baxter Springs. On January 30, 1956, she gave birth to a daughter and named her Judith.

Louise's own mother was furious with her, cursed her, and humiliated her. Louise was still married, but her husband was missing, so she gave the child her maiden name, Bryant. Not long after, she divorced and then married a local man. They had a son and daughter, but that didn't last either. In 1960 she married Charles Williams and took his last name to become Ethel Louise Williams. By then she'd given Judith up for adoption.

FIVE

As Louise told her story, Judith remembers trying to keep from laughing. Look at this poor woman, she thought, telling me that my father was a big oilman down in Texas. It was a strange way to assuage her guilt over giving Judith up for adoption. But now she at least knew who her birth mother was. She also found out that she had seven half-siblings and got in touch with one of them, Louise's oldest daughter, Diana Stiebens, who lived in Kansas.

As the two were getting to know each other on the phone, Judith brought up what her mother had told her. "Can you believe this crazy story that my father was M. A. Wright?" she said. "How ridiculous is this?"

"It's not ridiculous at all," Diana told her. "That is your father. I met him."

Stunned but still suspicious, Judith decided to do some research of her own. She started with the library in Joplin, where the librarian found news stories about an M. A. Wright meeting with politicians. Then she called the Tulsa library, which sent her an article with a picture of an M. A. Wright who had been an executive at Exxon.

His name was not Marcus Arrington but rather Myron Arnold Wright, and he had been born in Blair, Oklahoma, in 1911. As a child he'd moved with his family across the state from one tiny town to another, from Altus to Shattuck to Waynoka. Wright was industrious even in his youth, working his way through Oklahoma State, where he captained the tennis team while earning a degree in civil engineering. After graduating in 1933, he passed on a municipal engineering position in favor of an $87.50-a-month job as an oil field roustabout for Carter Oil, a division of Standard Oil of New Jersey.

It was a gamble for an educated young man in the thick of the Great Depression, joining an Oklahoma pipeline gang, living in a four-dollar-a-month bunkhouse. When the business started to pick up, though, Wright's engineering background proved valuable; college graduates with technical skills were few and far between on the oil patch. He soon moved into management, and the company relocated him from Oklahoma to New York City.

Mike, as his colleagues called him, held executive jobs at two Jersey subsidiaries and eventually became the production coordinator for Jersey itself. He earned a reputation, as a profile in the company magazine *The Lamp* described it, of a corporate everyman who "enthusiastically tackles the mountain of paper that daily rises on his desk" and made his way through half a dozen cups of coffee before lunchtime.

"There's no magic about getting ahead in a corporation," Wright told an interviewer, "but you do have to work harder than the fellow next to you." In hiring, Wright said he looked for similar qualities, judging "how hard a man works, for one thing, and his determination to succeed." But he also looked at a man's "character, his integrity, basic honesty, his personal life—all of these things are also extremely important."

Wright and his wife, Izetta, an Oklahoma native, settled down in Scarsdale, New York. They passed the summers in Colorado Springs, and he filled his office, one visitor said, "with paintings of Indians and the Old West." The oil business over which he presided, meanwhile, was shedding its cowboy past and growing into a transnational colossus. In April 1955, around the time that Ethel Louise Williams boarded the bus for Tulsa, world oil output hit a record high, with U.S. production averaging 6.9 million barrels a day. At age forty-four Wright "had the looks of a streamlined John Wayne," as one interviewer put it, and had reached the top of the industry that powered the new American empire.

In 1966 Wright was named the CEO of Humble Oil, at the time the country's largest producer of crude. That same year he was made president of the U.S. Chamber of Commerce. By the late 1960s he was named to the board of governors for the U.S. Postal Service by President Richard Nixon.

Then in 1973 Humble and other Jersey companies were realigned under the name Exxon, and Wright was chosen as the first chairman and CEO of the new conglomerate, commanding one of the most profitable and powerful companies in the United States. He presided over a corporate structure known for its ruthlessness and enforced loyalty, along with a value system that preached faith and piety above all.

Wright finally retired from the company in 1978 and worked for another decade as the CEO of Cameron Iron Works. After retiring from Cameron, he returned to a kind of emeritus position at Exxon. He was in his office in the company's Houston offices one day in 1990 when he received a surprising phone call.

SIX

At the time she began digging into M. A. Wright's life, Judith was divorced and living in Joplin, the mother of her own teenage son. The details of Wright's ascent seemed like dispatches from another universe, and she was seized with the desire to know whether the man in the newspaper clippings was truly her father.

One day in 1990 she called Exxon's office in Houston, where she reached a man in the royalties and deeds department who sounded sympathetic to her story and gave her Wright's office number. Judith dialed the number the next day. When Wright's secretary put her through, she told him who she was. "This is kind of an awkward situation," she said, "but I've been told that you are my biological father."

"You've got me mixed up with somebody else," Judith recalls him saying. She apologized and hung up.

But Wright's answer did not sit well with Judith. She didn't want to accuse the wrong man of having a child out of wedlock, but the more research she did, the more the details of Louise's story seemed to point right back to the man from Exxon. So she called him again.

This time Wright was polite, and he answered her queries with an enigmatic question of his own. "What's this about, your grandmother?" she remembers him asking. "Let me ask you a question," he said when she seemed confused. "Is your mother's husband bothering you wanting money?"

"No, they've never asked me for anything," Judith said. But when she thought about it, it was strange how her mother had suddenly sought her out after all those years. "I will be honest with you," she told Wright. "I do think it was about money that they looked me up."

"Your thoughts are the same as mine," he said, according to Judith. "I don't want to talk anymore. I think this is blackmail." And with that, he hung up again.

Judith pulled out the document that her mother had written, the one telling the story of how she and Wright had met, and called him back. Before he could get out another denial, she said, "I have a transcript of detailed things that only you and my birth mother would know. I want to send it to you."

"Read it," he said.

She did. Before she finished, she remembers, she could hear him crying on the other end of the line. "I owe you an apology," he said. "This was not what I thought it was. You have not gotten what you deserved."

SEVEN

After that conversation, Judith would call and speak to Wright regularly. They talked about their lives, Judith says, and he peppered her with questions about her family. Wright would never fully admit to being her father, and after a while she decided not to press him on it and risk what little relationship they had. "I said, 'All I want is just to meet you,'" she later told me. "'Just meet me one time. I'll go away and never see you again.'" He said it wouldn't do either of them any good to meet. "I have a family, too, you know," he said. His first wife, Izetta had passed away in 1967, but he'd married again two years later, to Josephine Primm Wright, who had five children from her first marriage. And he had his own daughter to think about.

But Judith says that he apologized, at least, that he couldn't seek out more of a connection with her. "He said, 'This is not your fault,'" she told me. "If he said it once, he said it a hundred times." He warned her to be careful around her birth mother's family, even though he was never clear on why exactly.

One day in the late summer of 1991, finally feeling like she wanted answers, she called and confronted him with her research. "I know you were married at the time" of the affair, she told him.

"A lot of what you are saying is true," he said.

"I know that you are my biological father!"

Wright stayed on the line but didn't say anything.

She repeated herself. Finally, she hung up on him.

Over a year passed before she called him again. When she did, his secretary, whom Judith had come to know well, picked up. "Mr. Wright passed away," she said.

Some people might say that what Judith did next was about greed. But those people wouldn't understand how close she'd grown to the man she now believed was her father. Precisely because she felt so much for him, she also felt aggrieved by his silent rejection, his refusal to own up to her existence or complete the fragmented story she'd begun to assemble. "My thoughts weren't about money but that I could find the truth," she told me.

She'd never asked Wright for anything when he was alive. But now that he was dead, she began to think that maybe she was owed something. That phrase he'd once uttered was lodged in her mind like a splinter: *You have not gotten what you deserved.*

A few weeks after Wright's death, she got a lawyer down in Tulsa, a friendly ex–Marine Corps JAG officer named Terry Funk, to file a claim on the Texas estate of Myron A. Wright in Houston. Wright had died with a substantial fortune; a portion of his will later released in court showed that he held $7 million in stocks and bonds alone. Most of his assets were to be divided between his second wife, Josephine, and his daughter from his first marriage—unless, of course, Judith could prove that he was her father as well.

EIGHT

In February 1994 a lawyer for M. A. Wright's estate traveled from Houston to Tulsa to depose Ethel Louise Williams. Once Louise was sworn in, the lawyer coaxed from her an intimate and at times excruciatingly sad account of how she and Wright had become lovers. The lawyer pressed her on her specific memories of the man, asking if she remembered anything unusual about his physical appearance.

A: I recall his ears being big. He had huge ears, I mean—
Q: Big ears?
A: I mean, big ears. . . .
Q: Was he well built? I mean, was he muscular?

A: He was a very well-built man. He had a—large shoulders and he
  was—he carried hisself very well. . . .

Q: You did have an intimate sexual relationship with him?

A: Yes.

Q: Was he circumcised?

A: I don't think he was. . . .

Q: What sticks out in your mind as being the most—the thing you
  remember most?

A: The thing that I remember most was that he was—he was such a
  gentle person, you know. . . . I deeply loved him.

When it came to the events that occurred after their affair ended,
however, Louise's recollection grew muddled. She remembered that
he sent or gave her a deed—to what she couldn't say, maybe an oil
field in Texas. She remembered receiving some checks with little
holes punched along the edge, signed by M. A. Wright. She'd deposited a couple of them at a bank in Joplin, but they'd stopped coming.

She said she had not spoken to Wright after she last saw him,
at the foot of the stairs of the Mayo Hotel in July 1955, until March
1990, when Judith—who had already contacted Wright—had asked
her to call and confront him with the truth. "I don't want to hear
this," he'd repeated over and over when she told him who she was,
Louise testified.

"You don't want to hear no more about it because you, you made a
mess out of everything," she'd replied. "You didn't give a damn what
happened to me."

"There's nothing I can do about this now," he'd said. So she hung
up on him and never called back.

Judith had come down to Tulsa for the deposition as well; Funk
had told her to bring paperwork from a blood test, to be submitted
to the court. Louise, too, was to supply her medical records or a
blood test. If there was a match, Funk had told Judith, the estate
would likely want to settle.

After the deposition, Judith and her mother drove back north.

Then, a few weeks later, according to Judith, Funk called her and said that the estate was offering her $50,000 to end the case. "He said, 'Judith, you should take it,'" she told me. But something about it didn't feel right, not having the results of the blood tests, not having seen any documents. "I asked for some kind of paperwork," she said, "and that's went it all went strange."

In July 1994 Funk abruptly withdrew from the case. Not long after, the judge threw out Judith's claims. Her pursuit of a share of M. A. Wright's estate, and with it a court's seal of approval of her identity as his daughter, seemed to be over.

NINE

Judith's former life, the one in which she was just the daughter of George and Sue Adams, couldn't be recovered. She came from somewhere else, she now knew, not just a physical place but an unfamiliar world populated with rich and powerful people. But what good was that knowledge? It destroyed something and built little in its place.

The court case in Texas had ended mysteriously. She couldn't figure out why exactly she'd lost, why the blood test results that would've revealed the truth had never come back. In any case, M. A. Wright's money was gone. By the mid-1990s Judith was a struggling single mom with another young son to raise: Ryan, who had been born in 1993. Another marriage came and went, but she kept the man's last name, Patterson. She worked as a telemarketer and then sold cosmetics. There wasn't much time to dwell on what the money might have meant for her and Ryan.

But if Judith's newly discovered birthright hadn't brought her a fortune, her mother's reappearance had brought her a new family. Louise's other children came to accept her as a blood relative. She kept up with her half-sister Diana in Kansas and occasionally talked on the phone with Vicki, who was out in California.

Judith spent the most time with her half-brother Rick Harris, who turned out to live just a few miles down the road. In 1995 he had opened up Rick's Appliances in Joplin, which wasn't far from Carthage, where Judith and Ryan now lived. (Shawn, her older son, was in his early twenties by then and out of the house.) One day Rick called to ask if she could fill in for an absent employee at the appliance store. It soon became a regular job.

There was a darkness around the edges of her mother's family, though. It crept up on Judith slowly, as she and her son were drawn into Louise's orbit. Robert Harris, Louise's first husband and Rick's father, was said to have killed himself sometime in the 1960s or 1970s—"stuck a gun in his mouth and blowed his head off," Louise had said in her deposition, although she couldn't remember when. There were drug problems in the family. Vicki, Judith later told me, died mysteriously in 2001.

But Judith figured they were family now, and every family came with some drama. Maybe this one just had a little more than usual.

For several years Judith had a recurring dream. She was at an opera with M. A. Wright, sitting in an ornate hall. He was dressed in a suit and tie but never spoke. She couldn't remember much about the opera itself; in real life she'd never been to one. The vision haunted her in her waking hours. Every time she managed to bury her thoughts about the man she believed to be her father, the dream would exhume them.

After the dream came to her again one night in 2006, Judith called her friend Alice Burkhart. "We need to pray about this," Burkhart told her, and they did. Judith asked God to help her find out everything, to uncover the truth about who she was and what had happened to her family.

The first step was finding out what exactly had happened in the Texas case more than a decade earlier. So she called up the lawyer down in Houston who had represented M. A. Wright's estate in the battle over his will. "I really can't talk to you about this," the attorney said, according to Judith. "But it was that lawyer that you had." Judith hadn't actually lost the case; her filings had been thrown out because her attorney, Terry Funk, hadn't been licensed to practice law in Texas.

Judith asked what had happened to Josephine, M. A. Wright's widow. The lawyer said she heard that she'd died, but she didn't know the details.

Tracking down an obituary for Josephine, Judith discovered that Wright's widow had been living in Seattle at the time of her death. She located a lawyer in Washington who agreed to represent her on contingency and filed a petition in an attempt to recover something from Josephine's estate. The money had already been dispersed back in 2004, most of it to M. A. Wright's daughter from his first marriage. But under Washington law, if Judith could prove that she was unlawfully excluded from the will, she could still recover whatever portion of the money a court deemed should have been hers.

M. A. Wright's first daughter fought the petition—her name, incredibly, was also Judith. Judith's lawyer handed the case off to an accomplished litigator named Michael Olver, who argued in filings that Wright's will was written in a way that should include not just his legitimate daughter but Judith as well. The blood tests that could have proved definitively that Judith was Wright's daughter had never been completed, but DNA could now provide the answer just as easily.

To bolster the case, her Washington lawyers suggested she go to court in Kansas to have her adoption nullified. Josephine Wright happened to have moved to a state that specifically barred children given up for adoption from later claiming inheritance from their biological parents. A well-respected attorney in Kansas City named Gene Balloun agreed to represent Judith and filed to have her adoption vacated in the state of Kansas. To do so, however, he was going to need Louise's testimony.

So one morning in August 2006, Judith drove Louise two hours up to Kansas City. Ryan, now thirteen years old, came along, as did Judith's friend Alice Burkhart. That afternoon Judith and Louise sat in Balloun's office, and just like back in 1994, the lawyer asked Louise to recount her affair with M. A. Wright, from the bus ride to Wright's discovery of her pregnancy. The deposition was wrapping up when Balloun decided to clarify one detail for the record. "How long was it then before you ever saw your daughter again?" he asked.

"What was it, 'eighty-nine?" Louise said.

Judith turned to her mother. This wasn't right, she knew; she remembered the afternoon when she was sixteen, the strange woman on the porch, the men standing around the truck in the driveway. "You came to my house on 413 Twenty-second Street," she said.

"Oh yeah, sure," Louise said. "Probably around 'seventy-two, but I didn't actually see her."

"And how did that come about?" Balloun asked.

Louise suddenly looked scared, Judith remembers. "I came down there to see if Sue would let me take her to Houston," she finally blurted out. "Because they wanted me to—they wanted to see her. They didn't believe that there was a daughter or something."

Judith felt the room pressing in on her. For a second time, the woman sitting across from her had collapsed the story of her life as she knew it. After that last night at the Mayo Hotel in 1955, Wright *hadn't* disappeared without a trace. Louise had somehow been in contact with him, or his proxies at Exxon, and then he'd even sent someone to find her—to bring her to Houston so that he could see her for himself. *You have not gotten what you deserved.* Now that statement contained so much more meaning than Judith had understood.

When the deposition concluded, Judith drove back to Carthage, Ryan in the front seat and Louise and Alice in the back, all four sitting in near silence. When Judith and Ryan returned to their house late that night, there were messages on the machine from her half-brother Rick Harris wanting to know how the trip to Kansas City went. *That's odd,* Judith thought. She didn't recall telling him that they were going.

TEN

Up in Kansas City, Gene Balloun had obtained the depositions from the original court case over M. A. Wright's will, nearly fifteen years earlier. He mailed Judith copies, and when she opened them, her unease turned to dread. Now all the inscrutable things that Louise had said back then suddenly made sense. M. A. Wright had once tried to make things right, and something had gone terribly wrong.

At the end of the deposition, Louise had described to the lawyers how her mother and her aunt had taken the jewelry that Wright had bought her, along with the deed. Later, after she'd moved out of her mother's house, Louise had been back there and found "envelopes after envelopes from Humble Oil Company." They were empty, and her mother had told her that they'd just been utility bills.

Louise said that she wrote letters for years to Humble Oil in Houston, always addressed to "dear sirs," trying to get ahold of Wright. "I had built him on a pedestal," she said. "I felt like he would protect me and all my things was taken away from me, and I felt like that he would help me get Judy back."

She never got an answer, she said, but in 1972 she did get a letter from Humble Oil asking her to return any documents she had. So she decided to go down to Houston and try to find M. A. herself. After she was unable to convince Sue Adams to let her take Judith, she brought her third husband and her son Rick, now a teenager, and managed to meet Humble's then-president, Randall Meyer. "He said that he wanted me to come back that afternoon, and we would probably get this matter all straightened out," Louise recalled. But her husband had gotten a parking ticket when they went for lunch. Flustered and fed up with his wife's oilman tales, he demanded that they drive back to Kansas and abandon the whole thing.

Louise's memory seemed uncommonly sharp on certain details but foggy on others. "A lot of this stuff is blank in my mind," she said at one point. "My mother beat on me ever since I was a child, and my mother was very angry with me when I got pregnant by M. A., because back in the fifties, you didn't get in trouble."

The family Judith had begun to feel close to, she now saw, had some connection to M. A. Wright beyond just Louise's several-month affair. And yet the story remained a collection of fragments: Wright had somehow tried to send money and oil deeds to Louise and maybe even to Judith. They had been intercepted along the way. It was unclear if her mother was a perpetrator or—if her deposition was to be believed—a victim of her own crooked family. Whichever it was, Judith was beginning to suspect that the new family she'd embraced had drawn her close for reasons she'd never imagined.

Still, Judith pressed on with her attempt to nullify her adoption. In November 2006 a district judge in Cherokee County, Kansas, issued a judgment confirming the facts of the case as Judith herself now understood them. "Ms. Patterson was born Judy Diane Bryant on January 30, 1956," he wrote. "Her birth mother was Ethel Louise Harris, also known as Ethel Bryant, and now known as Ethel Louise Williams. Her birth father was Myron A. Wright."

There it was, at last, on paper. Judith started going by Judith Wright Patterson.

ELEVEN

When I called Judith for the first time in the spring of 2008, it had
been two years since her adoption had been dissolved. Her suspicions about her mother's family had calcified into a certainty shot
through with anger and fear. She knew now, she told me, that her
mother's family had robbed her of the money that M. A. Wright had
sent her for decades. "My life will never be the same," she told me.

In September 2007 Judith had lost her initial lawsuit in Washington over Josephine Wright's will. The case hinged on the fact that
the will specifically bequeathed most of M. A. Wright's remaining
fortune to his "lawful issue," excluding any illegitimate children.
Her lawyers were appealing the verdict. Meanwhile she was engaged
in a new legal battle, this one in Missouri, against her mother's family. She'd enlisted a local lawyer to pursue a civil case alleging that
her mother and her half-brother Rick—along with half a dozen other
relatives—had intercepted money from Wright intended for her.

"I think basically my dad did try to stop this, at least make sure
this money was going to me," Judith told me on the phone. "But I
think these folks stepped in and had him over a barrel, saying that
we are going to expose you."

"Were they living high on the money?" I asked her.

"That's the catch: this is where they fooled everybody," she said.
"To look at these people, around this area right here, you would not
suspect them in any way."

Bit by bit over months, Judith described to me the scattered but
tantalizing documentation she'd collected, through a blend of mid-
western friendliness and an almost frightening persistence, to
prove that her family was not what it seemed. She'd employed private investigators in Texas, Oklahoma, and Missouri to run traces on
family members immediate and distant. They'd found evidence, she
told me, of aliases and hidden bank accounts, of money-laundering

vehicles and strange trusts in distant states, of oil wells deeded to names that matched up with members of her family.

She'd pried loose some documents from Exxon, too, including one concerning an oil field that Louise had mentioned in one of her depositions. It was in Tomball, Texas, just outside Houston. The field had changed hands over the years, but Judith had followed the trail of ownership until she found a link between one of the Tomball leases and an address Louise Williams had once used in Coweta, Oklahoma.

The documents indicated that some oil royalties had been sent to that address. According to a letter she received from Exxon, the payments had begun in the 1950s, only to be suspended sometime in the next decade. "It dawned on me: That's why my mother contacted me in 1972!" she told me. "My father must have known that the money wasn't going to the right people, so he sent an investigator down and stopped the payments." She suspected that her mother had used another relative to impersonate her—which would explain some of the confused conversations she'd had with Wright on the phone before he died.

The most important document that Judith had gotten out of the Exxon archives, however, was a handwritten letter that the company had received back in 1958 when it was still Humble Oil. The letter read:

> *Humble Oil and Refining Co*
> *dear sirs,*
> *m. a. wright passed away after spending 3 years in a state mental hospital. I cashed his checks and sent him clothes until he died the bank will no longer cash them unless they are made to me. I am his sister the last in his immediate family the checks are not much but I am nearly blind and I can use it I want to put a marker at his grave. Wright's funeral home Coweta okla could furnish death certificate.*
> *Ethel Williams*
> *Coweta, OK*

Enclosed with the letter was a copy of a half-filled-out document marked "Record of Funeral" for one Marcus Arrington Wright. It was the name that M. A. Wright had given Louise during their tryst at the Mayo Hotel.

Judith and her lawyers were certain this meant that Louise had tried to extract money from Wright's company by duping its executives into believing their employee was dead. It seemed like a clumsy con, but Judith believed it proved that her mother had been trying to get her hands on Wright's money.

Judith took the information she had gathered to the police department in Carthage, but they were flummoxed by the allegations. They quickly ascertained that whatever had happened had occurred mostly outside their jurisdiction; Judith's story ranged across Texas, Oklahoma, Kansas, and New York.

But before the police dropped the case, Judith managed to procure one more piece of evidence. One afternoon she went to Louise's house and—despite their ongoing legal dispute—convinced her to ride down to the police station and give a new statement. Why her mother agreed to it is entirely unclear. Later she'd claim that her daughter had "kidnapped" her—raising the question of whether the statement was written under duress. But at the station that day, Louise handwrote and signed an affidavit witnessed by a clerk. "My entire family blackmailed M. A. Wright for money for gas and oil stocks property trust fund," she admitted.

The document, like all the scraps that Judith had gathered, seemed at once to suggest everything and add up to nothing. But at the very least, someone had admitted, on paper, to blackmailing Wright.

TWELVE

In early 2009 Judith's lawsuit in Missouri was thrown out. If the family had stolen money from M. A. Wright, the court concluded, the proper place to pursue the claim would be in Harris County, Texas, where Wright's estate had originated. Judith found a lawyer there and filed suit in Houston.

It was at this point that I began to discern a pattern in Judith's legal representation. Her lawyers almost always took up her case on contingency, hoping to make their money back when she won. But Judith would inevitably part ways with them along the road to justice. Every time I talked to her, she'd added one lawyer and subtracted another, to the point where, after several years, I had trouble keeping them straight. There was Terry Funk, of course, and a character named Jim Lloyd who had once represented her mother. There was Daniel Whitworth, a local attorney, and Gene Balloun, out of Kansas City. There'd been Michael Olver and Richard Wills in Washington, and then there were others who seemed to pop up in our conversations once and then never appear again.

When I tracked down Judith's lawyers and investigators, they usually told me versions of the same story. "Normally, when you talk to people like that, you weigh it with a grain of salt," Whitworth told me. "But the interesting thing is that when you dig into it, there appears to be merit in what she is saying. My opinion is that she's right." He paused. "I suppose I represent her, so I'm supposed to say that."

When Michael Olver first heard Judith's story, it sounded to him like "a Friday night movie of the week." But over time, he told me, "in dealing with Ms. Patterson, every time we've heard her describe something and we've checked it out, it's been accurate," he said.

Then there was Joseph Norwood, another Tulsa attorney who Judith had described as "kind of like my spokesperson" at one point in 2008. "Right now I'm still kind of getting my head wrapped around it," Norwood told me when I reached him at his office. "I do believe there is merit." I began running through the litany of accusations and conspiracies that I'd piled up in my notes. "Here's the problem," he said. "Judith has been completely overwhelmed and turned obsessed on this situation. She sees things that are not there. She's become damn near full-blown paranoid."

A few months later, when I brought up Norwood, Judith told me he was no longer representing her. "He's not wealthy enough to put together the case," she said. "Brilliant man."

And so lawyers came and went, drawn in by Judith's story and then driven off by its complications. Judith herself, however, remained undaunted. By 2010 she had lost her appeal in Washington but was still confident that she could win in Texas. "I think this thing is going to blow wide open," she told me. She had enlisted the services of Jeff Zimmerman, a litigator from Kansas City, who had found out about Judith's case when she rented a house from a former client of his.

When I called Zimmerman, I found myself listening to a familiar refrain. "If you asked Judith to sit down for a couple of hours and tell you the story, you'd say 'That's really kooky,'" Zimmerman told me. "But when you start to tie together all the evidence—I tell you, it's probably the strangest case I've ever been involved with."

Even as her legal battles were flagging, Judith was at last finding some purchase in the world Wright had inhabited. In 2005 she had looked up the phone number for the Oklahoma ranch that had belonged to the Phillips oil dynasty. In her depositions, Louise had described a pair of Phillips sisters and Waite Phillips as being close friends of Wright. Judith eventually found her way to Jean Phillips, one of the few remaining members of the Phillips family from the same generation as M. A. Wright. Phillips "wasn't surprised at all when I contacted her," Judith told me. "She said, 'You were a secret through the Phillips family and in the oil industry for years.'"

The two women became friends. Phillips was one of the few people who accepted Judith for who she now wanted to be. "It was never like 'What makes you think he's your father?'" Judith told me. "She knew he was. She said, 'Honey, you need to hold your head up high. You come from good blood.'"

Phillips took a particular interest in Judith's son Ryan, then a teenager, and once invited the two of them to Tulsa. "This was a million-dollar neighborhood; J. P. Getty had lived across the street," Ryan recalled. "And walking in there, it was a whole different world." Phillips, he said, told him that he should get into the oil business like his grandfather. "She said right off the bat, 'That was your grandfather, be proud.' We hadn't taken any DNA or brought pictures."

But at the end of the day, it was time to go back. "You come back to your little town where you grew up, and you don't see the same future in it," he said. "You suddenly don't feel like you belong. You go back to your friends—you can't be that and be here. You're in a Cinderella world. And you come back to this world, and you are trapped in between."

THIRTEEN

In December 2011 I went to visit Judith in Carthage. I pulled my rental car up to a yellow one-story condo with a gravel front path, in a new-looking development of cookie-cutter buildings on the east side of town. When Judith opened the front door, she greeted me like an old friend. Which, in a way, I was; we'd talked every few weeks or so for the better part of three years. She had dyed her hair black and wore it long. Her eyebrows were painted on, and her face was framed by oversize hoop earrings.

By this point, I'd evolved almost by sheer force of exposure from a reporter to someone she seemed to view as a mixture of confidant and potential advocate. Now, at least, I could cross-reference her tale with the evidence she'd described to me so many times on the phone, contained in bankers boxes of documents stacked up in her closet.

By the afternoon, we were sitting in her living room—decked out for the holidays with wreaths and a tree—with papers and photographs stacked in concentric circles around us on the carpet. On the phone, Judith had recounted evidence that seemed to fit perfectly into the narrative she had assembled. When I went through all the documents myself, the puzzle was more challenging. It wasn't that the documentation didn't exist; it was that the conclusions Judith drew from it required a baroque chain of connections. Documents like her mother's letter to Humble Oil seemed tantalizingly close to proving her story but also invited more questions.

The evidentiary touchstone to which Judith kept returning was always Tomball. The oil field outside Houston that Humble Oil once operated had been transferred to another company and then another. But Judith had called all of them and eventually turned up a record of unclaimed money in M. A. Wright's name, which indeed appeared to have been headed for Rural Route 1 in Coweta, Oklahoma, and was now held by the Oklahoma state treasury. One of her investigators found the same Rural Route 1 address associated with Louise Williams. That much of the story seemed tangible: At some point, oil companies had been sending checks in an M. A. Wright's name to a Louise Williams, whether he knew it or not. Judith even convinced the Oklahoma Unclaimed Property Division to send her one of the checks, for $76.96.

Where the conspiracy had gone from there was a matter of speculation. Judith met and befriended a local woman named Violet Jean Vasquez, who had grown up down the street from Louise's family and described having heard, while playing at their house as a child, Louise and her relatives discussing how they were collecting money from an oilman. Vasquez later dated Rick Harris and worked at Rick's Appliances and reported a wealth of suspicious details to Judith: his handling of large amounts of cash, strange life-insurance policies, and mysterious government checks.

By this point, Judith's relationship with her mother's side of the family had long since soured. This wasn't surprising, given that they'd all been served papers for the fraud lawsuit she'd filed against them. Her half-sister Diana, who had once described to her meeting M. A. Wright in Tulsa as a child, now refused to speak to her. Things only worsened after a 2007 story on Judith's lineage by local TV news anchor Dowe Quick. Quick managed a brief interview with Louise at her front door in which she angrily declared, "I'm the victim of all of this. I've had this stuff stolen from me, years ago."

After that, strange events kept happening around Judith's home. Her car's engine went haywire, and one of her tires blew out not long after. She called the police about possible prowlers out behind the house and to report that someone may have tampered with her heating vents when she was out. Judith became convinced that it was all connected to Rick Harris.

Years before, when Judith worked at Rick's appliance store, she and her sons would attend weekend barbecues at his house. But as they grew close, Harris had always struck her as a volatile man, with a lightning-quick temper and a haughty pride. To outward appearances, his appliance store never seemed like a thriving business, but he was extravagant with his money, flashing it around and taking spur-of-the-moment jaunts to Las Vegas. He bought new cars and a wood-paneled hot tub that he put in the yard behind his house.

In July 2008 I called Judith and found her in an unusually agitated state. "I had something very traumatic happen today," she told me. "There wasn't much air coming in, and I called somebody to look at the air conditioner. And the guy said, 'Ma'am, you better come out and look at this. Somebody has opened up your box and pulled out one piece, the relay. You've got somebody mad at you.'"

After one too many scares, she stopped letting Ryan ride the bus to school. He took to sleeping with a butcher knife between his mattress and box spring. Judith started sleeping in a chair in the living room, not knowing if she would wake up with someone standing over her. "I was scared to leave my own house for a long time," she later told me. "I didn't know if I was going to get a bullet put to me or what." For a while she and Ryan moved into Alice Burkhart's house and only returned home by day to pick up clothes.

By then, however, it was too late for Judith to turn back. Unraveling the story of M. A. Wright had become her full-time occupation. The job at Rick's shop had ended, predictably, when she served him with papers. She had thrown her back out working as a massage therapist back in 2006 and was living off the disability payments. By the end of 2008, she'd lost the house in Carthage and moved out of town temporarily, to a cheaper place in Loma Linda, a town outside Joplin. But the Texas lawsuit was up and running, and she felt like there was light coming at the end of a very long tunnel.

In April 2009 she flew down to Houston for a few days to meet with her lawyers. Ryan stayed with Alice, and they picked Judith up from the airport when she returned. As they made the last turn back to the house in Loma Linda, they passed a car coming the other direction.

"There's Rick," Ryan said.

"No way," Judith replied.

When they pulled into the driveway, however, Rick pulled in behind them, blocking the way out. "He didn't get out of his car," Judith told me. "He just sat there" and stared. Ryan jumped out and ran to the neighbor's house, but no one was home. So the three of them made a break for the garage, and inside Judith called the sheriff. Harris left before the police arrived.

The next week Judith went to court and got an order of protection against Rick. By the time I visited her in Carthage, she had become convinced that her half-brother was the linchpin to the whole conspiracy and the reason she'd feared for her and her sons' lives for years. But after reading the police reports from the incidents Judith had described, I'd begun to wonder if they were really anything more than the confrontations you'd expect between feuding relatives. The only way to find out, I figured, was to go to Joplin myself.

FOURTEEN

Joplin, like Carthage, is nestled in the southwestern corner of Missouri, where it meets Kansas and Oklahoma. Once famous for being the site of some of Bonnie and Clyde's first bank robberies, it acquired a grimmer place in the national consciousness after the 2011 tornado that killed 158 people. Driving toward downtown, I could still see the lingering devastation: whole tracts of suburban-style homes had been obliterated down to their foundations and never rebuilt. The local high school looked as if it had been hit with a bomb.

The section of Joplin's Main Street where Rick's Appliances was located had seen better days, but it at least appeared to have been spared the storm's wrath. It was four-thirty p.m. on a Thursday when I pulled up. The place was locked, despite the sign out front that said it was open until five. At first it wasn't clear that the store was in business at all. The showroom was virtually empty, with a few battered-looking washers and a refrigerator haphazardly arranged across a stained carpet.

I cupped my hands to the glass to get a better look and noticed a bearded, heavyset man visible through an open doorway to a back room. I knocked loudly on the glass and waved. The man turned his head slowly toward me, then turned back and wandered away. A moment later another man walked out from the back and approached the front door.

He was small—five foot eight, according to the arrest records I later obtained—with brown hair and brown eyes, wearing a pair of large metal-rimmed glasses. His hair was slicked over to one side. He unlocked the front door and cracked it open, glaring at me suspiciously.

I introduced myself as a journalist and said I was writing about a lawsuit related to M. A. Wright. Did he know anything about it?

"Yeah, and it's bullshit!" he shouted.

"Okay, I just wanted to find out what you thought about it," I said. "That's all."

"Get in here," he said, opening the door wider and waving me inside.

He slammed the door fully open against the wall and held on to it while the sound reverberated through the mostly empty shop. He clenched his teeth and closed his eyes, as if he were trying to hold back a tide of fury and anguish that was about to pour forth. "That fucking lawsuit is by Judy"—here he let out a kind of angry grunt—"fucking Patterson over in Carthage. That sonofabitch needs to be arrested!"

He leaned in toward me, and for a moment he looked as if he were going to hit me.

"She had that same goddamn lawsuit here in Joplin, back in oh-eight, and had three court hearings here! The case was dismissed because there was no damn truth to it whatsoever," he said. "She's a worthless motherfucker, man." He slammed the door against the wall again. "Fucking sonofabitch pisses me off, man!"

"I can tell," I said.

"Nobody owes her nothing!" he shouted. "My family don't owe her a goddamn fucking dime."

Harris started backing me out of the store, stepping in close enough that I was forced into the threshold and then onto the sidewalk. I asked if there was a phone number where I could reach him. He stared at me blankly. "I'm not going to be here," he said. "I'm locking this sonofabitch up." He closed the door and disappeared into the back.

Judith wasn't surprised that Rick had come undone, nor that

the store itself seemed to be barely functioning. "That place should have been folded up beaucoup long time ago," she said. "There's not enough money there to keep the place going, but he was laundering money through that business."

If that was the case, however, none of Judith's investigators or lawyers had ever managed to produce any hard evidence of it. And the visit to Rick's Appliances had brought to mind a lingering question I'd had since Judith first told me about the money that her family allegedly had stolen: Where had it all gone? Rick struck me as an unlikely financial mastermind. His house was small and simple, on the edge of a trash-filled culvert. From what I could discern, none of the other relatives seemed to be living much better.

Louise, meanwhile, had gone missing. Judith hadn't seen her in over a year. Judith was, in some sense, back where she'd started. And it wasn't clear if by pressing on, she had any hope of winning back more than she'd already lost.

Something extraordinary had happened to her, that much was certain. And something dark clearly had taken place in her family—indeed, it seemed to still be happening. But a great many of the answers lay in a time that was now out of any reasonable reach of memory. Judith was fighting a war against a basic erosion of historical facts, and I had unwittingly ended up fighting it alongside her.

At times her motivations seemed to slip into something like revenge. "I probably will never be able to ever, ever get back all this money that these people have taken," Judith admitted to me at one point. "I hate the fact that Rick has any of this. But the public humiliation that he is going to have to deal with down the line, I wouldn't want to be walking in his shoes."

Several months later I was reading through the court filings for Judith's lawsuit in Texas, as it wended its way toward trial, when one document caught my eye. It was a note postmarked November 29, 2010, from Louise Williams to the court:

Dear Judge Weiman,

I have no money to travel and my Doctor won't let me go that Far because of my Health. And Just about everything Judy Patterson has Said is a Lie. . . . This is about the Fourth time She has Done this she Wants to make a Movie of me and my family & Smear our names all over the world. If I had any money I would sue her.

Something Bad is going to happen to [. . .] Because [God] Don't like ugly.

Sincerely,

Ethel Louise Williams

Smear our names all over the world. Was she referring to me? I remembered back to my visit, when I'd been sitting in Judith's living room and she'd answered a call on her cell phone. "Can I call you back?" she'd said. "Evan is here." Not "that reporter" or writer or any of the ways I'd described myself to try and make clear the boundaries of our relationship. As many times as I explained to her that we weren't really on the same side, it never seemed to sink in. "I'm beginning to think that some sort of media attention would help us," she confided to me at one point.

Reading Louise's letter, though, I realized it was more than that. I'd set out to make Judith a character in my story, and instead I'd become a character in hers.

FIFTEEN

On January 30, 2012, Judith Wright Patterson finally got her day in court. She and her lawyer Seth Nichamoff appeared before Judge Larry Weiman of the 80th District Court in Harris County, encompassing Houston. By this point, the defendants in the case had been whittled down to Ethel Louise Williams and Rick Harris.

Neither Rick nor Louise had ever hired a lawyer to defend themselves, nor did they show up for the court appearance. Even so, the judge proceeded to rule against Judith. Whatever her relatives might have done to M. A. Wright, she hadn't proven that they'd stolen from her, and they didn't owe her anything as a result. And that was it.

I was relieved to find that Judith considered the verdict final and, oddly, something of a victory. Even if the judge hadn't ultimately ruled in her favor, she told me when I talked to her just after her court date, his comments in open court had persuaded her that he believed M. A. Wright had been defrauded. He just didn't believe there was enough evidence that she had been. Her decades of legal battles were over, and she'd lost nearly all of them. She would never see a dollar from Wright's family or her mother's.

Later Nichamoff admitted to me that while he had hoped for a different outcome, he knew they'd never truly tied together the story's loose ends in a way that would satisfy the judge. "Did they take property that specifically belonged to Judith?" he told me. "We just don't have any evidence of that. We never did.

"My guess," he went on, "at the end of the day, did these people extort money from Myron Wright? Yeah, it did happen. Absolutely, there is no doubt. But then what? These are people living in trailer parks. There is no honor and no victory, morally, legally, or financially, in making people's lives more miserable than they already are."

SIXTEEN

My conversations with Judith tapered off after the verdict, but a year later, in early 2013, I decided to go back to see her. I flew first to Tulsa and spent a few days driving around town, looking for the landmarks that had figured into Louise's account of her affair with M. A. Wright. The Dutchman's steak house where she'd worked is now a small strip mall anchored by an out-of-season Halloween store. The Adams Hotel has long since been transformed into an office building, with a Mexican restaurant on the ground floor.

The Mayo, next door, fell into disrepair in the 1980s, but it recently came under new ownership and has been restored to something approaching its original glory. It now houses a small museum dedicated to its history, and I wandered through it, past the photos of the celebrities and politicians who'd stayed there in its heyday: John F. Kennedy, Lyndon B. Johnson, Marilyn Monroe, and Elvis Presley. I stood atop the steps where Louise remembered standing when M. A. Wright told her that she'd never see him again.

The next day I drove up to Carthage, to try one more time to talk to Rick Harris and Ethel Louise Williams, the two people who could still, if I managed to get them to talk, fill in the story's gaps. With the legal battle over, I figured, maybe they would finally tell their stories.

Judith had told me that she'd heard that Rick had grown more erratic, attacking customers at the store. Indeed, on the website for the Joplin police, I found the record of an arrest the previous year for assault, disturbing the peace, and resisting arrest. He'd failed to show up in court several times since. Now, she said, he'd disappeared, having moved out of his house to nobody knew where. When I drove by his shop, I saw it had been transformed into an antiques store. The proprietors had never met him but had heard stories of his outbursts.

The next day, on an oppressive ash-sky afternoon, I drove across the Kansas border to Baxter Springs, to the last address I could find for Ethel Louise Williams. The house was just off the old Route 66, but without the historical markers the street looked like any other in a small town. Williams's home was a gray two-story house with a green roof. The yard was overrun with junk: an empty blue barrel, a small sculpture of a lighthouse, a green plastic cactus. The most prominent item was a wood-paneled hot tub with one side caved in.

There was a car in the driveway; I parked behind it and walked up to the front door. A sign on it read, THIS IS A NO SMOKING HOUSE.

OXYGEN TANKS IN USE. Through the little window in the door, I could see tanks strewn around and a stack of moldy-looking mail on a nearby table, but not much else. I knocked, then rang the doorbell. Nothing stirred.

I drove over twice more in the next two days, but nobody ever came to the door. In truth, I felt relieved. Ethel Louise Williams would be seventy-nine years old and apparently was in poor health. Her doctor had written a note to the court saying she had dementia.

Most of our stories pass into oblivion along with the dead. M. A. Wright died in 1992. Jean Phillips passed away in 2010. Wright's second wife, Josephine, died in 2004, followed by Wright's daughter by his first marriage, Judith Wright Reid, in 2008. They all died before I found time to call and ask them what in Judith's story was true to their own experience. Even Dominick Dunne died in 2009, suggesting the counterfactual possibility that if Judith had really gotten to him, the account of her story might've died with him. I doubt it, though. Judith would have found someone like me eventually.

There are dozens of possible versions of the truth in Judith's life story, alternate explanations for all the pages in the boxes stacked in her bedroom closet. After years of wading through it all, my own best guess at the truth is this: That M. A. Wright likely did have that affair with Ethel Louise Williams, and Judith was the result. That Louise, by her own admission, tried to obtain money from Wright after putting Judith up for adoption—money that, it should be said, she and Judith both would have deserved from him. That her family tried to get that money, too, an effort that may very well have metastasized into decades of blackmail and grifting. That Wright made a mistake of passion fifty years ago and largely avoided the consequences.

But that's all it really is, in the end: a guess. I'd be lying if I didn't say that sometimes I still wonder if this all could be some great hoax. That I sometimes wonder how Ethel Louise Williams's memory of those days in 1955 could be so cloudy at times and yet so perfect when it came to the details that mattered. That after examining the chains of evidence, I have concluded that they are almost all circumstantial and sometimes even contradictory. That I, with a vested interest in my guess being correct, am perhaps no more reliable a narrator of Judith's story than she is.

One day not long ago, I finally managed to track down Diana Stiebens, Judith's half-sister, and reach her by phone. She had long since stopped talking to everyone in her family, she said. She'd felt betrayed when Judith named her in a lawsuit, and she'd spent thousands of dollars defending herself from accusations she claimed to not even fully understand.

But she was willing to tell me what she remembered about M. A. Wright. "He came to a boardinghouse where I was staying with my mother," she said. "He was very, very pleasant, kind, spoke to me very nicely." She remembered the nice preschool she'd been put into but had only been told years later by her mother that he was responsible for it. I asked her if he seemed like a wealthy man. "This was from a child's point of view," she said. "It was a man dressed in plain khaki clothes, and he took his hat off in the presence of ladies. I remember those kind of things."

As a girl, she'd heard her family talking about a child that Louise had given up for adoption, and she pieced together herself that it was the young girl named Judith in her town. She used to follow Judith around at a distance sometimes, she told me, curious about her mysterious sister. Diana had run away from home not long after, and she ended up in foster care as a teenager.

As for M. A. Wright's money, she said, she'd never seen any of it. "The only thing that was ever given to me, that I know, was that he bought me a pretty dress and put me in a preschool," she told me. In any case, she said, "what difference does it make? My mother is probably about seventy-nine now. My brother is about three years younger than me. I'm sixty-two. My point of opinion is, why do we have to continue this on? There's really nothing that can be done about it."

SEVENTEEN

Early on the morning before I was scheduled to leave Carthage, I awoke at the Best Western to the sound of my phone ringing. It was Judith, calling to make sure I had directions to get over to the police station, where I had an appointment to catch up with a sergeant there. As always, a brief call turned into a longer one, and she told me that she'd finally decided that she needed to get out of town. There were just too many bad memories here. Her adoptive sister had been in the hospital for years, unable to communicate after a brain aneurysm. Her adoptive father, now ninety-five, didn't really even speak to her anymore. He'd remarried, and his wife didn't want Judith to have anything to do with him since she'd dissolved her adoption. "I want out of here so bad, I can't stand it," she said.

She still had her sons, at least. Twenty-year-old Ryan was doing well in his job as a legal clerk and going to school part-time at a local college. But beyond that she had few connections, just friends like Violet who'd backed her through the ordeal. "People like you, people like lawyers became my family," she said. Over the course of a decade of lawsuits, Judith had managed to lose both her old family and her new one. I remembered something Jeff Zimmerman had said when the three of us were sitting in Judith's living room one evening more than two years earlier: "I've told Judith several times, 'You know, you might have been happier never knowing this.'" The danger of putting your life into the legal system, Zimmerman always warned his clients, is that "it requires you to live your present in your past."

Judith didn't deny that she might have been better off if she'd never responded to that first entreaty from her mother. But something had steeled her resolve. "I've got some pictures in my room that I'm going to show you," she said. "When you see this, you'll understand." For a long time she'd seen photographs of M. A. Wright only in his later years, as president of the U.S. Chamber of Commerce or giving corporate speeches for Exxon: an older man with thinning hair, standing at a dais in a boxy suit. But a few years ago, one of her investigators had found a photo of him as a young man, just after he graduated from Oklahoma State.

"Ryan always had this look of his own," Judith told me. "And when I got that picture of my dad—oh, my God. I went around the house for, I don't know, a good month off and on and all I did was cry. I saw my son."

Judith had blown up a photocopy of one of the pictures and hung it on her bedroom wall. Looking out from the wooden frame was a relaxed and confident young man, with his prominent ears and his hair swept across his head. His mouth was set in a line, with just a hint of a smile reflected in his eyes. Below it was a framed picture of Ryan in high school, his lips pursed in the same way, his eyes displaying the same look of assured intensity. The more I stared at them, the more the two men seemed to resemble each other.

THE
SINKING
OF THE
BOUNTY

MATTHEW SHAER

And tell me, wasn't that the best time, that time when we were
young at sea; young and had nothing, on the sea that gives nothing,
except hard knocks—and sometimes a chance to feel your strength.

—*Joseph Conrad, "Youth"*

ONE

Monday, October 29, 2012

5:30 A.M.

Five hundred feet over the Atlantic Ocean, Coast Guard Petty Officer Second Class Randy Haba jammed himself into the rear bucket seat of the Jayhawk helicopter and waited for the doomed ship to come into view. Through the window he could see the crests of the waves and a flotilla of detritus that seemed to spread out in every direction toward the horizon—wormy coils of rope, sharp splinters of yard, tatters of sailcloth. The phosphor screens of his ANVIS-9 night-vision goggles rendered the ocean neon green—the kind of green that made it difficult to distinguish distance or depth of field, let alone the blink of the chest-mounted strobe that the guys up in the C-130 transport airplane had sworn was out there, somewhere in the hurricane-roiled sea.

Haba felt the helicopter lurch into a hover. The winds were blowing at close to ninety miles an hour, and in the cabin, Lieutenant Commander Steve Cerveny was fighting the sticks. "Left side," Lieutenant Jane Peña, the safety pilot, called over the radio. "Got it?"

"Roger," Haba, the crew's rescue swimmer, replied. Setting down the ANVIS-9s, he pulled on his fins, dive helmet, mask and snorkel, and thick neoprene gloves. He checked the neck seal of the flame-retardant dive suit and the pockets above the harness, which contained flares, a radio beacon, and one very sharp, spring-loaded knife.

Haba, a six-foot-three former high school football star with hard blue eyes and a weather-beaten face, had been based at the air station in Elizabeth City, North Carolina, for more than eight years, the majority of his coast guard career. He'd participated in plenty of rescues in the waters off Cape Hatteras, a dangerous patch of sea known by generations of mariners as the "Graveyard of the Atlantic." There, past the pastel beach houses and salt-stained crab shacks, the North Atlantic's cold Labrador current collides with the warm waters of the Gulf Stream, yielding frequent storms and high waves capable of swallowing a ship whole.

But Haba had never encountered a situation like this. An hour and a half earlier, he'd been snoozing on a lumpy leather couch at the air station when the call came in: a large wooden ship was in trouble a hundred miles east of Elizabeth City with sixteen people on board. The ship's water-removal systems were malfunctioning, and it was limping into the path of Hurricane Sandy, the vast superstorm swirling over the North Carolina coast. Haba had trotted downstairs and rendezvoused with his helicopter crew. One of the command center staffers had printed out a picture of the ship in question from Google Images, and only when he saw it did Haba grasp how strange his morning was about to become. Because the distressed vessel wasn't a yacht. It wasn't a schooner. It looked more like a pirate ship.

The *Bounty*, as she was known, was a working replica of the eighteenth-century tall ship of the same name, commissioned half a century earlier for a film. She measured 120 feet from stern to bow, and 128 feet from keel to masthead. Her three wooden masts held ten thousand square feet of sail. A couple of days earlier, she'd departed New London, Connecticut, under the command of Robin Walbridge, a veteran tall ship captain. At first she'd tacked east, in an effort to avoid the worst of the storm, but at some point, Walbridge had turned the ship southwest, toward shore and Sandy's perilous center mass. Until four a.m., when the crew abandoned ship, she'd been in contact with a C-130, which was still circling overhead at one thousand feet. After that there was only silence on the radio.

THE SINKING OF THE *BOUNTY*

The number of survivors was uncertain. But the C-130 crew had spotted at least one figure bobbing alone amid the debris—a small shape swaddled in an immersion suit, with a blinking strobe on his chest. The straggler, they called him. Maybe he was dead—a floater— but maybe he wasn't. Either way, Haba was about to find out. He clipped into the winch, gave a thumbs-up to the flight mechanic, and, the cable whistling behind him, dropped into the waves.

Almost immediately, he began to eat seawater. He was swimming against the current, against the wind. It didn't help that Cerveny had the Jayhawk so low. The rotor wash was spectacular, drowning out any other sound. Still, Haba paddled like hell, and a minute later he reached the straggler. The hood of the immersion suit was pulled tight around the guy's head, and all Haba could see was his face, which was covered in fresh lacerations. One arm hung limply at his side.

With some effort, Haba angled the sling under the man's other armpit and pulled the man close to his chest. Sometimes survivors fight back, out of confusion or panic—*the surest way to drown is to fight us*, rescue swimmers like to say. But the straggler was docile, barely even able to talk, and Haba made good time back to the winch. He gave the thumbs-up to the mechanic and waited for the cable to pull them skyward. Beneath the Jayhawk, illuminated by the rising sun, the tall ship *Bounty* was slipping under the surface of the sea.

TWO

Thursday, October 25

11:00 A.M.

It amused the hands on the *Bounty*—a motley collection of retirees, bearded and tattooed twenty-somethings, and midlife reinventionists—

to watch the navy guys go all weak-kneed at the sight of the 112-foot masts. *Bounty* sailors knew every inch of that rigging, from sheets to spar. But to the local nuclear submarine crew in New London, who had come aboard that afternoon for a demonstration in square-rig sailing, it was utterly unfamiliar territory. In the end, only a few of them were brave enough to strap up and attempt a climb. The weather was calm and overcast, a pleasant fifty-eight degrees.

Later that day, after the sub crew departed, Captain Robin Walbridge convened a brief all-hands meeting. Walbridge was a naturally reserved man, but at musters he presented a calmly confident mien. Peering out over the top of his eyeglasses, a ball cap partially obscuring his brow, he outlined the course for the two weeks ahead. The *Bounty* would depart New London that night—setting sail on a Friday was considered to be bad luck—and head south. If they kept up a pace of one hundred miles a day, they could easily make Florida by the second week of November.

That would allow them to meet an obligation in St. Petersburg, a tour for members of an organization that promoted awareness of Down syndrome—and maybe even make a pit stop in Key West, where the crew could swim, hit the bars, and recharge after what was sure to be a difficult voyage south. In mid-November the *Bounty* would sail around the tip of Florida, across the Gulf of Mexico, and into Galveston, Texas, where she'd be put up for the winter.

Walbridge was sixty-three, with unruly silver hair and meaty, callused hands. He had come relatively late to professional seafaring, after a series of stints on oil rigs and a short career as a long-haul trucker. He'd grown up in St. Johnsbury, a cloistered town in northeastern Vermont, and claimed to have first sailed at the age of eighteen, although he was tight-lipped about that part of his life; when his crew members asked his age, he would offer an array of different numbers. Perhaps something painful lurked in his past, they thought. Or perhaps Walbridge simply preferred to talk about his ships.

He'd worked on plenty over the previous two decades, all of them throwbacks in one way or another. There was the nineteenth-century schooner *Governor Stone* and the HMS *Rose*, a tall ship built in 1970 to the specifications of eighteenth-century British Admiralty drawings. But his true love was the *Bounty*, a vessel he'd captained since 1995.

Tall ship crews are usually drawn from two cohorts of people. First there are the amateur adventurers—the retirees and armchair admirals, the recent college graduates putting off adulthood. These volunteers might sail with a tall ship for a week, or a few months, or a year, but they are not paid; in many cases, they are actually billed for berth and board. The second cohort, the mates, tend to be experienced sailors who have decided to make a career out of tall ship sailing. Generally speaking, they have worked their way up the totem pole, from volunteer to paid hand.

On average, the crew of the *Bounty* numbered around eighteen, with a small cadre of paid officers, a paid cook, a few lower-ranking hands, and the occasional volunteer. Walbridge never discriminated among the various groups. If anything, he seemed to lavish more attention on the sailors who were still learning to navigate the ship, to take in line and climb the rigging. He was intoxicated by the old-fashioned way of doing things, and he was pleased to be around those who were in the process of becoming intoxicated themselves. "He considered square-rigged sailing a truly dying art, and he was the one keeping the idea alive," one longtime *Bounty* hand has said.

And yet Walbridge was no fusty antiquarian. He had sailed the *Bounty* up and down the East Coast, through the Panama Canal and over to the West Coast, and twice across the Atlantic. Along the way, he'd seen plenty of bad weather, including a pair of hurricanes and pants-shittingly high waves that heaved across the decks, and he had acquired a certain bravado about it. Walbridge was "clearly brilliant," says a former first mate of the *Bounty*, speaking on the condition of anonymity. "The kind of guy who could play three games of chess at once, who could take apart a diesel engine and put it back together with his bare hands. But the term 'prudent mariner' doesn't really enter the mix."

The former first mate recalled a series of harrowing close calls aboard the ship, including a "thirty-six-hour nightmare ordeal" off Cape Hatteras in 1998, when rough seas sent water pouring into the *Bounty*'s engine room. Both the coast guard and the navy had sent vessels to the scene, and extra pumps had to be dropped on board to clear out the water.

Around the same time that Walbridge was convening his crew on the *Bounty*'s deck in New London, on October 25, a different storm, Hurricane Sandy, was arriving on the Florida coast, a thousand miles to the south. Several crew members who were in the meeting on deck say that Walbridge believed Sandy would barrel up the coast and eventually track inland, somewhere near North Carolina. By sailing southeast before turning south, the *Bounty* could stay windward of the storm. Remaining in Connecticut, Walbridge felt, wasn't an option—he subscribed to the old maxim that a ship was always safer at sea than at anchor. In a crowded port like New London, there would be practically zero "sea room," and the *Bounty* would be hemmed in, dangerously close to the docks. Better to take our chances "out there," Walbridge told the crew.

It was an unusual decision—few other captains in the region, and no other tall ship captains, were taking any such gamble. And Walbridge, likely mindful of his less experienced hands, was careful to stress that no one was obligated to stay on the *Bounty*. "I know that quite a few of you all are getting phone calls and emails regarding the hurricane," Chris Barksdale, the fifty-six-year-old engineer, recalls Walbridge saying. "I wouldn't blame anyone if you want to get off, and I won't think any worse of you, and I won't hold it against you."

Josh Scornavacchi crossed his arms and nodded. Scornavacchi, twenty-five, was short and stoutly built, with an earring in his left ear and a mop of unruly reddish hair, which he wore swept across his forehead and cowlicked up in the back. He'd grown up in landlocked Mohnton, Pennsylvania, and studied biology at Penn State before signing on as a whitewater kayaking guide in the Lehigh Gorge. It was there that he'd caught the adventure bug and hatched a series of increasingly grandiose plans—someday he would hike Everest, float down the Amazon, travel to Congo and Papua, New Guinea. He would buy a boat and sail around the world. But in order to do that, he'd first need to learn how to sail, so in 2011 he'd signed on for a Hudson River tour aboard *Clearwater*, a sloop owned by the folk singer Pete Seeger.

After the tour, Scornavacchi returned to Mohnton, where he worked shifts at the local Red Robin and looked for another opportunity to ship out. The world of tall ships is tight-knit, and through a friend on *Clearwater*, Scornavacchi heard of an opportunity on the *Bounty*. He interviewed with John Svendsen, the ship's forty-one-year-old first mate, and in the spring of 2012, he flew to Puerto Rico to start a stint as a paid deckhand. The money wasn't much, but Scornavacchi was deeply enamored with the ship. He loved scrambling up the high masts, loved the sight of the big canvas under sail, loved the rhythm of life on board—the nights in his gently rocking bunk and the days exploring strange new cities.

With the *Bounty*, Scornavacchi had sailed from Puerto Rico to Florida, up the East Coast to Nova Scotia and back down to Maine, stopping in dozens of ports along the way. Now he would have the chance to experience his first real hurricane. It was a prospect that had not particularly delighted his mother. Earlier that day he had spoken to her on the phone and listened to the way the worry made her voice heavy and syrupy. "Mom, I'm not going to die," he told her. "I promise." Walbridge was a veteran sailor, he assured her, and he was backed up by a pair of extremely able lieutenants: Svendsen, the long-haired and taciturn first mate, and second mate Matthew Sanders, an affable thirty-seven-year-old with a degree from Maine Maritime Academy. Together, Walbridge, Svendsen, and Sanders had decades of storm experience. "We trusted them," Scornavacchi recalled later. "We all did. And we trusted the boat."

In the end, none of the crew members took Walbridge up on his offer to get off in Connecticut. Around eight p.m. that evening, the *Bounty* glided out of the New London harbor, past the navigational buoys and the shuddering glow of the nearby boats, her dual John Deere engines rumbling underfoot, Long Island Sound opening up before her.

THREE

Friday, October 26

8:00 A.M.

All storms start in miniature, sucking in moisture and matter as they grow, and in this respect at least, Hurricane Sandy was no different. She had been spotted in the radar images for the first time on October 19, in the Caribbean Sea, that blue breeding ground for hurricanes, an unspectacular whorl of cloud perched southwest of Puerto Rico. Meteorologists dubbed her Tropical Depression 18. She worked her way west, along the coasts of Venezuela and Colombia, before turning north toward Jamaica. Her status was upgraded with alarming regularity, from a tropical depression to a tropical low—a cyclone with a low-pressure core—to a full-fledged hurricane.

Still accumulating size and strength, Sandy rumbled northward. By

October 25 she was just southeast of Florida. News reports indicated that she could eventually reach the magnitude of Katrina and impact the entire eastern seaboard from the Southeast to New England. The National Oceanic and Atmospheric Administration (NOAA) predicted gale force winds of up to seventy miles an hour in some areas and widespread storm surges—the rising of the Atlantic Ocean itself.

But the morning of October 26, standing on the stern deck and gazing out in the direction of the Maryland shore, Doug Faunt found it hard to believe there was a storm out there at all. The day was calm and comparatively mild, and above the *Bounty*'s towering masts, the gulls were circling. *Robin is right*, Faunt thought. *Get clear of the hurricane to the east, and then tack south. Nothing to it.* They'd be in Key West in no time, drinking Coronas on the beach.

At sixty-six, Faunt was the oldest person on the *Bounty* and the only volunteer. For most of his life, he'd been a computer engineer in Silicon Valley, a job that had made him plenty of money—not enough to be filthy rich, but enough that he was able to fully retire, without worry, shortly after his forty-eighth birthday. He'd always been an avid reader, and among his favorite books were nautical adventures. And so in the late 1990s, married but without kids, Faunt had set about finally fulfilling his sailing dreams. He'd taken a tour on the *Rose*—the same vessel that Robin Walbridge had once helped helm—and sailed across the Atlantic on a century-old steel-hulled barque called the *Europa*. In his spare time, he rode motorcycles in the war-torn Balkans and backpacked through the western Sahara.

In 2008 Faunt had learned of a vacancy on the *Bounty*, a ship whose history he had studied extensively. The original vessel, he knew, had been built in 1784, in the city of Hull, and christened *Bethia*, only to be purchased by the British Royal Navy and renamed HMS *Bounty* three years later. In December 1787 the *Bounty* had sailed from the port of Spithead, in Hampshire, England, under the command of William Bligh, a thirty-three-year-old lieutenant who had once served with Captain James Cook. Bligh was bound for Tahiti,

where the *Bounty* would pick up a hold's worth of breadfruit trees
and transport them to the West Indies. Sir Joseph Banks, a prominent naturalist with the ear of the king, hoped breadfruit, a meaty
and filling food, could eventually become a staple in England.

But the *Bounty* was cursed almost from the outset. She ran into
extremely rough weather near the southern tip of Chile, and after thirty
days of unsuccessful attempts to round Cape Horn, Bligh was forced to
head east, for the Cape of Good Hope and the Indian Ocean. Over the
ten months it took to reach Tahiti, a deep tension developed between
Bligh and his crew, especially the master's mate, Fletcher Christian.

In early April, after half a year in Tahiti, Bligh announced that
the procurement of the breadfruit trees was complete—the *Bounty*
would set sail for Jamaica, unload her cargo, and return to England.
The members of the crew boarded the ship as ordered, but unhap-
pily; many of them had started relationships with Tahitian women,
and none of them much enjoyed the prospect of a return voyage as
arduous as the first. A few days later, on April 28, 1789, eighteen crew
members under Christian's direction led Bligh out of his chamber
at gunpoint and deposited him in a twenty-three-foot launch along
with twenty-two loyal sailors.

In an exceptional display of seamanship, Bligh managed somehow to pilot the boat 3,618 nautical miles to the Dutch-held port
in Timor and went on to enjoy a long if unspectacular career in the
Royal Navy. The mutineers, meanwhile, sailed to Pitcairn Island
via Tahiti—where they deposited a few of their number—and, after
burning and sinking the *Bounty* there, established a small, self-
sufficient colony. The mutineers who remained in Tahiti were eventually apprehended and sent in chains to England to stand trial.
The Pitcairn crew, however, succeeded in staying out of view of the
Admiralty. Their outpost was discovered only in 1808, at which point
almost all the mutineers were dead or gone, including Christian.

Beginning with Bligh's publication of his own account in 1790,
the *Bounty* mutiny became an enduring subject of public fascina-

tion, the facts of the incident increasingly obscured beneath layers of speculation and literary invention. Charles Nordhoff and James Norman Hall's popular 1932 novel *Mutiny on the Bounty*—in which Bligh is cast as a sadistic disciplinarian and Christian a brave upstart—was adapted four times for the screen and once for the stage, with Christian portrayed by half a century's worth of leading men: Errol Flynn, Clark Gable, Marlon Brando, and Mel Gibson.

It was for Brando's outing that MGM Studios had asked the Smith & Rhuland shipyard in Lunenburg, Nova Scotia, to build a replica—the most exacting and accurate that had ever been created for a film. The shipbuilders consulted the *Bounty*'s drawings in the archives of the British Admiralty. Their only significant amendments to the original were the ship's size—the eighteenth-century ship was ninety feet from stem to stern, close quarters for a film crew—and a pair of diesel engines.

In 1986 Ted Turner, the founder of CNN, acquired MGM's entire library of film props, including the *Bounty*. In the years that followed, the ship appeared in a handful of other movies—among them a 1990 *Treasure Island* adaptation starring Charlton Heston—but Turner had no great desire to hang on to the ship. In 1993 he donated her to the Fall River Chamber Foundation, in Massachusetts, which in turn established the Tall Ship Bounty Foundation. Robin Walbridge was brought on a year later.

Under Walbridge's direction, the *Bounty* joined the community of tall ships that crisscross the globe in the summer months. It was a sort of inverse tourism circuit: the ships would lay up for a few days in one harbor, long enough for locals and visitors to admire the high masts and ballooning sails, then push off for another port of call. Maintenance, supplies, and crew salaries were financed with ticket sales, the ten bucks they charged people to climb aboard, wander belowdecks, or pose for pictures beside the replica cannons.

And yet Faunt was not unaware of the subpar condition in which the *Bounty* found herself at middle age. In 2001 Robert Hansen, the millionaire founder of Islandaire, an air-conditioning company, had purchased the *Bounty* from the Tall Ship Bounty Foundation. He had kept Walbridge as captain and also provided a much-needed infusion of funds to help maintain the vessel and pay the sailors. But even with his respectable fortune, he seemed unable to keep up with the intensive and regular maintenance a ship of the *Bounty*'s size required.

Before arriving in New London, the *Bounty* had spent several weeks in dry dock in Boothbay Harbor, Maine, where workers and crew members replaced some rotted planking and installed a pair of new fuel tanks. In Connecticut two new stoves had been driven down by Tracy Simonin, an employee of the HMS Bounty Foundation, and installed by Faunt and Barksdale. *Very much a work in progress* was how Faunt referred to the ship. Still, like practically all the hands on board, Faunt believed the ship would get them to Galveston, where he had planned to undertake an array of improvements.

Now he leaned against the railing on the stern deck, listening to the reassuring gurgle of the John Deeres. They were at full power, motoring fast southeast, and the entire ship shook with their effort. The wind was blowing, but not violently, and he could feel the sun on his neck.

FOUR

Saturday, October 27

11:00 A.M.

The Saffir-Simpson hurricane scale separates storms into five categories. A Category 1 hurricane, the weakest on the spectrum, is defined as having sustained winds of 74 miles per hour; in a Category 5 storm, winds regularly reach 157 miles per hour—enough to rip the roof off a house. On Saturday, October 27, two days after the *Bounty* left New London, Sandy was a mild Cat 1, flirting with tropical storm designation. And yet her low intensity belied her remarkable size. NASA satellite images taken at the time show a swirling gauze knot, with a compact core and tendrils that extended across a thousand-mile swath of the Atlantic Ocean, from Florida to the Chesapeake Bay.

According to Laura Groves, the *Bounty*'s twenty-eight-year-old boatswain—an officer in charge of equipment maintenance—beginning on Friday, the crew had printed out maps from the ship's weatherfax. They posted them in the hallway belowdecks so all hands would have a chance to track the storm's progress and the location of the *Bounty* relative to it. Those maps would have shown the *Bounty* approximately two hundred miles from the Virginia shore, on the eastern edge of the storm. So far, so good—if the storm kept up its current pace and trajectory, the ship could still skirt the worst of the winds and bypass Sandy once she turned inland.

But it seemed increasingly probable that Sandy would soon clash with a fast-moving cold front, which had swept down from Canada and across the Midwest. As NOAA forecasters pointed out, the two systems, both dangerous in their own right, threatened to merge into one colossal "Frankenstorm." The prospect was terrifying. The last major hybrid storm to hit the East Coast was the Halloween Nor'easter of 1991, which occurred when a low-pressure system from Canada swallowed Hurricane Grace and slammed into the coast of Massachusetts, killing thirteen people.

On the *Bounty*, sea-stowing preparations began in earnest. Anything loose, from heavy appliances to the crew's baggage, had to be lashed down. The crew furled most of the sails to reduce weight aloft, leaving only the forecourse, the lowest sail on the foremast. This was the *Bounty*'s storm sail—it would be needed to help steady the ship in a gale.

Doug Faunt spent most of the morning belowdecks. An inveterate radio geek, a couple of years earlier he'd installed a Winlink system that could be used to transmit email messages via shortwave radio signals in the event of an emergency. Faunt booted up the system—all was in working order. Next he made his way aft, where the washer and dryer, previously secured, had moved six inches. They had to be tied down again, this time with extra line.

Faunt was joined for part of his shift by Claudene Christian, one of the newest members of the *Bounty* crew. Christian had grown up in Alaska, where she'd competed in pageants from an early age. At the University of Southern California, in Los Angeles, she'd been a cheerleader—experience she parlayed into a career when she founded the company Cheerleader Doll. In 1997 the Barbie manufacturer Mattel sued Christian and her father, Rex Christian, for patent infringement, and Claudene was forced to abandon the company. According to *Los Angeles* magazine, Christian subsequently sued her own lawyer for "gross misconduct" and settled out of court for $1 million.

Suddenly flush with cash, Christian bounced around the West Coast. She sang with a band named the Mad Tea Party, did PR for a racetrack in Hermosa Beach, and became a partner in Dragons, a trackside bar.

She shipped out for the first time in 2011, as a cook on the *Niña*, a sixty-five-foot replica of Columbus's ship. She spent three months on board, lived for a time in rural Oklahoma—where her family had moved—and in May 2012 trucked out to Wilmington, North Carolina, to join the crew of the *Bounty*. When she was growing up, Rex Christian had always told his daughter she was a descendant of Fletcher Christian, the leader of the 1789 mutiny. This may or may not have been true, but Claudene certainly believed it; it was one of the first things she told the other *Bounty* hands.

For Christian, the *Bounty* was a chance to start over—to make up for what she described as her "failures" in California. She threw herself into her daily duties with alacrity, taking on tasks others tried to shirk. In the evenings, sweaty and soused with salt water, she'd often join Josh Scornavacchi on deck for an impromptu jam session. Scornavacchi had brought a pair of bongos, and Christian sang along to old rock songs, her voice bright and unwavering.

Shortly before the *Bounty* departed from Boothbay Harbor, Christian was promoted by Walbridge from volunteer to paid hand—a position for which she'd earn a hundred bucks a week. "Volunteer with drinking money" was how Walbridge phrased it, but Christian was immensely proud of her new position: it validated her feeling that she belonged on the *Bounty*.

But Christian was still a green sailor, and she had never experienced bad weather at sea. The approaching storm clearly scared her in a way that it did not scare the more seasoned hands. In an email conversation with her friend Rex Halbeisen after leaving Connecticut, she said she was "praying to God that going to sea was the right decision" and expressed concern with the equipment on the *Bounty*. "You know me, I am not a mechanical person, but the generators and engines on this ship are not the most reliable," she told Halbeisen. "They are always stewing over them. I would hate to be out to sea in a storm and the engines just quit or we have no power."

But by the time she sent a subsequent text message to her mother, probably late on Saturday night, Christian seemed to have made peace with her misgivings. "Just be sure that I am ok and HAPPY TO BE HERE on *Bounty* doing what I love," she wrote. "And if I do go down with the ship & the worst happens . . . Just know that I AM GENUINELY HAPPY!!"

FIVE

Saturday, October 27

1:00 P.M.

By Saturday afternoon the *Bounty* was a couple of hundred miles due east of the border of North Carolina and Virginia, and Robin Walbridge made the decision to change course. He would now steer the ship southwest, toward the coast.

It was a tactic he had used before when sailing in the vicinity of large storms. "You try to get up as close to the eye as you can, and you stay down in the southeast quadrant, and when it stops you stop, you don't want to get in front of it," he said in a 2012 television interview. "You'll get a good ride out of the hurricane." Walbridge reasoned that by October 27, the *Bounty* had made it out far enough beyond Sandy's eye that if he steered inland again, the winds whipping counterclockwise out along the margins of the storm would help propel the ship to St. Petersburg.

Walbridge reminded his senior officers that he had a good sense of how storms behaved. "He [was] never a yeller or a screamer," third mate Dan Cleveland later testified. "When things would go wrong, you'd never see him freak out, he'd handle situations in a calm manner. I never saw him get nervous or scared. It made you feel like you could handle things."

In the end, neither Cleveland nor the other senior officers who might have had a say in navigational matters ever objected to the new southwestern tack.

But Walbridge had made a miscalculation. His plan assumed both that the forecasts of Sandy's path would hold, and that it was possible to get around Sandy at all—that she was a hurricane of normal size, a few hundred miles across. Irene, in 2011, had been six hundred miles in diameter; Katrina, in 2005, measured only 415 miles from edge to edge. Skirtable distances, if your ship was well equipped and moving fast. But Sandy was not skirtable. Meteorologists later estimated that she was the largest hurricane ever recorded in the Atlantic Basin, with a diameter of a thousand miles and a wind swath of 2 million square miles. If Walbridge had kept to his original southeasterly course, it was conceivable that he might have made it to Sandy's edge. Instead, he was now unwittingly sailing the *Bounty* directly into her maw.

That afternoon the weather worsened. Winds were now reaching over thirty miles per hour, waves were climbing to fifteen and twenty feet. A cold rain fell periodically overhead. The *Bounty* rocked irregularly, making it hard to get any rest belowdecks. Even a simple action, like moving around the cabin or walking down the passage-way to the head, required concentration and energy.

More distressingly it had become clear that the *Bounty* was tak-ing on a considerable amount of water. It seeped through the ceil-ing and across the floorboards and through the forepeak. It spouted through the walls and squirted down from the ceiling and collected in greasy little pools in the corners of the cabins. All wooden ships leak, of course, and some of the crew members comforted them-selves with the fact that the *Bounty* had pumped herself out of a few disasters before. There were five pumps on board—two electric, two hydraulic, and one "trash pump," a smaller unit that could be hauled around to different locations on the ship. But the hydrau-lic and electric pumps were working at peak capacity, and still the water was rising.

At eight a.m. on Sunday morning, after a long and mostly sleep-less night, Walbridge gathered his mates in the navigation shack for a meeting. Chris Barksdale, the engineer, was also invited. Barks-dale, a handyman by trade, was already seasick—later that day, when a crewmate gave him a pill for it, he vomited it back up. Walbridge pinpointed the *Bounty*'s location on a map and reviewed the plan for the day ahead: southwest and then south and straight on toward St. Petersburg.

At this point, boatswain Laura Groves later recalled, the seas were twenty-five feet and the wind was blowing at nearly sixty miles per hour. After the meeting concluded, around 8:45 a.m., she departed to help adjust the jack lines, the bow-to-stern lines that allow sail-ors to move safely around the deck of a storm-struck ship. Groves believed that the end was in sight, especially once they'd swung over the bottom quadrant of the hurricane and put the storm behind them. There was not yet much cause for concern, she thought.

This was not an opinion shared by Doug Faunt, who had spent

Saturday night and much of Sunday morning in the engine room, monitoring the pumps. If the devices were unable to keep up with the seawater, the engine room would flood. And if the engine room flooded, the *Bounty* would eventually find herself entirely at the mercy of the growing storm, batted about by the waves like a toy boat. The replica *Bounty* would be forced to rely solely on her sails, just as her namesake once had.

Faunt dashed from one engine to the next, minding the meters, tinkering with the levers, cursing under his breath. It must have been 120 degrees in that room, and humid as hell. He stripped down to his T-shirt and underwear and hiking boots, occasionally ducking through the hatch for a breath of fresh air. It was exhausting work, and at noon he handed off the baton to another crew member and crawled back upstairs to try to catch a few hours of sleep. When he got to his cabin, he found the room flooded and his gear soaked. He climbed naked into his sleeping bag. The bag was polyester, not cotton, and although the sensation was uncomfortable—not unlike folding your body into a used athletic sock—it did afford a bit of warmth.

Faunt had barely closed his eyes when he heard someone shout the "all hands on deck" call. *You've got to be kidding me,* he thought. He shouted his acknowledgment, fumbled for his sweat- and seawater-soaked clothing, and dressed in the damp darkness.

SIX

Sunday, October 28

12:30 P.M.

Josh Scornavacchi made it on deck a few minutes before Doug Faunt. Looking up at the masts, he saw the reason for the all-hands call: the forecourse was split, and the canvas was flying free. The forecourse was the *Bounty*'s storm sail; it helped steady her. It had to be furled.

So Scornavacchi began to climb. He was a strong climber, comfortable with heights, but the rigging seemed to just get smaller and wetter as he shimmied upward. The wind whipped the ropes around him into a fury, lashing him on the arms and neck hard enough to draw welts. Nevertheless, within the next hour, Scornavacchi, Laura Groves, and John Svendsen were able to secure the sail to the gaskets on the top of the yard.

While Scornavacchi was aloft, Faunt and Claudene Christian were taking up or paying out the lines as needed. The task had fallen to them partially because they were late in arriving on deck but mostly because Faunt was fatigued and Christian couldn't be trusted aloft. Despite having been on the *Bounty* for several months, Christian was still very much a novice when it came to the workings of the ship. Faunt, who often shared shifts with her, regarded her as something of a slow learner. "It wasn't that she wasn't brave," he would later recall. "She was. She was brave and she had a lot of heart and she had passion for the *Bounty*. But you usually had to repeat things several times before she really got it."

Now she fixed Faunt with an intent stare and complained that no one on the ship was listening to her.

"What aren't they listening to?" Faunt asked. He had to holler over the roar of the storm. Behind them, thirty-foot waves were breaking over the foredeck.

"We're taking on too much water. The pumping isn't going well. We've got big problems."

"I know," he said. "We all know." There wasn't a person aboard the *Bounty* who didn't know the ship was in trouble. But it did no good to complain about it. Faunt tried to reassure Christian. "Listen," he said. "It's going to be fine."

That evening Sandy closed in on Cape Hatteras. The storm had now merged as predicted with the easterly moving cold front. Meteorologists were reporting a noticeable drop in the atmospheric pressure off the coast of North Carolina, a sign that the storm was entering an even more dangerous phase. The *Bounty*, a couple of hundred miles southeast of the cape, had found herself square in the middle of the storm system, with little hope of sailing her way back out.

As night fell over the *Bounty*, visibility that had been limited enough at twilight, when a veil of rain enclosed the ship, was whittled down to practically nothing. The swells rose like battlements around her. Scornavacchi ducked through the aft hatch to check on his cabin. What he saw startled him: several boards had been ripped up from the floor and were swirling around in the wash. He understood the gravity of the situation, but he also felt strangely energized. Back home in Pennsylvania, he had longed for an adventure. Now he had found one.

Around eight p.m., the winds again tore the forecourse loose, and again Scornavacchi was sent aloft to deal with it. He scaled the foremast with extreme caution. A hard hail pelted him in the face; he could barely see, let alone hear anything. A couple of dozen feet below him, the bow of the ship shot down the trough of one wave and up the sheer face of the next. Black water coursed across the deck. Occasionally, the ship would list nearly at beam ends, the deck at an almost perpendicular angle to the sea and the crew clinging to anything they could get their hands on.

At this point, there were already two injured sailors aboard the *Bounty*. One was a twenty-seven-year-old named Adam Prokosch, who had been tossed headfirst across the mess by a particularly high wave. Christian set up a mattress in a dry part of the ship and made Prokosch lie on his back, with his hands at his sides. It was clear that he was badly hurt; Christian worried that he might be partially paralyzed. She told him not to move.

Meanwhile Walbridge had suffered an injury of his own, likely caused when he collided with the table in his cabin. Several sailors on board later recalled that he was moving only with extreme effort, bracing himself with both hands. Scornavacchi believes Walbridge broke his back; Faunt thinks it may have been a leg. Either would have been an ominous development. Unless you're extremely lucky, escaping a sinking ship without full ambulatory control is all but impossible.

As the *Bounty*'s engineer, it was Chris Barksdale's job to maintain the generators, the pumps, and the diesel engines that powered the ship. In a subsequent interview with *Popular Mechanics*, Barksdale recalled that the pumps became clogged early Sunday afternoon; Walbridge himself did the unclogging, but it was to little avail. The water was flooding into the *Bounty* much faster than it was going out. As the ship rolled, the water in the engine room and the bilge would heave up the walls and slosh back down over the equipment. The engines sputtered, churned, and sometime after nightfall, with a dull whine, gave out completely. The *Bounty* was now adrift.

At nine p.m. Walbridge and Faunt descended to the radio room to call for help. The *Bounty* was noticeably light on communications systems—most of the time, the crew members relied on their cell phones. Closer to the coast, in calm weather, this wasn't a problem. But the *Bounty* was now a hundred-odd miles out to sea, and no one on board had any reception. So Walbridge and Faunt decided to issue the Mayday call on the Winlink system. You almost had to laugh, Faunt thought—they were going to peck out their damn SOS via email.

Still, the system worked fine, and after confirming that the message had gone through, Faunt left Walbridge and made his way forward toward the galley, bracing himself with both hands. The generators were surging badly, and the lights were flickering on and off like disco strobes. After a while the backup generator kicked in. In the yellow glare of the emergency lights, Faunt could see the other crew members organizing emergency supplies and tending to Prokosch, who was on his back on the mattress.

He dashed back to his cabin and took a quick inventory. He wouldn't be able to bring much with him—he was going to lose his bicycle, most of his clothing, his radio gear, and his books. In the end, he settled on his rescue knife and his teddy bear, Mush, which he strapped to his chest.

Engineless, the *Bounty* spun windward up the crest of one three-story wave only to be knocked leeward by the next. At around midnight the first coast guard C-130, piloted by Lieutenant Wes McIntosh, came into range, and the *Bounty* was able to establish radio contact. There was a small cheer from the navigation shack. McIntosh requested that the crew shine a light on the rigging, and Faunt activated the search beam.

For the next couple of hours, the C-130, heavy with fuel, circled overhead, sometimes at a thousand feet and sometimes at five hundred. "Someone tell that guy we're 110 feet," Walbridge joked. "He's going to clip us!" There was still time for levity: according to Faunt, despite the six feet of water in the belly of the ship, Walbridge and Svendsen believed that the *Bounty* might yet be saved if the coast guard could find a way to lower some working pumps. But McIntosh could barely see half a mile in the rain, and the winds were blowing at between eighty and ninety miles an hour. A gear drop was impossible. The only thing the crew of the *Bounty* could do was hold on until morning, when a helicopter could be summoned from Elizabeth City. It seemed to Faunt an awfully long time to wait.

SEVEN

Monday, October 29

2:00 A.M.

Around two in the morning, the crew donned their bright-orange survival suits. Josh Scornavacchi was still not convinced that the

Bounty would have to be abandoned, but he knew it was better to be safe than sorry. The suits—what sailors call "Gumby suits," after the bulbous, ungainly form their wearers assume—were made of heavy neoprene. They would protect against both cold water and flame, in the unlikely event that the electrical fires spread through the *Bounty*. Scornavacchi zipped the waterproof seal on the collar closed and attached a small rubberized plastic bag to his climbing harness with a carabiner. Inside the bag was his ID, a pocketknife—the essentials.

Svendsen, the first mate, was in the navigation shack, his Gumby suit only halfway zipped. He seemed to Scornavacchi to be much less concerned with his own safety than with the safety of the crew. He inspected each sailor carefully, like a commanding officer before a battle, tugging on straps, double-checking rescue lights, slapping shoulders, and patting backs.

Scornavacchi thanked Svendsen and joined Claudene Christian near the mizzen fife rail, which surrounded the aftermost mast. The clouds he could make out overhead in the darkness were low-bellied and full, and a strong wind blew across the deck. Christian was clearly scared but was putting on a brave face for her friend, and she smiled brightly at Scornavacchi.

He looked up at the ghostly lights of the C-130 circling above him in the rain. Then he felt the deck lurch violently beneath him. The *Bounty* was once again leaning perilously over on her side. Bodies slid past him in the night, some silently and acquiescently, some with horrific screams, their hands desperately clawing for a handhold, a stray piece of rigging, anything at all.

He took a deep breath and jumped.

After receiving the okay from Svendsen, Doug Faunt waddled sternward in his Gumby suit and lay down on the deck alongside Adam Prokosch, the sailor with the injured back. Prokosch was not para-

lyzed, as Christian had feared; he would later learn that he had separated his shoulder, broken two ribs, and severely damaged a pair of
vertebrae. But it had taken time to get him up on deck, and he looked
bad: his eyes were half closed, and he had his hands crossed over his
chest, kind of like a corpse.

The *Bounty* was heeling badly to starboard, forty degrees or more,
Faunt guessed. He wasn't so much lying down as standing up now,
with his feet on the railing, the sea frothing below him and lapping
at his feet, the ship looming over him. The C-130 passed once overhead, the sound of its engines reduced by the storm to an insect-like
whine. Gazing up, Faunt caught a glimpse of the big silvery wings
of the plane and the moon glowing faintly through the clouds, and
then he was asleep.

That he was able to nod off on the deck of a doomed ship was a
testament to the extent of his exhaustion. He had been working for
forty-eight hours straight, give or take, many of them in the swel-
tering hell of the engine room. He was dehydrated, he was hungry,
his joints ached, and his lungs burned. He was strong, but he was
also sixty-six years old, and he had his limits. Faunt later figured
that he might have slept for an hour, but given the speed at which
the *Bounty* rolled over, it was probably half that. When he opened his
eyes again, the deck was fully vertical. He bent his knees and pushed
off into the sea. The storm swallowed him.

Now commenced a jarring, vicious cycle. Faunt would push his
way to the surface, and a wave would drive him back under like a
hammer pounding the head of a nail. The *Bounty*'s engines were
submerged now, and there was plenty of diesel in the water. Faunt
was an experienced diver, and he did his best not to open his mouth.
But the strength of the ocean was stupendous, and he couldn't keep
the salt water and diesel out of his throat.

At irregular intervals, a body in a survival suit would float past
him, and Faunt would holler and wave, but it was useless. Nobody
could hear him, and he couldn't distinguish one sailor from another.

Zipped into the Gumby suits, they all looked the same, cartoonish orange shapes silhouetted against the dark sea. He caught hold of a life preserver, but it appeared to be tethered to something—maybe to the ship herself, he thought. He was afraid she would plunge, and he would plunge with her. So he let go.

What surprised Faunt—what he would often think about in the days to come, first back at the coast guard station, and then in his cluttered bedroom in Oakland—was the strange tenacity of the human brain. The brain, the mind, maybe the spirit—whatever you wanted to call it, the thing that did not allow Faunt to give up, even when he probably *should* have given up, dropping his hands and surrendering to the ocean. It simply never crossed his mind that he might be dying. The fact that it didn't, he figured, probably saved his damn life.

A sinking ship creates a funnel on the surface of the sea—planks of wood, life rafts, and human bodies can be sucked down behind her. From his training, Scornavacchi was familiar with this effect, and after jumping clear of the *Bounty*, he fought hard to get a safe distance away from her. But swimming in a Gumby suit is incredibly awkward, and his progress was maddeningly slow. The sea around him looked like a flushing toilet.

Everything he grabbed at—stray planking, strands of line—was ripped out of his hand. Gasping, his lungs filling with salt water, he fought his way back to the surface. There appeared to be no one left on board the *Bounty*, which had now fully capsized. Indeed, there appeared to be no one around at all. Before he could ponder the particulars of his plight, he was yanked underwater again by some invisible force.

In movies, sinking ships lurch through the deep like whales, their every contour visible to the camera. Scornavacchi could see nothing. It was dark enough on the surface, and an inky pitch underwater. But groping around with both hands, he did figure out what was pulling him down: some of the rigging had caught onto the small bag of essentials lashed to his harness. The weight of the ship pulling on him made it impossible to unhook the carabiner, and the bag was made of heavy-duty PVC plastic, which offered little hope of breaking. He was going down—five feet, then ten, fifteen. He could feel himself starting to drown, losing the ability to think or use his muscles. His lungs were filling with seawater and diesel.

Just before the *Bounty* left New London, Scornavacchi's mother had fretted about the storm. "Mom, I'm not going to die," he had told her. Now here he was, about to break his promise. He was furious with himself. He thought about his eleven-year-old brother, too, and of all the other people he would never see again. *I'm sorry*, he thought. *I'm so sorry.*

EIGHT

Monday, October 29

4:15 A.M.

The two emergency life rafts on the *Bounty* were rated for twenty-five passengers each—nearly twice the number of sailors abandoning the ship. Inflated, the rafts resembled orange polyurethane igloos, with a wide base and a domed roof. Sausaged into their silvery casings, they were just a couple of feet long and pellet shaped. Now Chris Barksdale saw one of the capsules float past him. He instinctively reached out and grabbed hold of the line, he later told a reporter for *Popular Mechanics*. His other hand clutched a heavy piece of wooden grating, which the *Bounty* had shed as she sank. He was sharing the grating with a couple of other sailors, including Cleveland.

"Don't let loose!" Cleveland shouted to him.

"You don't have to worry about me letting loose of this son of a bitch," Barksdale replied. "I'm going wherever it goes."

Within an hour or so, Barksdale and Cleveland had inflated the raft and helped four other sailors inside: Drew Salapatek, Jessica Hewitt, Laura Groves, and Adam Prokosch. They tried to be optimistic, but it wasn't easy—the storm, far from weakening, actually seemed to be blowing harder.

Several months after the sinking, Josh Scornavacchi still could not explain his salvation in practical terms. He was drowning, he was going under, he was dead—and then he was not. The bag on his harness had somehow broken free of the rigging. He climbed fast upward, pulling with his hands and kicking his feet. "I believe God did it," he says. "That he helped me in some way."

He surfaced, sputtering and coughing, alongside a makeshift raft of emergency supplies that Claudene Christian had assembled hours earlier. He clung to the side and took stock of his location. He was still dangerously close to the *Bounty*, which had rolled temporarily back to an upright position.

After a while, he saw Jessica Black, the ship's cook, drape herself over the other end of the raft. Black was clearly panicking; her face was a mask of shock. Scornavacchi was making his way toward her when he heard a sharp crack, like a rifle shot. It was a large piece of the mast, breaking loose and crashing down toward the raft. The masts on the *Bounty* weighed several tons apiece; a direct hit would have been fatal. Instead, the piece of mast fell neatly between them and sent both sailors flying high into the air, as if they'd leaped off a trampoline.

Black vanished into the waves. Plunging back into the water, Scornavacchi cursed to himself. He'd finally found another survivor, and now she was gone. He was alone again.

Nearby he could see the *Bounty*'s mizzenmast, the aftmost mast on the ship, lying flat across the surface of the sea. Out of other options, he hauled himself up on top of it and held on.

Suddenly the *Bounty*, buoyed by a large swell, began to roll back upright. Scornavacchi, both hands wrapped tightly around the miz-zenmast and hanging on for dear life, went with it. Soon he was more than forty feet in the air. From somewhere out in the storm he heard a voice. "Jump," the voice said. "You've got to jump." And he did.

The next day, safe on shore, Scornavacchi would ask his ship-mates who had issued the order, and receive only blank stares. No one remembered telling him to jump. No one had seen him up on the mizzenmast at all.

It was about four-thirty a.m. by the time Scornavacchi managed to reach one of the life raft capsules. He was working to get it open when his shipmate John Jones bobbed up alongside him. Soon they were joined by two more, Mark Warner and Anna Sprague. For hours Scornavacchi had thought that everyone else was gone; now it seemed like a familiar face was popping up every few minutes.

Once the raft was inflated, the four survivors were faced with the prospect of actually boarding it. The hatch was far above the water, the rubber was slick, and the whole craft was pitching wildly in the waves. They were all exhausted from battling against the ocean for hours; Scornavacchi's forearms were burning, and he found he could barely make a fist. He was helping to boost up Sprague when he heard voices nearby. On the other side of the raft were Doug Faunt, Matthew Sanders, and Jessica Black. One by one they all piled inside and, shiv-ering in the cold, settled down to wait. Scornavacchi, Jones, Warner, Sprague, Sanders, Black, and Faunt—seven in all. As far as they knew, they were the only surviving crew members of the tall ship *Bounty*.

Ingested in trace amounts, salt water is not particularly harmful to the human body. But swallowed in large quantities, it wreaks havoc on the metabolism, impairs the nervous system, damages the kidneys, and dangerously elevates blood pressure. By the time

Faunt climbed aboard the inflatable emergency raft, he had consumed, by his estimate, a couple of gallons of salt water. He could still breathe normally, and his brain was functioning, but there was an ominous ache in his stomach. He lay back on the floor of the raft and evacuated his bowels into his Gumby suit.

To either side of him, the six other survivors had assembled in a circle, leaning back against the walls in an effort to keep the raft stable. They did their best to keep spirits high. They told stories about happier voyages aboard *Bounty*, days when the weather was fair and the sailing smooth. They reminisced about the missing shipmates. They wondered when day would finally break. As they waited for dawn, Scornavacchi, Sprague, and Warner sang "Mingulay Boat Song," a Scottish sea chantey. Lying on his back, Faunt listened to the words:

> *What care we, though, white the Minch is?*
> *What care we for wind or weather?*
> *Let her go boys; every inch is*
> *Sailing homeward to Mingulay.*
>
> *Wives are waiting, by the pier head,*
> *Or looking seaward, from the heather;*
> *Pull her round, boys, then you'll anchor*
> *'Ere the sun sets on Mingulay.*

NINE

Monday, October 29

5:30 A.M.

By dawn there were two coast guard helicopters hovering over the wreck of the *Bounty*. It was Randy Haba, the rescue swimmer from the first of the two, who scooped up Doug Faunt. The first thing Faunt glimpsed when he was hauled into the cabin of the Jayhawk was the face of John Svendsen—the straggler that Haba had spotted amid the wreckage of the *Bounty*. Svendsen had remained in the navigation shack long after the rest of the crew jumped overboard, but eventually the *Bounty* heeled so vertiginously that he had no choice but to leap clear of the deck and into the water. Behind him, he could hear the VHF radio sputtering: *Are you still there,* Bounty? *Do you read me,* Bounty? *Come in,* Bounty.

Faunt was ecstatic to see Svendsen—he'd worried that he had gone down with the ship. But he hardly had time to greet the first mate before the coast guard helicopter's mechanic, Petty Officer Third Class Mike Lufkin, was hollering in his ear, "Take off the suit."

"I can't," Faunt replied. "I'll foul your bird."

"Just take it off," Lufkin said.

Faunt knew Lufkin was right. The cabin doors were open and the wind was blowing cold and Faunt was drenched. It was a recipe for hypothermia. He unzipped the suit and dropped it onto the floor.

Haba was able to make three more trips to the raft to retrieve more survivors before the Jayhawk was low enough on fuel that the pilot announced he was turning back toward Elizabeth City. He had six survivors on board. It would be up to the other Jayhawk crew that had just arrived from Elizabeth City to retrieve the rest.

Scornavacchi, Jones, and Sanders spread out across the floor of the rubber raft in an effort to keep it steady. Without the presence of the four other bodies, the craft had turned skittish, scudding over the sea like a skipping stone. All Scornavacchi could do was hold on.

Around eight a.m., Petty Officer Third Class Dan Todd, the rescue swimmer from the second Jayhawk, poked his head into the raft's hatch. Scornavacchi allowed Todd to strap him into the basket and, leaning on his side, took in the view. He could see the flank of the *Bounty*, lying on her side, and the snarled remainders of the ten miles of line that had once kept her at sail.

The basket swung higher. There was a clank, and Scornavacchi pulled himself into the cramped cabin of the Jayhawk. Pretty soon there were eleven people crammed inside: Sanders, Jones, and Scornavacchi from the first raft; Barksdale, Cleveland, Salapatek, Hewitt, Groves, and Prokosch from the second; plus Todd and the coast guard flight mechanic.

Two hours later the helicopter set down in Elizabeth City. In a single-file line, the survivors limped across the tarmac. A pack of local news photographers waited nearby, jostling against hastily erected barriers. There were camera flashes, shouts, the sound of someone crying. Scornavacchi kept his head down.

Inside the coast guard station, the tallying-up began in earnest. The *Bounty* had left New London with sixteen sailors. Fourteen had been rescued. Robin Walbridge and Claudene Christian were still out there somewhere.

Among the last crew members to see them on board the ship was Laura Groves, the boatswain, who had helped conduct a headcount of the crew in the frantic last moments before abandoning ship. She would later remember that Svendsen was in the navigation shack, communicating with the C-130 pilots, and that Dan Cleveland was beside her, his Gumby suit halfway on, working on connecting a line to the capsules that held the inflatable life rafts so they'd be easier to find if the ship capsized. Christian was on the mizzen fife rail. Walbridge was just forward of Groves, on the weather deck.

Time had gone baggy, elastic. Groves heard Svendsen shout that the foredeck was underwater, and she raced to help Cleveland get the rest of the way into his Gumby suit. Then the ship was on her side, Groves was kicking as hard as she could to keep her head above water, and Walbridge and Christian were gone.

Scornavacchi was in his room in an Elizabeth City motel when definitive word arrived. The crew from a third coast guard helicopter had finally found Christian in the water near the *Bounty*, but she was unresponsive, with no vital signs. Two *Bounty* crew members later said that her corpse bore the signs of severe cranial trauma: heavy bruising on one side of the face and a partially crumpled skull. That could have meant that she was killed by a blow from one of the falling masts, or it could have meant that she slipped unconscious into the water and quickly drowned. As for Walbridge, the search was ongoing. A day later it would be called off.

Unresponsive, no vital signs. The official terminology, the way it depersonalized the dead and the lost, unnerved Scornavacchi. He summoned an image of Christian as he had last seen her, lashing together the gear and supplies on the deck of the *Bounty*. She had looked almost peaceful there, even as the ship was going down, an easy smile on her face.

That night Scornavacchi called his mother in Pennsylvania. She'd seen the news—she knew what had happened to the *Bounty*. "But I'm alive, Mom," he said. "I made it." He held the receiver to his ear and listened to his mother sob.

TEN

February 12, 2013

9:00 A.M.

It was not hard to pick out Dina and Rex Christian in the crowded ballroom. They sat a couple of rows back from the microphones, alongside their lawyer. To their left was a battery of television cameras, and behind them, arranged across a wide expanse of brightly patterned carpeting, were the reporters, maritime lawyers, and local sailors with a few hours to kill.

Dina Christian passed most of the hours of the coast guard's hearing on the *Bounty* sinking in rigid silence, sometimes dabbing her eyes with a tissue, sometimes shaking her head furiously, and sometimes leaning in to whisper to Rex, a rumpled man in his sixties. Anyone who looked closely at Dina—small, blond, with a gently upturned nose and round cheeks—would have noticed the striking resemblance she bore to her only daughter, Claudene.

The Renaissance Portsmouth Hotel and Conference Center in Portsmouth, Virginia, where the hearing was held, looms over the Elizabeth River. From the hallway outside the second-floor ballroom, you could look out across the wind-chopped water to Norfolk, where a navy aircraft carrier and a handful of smaller ships, bristling with scaffolding and plastic tarp, awaited repairs. Every morning, at precisely 8:50 a.m., Coast Guard Commander Kevin Carroll, clad in his dress blues, arrived and took his place in the front of the ballroom, a few yards from where the Christians sat.

Carroll is in his forties, thickly built and tall, with a high-and-tight military style haircut and a brusque, if not entirely unfriendly, interrogative style. Three and a half months after the *Bounty*'s sinking, he had been tasked with conducting the official inquiry into the incident, with sorting out the messy particulars of what exactly had gone wrong.

It had taken only a few days after the sinking for the second-guessing to begin. The questions percolated in the comments sections of articles about the incident, on the message boards and Facebook pages frequented by tall ship buffs, in the letters pages of sailing magazines. Although they spoke fondly of him as a person, few of Robin Walbridge's fellow tall ship captains seemed able to comprehend his decision to sail through the hurricane—or more bafflingly, to cut across its center mass on October 28.

In an open letter to Walbridge circulated in mid-November, Jan Miles, the captain of the schooner *Pride of Baltimore II*, had compared the *Bounty*'s sinking to that of the *Fantome*, a schooner that went down off the coast of Belize in 1998, killing all thirty-one crew members aboard—the worst Atlantic sailing disaster in forty years. Like Walbridge, Miles wrote, the *Fantome*'s skipper had tried to outrun a hurricane on a set of underpowered engines and had placed too much faith in the accuracy of hurricane forecasts. Addressing his still-missing colleague, Miles wrote, *Yeah, you were a reckless man Robin. I would not have continued to proceed as you did.*

Joining Miles in his criticism were the Christians, who believed that their daughter would still be alive if Walbridge had kept the *Bounty* in port. "Fact: Walbridge took [Claudene] into the worse hurricane & did not except help from the [coast guard] until it was to late for her," Dina wrote on Facebook in January. "After reading all this, how can any of you defend this Crazy Nut?"

There was one group of people who did not buy the emerging consensus that Walbridge's navigational errors and hubris were wholly responsible for the *Bounty*'s end: the ship's crew. As many of them would point out, the ship had been through bad storms before and survived them all. The *Bounty* had crossed the Atlantic in foul weather, motored through gales in the Gulf, and threaded some of the most treacherous passages on earth. And in each circumstance, Walbridge had acquitted himself well.

It stood to reason, then, that the sinking was not only a matter of the *Bounty*'s position relative to the hurricane on October 29—that factors beyond Walbridge's control had turned an ill-advised voyage into a doomed one. In this scenario, the blame that had fallen on Walbridge belonged more properly to Robert Hansen and the HMS Bounty Foundation.

Hansen had long struggled to adequately maintain the ship with the meager funds earned from dock tours and day sails. Patchwork measures had been undertaken to get the *Bounty* from one port of call to the next. According to one legend that circulated among new crew members, shortly before a coast guard inspection in the 1990s, a small fire had broken out on the *Bounty*. It allegedly smoldered for a full three days and was smoldering still when the coastguardsmen came aboard, but the crew—in a scene that sounded like something out of a bad sitcom—was able to keep the inspectors distracted and away from the fire. "I learned a lot about how to handle boats from Robin," a former crewmember says. "And I learned far more about how to handle people."

Coast guard hearings do not have the authority to determine criminal responsibility or levy civil penalties; Carroll was in Portsmouth as an investigator, not as a jurist. But his findings—drawn from nine full days' worth of testimony of survivors, coastguardsmen, surveyors, and ship inspectors—would be admissible in civil or criminal court. And since the Christian family was widely believed to be preparing a lawsuit against the HMS Bounty Foundation, the hearings had the feeling of a practice trial.

On one side were the Christians and Jacob Shisha, their lawyer, a veteran maritime litigator with a showman's demeanor and a trace of a New York accent. On the other side were Tracie Simonin and Robert Hansen of the Bounty Foundation, and their two attorneys, Frank Ambrosino and Leonard Langer.

John Svendsen was the first witness Carroll summoned when the hearing commenced on the morning of February 12. The first mate had sustained serious injuries to his face, hand, shoulder, and torso during the storm, and he moved slowly and deliberately to the front of the ballroom. He was dressed in a floral button-down under a black fleece, and his dirty-blond hair hung lankly to his shoulders. A conspicuous murmur arose in his wake. Seating himself in front of the microphones, Svendsen steepled his long fingers on the table and allowed Carroll to walk him through the days leading up to the sinking of the *Bounty*.

Of particular concern to Carroll was Walbridge's August television interview in which he had spoken of chasing hurricanes. At the time the comments had seemed like the boasts of a daring sailor. Now they looked a lot more like tragic foolhardiness—proof of Walbridge's poor judgment.

"Did the *Bounty* chase hurricanes?" Carroll asked Svendsen bluntly.

"Not in my opinion," Svendsen replied. He maintained that Walbridge's comments had been widely misunderstood. The captain had not been advocating the "chasing of hurricanes" as a matter of pleasure or thrill, he said. He had simply been stating the truth—that hurricanes can generate a strong but manageable boost of wind power to a full-rigger like the *Bounty*.

Svendsen, however, made it clear that he did not hold Walbridge entirely blameless for the sinking. He recalled that he had stressed to Walbridge the historic nature of the storm and worried aloud about the *Bounty*'s ability to withstand it. "I had mentioned other options as far as staying in and not going out to sea," Svendsen said.

These pleas were apparently offered semiprivately, in the presence of other mates, and in at least one case, privately to Walbridge. But Walbridge, Svendsen testified, had faith in the *Bounty* and was determined to press southward. "Robin felt the ship was safer at sea," he said.

Equally striking was Svendsen's recollection that twice in the early morning hours of October 29, he had requested that Walbridge issue an abandon ship order. Twice Walbridge refused. The captain apparently believed that the *Bounty*, even without power, would remain afloat, and that the crew would be safer on board than in the life rafts. In hindsight, Walbridge had badly misjudged the condition of his ship. It was not safe at all—it was sinking fast.

Had Walbridge issued the abandon ship order earlier in the morning, when the ship was more stable, an orderly procession to the life rafts might have occurred. Instead, she began to roll over before the rafts were even fully inflated. For an inexperienced sailor like Claudene Christian, an earlier order might have meant the difference between life and death.

ELEVEN

Wednesday, February 13

10:00 A.M.

Hardly anyone on board the *Bounty* during her final voyage in October had failed to note that the ship was taking on water. Even in relatively calm weather, there was always a leak—a trickle here, some seepage there. Were those leaks ordinary for a wooden ship her age? Or were they evidence that the *Bounty* was dangerously dilapidated?

The task of answering those questions fell to Todd Kosakowski of the Boothbay Harbor Shipyard, who had worked on the *Bounty* during the month she spent in dry dock in the fall of 2012, shortly before she sailed for St. Petersburg. The crew at Boothbay had caulked leaky seams, installed new fuel tanks, replaced rotten planks, and touched up the *Bounty*'s paint job.

Kosakowski told Kevin Carroll that shortly after the *Bounty* had been brought to the shipyard, he and his workers had pulled up some planking near the mizzenmast and mainmast and found significant amounts of rot—a "dry, almost charred-looking" kind of rot, Kosakowski said.

"Did you tell Captain Walbridge?" Carroll asked.

"Yes," Kosakowski said.

"What did he say?"

"He was a little shocked when we first started looking into it," Kosakowski admitted. "His shock turned to awe when we were prodding the other framing and finding the same signs of degradation. Once we started looking at the other frames, we saw it was more widespread." Kosakowski came to believe that as much as 75 percent of the framing above the vessel's waterline was rotten.

The rotten wood needed to be removed and replaced, Kosakowski said, and he had recommended to Walbridge that he allow the shipyard crew to inspect the rest of the *Bounty*, cutting out the worst of the damage and installing fresh white oak in its place. Kosakowski testified that Walbridge agreed to a few replacements but resisted a deeper—and inevitably more costly—investigation. "[Walbridge's] response," he said, "was that they would deal with the hull at the next year's hull exam"—the annual inspection conducted by the coast guard. But that exam wasn't scheduled until 2014.

Kowalski told Carroll that he met twice more with Walbridge to talk about the rot. On that second occasion, Walbridge told Kosakowski that he wanted the issue to "stay between the two of us," Kosakowski testified, "and that he explained these problems to the owner, [and] that I didn't need to be worried."

It wasn't hard to imagine the horrible bind in which the discovery of the rot would have placed the captain. For Walbridge, everything was riding on the *Bounty*'s fate. His sense of identity was irrevocably linked to the ship. Had she been mothballed, it might have been devastating to him. Would he have taken that risk and told Hansen? Or would he have done whatever it took to keep the *Bounty* sailing?

By the end of the hearings in Portsmouth, the *Bounty*'s loss had begun to take shape, in the way that shipwrecks often do, as an unsparing aggregation of mistakes. Any one of them, had it occurred in isolation, would not likely have been fatal; it was only gathered together that they acquired such terrible weight. Had Robin Walbridge kept the ship in port, the *Bounty* might have lived to sail another day, even in her decaying state. If the *Bounty* had been in better shape, the storm might have been survivable; Sandy was extremely large, but her wind speed never rose above Category 1 status, and vessels smaller than the *Bounty* have weathered much worse. If the generators had stayed online, if the pumps had been able to keep up with the rising water, the *Bounty* might have limped back to shore as she did during her near-disastrous trip past Cape Hatteras in 1998. These are the hypotheticals that haunt a lost ship and her survivors.

In an interview with CNN in February, Claudia McCann, Walbridge's widow, said she believed her husband had acted honorably in steering the *Bounty* south, and she has made it clear that she intends to protect his legacy. This will be no easy task—the captain's crew demonstrated loyalty in their testimony, but the story they told in spite of themselves was a damning one. In the most generous scenario, Walbridge made a single bad decision that was fatally complicated by terrible luck. But it was just as possible that he committed an act of unforgivable hubris, knowingly pushing a dilapidated ship beyond its limits and endangering the young, largely inexperienced crew he had sworn to protect.

In November 2012 the surviving crew members of the *Bounty* went to New York to tape a segment for ABC's *Good Morning America*. The producers shot more than an hour of tape but used barely two minutes of it, a fact that annoyed some of the crew members. After that they granted few interviews. Some took to switching off their phones or deleting emails from reporters without even reading them. Like soldiers returning from a particularly harrowing deployment, they worried that no one would understand what they'd been through. They became even closer than they'd been on the *Bounty*, sealing themselves off from the world. They started an email listserv to exchange memories from their time on the ship, and they posted reassuring messages on each other's Facebook walls.

It will get better, they wrote.

I'm having bad dreams, too, they wrote.

On a recent winter afternoon, Doug Faunt stood on the back porch of his house in Oakland, surveying his tangled, overgrown backyard. An aging cat wove between his legs. Even a couple of months on, his stomach still bothered him. "There's not a day that goes by that I don't think about the storm and what happened out there," he said, pushing a neon-yellow watch cap back over his brow. "I assume it will be that way for a very long time."

But the funny thing was, he also couldn't stop thinking of the things that he missed—the sound of canvas flapping overhead, the slap of salt water on his skin. Lately he had found himself returning often to tall ship forums online. Tall ships are typically taken out of commission during the winter months, laid up in October and back at sail by April or May. There was a ship sailing out of New York in the spring that he had his eye on—another full-rigger. Maybe she had room for one more sailor.

ACKNOWLEDGMENTS

It goes without saying that this book would not exist without the efforts of the authors contained within. But it's worth adding that many of them took a chance—with work they cared deeply about—on a young, unproven magazine. These pieces are constituted of those authors' obsessions, their reporting hours, and in some cases their own personal stories. We have always felt very fortunate to have them. So too are we grateful to the subjects of these stories, many of whom patiently gave swaths of their time, and the most personal details of their lives, to our authors.

Believing in great writing means believing in great editing, and these pieces would be equally impossible without the wonderful editors that *The Atavist Magazine* has been lucky to have over our five years. Alissa Quart, Charles Homans, Joel Lovell, and Katia Bachko have not only landed some of the finest writers working today but have helped them find their voices with the utmost skill and patience. Longform stories are a collaborative endeavor between writer and editor, and these editors are the best in the business.

We are in the debt of our agents, David Kuhn and William LoTurco, for helping shape the idea of what this book could be and then finding the best possible home for it at Norton. We were lucky to land in the experienced hands of the team there, particularly our editor, Tom Mayer, who amidst other invaluable assistance steered us through the impossible task of selecting the pieces. Ryan Harrington navigated us unfailingly through the whole publishing process, and Janet Biehl copyedited the manuscript astutely. Our thanks as well to the whole dedicated team at Norton, including production manager Lauren Abbate, art director Steve Attardo (for our beautiful jacket), managing editor Nancy Palmquist, and publicist Elizabeth Riley.

Many thanks go, as well, to the countless other people at *The Atavist Magazine* and Atavist, our company, who brought these stories to life. That includes five years of staffers and freelancers, from the designers and programmers who build our digital platform to the fact checkers we bring on for each story to ensure its accuracy. Specific, and immense, thanks go to Gray Beltran for his beautiful designs of these pieces online, Sean Cooper for his steady hand in copyediting, Megan Detrie and Olivia Koski for their story production, Thomas Rhiel for his design and art direction, and Crystal Fawn Williams for helping get them in front of readers. Finally, without brilliant co-founders Jefferson Rabb and Nicholas Thompson—and the many friends, family, and investors who put their support behind us—none of this would have been possible in the first place.

CONTRIBUTOR BIOS

CRIS BEAM is an author and professor in New York City. She is the author of *To the End of June: The Intimate Life of American Foster Care*, the young adult novel *I Am J*, and *Transparent*, a nonfiction book that covers seven years in the lives of four transgender teenagers. She is currently working on a book about philosophies of empathy.

DAVID DOBBS writes features and essays for publications including *The New York Times*, *The New York Times Book Review*, *National Geographic*, *The Atlantic*, *Slate*, *Mosaic*, and *Aeon*. Several of his stories have been chosen for leading anthologies; most recently, his *Pacific Standard* feature "The Social Life of Genes" was selected for *The Best American Science and Nature Writing 2014* as well as the 2014 AAAS/Kavli Science Journalism Award, Magazine. He lives in Vermont.

ADAM HIGGINBOTHAM began his career in magazines and newspapers in London, where he was the editor-in-chief of *The Face* and a contributing editor at *The Sunday Telegraph*. Based in New York for the last twelve years, he has written for *GQ*, *The New Yorker*, *The New*

York Times Magazine, and *Smithsonian Magazine*. He is currently at work on a book about the Chernobyl nuclear accident, which will be published in 2018.

LESLIE JAMISON is the author of the essay collection *The Empathy Exams* and the novel *The Gin Closet*. She is a columnist for *The New York Times Book Review*, and her work has also appeared in *Harper's, Oxford American, A Public Space, Virginia Quarterly Review*, and *The Believer*. She is an assistant professor at Columbia University and lives in Brooklyn.

BROOKE JARVIS is an independent journalist who focuses on longform narrative and environmental reporting. She has written for *Harper's Magazine, The California Sunday Magazine, National Geographic*, and *Rolling Stone*. Her work has been published in *The Best American Science and Nature Writing* and supported by the Alicia Patterson Foundation and the Middlebury Fellowship in Environmental Journalism. She lives in Seattle.

JON MOOALLEM is a contributing writer to *The New York Times Magazine* and the author of *Wild Ones: A Sometimes Dismaying, Weirdly Reassuring Story About Looking at People Looking at Animals in America*, one of *The New York Times Book Review*'s 100 Notable Books of 2013.

EVAN RATLIFF is co-founder of Atavist, a media and software company that produces a digital storytelling platform, and editor-in-chief of the award-winning flagship publication *The Atavist Magazine*. His writing also appears in *The New Yorker, National Geographic*, and *Wired*, where he is a contributing editor. And he is the co-host of the Longform Podcast.

MATTHEW SHAER's last story for *The Atavist Magazine*, "The Sinking of the Bounty," was a finalist for the 2014 National Magazine Award for Reporting. A contributing editor at *Smithsonian Magazine*, he has written for *GQ*, *Harper's*, *The New York Times Magazine*, and *Men's Journal*, among other publications.

JAMES VERINI is a writer based in Africa. His last story for *The Atavist Magazine*, "Love and Ruin," won a 2014 National Magazine Award for feature writing.

VANESSA VESELKA is the author of the novel *Zazen*, which won the 2012 PEN/Robert W. Bingham Prize for fiction. Her short stories have appeared in *Tin House*, *Yeti*, and *Zyzzyva*. Her nonfiction can be found in *The American Reader*, *The Atlantic*, *GQ*, and *Medium* and was included in the 2013 *Best American Essays* anthology.